TAMING THE BEAST

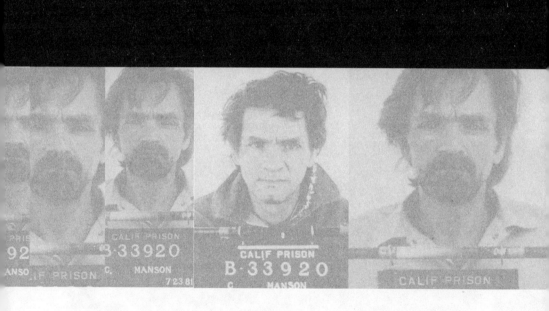

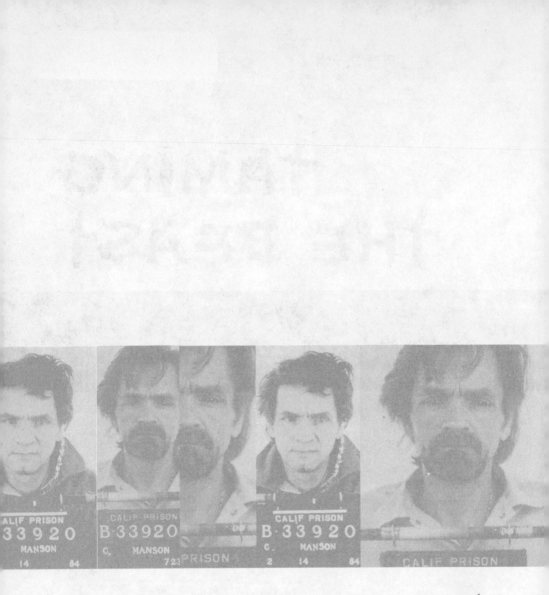

ST. MARTIN'S GRIFFIN
NEW YORK

TAMING THE BEAST

CHARLES MANSON'S LIFE BEHIND BARS

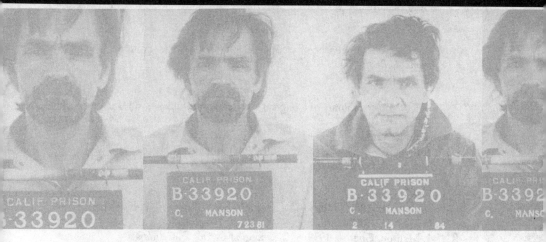

CALIFORNIA CORRECTIONS OFFICER

EDWARD GEORGE

WITH

DARY MATERA

Library of Congress Cataloging-in-Publication Data

George, Edward.
  Taming the beast: Charles Manson's life behind bars / by Edward George with Dary Matera.
    p. cm.
  Includes index.
  ISBN 0-312-18085-3 (hc)
  ISBN 0-312-20970-3 (pbk)
  1. Manson, Charles, 1934- . 2. George, Edward. 3. Criminals—California—Biography. 4. Prisoners—California—Bibliography. 5. Correctional personnel—California—Biography. 6. California State Prison at San Quentin—Officials and employees—Biography. I. Matera, Dary. II. Title.
HV8658.M2797G46 1998
364.15'23'0979493—dc21

                                  97-37965
                                    CIP

First St. Martin's Griffin Edition: August 1999

10 9 8 7 6 5 4 3 2 1

AUTHOR'S NOTE

The conversations throughout the book, including my conversations with Charles Manson, have been reconstructed from my recollection and, in some instances, from notes made immediately after those conversations.

—Ed George

CONTENTS

INTRODUCTION

ELECTED EXCERPTS FROM Charles Manson's statement to the California court that convicted him of seven counts of murder conspiracy in the first degree and sentenced him to death in 1970:

"These children that came at you with knives, they are your children. You taught them. I didn't teach them. I just tried to help them stand up. Most of the people at the ranch that you call the Family were just people that you did not want, people that were alongside the road, that their parents had kicked out or they did not want to go to Juvenile Hall, so I did the best I could and I took them up on my garbage dump and I told them this: that in love there is no wrong.

". . . It is not my responsibility. It is your responsibility. It is the responsibility you have toward your own children who you are neglecting, and then you want to put the blame on me again and again and again. . . . You eat meat with your teeth and you kill things that are better than you are, and in the same respect you say how bad and even killers that your children are. You make your children what they are. I am just a reflection of every one of you.

". . . I have nothing against none of you. I can't judge any of you. But I think it is high time that you all started looking at yourselves and judging the lie that you live in. I sit and I watch you from nowhere, and I have nothing in my mind, no malice against you and no ribbons for you. . . . You are just doing what you are doing for the money, for a little bit of attention from someone. I can't dislike you, but I will say this to you. You haven't got long before you are all going to kill yourselves because you are crazy. And you can't project it back at me. . . .

"You can say that it's me that cannot communicate, and you can say that it's me that don't have any understanding, and you can say that when I am dead your world will be better, and you can lock me up in your penitentiary and you can forget about me. But I'm only what lives inside of you, each and every one of you. These children . . . you only give them your frustration. You only give them your anger. You only give them the bad part of you rather than give them the good part of you. You should all turn around and face your children and start following them and listening to them.

". . . If I could get angry at you I would try to kill every one of you. If that's guilt, I accept it. These children, everything they have done, they done for love of their brother. . . .

"I may have implied on several occasions to several different people that I may have been Jesus Christ, but I haven't decided yet what I am or who I am. I am whoever you make me, but what you want is a fiend. You want a sadistic fiend because that is what you are.

". . . My father is the jail house. My father is your system. . . . I have ate out of your garbage cans to stay out of jail. I have wore your second-hand clothes. I have given everything I have away. Everything! I have accepted things and given them away the next second. I have done my best to get along in your world and now you want to kill me, and I look at you and I look how incompetent you all are, and then I say to myself, 'You want to kill me? Ha, I'm already dead! Have been all my life!' I've lived in your tomb that you built.

"I did seven years for a thirty-seven-dollar check. I did twelve years because I didn't have any parents, and how many other sons do you think you have in there? You have many sons in there, many, many sons in there, most of them are black and they are angry. . . .

"Sometimes I think about giving it to you. Sometimes I'm thinking about just jumping on you and let you shoot me. Sometimes I think it would be easier than sitting here and facing you in the contempt that you have for yourself, the hate that you have for yourself. It's only the anger you reflect at me, the anger that you have got for you. . . . If I could I would jerk this microphone out and beat your brains out with it because that is what you deserve! That is what you deserve.

". . . I live in my world, and I am my own king in my world, whether it be a garbage dump or in the desert or wherever it be. I am my own human being. You may restrain my body and you may tear my guts out, do anything you wish, but I am still me and you can't take that. You can kill the ego. You can kill the pride. You can kill the want, the desire of a human being. You can lock him in a cell and you can knock his teeth out and smash his brain, but you cannot kill the soul.

". . . I don't care what you believe. I know what I am. You care what I think of you? Do you care what my opinion is? No, I hardly think so. I don't think that any of you care about anything other than yourselves. . . .

"You made me a monster and I have to live with that the rest of my life because I cannot fight this case. If I could fight this case and I could present this case, I would take that monster back and I would take that fear back. Then you could find something else to put your fear on, because it's all your fear. You look for something to project it on and you pick a little old scroungy nobody who eats out of a garbage can, that nobody wants, that was kicked out of the penitentiary, that has been dragged though every hellhole you can think of, and you drag him up and put him into a courtroom. You expect to break me? Impossible! You broke me years ago. You killed me years ago!"

TAMING THE BEAST

CHARLES MANSON ARRIVED at San Quentin in June 1971 shackled in heavy chains and basking in the glow of a frenzied media. As he trudged across the garden plaza on his way to the prison's notorious death row, an officer whispered a remark that would be repeated often that morning.

"Look at him! He's such a little motherfucker!"

The world's most famous "little motherfucker" had just been convicted of multiple counts of homicide for orchestrating the infamous Tate-LaBianca murders, a two-night slaying spree that left eight people dead and shocked the world in 1969.

Manson remained on death row at San Quentin until capital punishment was overturned by the Supreme Court thirteen months later. The ruling automatically reduced his sentence to life (with parole)—and created a massive headache for the American corrections system. If society didn't have the stomach to execute a man who appeared to be evil incarnate, then what the hell were we supposed to do with him? It's a question that's never been sufficiently answered.

To get rid of him, San Quentin officials quickly transferred Manson to the California Medical Facility (CMF), Vacaville, for a psychiatric evaluation. Found to be mentally stable, he was sent to Folsom State Prison, a hellhole that even a prison-scarred sewer rat like Manson found to be repugnant. Instead of the relative tranquillity of a federal prison, Manson now had to survive among vicious gangs like the Aryan Brotherhood, the Black Guerrilla Family, the Mexican Mafia, and assorted other friendly groups. Some members of these organizations itched to create a name for themselves by "offing" the world's most famous felon.

For the next three years, Folsom and CMF played Ping-Pong with the demon-eyed cult leader, bouncing him back and forth between the facilities. Folsom's medical staff claimed he was a stark raving lunatic who belonged in a straitjacket at CMF. CMF's doctors insisted that he was not psychotic, never had been, and should reside unencumbered at Folsom. The one thing everyone agreed on was that nobody wanted the little bastard under their roof. Even locked in a cell under heavy guard, Charlie Manson was one scary dude.

Manson, true to his master-manipulator, antiestablishment form, created most of the dilemma himself. He could play crazy or sane. Wherever he was at the moment, he'd play the opposite role.

In June 1975, Folsom officials found a way to expand the circle. Complaining that the Manson clan was camped outside the prison, harassing the staff and making everyone miserable, they appealed to the mercy of Bob Rees, San Quentin's warden. Rees, figuring that his savage inferno couldn't be any worse with Manson around, decided to help his fellow jailers. Rees's act of compassion brought Charles Manson to San Quentin six weeks prior to my own reluctant arrival. When I got there, I was promptly placed in charge of the lockdown unit—the ominous section that housed prisoners so crazed and violent they couldn't even coexist in a society made up of their criminal peers. Manson, naturally, was housed in my unit. That made him my responsibility.

Along with Charlie came his bizarre group of fanatical followers. Led by his chief lieutenant on the outside, Lynette "Squeaky" Fromme, the persistent mob had assaulted Folsom and CMF officials with daily calls begging for scraps of news about their beloved leader. They also demanded mail and visitation privileges. As with everything else dealing with Manson, Warden Rees dumped Squeaky and gang into my lap. "I don't want to be bothered by those freaks," he growled. "You handle it. And for God's sake, make the right decisions!" Wonderful. I was now the chief ringleader of the entire Manson circus.

The irony was that I never wanted to be at San Quentin in the first place. I'd previously served as a program administrator for the Sierra Conservation Center, a minimum-security facility in Jamestown, California, that was designed to give nonviolent prisoners a chance to work in the forestry service. The gentlemen cons spent their days building hiking trails, battling floods and forest fires, searching for lost children, and for the most part, enjoying the great outdoors. Set in the rolling, oak-studded hills on the western slopes of the Sierra Nevada, it was an idyllic place to work and live.

Naturally, I took the transfer to San Quentin hard. That was going from one extreme to the other, from paradise to hell. San Quentin was a rancid rathole festering with violent, high-security felons. At the time of my assignment, the facility was a virtual chamber of horrors. A deadly riot had broken out four years before, resulting in the savage murder of three guards and two prisoners, along with the sadistic torture and mutilation of three additional correctional officers. After numerous delays, the inmates responsible were finally going to be tried, an event that brought the violent nightmare back to life in everyone's mind. The place appeared on the verge of blowing out of control.

The thought of working there depressed me. I furiously fought the transfer, all to no avail. A new team of top administrators was being assembled to try and keep the lid on the place, and I'd been handpicked to join them. The higher-ups apparently figured that my unique background as a former seminary student turned navy fighter pilot would come in handy. They felt that it gave me both the compassion and the authority San Quentin needed.

I'd barely settled in for my first full day on the job when the insanity began. A chipper voice greeted me on the phone. "Have you met Charlie?" Squeaky asked.

"No, I haven't."

She appeared shocked that I hadn't rushed right over to his cell for an autograph. For the next twenty minutes, Squeaky proceeded to extol Manson's mythical charms. "Can I visit him?" she finally asked, getting to the point. Her birdlike voice hungered for an immediate answer. I knew that Manson's previous prison administrators had refused to let him meet with any known Family members. The officials were afraid that Manson would use the visits to pump up his followers and send them out on horrible new missions. Those were my sentiments, exactly.

After years of legal fights, appeals, and bitter frustration, Squeaky came at me with a new tack. "Charlie wants to marry me. I demand to see him!"

"Does Charlie really want to marry you?" I asked, aware that such a request must originate with the inmate.

"Ask him," she squeaked, quickly changing the subject. "What about Charlie's cell? What does it look like? How is it furnished? Does he have enough underwear, socks, linens? Does he see the sun? Does he have some earth to grow things? Books to read? A guitar to play?"

Squeaky asked question after question, hanging on my every answer. I sensed that any speck of information about him was sacred to her. Before I could wring her from the phone, she made me promise that I'd visit Charlie the next day.

I was so nonchalant about it that I didn't remember my promise until late the following afternoon. Behind the cells in the high-security Adjustment Center was a dank, narrow utility alley. There was a small barred opening in the back wall of each unit approximately eighteen inches square. This allowed staffers to converse with an inmate without the other prisoners' seeing them. The opening, at eye level, was secured with a steel door and was kept locked when not in use. During my rounds, I normally remained in the well-lit areas in front of the cells, casually chatting with the men behind the bars. That afternoon, I maneuvered through the old pipes, ripped-out wiring, and rusted ventilation ducts that cluttered the grimy alley and made my way toward the rear of the cell that housed Squeaky's idol.

Before reaching it, I heard a clank inside a metal drainpipe that ran the length of the alley. The sound gave me a chill. I knew that inmates transfer weapons to other prisoners by tying them to homemade fishing lines and flushing them down their toilets. Was that a knife or a zip gun I heard traveling the inmate highway? A knife or zip gun that would one day be aimed at me?

I approached Charles Manson's cell, quietly unlocked the steel viewing door, and took my first glimpse at the most feared man in the world. I instantly recoiled. There he was, hunched on his bunk like an ugly troll from a child's nightmare. His fingernails were long and stained yellow from nicotine. His stringy black hair was draped around a chalky, almost inhuman face. The faint outline of a swastika scarred his forehead. He was thin, small, not physically threatening in any way, but boy was he creepy.

Turning slowly, the demon looked up at me. Our eyes locked. I felt my blood run cold as Manson studied me like a predator, twisting the tip of his goatee between his thumb and his index finger. Suddenly, a demonic snarl formed on his face. I backed away, totally spooked by his appearance. I tried to catch myself and overcome my fear. Hell, I was no stranger to prisons or crazed prisoners. I'd spent half my life surrounded by the most vicious criminals one can imagine. Before that, I'd landed propeller-driven fighter planes on bouncing aircraft carriers at sea. Nothing could be scarier than that. Or so I thought. Why, I asked myself, was this goofy pip-squeak affecting me so?

Gathering my nerve, I eased toward the door, found my voice, and introduced myself. "Hi. I'm Ed George."

Manson stared for a moment, then responded in an austere, almost grandiose manner. "Do you know who I am?" I nodded. We looked at each other for what seemed like forever. I studied his eyes. They were every bit as hypnotic and frightening as I'd been warned. Whatever depraved energy burned inside this man was very real.

"Lynette Fromme called," I began, breaking the tension. "She said that you want to marry her. Do you?"

Charlie slowly turned away. His gaze traveled to a picture of a crucifix that hung from his cell wall. After studying it for a few seconds, he responded in an eerie whisper. "Imagine me coming down from the cross to get married in front of myself." His eyes turned back toward me, his face bathed in a devilish glow. I felt myself weakening again.

"Charlie," I coughed, forcing away the dread. "I don't have time for any bullshit. Do you or don't you want to marry her?"

In a flash, Charlie sprang from his bunk and was suddenly standing inches away from the door. He pressed his face against the bars of the tiny aperture and began to speak with a savage intensity that was foreign to me. I stood riveted in place, paralyzed by some unknown force, soaking in the moment. His language was strangely exotic, gushing forth with great emotional energy. Time stood still as he lectured me about everything from his "fraudulent" conviction, to racism, to world pollution. His words were like a whip lashing at my conscience, making me feel that I was personally responsible for everything that was wrong with the world.

He poured it on, painting a horrific portrait of environmental corruption and the criminal neglect of children, which he blamed on the entire human race. I felt my intellectual side feasting on the stimulating thoughts and hungering for more. His twisted logic and garbled half-truths somehow began making sense.

"I live not by your laws, but by my laws, the laws of the Great One of whom I am and of whom all of us are a part," he seethed. "I am the one, the one who can save the world. The one who gave his life so that you could live. I am holding him for you, but you try to destroy me, yet you are really destroying yourselves. You fool! Can't you see that I am you and that I am your reflection? I am your child, your creation. If you kill me, you kill yourself."

It wasn't so much his words, but the power, the energy, the charged charisma that emanated from his grubby little being. I began to understand why his troubled followers literally worshiped the man, why they would do anything, good or horrendously evil, to please him.

"The world is rotting," he continued with escalating intensity. "Can't you see it? Open your eyes. Pollution is all around you. Money is raping the earth, destroying the trees, polluting the air and water. Your children are choking and dying under your money noses. Your children cry for help, but you don't hear them. You ignore them and they come to me. The children you ignore, I will keep. Someday they will rise up and kill you to save the world."

After a pause, Manson cried out with resounding fervor: "I have a mission that makes my life worth something! You have sold your planet and your children. I have come to buy them with your blood!" With that, he darted from the door and retreated to his bunk.

I staggered down the alley, my head spinning from everything I'd just heard. It wasn't until I was halfway down the hall that my senses returned. Thank God this man was locked in a cell, I thought. Thank God I could walk away from his hypnotic influence. What must it have been like for those who followed him when he was free, the impressionable young women who barely had any thoughts of their own? They were the perfect empty vessels, and Charlie had filled them with the most beguiling poison.

How could those disfranchised little girls from broken, dysfunctional families have fought it? I was a prison-hardened ex-cop and ex–navy fighter pilot trainee who had studied for five years to be a secular Sulpician Catholic priest, with additional Jesuit studies at the University of San Francisco. My head was clear, my will strong, my cynicism sharp, and my faith unbending. And yet, because of my open mind, I had temporarily fallen under this criminal's spell. No wonder his followers had chosen to spend the best years of their lives camped around the entrance of a dank, foreboding prison, waiting for a sound, a glimpse, a fleeting thought to drift down from their imprisoned guru. I knew then that they would never leave. Squeaky's calls would never let up, and the letters that poured in from troubled souls around the world would continue to arrive as long as Manson was alive.

From that moment on, I was hooked on Charlie and his Family. Not as a follower, but as a professor studying a strange, mystifying phenomenon. For the next eight years, I would be Charles Manson's jailer, protector, and counselor. I would oversee the security and treatment of this strange, elfin man on a daily basis. I would control his life. In a way, he would also control mine.

The next day, while making my rounds, I stopped in front of Charlie's cell. This was a different approach, a more public and casual visit. Charlie, a master of the moment, sensed that this wasn't the time for a serious discourse on the meaning of life. His demeanor completely changed. He was less agitated, his voice was quiet and restrained, and his speech was clear and to the point.

"Do you know who I am?" he asked again.

"Of course."

"No. I mean, do you know about me? Who I really am?"

"No. I know why you're here, but I don't know much about you."

Charlie skittered to his bunk, grabbed a book, and stuck it through the cell bars. It was *Helter Skelter*, former L.A. prosecutor Vincent Bugliosi's best-seller about the sensational Manson trial.

"Take it. There's lots of lies in it, but it tells about me," Charlie insisted. I thumbed through the pages, then handed it back.

"Thanks, but I'll get my own copy."

I was surprised that Manson was promoting that particular book. It painted a horrendous picture of him, at least from a sane person's perspective. Then again, maybe Charlie reveled in the demon-possessed, murderer-controller, modern-day Adolf Hitler image Bugliosi presented. It's difficult to fathom what feeds a felon's self-image. Whatever Charlie's reasoning, he would have to be more careful about his literary boastings in his current surroundings. There's a strange, harsh, and totally inexplicable morality that exists among prisoners. While many ruthless and sadistic behaviors are accepted, even celebrated, others, like child molestation and crimes against women, are generally condemned. Manson's offenses didn't fall squarely into the banned categories, but he was still considered to be weird and sick. Like the "chomos" (child molesters) and rapists, he needed protection. He'd never admitted it, but he was aware of it. Manson was one of the best I'd ever seen at manipulating the system to keep himself out of danger.

I bought *Helter Skelter* that weekend and read it again with renewed interest. The horror of what Manson and his followers had done terrified me. The savagery and lurid detail surrounding the murders was staggering. I couldn't shake the eerie images of drugged, homicidal zombies invading Hollywood and cutting up eight socialites — including *Petticoat Junction* actress Sharon Tate's unborn baby. In a particularly gruesome touch, Charlie's depraved crew used their victims' blood to write cryptic messages like "Pigs" and "Helter Skelter" on the walls.

Although Charlie himself had not participated in the first set of murders, he went out the second night and personally selected supermarket magnate Leno LaBianca and his wife, Rosemary, to be his clan's next victims, breaking into their home and tying them up. Once they were so secured, he left and ordered his followers to do the dirty work.

I again wondered why Charlie would want me to read such a disgusting depiction of his madness. Was he bragging, or was it merely an attempt to fill me with fear? I was sure it was both. The cunning little bastard believed that fear motivated everyone. What better way to instill fear than with that book?

My initial experiences with Charlie made me recall an article I'd recently read about Dr. Albert Speer, Hitler's chief architect. Speer described his first impression of Hitler, catching one of his speeches in a "dirty, ill-lit beer hall" in Munich. Until then, Speer had viewed Hitler as nothing more than a "vulgar, rabble-rousing fanatic in a comic-opera Brownshirt uniform." That changed as Dr. Speer listened.

"Hitler started to speak earnestly, persuasively, almost shyly," Dr. Speer recalled. "His manner was completely sincere, more like a dedicated professor delivering a lecture than a screaming demagogue. Within a few minutes, he had the entire audience in his grip, and by no means was everyone there his supporters. Soon, his low-pitch manner disappeared, his voice rose to a hypnotic pitch, and there was a palpable aura of tension and excitement in the hall, a crackling emotional voltage. . . . His dynamic presence filled the room. His voice swelled, his eyes transfixed the audience. It wasn't so much what he said, I hardly remembered afterwards, but the mood he cast over the entire hall; it had an almost orgiastic quality."

This was exactly the way I reacted to Manson. I was thankful that the cult leader had been caught and cut down when he was, because, like Hitler, he would have done a hell of a lot more damage had he remained free.

Part of me wanted to stay away from this man, to keep my distance and treat him like any other prisoner. Another part sucked me in, drew me to him like a heroin addict to a needle. I'd abstain for a few days; then I couldn't stand it anymore and would have to go to his cell for my next "fix."

One afternoon, this feeling was so overpowering that I was moved to pull Charlie from his cage and bring him to my office for a chat. Charlie sensed it was time for another royal performance and obliged. Like Dr. Speer, I sat in rapt attention as he put on his latest show, this time giving me a rousing rendition of his life story. He began by conjuring primitive images of serpents and other animals and weaving them into spectacular metaphors. He spoke for an hour about the horrors of his life, how he'd walked out of prison the previous time with good intentions, then encountered his female followers and started his "Family." He described in detail how he used LSD to turn them on, and made love to each one. He expressed an amazement at the emergence of his own persuasive powers, discovering for the first time that people would follow him and that he could control them.

He continued by reciting a chapter from what I can only describe as Manson's personal book of Anti-Proverbs, a stream-of-consciousness series of loosely connected nuggets of disturbed, life-guiding thought.

"What do you know about fear? To save people from what they do to themselves, it would take a greater fear than the earth has ever seen. A fear only I can unleash! Fear is nothing more than awareness. Awareness is love. Absolute fear is absolute awareness. Give in to your fear and it will cease to exist. All you are left with is the awareness. And that awareness is love.

"See, all is love? There is nothing that's not love. Confusion is love in another form. But what really is love? Love is a word we used for God. But even that's misguided. What we mean by love in that form is intelligence. The understanding of things that are beyond you. Beyond you, but not beyond me. Because I can see. I understand. That's what you people can't accept in your paycheck-whore worlds. It blows your mind to confront the truth that I've been enlightened, and the rest of you haven't.

"I've been charged with waking up the world. But why should I? I tried that before and look what you did to me? The people, they're not worth the trouble! Humanity as a whole isn't worth shit. You could search the earth before you could find five honest adults. A few individuals out there understand and touch life, but the rest are spineless predators trying to get over on someone else to justify their own existence. The ego gets so big they don't realized their dick's gone soft.

"So why should I care anymore, even with my knowledge? The people don't care enough about themselves to listen! No one wants to do it themselves, man. They all want to follow a leader who tells them what to do. Believe me, I know that trip. If there's anything I know, it's that. Everybody wants to be saved, but they won't take the first step necessary to rescue their damned souls. They're out there in their little churches waiting for Jesus to come back and save them from the doom and gloom of their meager existence. But Jesus already came! He left his message two thousand years ago. Wasn't that enough? Hell no! Greedy paycheck whores want him to come back. They missed him the last time, so they plead, 'Please come back during my time.' That's crazy, man! You know what I tell these people? How many fucking times do you want him to come back? Every time he comes back, you turn on him like rabid rats and give him nothing but shit—just like you've turned on me! He came back in

Germany during the 1930s and people are still bitching about that. The Iron Cross replaced the wooden one. Millions of people died trying to put order in the world, and when the forces of greed and evil rebelled, the truth was lied about and covered up.

"What if he don't come back at all anymore? What if he sees what you did to me and says, 'Fuck you all. You don't deserve it.' Humans need gods. God don't need humans. That leaves us on our own, man. All we have is our mind. But that's all we need! The mind is everything. It's Christ, Buddha, the devil, it's God himself. It's where the music plays and the passion simmers. It pumps the energy of life up from the heart.

"People say I'm bad. I'm evil. I'm a beast. But what do they know about good, bad, and evil? They know nothing! There's no good or bad in my world, just 'is.' It doesn't make a difference what I've done, what I want, my hopes. Good or bad has nothing to do with it. A wolf jumps on a precious baby squirrel and swallows it down while the mother watches in horror. What could be more horrible than that, watching a mangy wolf eat your child? But is the wolf bad? Is the wolf a monster? No! The wolf's only doing what nature has programmed it to do. Nature put it on the earth and said it has to eat to survive. Baby squirrels are on the menu. Even the mama squirrel eventually comes to understand this. The only ones who don't are humans. People don't understand the order of nature. All they know is how to screw it up. A dog wags its tail and plays fetch because humans give it food and water. But take away the humans and their handouts, and those sweet little puppies will turn into snarling beasts tearing apart rabbits and cats and small children and eating their bloody carcasses to survive. And those are our beloved pets that share our homes and beds. What makes us think that we're any different? This innate human arrogance is why I'm in a cage and the animals are in cages in zoos and all of you are on the outside blighting the planet.

"Humans are worse than dogs because it wouldn't even have to come to survival. If people knew they couldn't die, if they couldn't be punished for anything they ever did, what do you think would happen? Absolute evil. Strip away the concept of retribution, bring down the walls of fear, and the true evil nature inside humans will gush forth. To keep control, we are schooled, taught and programmed against our own natures by the fear instilled in us by grown-ups and authority figures. And it's all a lie! We are warned not to lie, that it's bad to lie, but the people who are telling us that are lying to us all the time! You see, doing good, that's easy. Being good is a breeze, man. Just stand in line and do what everybody else is doing. Doing evil, that takes effort, work, and creativity. The hardest part is afterward, when you have to step back and deal with the rewards. And one of the most important rewards is that you can never truly understand good until you've done evil. That enlightenment will lead to a perfect universe within oneself and a balance between good and evil.

"You may be free in what your tiny, schoolbook minds know as freedom, but you tell me who's free. Are you more free than me? I'm a hundred different things. I'm a glass of water, a rock, a grain of sand, a guitar, a rattlesnake, a young girl, an eagle, a cactus in the desert sun. I can be all of that, but you can be nothing but the one simpleton human that you are. You have no thoughts of your own, just what others have programmed in you.

"I confess! I'm not human! People have cried that derisively, tried to sear me with that stinging brand, but they're too lost to know how right they are. I am beyond human. I am everything and everybody! Because of this, you think I'm insane. You tag me as crazy. But it's you who are crazy! You don't have the intellect to understand an entity that is a cobra, a wolf, a scorpion, or sometimes, nothing at all. I'm just a reflection of what you are thinking at any given time. Yet, you can't see the beauty there. You can't see the power. You think I'm insane because I'm angry about the lies of this world, the greed, the lust for money, the rape of the earth, the pollution, the mass confusion, and the relentless inbreeding of fools with no intelligence whatsoever.

"Even locked in here, I can see what's out there better than you! Self-ishness! The whole world is awash in a black plague of selfishness. Every-body spends their every waking second chasing after what's best for them and them alone. They're all lost! A total lost cause! How long can I scream that this is the true insanity? How long can my followers keep screaming the truth? Our very existence lies in the air, trees, water, and animals. Ignore this, and we all die. Not just me. You've condemned me to death in your corrupt courtrooms, but I'm not going out alone. You're all sen-tenced to die with me. And even while you're dying, you continue to reach out with your shriveled fingers to grab little green pieces of paper with dead people's pictures on them.

"When the end comes, and chaos rules, and the ordered world you've created crumbles to dust, you won't know how to survive. You're weak. You've depended upon your own corrupt universe instead of the natural order. You're chasing your tail, and it will lead you into a black hole worse than anything you've accused me of.

"So what do you do? Instead of listening, you hang it all on me, Charles Manson. You want me to fight all your fears and die all your deaths. You're trying to kill me over and over, but I won't die. You tried to march me into that gas chamber with the preacher on each side and the pigs in front and back, but you couldn't do it. My power was too strong. You couldn't extinguish the light! And you know why? Because deep inside every one of you, you know I'm right. You have the proof. An ex-con comes out of jail, and all your children, the children of your doctors, lawyers, Harvard grads, they come flocking to me for the answers. To me! Not you who raised them, but to me, a man with no formal education. And I told them to go away, not to follow me. I told them to go home and ask their moms and dads. And you know what they said. They begged, 'Please, Charlie, don't send me away. My mother and father won't let me come back. They hate me. They don't understand. Only you understand. Please, Charlie, let me stay.' So I let them stay. And people say that terrible things resulted. Whose fault was that? Mine? You can't hang that on me. You can't even hang your hate and revulsion on me. How do you feel about the murders? That's all that matters. Not what anyone did, but how the rest of you feel about what your children did. It happened in your world, not mine. Nothing like that ever happened among my people. Strange how that was lost on everybody. It's like this prison. Terrible, savage men in here, did brutal things on the outside. But what they all did combined wouldn't equal what would happen if you opened these bars and left them to themselves for a few hours. The blood and savagery against each other would be unspeakable. It wasn't like that in the desert. My children lived in perfect harmony. Do you think I would have tolerated any bullshit like that among the kids? We weren't about murder! We were about fucking and blow jobs and eating pussy and playing music and getting high and doing our thing and having sex all day and night. It was your world that wouldn't leave us alone. It was your world where the sickness and madness existed.

"What is murder anyway? There's no murder in a holy war. That was a holy war. Everything's a holy war. You don't draw a line and say killing these people in Germany and Vietnam is okay, but killing these people in Hollywood isn't. That's the height of hypocrisy.

"How can you pretend to know me and my motivations when you don't even know yourself? Our brains are like spaceships from another planet that the best scientists in the world can't figure out. It's ten thousand light-years beyond mortal comprehension. There are five computer chips to grow one fingernail and ten fibers just to let you take a shit and a hundred million satellites to move thoughts around. It's operated by flies, snakes, beetles, mice, and cockroaches. Yet, take the brain of a human and put it in a maggot's head and it will go crazy. It will convulse and die from the horror of human thought.

"After all this, all this hate, greed, madness, violence, and murder festering inside you, your children still turn to me for deliverance. And let me tell you something. By the time you assholes wake up and find your father God, I'll be too old and beaten down to piss on you to put out the fire that is destroying your souls. So wake up. The only chance this planet has is to unite as one world under the last person. I am the last person. You will do what I say or there will be nothing!"

My head was spinning so wildly that it took me a while to realize that he'd finished. Actually, he hadn't. Charlie capped the glorious oratory with what I would come to experience as a typical incongruity. After going on about his supernatural force and mystical abilities, specifically about his powers to persuade and control—powers that were obvious to me from the moment we met—he suddenly remembered where he was and whom he was talking to. Backpedaling, he tacked on a totally conflicting epilogue, repeating his standard cop-out for the Tate-LaBianca murders. He blamed his followers for what they did and professed to have no influence over them whatsoever.

Inconsistencies aside, it was a spellbinding performance, one of his best. After he finished, I fought the urge to stand and applaud.

It took about a month for Squeaky and her cohort, Sandra Good, to make their most defiant stand at the prison gates. "They're demanding to visit Charlie," the gate officer radioed. "I told them they can't because they haven't been approved. Now they say they're not leaving until they talk to you."

"I'll be right down," I said, eager to meet the two main Manson groupies after having jousted with them on the phone for weeks. As with everything involving Charlie, the meeting was a trip. The pair, original Family members and Manson favorites who had not taken part in either set of murders, were standing together like Technicolor monks draped in full-length hooded robes. Squeaky's was red, Sandra's blue. I knew the colors stood for something—everything with Charlie stood for something. (I later learned that he had dubbed Lynette "Red" and given her the task of saving the great redwood forests. "Blue" Sandra was responsible for the air and the water.)

From the moment I laid eyes on Squeaky, I wanted to reach into her soul, push some inner reset button, and get her back on track. How could this soft, frilly creature worship a cretin like Manson? To have once fallen under his spell was understandable. He had found her right after a bitter falling-out with her father. Charlie took her in when she was lost and alone. But why hang on now? They had been separated for more than five years. He was trapped in a wretched prison, and would be forever. What was the point?

I studied the pair up close. Lynette and Sandra were the stereotypical girls next door. Squeaky was cute, freckle-faced, with chestnut eyes and fiery auburn hair. Sandra was softer, more feminine. Her blue eyes matched her robe, and her striking sandy hair was the kind of mane most women would kill for. Both were attractive women with definite sex appeal. Neither wore a trace of makeup, which gave them an innocence that belied the truth.

As they spoke, I could sense their darker sides emerge, slowly at first, then with a cascading force. Squeaky started right in with her veiled threats, implying that unpleasant things would befall me if anything bad happened to Charlie. I brushed that aside, explaining for the umpteenth time that it was extremely doubtful that she would be approved to visit or write Charlie if she maintained that attitude. Seeing them now, I knew the decision would hold. It was obvious that the pair were programmed to do anything Charlie wanted.

"Mr. George, don't you know your life depends on it?" Squeaky said, her birdlike voice eerily conflicting with the menacing message.

"Are you threatening me?"

She did a quick soft-shoe. "What I meant was, if Charlie isn't allowed to be free, we're all going to die. He's the only one who can save us from the destruction, save the earth, the air, and the water. When that's gone, we're all going to die!"

Nice rebound. Charlie had taught her well. It didn't serve her purpose to infuriate me. Like it or not, I was the only conduit to her master. And I'd treated her with a measure of respect, better than most. Shrewd as she was, she shared another trait with Charlie that didn't serve her, or his, best interest. Although neither was foreign to lies, they could both be painfully honest, usually at the wrong time.

"Would you help Charlie escape?" I asked.

"Yes!" she answered, as if the question were more about her loyalty than her desire to break the law.

"There you have it," I sighed. "How can you expect me to approve a visit or a letter when you admit you'd help him escape?"

"But we need him, Mr. George. We all have to help him."

Putting aside her threats, I was impressed with Squeaky's spunk. She was ruthless and daring, and had an air of sophistication and mystery about her. Staring at this lonely young lady, some basic instinct flickered inside me. I felt envious of her commitment to Manson. I imagined myself wooing her away from him, straightening out her head, and returning her home to her parents a changed, remorseful woman. To accomplish that, I didn't know if I should take her in my arms and give her a hug, or slap her across the face and scream some sense into her. I even contemplated dragging her kicking and screaming to the psychiatric ward and pumping a few thousand volts of electricity into her messed-up brain. I dreamed about helping her escape a decade-long nightmare, but it was only a seminary student's fantasy. There was nothing I, or anyone else, could really do. Short of a biblical miracle, the only person who could free her was Charlie himself, and even if he tried, she probably wouldn't accept it.

Tossing the young ladies a bone, I set up an interview at a later date to be held in the records office of the administration building. I had a few more questions I wanted answered before I filed my final ruling on their visitation request. I also needed the time to determine if either had a criminal record. I knew they weren't felons. If they were, the point would have been moot. Convicted felons aren't allowed to visit prisoners. On the other hand, I suspected that the girls might have picked up a misdemeanor or two along the way. Sure enough, they had, but their official offenses seemed mild in comparison with some of their cohorts'. Squeaky had been arrested during the Manson trial and charged with conspiracy to spike a witness's hamburger with LSD to prevent her from testifying. She was given a ninety-day sentence. Police also had questions about what part, if any, Squeaky might have played in the murders of a couple of Manson hangers-on in Stockton. However, she was never charged in connection with those crimes.

Sandra Good's major post–Helter Skelter blemish was being friends with a group that tried to rob a gun shop. The motive was to arm themselves for an attempt to storm Folsom prison and free Charlie. Good was not arrested when the culprits were rounded up. She was later charged, and convicted, of giving a lift to a Manson supporter who had escaped prison. The helpful ride cost her a few months in jail. The most disturbing thing I had read about Sandra's life was the mention in *Helter Skelter* of the mysterious demise of her husband, a onetime Family member named Joel Pugh. On December 1, 1969—the same day the main players in the Tate-LaBianca murders were arrested—Pugh was found dead in a London hotel room. Although his throat had been slashed twice, both wrists cut, and no note found, the London authorities ruled it a drug-induced suicide. The question in everybody's mind was, had Pugh run all the way to London to escape the coming Manson Family Armageddon? And if so, had Manson dispatched an assassin halfway around the world to go after him? Bruce Davis, a Manson Family hatchet man and convicted murderer, had been in London earlier that year. English authorities were uncertain whether he was there the day Pugh died. Wherever he was, Davis didn't resurface in California until February 1970.

As with Charlie, my fascination with these dangerous women overruled my good sense. I should have run them off and barred them from coming on the prison grounds. Instead, I stretched out the investigation and promised to reconsider the possibility of a future visit or letter. I was flirting with disaster, toying with frayed personalities and damaged souls. Yet, my innate hunger to learn more about the criminal mind, about people like Charlie, Squeaky, and Sandra, pushed me into the abyss.

I recalled some poems I had read in the seminary about the desire of man to soar beyond the ever moving arches of experience that forever drifted farther away, chasing the unknown, seeking something just beyond the next mountain range. Maybe I could make a difference. Maybe one day, with my help, Charlie would stop performing like a circus freak, put on a suit and tie, cut his hair, and promise to join the human race. Maybe Squeaky and Sandra would find some decent men, get married, have babies, and direct their energy toward more positive causes. Maybe I was the one who was crazy.

Whatever my motives, I was determined to closely observe this man and his disciples, if for no other reason than to see where it took me.

That night, something I'd read kept tearing at my mind. I checked my personal files and found it. It was Squeaky's assessment of the Tate-LaBianca murders. "Stone souls, prowling the neighborhoods, out on the town, looking for a bloodbath. Five or six people get murdered and everybody panics. So what's the big deal? People die every day." Hooded or not, this was one sick child. I memorized the quote to keep it in mind whenever I found myself succumbing to her relentless pleadings.

The twin terrors arrived on schedule seven days later. They were draped, as usual, in their colorful robes. I escorted them inside the compound and watched as they followed without hesitation. There were plenty of men inside those gates eager to ravage them on the spot, rape them repeatedly. Most sane women would be terrified by the mere thought of entering such a place. Not Squeaky and Sandra. Totally consumed with their mission, the strange pair readily marched inside this craven environment. Their only concern was getting closer to their master. Their only fear was being prevented from doing so.

A guard ushered them to a conference room normally used for parole board hearings. The mahogany walls, high-backed leather chairs, and polished table offered the formal atmosphere of a court hearing. Squeaky and Sandra seated themselves and waited for the questions. Sitting back in my chair, I plopped Manson's thick file on the table, then got down to business.

"Why don't you just tell us what you want?"

Squeaky, as usual, did all the talking. "We want to visit Charlie."

"You requested visitation rights at every institution Charlie's been in. They all turned you down. Why should we be different? Has anything changed?"

"You don't understand. Charlie is our life. He has the answers that will save the world. It's dying, can't you see that? He can save it. He can save you and me. Look around you. The air is dirty. The water is polluted. The trees are being cut down to build beautiful homes for the rich. The earth is being raped and scarred by tractors and bulldozers. Money and greed are killing the earth. We must stop it before it's too late! . . . See our robes? We're nuns waiting for our lord to be set free. The only thing we can do before he comes off the cross is clean up his earth for him. Our robes symbolize a new era. We must protect the air, water, and land. My robe is red with the blood I've vowed to shed to save our lord's precious environment. . . ."

Squeaky went on like that for more than an hour. I couldn't help noticing how her words and phrases and the rhythm of her language matched Charlie's. Some of his oddest statements came out of her mouth in the same exact sequence. I could sense that the concepts she parroted were beyond her comprehension. They reached levels of philosophy that would make a college professor woozy.

"Lynette," I interrupted. "Did you come here to lecture us or to discuss visiting Charlie?"

"Both!" she snapped, once again exhibiting her stark honesty.

"Well, I only have time for one."

"You better listen to us, Mr. George," she threatened, her eyes suddenly on fire. "Your life depends on it."

"Damn it, Lynette, you can't keep going around talking like that. That's it. No visits. The meeting's over. It's time to go."

As we stood, I heard a soft, cold, emotionless voice break the silence.

"Can we write?" Squeaky asked.

"No. I'm sorry."

Once again, I'd let my heart overrule my head. I wanted to give these women every opportunity to present themselves in a manner that would enable them to see Manson, if only for a few minutes, but they couldn't even pretend to suppress their violent rhetoric or emotions.

Both Squeaky and Sandra were now fighting for control. Their faces twisted and contorted, warning of an explosive anger born out of a catastrophic disappointment. Then, as quickly as it built, it dissipated. "You are our only hope," Squeaky pleaded. "The others have all turned us down. They wouldn't listen, even to save their own lives."

She continued her pleas as I escorted her out of the office. "Charlie went to prison for us. We are responsible. When we were arrested, he came to us. He gave up the freedom that he loved so much because he wanted us to be free. Now he's in a tomb, suffering. His blood is being sucked from his life and no one listens. Listen to him," she whispered, as if she were telling me some great truth so special she couldn't say it out loud. "He is ever changing. He has majesty that will blind you. He is everything you are not. He can help you."

As we were coming down the stairs, Associate Warden Ted Rinker,* a stiff, hard-line guard turned no-nonsense administrator, burst through the door. "What the hell is going on here?" he demanded. "Who are these people?" I knew exactly what he was thinking. Because of their strange outfits, Rinker figured we'd slipped some of the inmates' wives or girlfriends into the conference room for some hanky-panky.

"They're two of the Manson Family women, the ones who have been picketing the front gate, Ted," I answered matter-of-factly. "We were interviewing them to determine whether they should be allowed to visit

---

*This name is a pseudonym invented by the authors.

Charlie." For a few seconds, Rinker searched our faces and theirs, wondering if I'd come up with a great dodge.

"Well, you've been in here long enough. I want you both back in the unit where you belong," he groused, never missing an opportunity to pull rank and bully. It was Sunday. I had specifically scheduled the meeting on the weekend to avoid Rinker, San Quentin's annoying assistant principal.

"Doesn't that jerk ever go home?" I muttered when he was out of range. "Get a life, Rinker."

Outside, I watched as Lynette and Sandra glumly walked away, their dreams once again shattered. I would never see Lynette again. Her date with infamy was fast approaching. But she would continue to call and write.

Relentlessly.

2

A MONTH AFTER arriving at San Quentin, I bumped into Warden Rees at the prison snack bar, which was actually a neat little café outside the prison walls overlooking San Francisco Bay. Our conversation naturally turned to Manson. "How's he doing?" Rees inquired.

"Not bad. He's still in the Adjustment Center, max security."

"Behaving himself?"

"Pretty much. Everybody caters to the little bastard. It's like we have this celebrity over there. He's a weird guy, hard to figure," I said.

"Have you thought about reducing custody?" I was surprised that Rees posed the question. That was something that I'd been toying with in my own mind.

"We're seeing him next week in classification," I explained. "If he comes across okay, the committee might lower his custody and give him a try in B section. He's ready for a shot. I think he'd do okay."

"That sounds good," the warden responded. "He's been locked up at max custody for what, five years now?"

"Yeah, nobody wants to take a chance."

Well, maybe you should."

"Lynette got to you, didn't she," I said, smiling.

"Yeah," Rees confirmed. "She's an aggressive little bitch."

"Hey, I've been there." I laughed. "She bugged you about getting him out in the sun, giving him a guitar, and a place to grow some flowers, right?" The warden's smile confirmed that he was familiar with the rap. "Hey, I thought I was supposed to handle all her calls," I jokingly protested.

"You are," he grunted. "She's still your responsibility. She just lucked out and got through to me."

"Seriously, Bob," I continued. "He's been a good inmate so far. He deserves a break. I'll get him psyched. If Dr. Sutton thinks he looks okay. I'll give him the shot."

Taking the cue, I transferred Charlie to the more populated and less restrictive B section after an exhaustive investigation of the inmates who would be housed around him. The trustees gave me an inside scoop on the mood of the cons, while the correctional sergeants relayed the feelings of the guards. We determined that no one was likely to try and whack him or carve out a piece of his neck for a souvenir.

Charlie had kept his nose clean and earned the right to escape his suffocating twenty-four-hour lockdown. In B section, he'd be able to catch a ray or two of sunshine out in the yard with the other inmates. Remembering Squeaky's request, I noted that there was a small plot of dirt by the hospital morgue against the west wall. Charlie could plant some seeds, stroke his guitar, and serenade the flowers to his heart's content.

The Adjustment Center classification committee approved the transfer and reduced his custody from maximum to close supervision. After his first week, the prison psychiatrist informed me that Charlie had settled in and was behaving himself.

The same couldn't be said for Squeaky. In one of her calls, she announced that she was holding me personally responsible for Charlie's well-being. I explained that all of the prisoners were my responsibility. They were there to serve their time, not to be beaten, tortured, raped, or abused in any way. Charlie was no different from the rest in that respect. He was, of course, unique in virtually every other category. I found it ironic that the man who preached living free in the wilderness, and castigated those wedded to money and possessions, had more "stuff" than any other prisoner. Charlie's fans and Family sent him multiples of every item on the approved property list—sweaters, shirts, socks, underwear, books, magazines, television sets, radios, even an acoustic guitar. (He had to check the instrument in and out with the guards, and could only play it during designated times.)

One day, a beautifully crocheted vest arrived through the mail. It was decorated with the most brilliant display of intricate, multicolored scenes I'd ever seen. It was cut like one of those leather biker vests, only the embroidery was truly a masterpiece. Studying it closer, I was amazed to see that it was an artful history of the Manson Family. There were scenes of sex and murder, and images of snakes, spiders, wounded bodies, swastikas, and black-magic symbols harmoniously balanced with clusters of flowers, birds, butterflies, dancing children, musical notes, and natural panoramas. The garment, custom-made by Squeaky and friends, reflected long hours of meticulous, painstaking work. Elaborate and delicately woven, it clashed severely with the ugly, drab monotony of the prison.

Vests were not approved items. Because it was such a work of art, I made an exception, slipping it to Charlie under the loophole that allowed handmade cardigan sweaters. Charlie played it cool when I presented it to him. That was smart. Veteran cons like Charlie know better than to become attached to anything in prison, especially something unusual or special. I could tell, however, that he cherished it.

Two days later, a sergeant strolled into my office with some startling news.

"You know that vest you gave the little motherfucker?"

"Yeah?"

"Everyone's got it now."

"What?"

"Just what I said. It's all over the tier."

I bolted from my office and immediately began to investigate. I couldn't believe Charlie, even a homicidal creep like Charlie, could do such a thing. Turned out that it was another example of Manson's keen survival instincts. A few of the bigger, meaner inmates became jealous and tried to take it from him. Charlie, as weak and helpless physically as he was strong mentally, saw where that was heading. A violent confrontation was inevitable. To save face, he decided, King Solomon style, to cut up the vest and bestow it upon everybody. It was a brilliant move. He not only ingratiated himself with inmates longing for a keepsake from the famous cult leader, he frustrated the thugs who wanted it.

Despite the logic of the action, I was still upset that he had destroyed so precious a gift just to save his butt. When I told Lynette, she let out an emotional wail. "Why did he do it?" she asked in a horrified tone. "Doesn't he understand what that meant to us? How much love we put into that? That was our souls, the souls of the people devoted to him." It was the first and only time in my decades-long association with her that Squeaky questioned the actions of her master.

"I have no idea, Lynn," I ducked, praying that the incident would be the catalyst to help her break away. "You'll have to ask Charlie that." There was a long pause, followed by some rare sobbing. Then the phone went dead. That was really unusual. Squeaky was never one to cut short a conversation with someone close to her prince.

Charlie saved his butt all right, but he nearly lost his most faithful follower in the process. Nearly. When I told Charlie how devastated Lynette was, he immediately put pen to paper. His explanation was short, and rather well stated. "It will always live in my mind, where no one can destroy it or take it away from me." That was it. He said nothing more. I sensed that because the gift was so special, he indulged her brief defiance, but only to a point.

The next time she called, she was her old Squeaky self, as devoted to her sinister master as ever. She never mentioned the vest again. Yet, as the weeks passed, I sensed something different about Squeaky, an unraveling of her already loosely knit psyche. There was a tension and desperation building inside her that was unnerving. Her desire to visit Charlie grew into an obsession that consumed what little remained of her outside life. It seemed as if she had a burning question she needed answered, and approval for something big she was planning. That, or she desperately needed to confirm or challenge some order she had already received. Whatever the reason, Squeaky was coming unglued.

Her threats increased so much that a public advocates attorney in San Francisco, whom Squeaky and Sandra had been consulting in their efforts to obtain visiting privileges with Manson at San Quentin, went to the police. They had began writing to and appearing at the attorney's home. When he felt their implied threats were becoming dangerous to his welfare, he reported their strange behavior. According to deputy chief William Keayes, the two women were interviewed at the Hall of Justice by police investigators and admonished that legal action could be taken against them.

On Tuesday, September 2, Associate Warden Rinker held a routine staff meeting. The chats were highlighted by each program administrator giving a progress report on his unit's operation. When it was my turn, I suppressed my concerns about Squeaky and addressed the issue of how Manson was handling his newfound freedom. Although everybody in the prison was talking about it, the transfer was news to Rinker—bad news. The wrinkles on his forehead deepened and his eyebrows darted upward in shock.

"Are you sure he won't get killed over there?"

"I checked it out before I made the move," I countered. "There's no reason to worry. He's working as the first-tier tender, so he's screened off except for some outside exercise. And we only exercise him with those who aren't a threat. It's working great."

Rinker glared at me. "How do you know there's no threat?"

"I had my staff question and investigate all the inmates housed in B section. He's safe. Even Pin Cushion says he'll be safe."

"Pin Cushion? That's a joke," Rinker sneered, attempting to solicit a laugh. "Do the rest of you think Manson is safe in B section?"

Rinker's yes-man, a lower-ranking associate warden, shook his head, supporting his superior. Rinker then turned to his buddy, the head of the prison security squad. Before the man could second his boss's opinion, I cut in.

"Wait a minute. He's there already. He's been there over a week. This isn't speculation. It's past history. He's hasn't had a single problem. Besides, he's no dummy. He knows how to survive."

"Does Manson have enemies in B section?" Rinker asked the security chief.

The officer cleared his voice and glanced around the room for support before answering. "Yes, I think he has enemies there."

"That's bullshit and you know it," I argued. "I checked with Smokey Thompson, your squad sergeant, long before I moved Manson. He cleared it." I turned back to Rinker. "Our unit classification committee agreed and endorsed the move. Dr. Sutton wrote a report stating that it would bene-fit—"

"I think you better move him back to the AC," Rinker interrupted.

"What—?" I began before cutting off my protest. I knew it was no use. Once Rinker started in a direction, he couldn't be budged. I decided to let it rest, then appeal the decision to Warden Rees.

The following day, Wednesday, September 3, 1975, Squeaky phoned me with an urgent message for Charlie. She was happy and upbeat, as if she had finally come to grips with the issue that had been tormenting her. "Tell Charlie I've found a way to save the redwoods!"

"Okay. Sounds good."

After that, however, her mood quickly darkened. She began rambling in a menacing tone. "Look, George, you've kept us apart long enough. We've tried to reason with you, but you're too stupid to see that you're killing yourself. Time is running out. There will be blood running in the streets. The people killing the planet will pay with their lives!" Squeaky's voice grew harsh and shrill. She spoke of murder and mass mayhem, and evoked scores of bloody images. Her tenses shifted oddly as she ranted. "The dagger was raised. Death was at hand. Nothing could stop it, only Charlie, who was in prison for something he didn't do. We are responsible for him being there and we must pay the price!" She began to cry, softly at first, then building to the point of hysteria. The tears fed a new round of razor's-edge doom and gloom.

Then, for a brief moment, she hushed. "I've sent you a book," she said. "It's about Charlie. *The Day They Murdered Christ.* I want you to read it."

"I can't accept a book from you," I explained. "It's against the rules."

That infuriated her, unleashing more verbal abuse. She raved about the children rising up against their parents, killing them and taking vengeance on those destroying the earth, water, and air. "Blood will wash down on the streets. People will die!" I couldn't stand it anymore. She had pushed my tolerance to the limit. I hung up.

The next day, before ending my shift, I paid Charlie a visit in his cell. His eyes sparkled with the prospect of outside news.

"I just talked to Lynette." At the mention of her name, Charlie cracked his sinister, dirty-old-man grin, as if some depraved erotic flashback from the past had flooded his demented little brain. Charlie liked to make love to his women "in the dirt," as he said, especially white, creamy, upper-middle-class girls like Squeaky. It was part initiation, part debasement to subjugate them to his will, and a large part pure perversion. "She asked me to tell you she found a way to save the redwoods." Charlie jumped from his bunk and started rubbing his hands together like a witch over a cauldron. I sensed that I'd just delivered some secret message that only Charlie and Squeaky understood. Never one to back away from a pending disaster, I pushed on. "She acted real crazy on the phone. She threatened me and everybody else, talking just like you about blood flowing in the streets, children rising up. She sounds more like you every day." My words jabbed him like a sharp stick. His face contorted with rage.

"Don't you know who I am, man?" he roared. "You should be on your knees, begging for your life. I hold it in the palm of my hand. I could have you killed anytime!" He rambled on for another three minutes before I cut him off. I found this dark, ugly side to be his least entertaining facet, and could only stand so much.

"Stop the bullshit!" I interrupted. "I don't have time for this."

As I walked away, I was more convinced than ever that something was up. Charlie had never threatened me like that before. For some reason, he wanted me to know that he had resources on the outside, that he still had power over life and death. Ominous as it sounded, I didn't take the threat seriously. Sure, Charlie continued to have tremendous control over his robotic minions, and they'd kill for him in a heartbeat. I knew that because I read his mail. I just didn't think Charlie would turn on me. I was the guy protecting his back and taking care of him in a hostile environment. I was also a gullible ex–seminary student who showed him more compassion, however undeserved, than anyone else had, or probably ever would. Now I was suspicious that Squeaky and Charlie had some plan afoot.

Twenty-four hours later, Squeaky shocked the world. At the Capitol Mall in Sacramento, Manson number-one follower Squeaky "make love to her in the dirt" Fromme, cast off her goofy robe, dressed herself in a slightly less goofy full-length fire red gown with a matching turban (so much for subtlety), and went to see the President of the United States. Her winning smile and cute freckled face excused her rudeness as she pushed forward through the throng, inching ever closer to the most powerful man in the world. She worked her way past spectators and grim-faced Secret Service agents until she was a mere arm's length from Gerald Ford. This was it, Squeaky's chance to join her master in heinous, historical glory. Through her shocking action, she would propel Charlie back into the limelight and establish his evil power like never before. Carving up a bunch of Hollywood types was one thing. Taking out the President of the United States was something entirely different.

As Ford leaned forward to shake her hand, Squeaky pulled out a massive .45 caliber automatic and shouted, "The country is a mess! This man is not your president!" She lunged toward Ford, aimed at his gut like Jack Ruby plugging Lee Harvey Oswald, and squeezed the trigger at point-blank range. Click. The weapon didn't fire.

One can imagine Squeaky's agony as a half dozen Secret Service agents swarmed her small body and knocked her to the ground. "It didn't go off," she wailed as the agents dragged her away. "Can you believe it? It didn't go off." Although she'd loaded the clip with four deadly rounds and popped it securely into place, she'd forgotten to slide the critical starter bullet directly into the chamber. Without the fifth slug, the only way the big gun could have fired was by snapping back the entire upper chamber and spring-loading it the hard way, a process that's difficult for many men, much less a one-hundred-pound woman. Familiar with weapons from her heavily armed, desert-rat days, Squeaky's baffling oversight can only be explained by fate. Ford's number just wasn't up.

One of the agents, Larry Buendorf, came away from the fracas with a cut on the web of skin between his thumb and forefinger, indicating that the determined Squeaky had pulled the trigger at least one more time during the struggle, slamming the hammer down on the alert Buendorf's hand.

If any doubt remained as to Squeaky's true intentions, best pal Sandra Good immediately appeared to dispell them. Squeaky, Good proclaimed, was only the beginning. "We're going to start assassinating presidents, vice presidents, and major executives of companies. I'm warning these people they better stop polluting or they're going to die."

Ultimate failure aside, Squeaky did take her place in history as the first woman ever to try to assassinate an American president.

Personally, Squeaky's attempt came at the worst possible time for me. Despite Associate Warden Rinker's unbending order, I'd yet to move Charlie back to his old, suffocating, high-security home. My plan was to run it by Warden Rees first. Now all hell had broken loose. Rinker led a team of FBI and Secret Service agents to the Adjustment Center to interrogate Charlie. The hotheaded Rinker flew into a rage when he discovered Manson wasn't there. He gathered a squad of security goons, charged over to B section, and banged on the locked door. "I'm taking Manson out of here, and don't anybody try to stop me!" he bellowed, intoxicated by his authority. The prison SWAT team, known as "gooners," marched through the halls, stormed Manson's cell, swung the door open, and ordered him out.

"What for?" Charlie asked, unaware of what had happened in Sacramento. A pair of officers rushed into the cell, grabbed Manson, and threw him violently against the screen just outside his unit, pinning him against it.

"When I say move, asshole, you better move!" a gooner shouted. Charlie was searched, cuffed, and dragged out of B section. Swept down the corridors in a mad rush, his route took him past Rinker, a man he was, surprisingly, meeting for the first time.

"Who the hell are you?" he asked.

"I'm Ted Rinker!" the starched officer announced with all the piss and vinegar he could muster. "Associate Warden!"

"Well, I'll be damned," Charlie responded. "Another fuckin' asshole!"

In the interrogation room, Charlie defiantly faced the army of accusers and denied everything, insisting that Squeaky had acted on her own and that he had had no prior knowledge of her plans.

The following morning, I received a call at my home from Warden Rees. The warden had handpicked me for the job of helping him clean up San Quentin. Until that moment, I'd always considered him to be an ally. "Ed," Rees opened in a stone serious voice. "Ted Rinker wants you fired."

"What? What for?"

"He said you disobeyed a direct order to move Manson."

"Well yeah, he did tell me to move him, but he didn't say when."

"Rinker said he told you Tuesday at his staff meeting, and expected it to be done the next day."

"The next day? I don't remember that," I dodged. "It was more like, 'I think you better move him.' That's how I read it. We disagreed about it, but he cut me off. I tried to explain what I was doing, but he wouldn't listen. So I waited to get a psych report from Dr. Sutton before discussing it with him again. If he didn't buy it after that, I was going to appeal to you." Rees said nothing, letting me twist in the wind. "Let's see," I continued. "He told me at the Tuesday staff meeting. I was busy Wednesday. I asked Dr. Sutton for a report on Thursday, then I took off Friday. So that makes two lousy workdays that I delayed. For that, he wants to fire me?"

"Well, damn it, it's bad," Rees said, finally speaking up. "Real bad. He wants you fired, and he has witnesses. It's a bad situation."

"He has witnesses? Who? That suck-ass associate warden and Rinker's pet security chief? Look, Bob, whatever I did, I didn't do it thinking I was disobeying a direct order. Rinker's directive didn't come across with urgency, like a command. It was more like a request, something I should do soon but not immediately. He's only making a big deal because that goofball Squeaky tried to shoot President Ford! Sure, that looks bad, but you can't hang that on me! I don't know why Rinker hates my guts. The day I got here, he told me I didn't have the balls for the job. He wanted one of his gooner buddies to get it. Ever since then, he jumps on my ass every chance he gets. He treats me like shit, and he's just using this Squeaky thing to try and get me. Frankly, I'm damn tired of him!"

By then, I was so angry I was shaking.

"Look, Ed," Rees said, trying to calm me down. "We can't solve this over the phone. We'll work it out next week."

Great, I thought, hanging up the receiver. String out the misery.

After a nerve-racking weekend, the other shoe dropped that Monday. I received a chilling letter from Squeaky that hit me like a sledgehammer. The newly imprisoned Manson disciple wrote that she had tried to kill the President to focus attention on my denying her access to Charlie. Fromme wrote: "Had I had a chance to see Charlie, most likely I would never have gone to confront the Pres." I put the letter down and sat stunned at my desk. It was only a one-in-a-million lucky break that kept Squeaky from being successful. The ramifications from my perspective were immense. In my dark corner of the world, a forgotten place populated by society's worst outcasts, I had made a decision that could have altered the course of world history.

I finally began to realize why nobody in the penal system wanted anything to do with Charlie Manson. Nobody except an idealistic ex–seminary student with a curious mind who thought he could save the world. I'd danced on the edge of the fire known as the Manson Family for nearly three months, all the while foolishly thinking I was shielded from the heat. Now, with my career in the balance and my resolve weakening, I'd been jerked into the blazing central core.

3

A S I WAITED for the warden to make his decision regarding my career, a vise seemed to tighten around my head. I had a wife and six children to support. Losing my steady income would be devastating. I stayed away from Charlie on the cellblock, not wanting to give him the satisfaction of knowing how deeply he'd messed up my life. I was in trouble because I had tried to show both Charlie and his followers a measure of kindness, but that sentiment would be lost on him. He was about power and control—with a good measure of evil insanity thrown into the bubbling cauldron inside his brain. Instead of sympathy, he'd get the perverse pleasure of knowing that Squeaky's assassination attempt might cost me my livelihood.

The vise clamped around my head didn't ease a notch when I punched the time clock and went off duty. Walking the emotional tightrope between work and home—especially when work is a hellish prison—is always a high-wire act for prison employees. The stress, tension, and gloominess can be unbearable, even for those of us on the outside of the bars. This week nearly pushed me over the edge. I was jumpy and irritable around the house, snapping at my wife and six children over every little thing. Eventually, I was forced to isolate myself physically and emotionally from them. It was obvious that something was eating me, but I refused to elaborate. It had long been my policy to leave the dark side of my profession at the office. I didn't think the family would appreciate lively dinner-table conversations about who got stabbed that day, or what poor sap was forcibly sodomized in the shower.

Sometimes, however, it's difficult to shed emotions the same way a person peels off his socks at the end of the day. This was one of those times.

The ironic part of my inner turmoil was that meeting Manson had initially revitalized me. I'd recoiled at the prospect of leaving the fresh forests of Northern California for the stale confides of San Quentin, but soon discovered that from a laboratory standpoint, the prisoners housed at San Quentin offered a far more insightful portrait of the damaged human psyche. That appealed to my Jesuit side, and fed my quest for knowledge about the criminal mind. My fascination with Manson in particular became so strong that it stayed with me even when I was off duty. He was the one prisoner that I couldn't restrain myself from talking about at home, a fact that alarmed my wife. She never shared, or even understood, my interest in Manson and his followers, and worried about the effect the hypnotic killer was having on me. It was as if she believed whatever Manson had might be catching.

"Honest, Beth, he's a real weirdo, but he's got this charismatic personality," I tried to explain one evening. "It's too bad you can't meet him."

"Don't worry, Ed. I have no desire to meet him." She shuddered. "He gives me the creeps. I think you should be careful."

"Be careful? About what?" I boastfully responded. "I can handle this."

Famous last words. You can imagine how reticent I was to admit that my current foul mood—not to mention my future career prospects—was directly related to my association with the famous cult leader. If Beth had known what was really going on inside my head during those days she probably would have freaked. Manson had planted some dark thoughts in my consciousness that I laughed off at the time, but were now eating at me like a cancer. "A woman hangs around a man because he's a meal ticket," he sneered on numerous occasions, promoting an oddly chauvinistic view for a man who depended so deeply upon loyal female followers. "Women are consumed by vanity. Their need to be beautiful and loved is more powerful than their instinct to be a loyal wife and mother. Given a chance, they'll choose their own selfish desires over the good of their family." That didn't sound like any woman I knew, especially Beth. It didn't even sound like Charlie's clan. Here he was, destitute and imprisoned, yet many of his girls were sticking by him as fervently as ever. Squeaky, for goodness' sake, had just tried to kill the President for him! Yet there he sat in his cell, spewing the poison that my wife was only in it for the money. "Lose your job and see how long she stays around," he chided.

"He has to be loving this," I muttered to myself. If Charlie knew how many times his childish cliché spun through my mind, he'd surely rub his goatee and cackle with hideous glee. Beth, of course, was above that kind of fickle thinking, I assured myself. Or was she? No man can really be sure until it happens. Manson had created a flicker of doubt, the same kind of flicker he fed upon in his followers, fed upon and stoked until it became a roaring fire. That's why I knew until my fate was decided, I had to steer clear of the little demon. I couldn't let him mess with my mind.

I shook my head and tried to cast off the increasing paranoia. In all probability, Manson didn't even know that my job was on the line. He was up to his neck in his own alligators, sparring with angry guards and federal investigators, feverishly denying that he had ordered Squeaky to clip the President. Still, news travels fast in prison. I couldn't take the chance.

Instead, I tried to comfort myself with positive thoughts about my personal life. Beth was a beautiful raven-haired Irish coed when we met. She was attending San Jose State, and I was a naval cadet undergoing flight training. Our paths crossed at a Christmas party while I was home on leave. I was so smitten by her that I immediately abandoned my date. By our second dance, I was already predicting we'd marry. Our subsequent whirlwind romance survived my leaving the service, her leaving college, our marriage, and our first child, all of which occurred in quick succession over the next two years. As our family grew and I settled into a career in corrections, Beth often struggled with the duality of my life. Once before, when the pressures of the job caused me to grow irritable and despondent, she suggested that I see a psychiatrist. In typical male fashion, I responded with wild anger, accusing her of knowing nothing about the tension I was under or the intricacies of mental illness.

"Lose your job, and see how long she stays around." Manson's words tore at my soul anew as I paced outside. "Could there be any truth to that?" I asked myself. "Would Beth be sympathetic to my current plight after having warned me about it for years? After having specifically warned me about this particular prisoner? Or would this be the last straw?"

I needed her support at that moment. I wanted to share how desperate and alone I felt. But instead of leaning on my devoted wife of seventeen years for the love and comfort she would have surely provided, I chose to heed the words of a certified maniac, suffer in silence, and wait for the storm to blow over.

At the office, I passed the hours boning up on the bloody 1971 prison riot that had everyone's nerves ready to fray due to the upcoming trial. The first thing that struck me was the date—August 21, 1971. I dug into the Manson file and confirmed my suspicions. Manson's previous stint at San Quentin began in June 1971. Although he was locked down on a different floor, and no one ever connected him to the horrors that occurred, I couldn't overlook the fact that he was there. It was almost as if the evilness inside his soul had washed over the place—just like it had now.

Poring over the files, I noticed other similarities. The riot began when notorious African American revolutionary George Jackson hid a handgun inside his huge afro and smuggled it into the cellblock. Like Manson, Jackson was a charismatic, verbose natural-leader type who had published a series of letters in a book entitled *Soledad Brother*. The gun was intended to be used at an appropriate time for a quick, quiet escape. Instead, a guard spotted something shiny in his hair, forcing Jackson's hand. The guard was immediately taken hostage and forced at gunpoint to open cells. In a flash, some of San Quentin's most violent prisoners were running loose through the corridors, slaughtering corrections officers with home-made knives, fingernail clippers, pencils, and anything else that could puncture or tear human flesh. The depravity and utter brutality instantly reminded me of another slaughter, the one so vividly described in the book *Helter Skelter*. Manson had unleashed his animals on a group of helpless celebrities and socialites in Hollywood to allegedly promote his bizarre agenda of a race war. Jackson had unleashed his animals on a group of helpless correctional officers—one with five children—to cover up his escape, an escape that would free him to ignite his own ideological race war.

Unlike Manson, however, Jackson's reign of terror lasted only thirty minutes before he was gunned down by a sharpshooter. That was still enough time to leave his blood-smeared mark: three corrections officers mercilessly hacked to death, three more mutilated to the point of death, and two informant prisoners similarly murdered.

Manson, no stranger to such carnage, had a typically selfish and callous reaction. Shortly afterward, he was overheard having a heated discussion with his lawyer. "George Jackson's attorney brought him a gun! Why can't you bring me one?"* (Immediately after saying that, Manson added that he was just joking.) I thought about that as the news of Squeaky's assassination attempt saturated the radio and television. Despite Manson's denials, my suspicion was that he might have known more than he let on.

Whatever the truth, it had all become personal to me. Usually an event of that magnitude is watched with detached disgust. Not this time. My life had somehow become intertwined with a group of violent loonies. And no matter where I went or what I tried to do, I couldn't escape it. Hardly a minute passed on television without photos of Squeaky, Manson, and the rest of the gang flashing on the screen. I retreated again, reading files at the office and working in the yard at home, isolating myself in my own emotional prison.

On Tuesday, a sergeant interrupted my misery by telling me that despite the way everyone felt about Manson and what had happened with the President, they were on my side. Rinker had bullied his way past a number of duty officers when he barged into B section to snatch Manson, and that caused them to lose respect.

"That little shit Manson hadn't done a thing wrong," the sergeant groused, "and they pounced on him like a pack of hound dogs."

Warden Rees finally summoned me to his office later that afternoon. We launched into a repeat of our previous argument. Rees, locked into the command structure, felt I should have followed Rinker's orders and removed Manson from B section without delay, regardless of how I felt about the decision, or about Rinker himself. By not doing so, and by intending to appeal, I wasn't taking the associate warden seriously. I countered that the order was ill-conceived, unfair, and illogical, and that Rinker's subsequent actions were heavy-handed and brutal. Rees wasn't buying it.

"I don't know what's going on between you two, but I'll tell you just once, you better start getting along," he ordered. "There's too much at stake for this kind of bullshit. You understand?" I was so locked into my fight-or-flight mode that I failed to realize that Rees's scolding meant that I wasn't going to be fired. Not this time, anyway. "If you can't work things out, somebody's got to go," he threatened. "And that's usually the guy lowest on the totem pole."

"Yes sir, I understand," I said, getting the picture. I had the Polaroid,

---

*Jackson's attorney denied smuggling in the weapon for his client. In 1985, he was acquitted of murder and conspiracy charges in connection with George Jackson's failed prison break.

but I still couldn't shut my mouth. "I know I've put you on a cross, Bob. I'm really sorry. That wasn't my intention. You can fire my ass, but let me say just one more thing. Rinker has little understanding of what motivates people. He thinks just like Manson, that fear is the only thing that motivates. That's how Rinker works. Fear does motivate some people, but it just pisses me off! Rinker busted into my unit and allowed the gooners to drag that little bastard the whole length of the upper yard with his hands cuffed behind his back. Many inmates saw that and by now the rest have heard about it. Further, he didn't tell my staff why the hell he was there or what the hell he was doing. He's on a power trip. They could have taken Manson out and lynched him for all my men knew. He let the gooners act like a bunch of vigilantes. This from a man who preaches treating inmates fairly, no more barbed wire and bullets? I'm sorry, boss, but that man's an asshole!"

My hands trembled with fear and frustration as I stormed out of the room. It was a great speech, filled with kindness and humanity for all, but I was talking about Charles Manson! Why was I taking such a fervent stand for that homicidal creep? The answer came to me as I reached my office. I remembered reading somewhere, or maybe hearing during an episode of *Star Trek*, that a society can be best judged by the way it treats its worst criminals. If we look the other way when someone — even a subhuman like Manson — is brutally dragged across a prison hallway, what does that say about ourselves? Will we still look the other way when it's a protester being manhandled instead of a condemned felon? Or how about a member of a rival political party?

Noble thoughts all. The bottom line was, I hadn't drawn the line in the sand because of a protesting college student or a rowdy libertarian, I'd done it for Charles Manson. That had to count against me. How much I'll never know. What I do know is that not only did I keep my job, but I wasn't even written up. My guess is that my mentor, Rees, respected my stance and defended me to some extent when Rinker roared in demanding his pound of flesh.

I tempered my elation and feeling of victory with the understanding that however intellectually founded my cause, I couldn't escape the fact that I had fallen, to some extent, under Manson's spell. Even if it was nothing more than a morbid fascination combined with a curious desire to know what made his twisted mind tick, I'd risked everything for a cause some might find hard to swallow. I'd have to be more careful the next time.

Two weeks later, I spent a few nervous hours convinced that "next time" had arrived. Another strange woman, Sara Jane Moore, forty-five, fired a shot at Ford in front of the St. Francis Hotel in San Francisco. For all his famous physical bumbling, Ford was certainly becoming nimble as a chipmunk when it came to sidestepping female assassins. Moore's shot missed. Everybody at San Quentin, including me, was convinced this was another

Manson production—even if Moore was a little out of fashion and thread-bare for his tastes.

"Don't look at me, I don't know the old bitch," Charlie, a spry forty-one, cracked. "She ain't one of mine. Don't be sending those FBI/Secret Service goons up here again gettin' on my ass."

Although Moore was indeed some kind of wacko revolutionary, Charlie was right—she wasn't aligned with him. Not only wasn't Sara a Family girl, she was a socialist and strongly anti-Manson. She and Squeaky ended up in the same prison and hissed like a pair of warring bobcats the entire time. Obviously, their shared failure wasn't enough to unite their troubled spirits.

It had, however, poured additional anxiety into mine. The way I saw it, I'd dodged a bullet again. To keep from catching the next slug squarely between my eyes, I thought it would behoove me to learn all I could about Manson. Not only him, but about his followers as well. I wanted to know who the next Squeaky might be, and get a head start on trying to figure out Manson's next move. I started by boning up on Manson's life in "the system," both before and after the Tate-LaBianca murders. That was crit-ical. The police detectives, prosecutors, journalists, and authors who had studied him in the past had centered their investigations almost exclusively on the small segments of time he spent on the outside. Yet, Manson him-self had said many times that he wasn't a product of the outside world. His strange persona was not a result of his broken home, Kentucky/Indiana/Ohio/West Virginia environment, a promiscuous, uncaring, bisexual mother, the copious amounts of drugs he ingested, or even the rebellious 1960s. He viewed himself as a casualty of the American prison system.

Manson had been in and out of boys' homes and jails since committing his first armed robbery at age thirteen. His much publicized twisted value system was little more than typical con behavior. He didn't fear social rejection, and seemed incapable of feeling guilt. The basic convict code was ingrained in him at a young age: One should be hedonistic, self-centered, and think only of survival; show defiance toward the system, and beat it any way you can; and never, ever snitch.

Hedonism, defiance, and hatred toward snitches were the tenets that the third-grade dropout later taught his gullible young followers. The "peace and love" flower children were simply fed a cherry-flavored syrup that disguised a bitter spoonful of jailhouse poison.

In order to do that, Manson had to first develop his extraordinary ability to collect, control, and manipulate people. Although manipulation skills are common among prisoners, Manson had apparently mastered the per-suasive arts long before his first bust. His relatives described him as a pleas-ant child who always knew how to get his way.

"If Charlie wanted anything, I'd give it to him," his mother told the *Los Angeles Times* in a rare interview before her death. "My mother did, too. . . . He never had to do a thing to earn what he wanted. . . . Charles had a wonderful personality and always charmed people at a first meeting. . . . He was real musical and had a real nice voice, so I gave him singing lessons. Then he got so conceited about his music that I made him stop, but he still sang special solos in church, and people always talked about how good he sang. I think that made him over-confident. . . . Everything was just handed to him."

Charlie's mother was just fifteen when she gave birth. A short-term marriage to William Manson gave the child a name, if not a father. In direct contrast to the plethora of books and articles written about him, along with dozens of psychological evaluations, Manson's life was influenced, possibly to a major extent, by his biological father—a man he's insisted he never knew. The elusive "Colonel Scott" didn't marry Manson's mother, and to this day, very little is known about him other than that he died in 1954. However, unlike previous reports, Mrs. Manson says that Scott was the love of her life and hung around long enough to establish a relationship with his bastard son. The Colonel (there was no record of a first name) was a wily young man with a weakness for pretty teens. His nickname, common in Kentucky, may have indicated that he had a military background. This would explain Manson's love for military ideals, as shown by his admiration for Rommel and Hitler, his collection of guns and swords, and the military-like maneuvers he performed in dune buggies during his desert-rat days. (Then again, Kentucky men with no military background are often called Colonel, like fried-chicken king Colonel Sanders. If Colonel Scott was merely a "Kentucky Colonel," the military influence obviously doesn't apply.)

Manson idolized his father and was deeply hurt when his mother moved from Ashland, Kentucky, to West Virginia. It was only after he lost contact with his dad, and his heavily drinking mother started bouncing from man to man, that the four-year-old's life began careening out of control. Knowing Charlie's "no pain, no regrets" thought process, it's obvious why he's always denied knowing his father. To do otherwise would force him to confront the anguish he still harbors. The prison-hardened Charlie I knew was not one to reveal anguish about anything.

Two years after leaving Ashland, his mother was convicted of robbery and sent to prison. Manson was passed around to relatives, one of whom, an uncle, made him wear a dress to the first day of school as punishment for whining and crying. The shame and humiliation were staggering, turning him into an angry whirlwind who lashed out at those who taunted him.

Manson's mother was released when he was eight. Charlie has often referred to her homecoming as one of the happiest days of his life. Four years, four states, and myriad towns and "uncles" later, his mom remarried and turned him over to the state, leaving her son angry and bitter.

Tragically, as with so many other felons, the beginning of Manson's lifelong criminal pattern coincided with the one-two punch of losing his parents. He hated the boys homes and juvenile halls and escaped whenever he could, stealing bicycles and food, unaware that he was building a rap sheet that would haunt him forever. He frequently fell to his hands and knees, asking God for deliverance, and for someone to come into his life who loved and needed him. Escaping again, he located his mother and begged her to let him stay. She did—for one night. The next day, she turned him in. Charlie had been snitched out by his own beloved mom! "I didn't feel like a boy anymore," he told convict turned author Nuel Emmons. "There were no tears, but I also knew I could no longer smile or be happy. I was bitter and I knew real hate."

More escapes followed, and Manson, now thirteen, was sent to the Indiana School for Boys in Plainfield, Indiana. The place was a barbaric misery pit teeming with psychotic youths and vicious, perverted guards. By his own account, he was repeatedly raped by older boys, sometimes after being prepared by a guard who rubbed burning tobacco juice up his anus for lubrication. "Every day was some kind of unimaginable experience," he confided to Emmons, who produced a revealing book entitled *Manson in His Own Words*. ". . . At an age when most kids are going to nice schools, living with their parents, and learning all about the better things in life, I was cleaning silage and tobacco juice out of my ass, recuperating from the wounds of a leather strap and learning to hate the world and everyone in it. . . . I had some help in becoming the person I am." The rapes ended when Manson clubbed one of his attackers with an iron window crank as the youth slept, severely wounding him. He hid the bloody weapon in the bed of another attacker, thus cleverly misdirecting the blame and killing two birds with one crank.

He escaped for good at age sixteen, making it to Utah before being arrested. This time, he was sent to a federal reformatory in Washington, D.C., that was far more civilized. The homosexual sex there, at least, was by consent. Manson, for all his bad experiences, freely admits he willingly participated when he was on the other end of the pitcher/catcher exchange.

The orphaned teenager kicked around three more federal reform schools, then was paroled when he was nineteen. He got a job shoveling shit at a racetrack and married the first woman he ever made love to, a coal miner's daughter he met inside a cardroom in Dean Martin's wild and woolly red-light hometown, Steubenville, Ohio. For a while, he was happy again. His wife became pregnant with Charlie junior (who has no doubt long since changed his name), and Manson was content to play the young husband role. Financial problems and the limited opportunities available to a man with his education and background caused him to turn back to crime. An auto theft arrest sent him to his first adult prison, Terminal Island in San Pedro, California. His son was born while he was on the inside. Mrs. Manson dutifully visited—for about a year. Then, without so much as a Dear John, she left him for another man. He never saw either her or the child again.

"I went back to being bitter and hating everyone," he told Emmons. "I had been bitter when my mom turned me over to the court when I was twelve. I hated her when she refused to let me stay with her after my first escape. . . . The bitterness I had learned at Plainfield never left me. And though I don't blame her or feel bitter toward her now, my wife had the full brunt of my hate then. . . . Until my wife left me, I was filled with honest thoughts for our future together. . . . The letdown I experienced when I realized I had lost her was the turning point in my life. I figured, screw all that honest-John bullshit. I'm a thief, and I don't know anything else."

Manson was released in September 1958 and set out to be a big-time Hollywood pimp, a profession he thought was at the top of the bad guy food chain. He ran a few girls with moderate success, fathered another son—this one he never even saw—took a fall for passing a bad check, took a bigger fall bringing prostitutes across state lines, hid out in Mexico, was shipped back to the United States, and was slapped with a new, ten-year sentence. He served seven, bouncing between McNeil and Terminal Islands in Washington and California.

With these critical pieces of the puzzle correctly in place, a picture emerges that better explains how Manson emerged as a 1960s guru. He merely had to look within himself to gain the insights needed to further alienate youthful recruits from their distracted parents. To this day, dysfunctional, loveless parents remain a constant theme with Manson.

Prison, combined with his diminutive adult stature (five three, 135 pounds), shaped Manson's well-known half-crazy mental attitude, along with his bizarre posturing. An unintimidating man who lacked physical prowess, he learned early on that in a grown-up prison, he desperately needed a psychological shield to ward off predatory inmates. He compensated for his shortcomings by enveloping himself in an aura of creepy evilness, spiced by a quick, sarcastic wit. Later, he added the body contortions and sudden jerky movements that would one day mesmerize the media. This gave him an air of unpredictability that scared bigger cons away. As every inmate knows, a "psycho" can go off without warning, inflict serious injuries, and/or force sudden confrontations that end with both participants being dumped into the dreaded isolation "hole." Thus, the crazier Manson acted, the safer he became.

Flush with success, Manson refined his new persona by practicing and perfecting a series of verbal outbursts and veiled threats, polishing the act until it was almost surrealistic.

Prior to Manson's 1967 release from Terminal Island, a counselor noted that "he has developed a casual glibness with words and certain techniques for dealing with people." They hadn't seen anything yet. Actually, Manson's oratory and self-preservation skills were probably obvious even then. The difference was that he was a nobody, just another dirtbag con going nowhere. At the most, his antics may have merely amused his guards, doctors, and administrators.

After leaving Terminal Island, Manson traveled to San Francisco and fell into the famous Haight-Ashbury flower children set. To Charlie, initially out of place and a decade behind the times, the bold new psychedelic world appeared like a carnival. Everyone dressed funny and people were doing drugs right out in the open! Going with the flow, he dropped his first tab of acid and went to a Grateful Dead concert, joining in with the frenzied dancers and wondering if he'd died and gone to heaven. Best of all, instead of being treated like an outcast because of his lack of roots, he was welcomed. Everybody was homeless in the Haight. Homelessness was hip! When night fell, people crashed wherever they happened to be. Charlie had suddenly become cool!

Using his con's instincts, he quickly discovered that many of the lost, aimless youth gathered around him were ripe for his antiestablishment, antiparents rap and were desperate for a leader. Listening as well as talking, Manson refined his prison tirades into a more polished and socially acceptable philosophy. Mary Brunner, his first recruit, influenced him greatly. Brunner, a librarian at Berkeley, was an environmentalist who preached the need to save the air, water, trees, earth, and animals. She gave Charlie a place to stay, and later became the mother of his third son. He rewarded the college-educated twenty-three-year-old by bringing in a young lover off the streets and laying down a "nobody belongs to anybody" rap. Brunner accepted it and became point zero in what was destined to be the strange and overflowing Family.

Thanks to Mary B, Charlie's new sermons went something like this: "The system that corrupted and caged me is corrupting the world. People have given up God to lust for money. Jews, the rich, and those in authority are destroying the planet by polluting the air and water. The black man is growing in power and polluting the races."

Manson found that Mary's "green" side, the environmental issues, was especially appealing to the longhaired, colorfully dressed hippies. The prison elements began to fade as the needs of the outside world took a firmer hold on his consciousness. The destruction of the environment was pushed to the forefront.

"It's not my world, it's yours," he lectured. "You let your parents destroy the earth while I was in prison suffering in darkness. Now you must change it. If the world dies, we all die, because we're all one. I've been sent to save you and your planet and to tell you what must be done. If you want to be in my truth and in your own truth, you must do something to stop the pollution. I'm already in trouble. They're watching me, waiting for me to make a mistake so they can drag me back to prison. But I'll show you the way and what you must do. I'll teach you so that you can survive, so that you can kill if you have to when the time comes."

The time for killing would be years later. In 1967, Manson was mostly about sex, freedom, and more sex. On that end, it was a kindhearted preacher who started Manson on his way. The reverend picked up the scruffy hitchhiker, brought him home to dinner, and when he learned of Manson's interest in music, generously gave him an old piano. Manson traded the piano for a Volkswagen van and hit the road, collecting young women like a snowball rolling down a hill. Squeaky was next, scooped off a street in Venice. Patricia Krenwinkel was rescued from a drug house in Manhattan Beach. Bruce Davis was the first male, swallowed up in the Pacific Northwest. The infamous Susan Atkins breezed in from the Haight in a haze of marijuana smoke.

Squeaky detailed her historic first encounter with Charlie in one of her numerous fanciful writings, offering a penetrating insight into both Charlie's style and the immediate effect he had on his potential recruits.

"Suddenly, an elfish, dirty-looking creature in a little cap hopped over the low wall grinning, saying, 'What's the problem?' He was either old, or very young, I couldn't tell. He had a two-day beard and reminded me of a fancy bum, rather elegant, but my fear was up. 'How did you know?' I started to say, and he smiled really bright, and I had the strangest feeling that he knew my thoughts. 'Up in the Haight, I'm called the gardener,' he said. 'I tend to all the flower children. . . . It's all right,' he told me, and I could feel in his voice that it was. He had the most delicate, quick motion, like magic, as if he glided along by air, and a smile that went from warm daddy to twinkly devil. I couldn't tell what he was. I was enchanted and afraid all at once, and I put my head down and wished he would go away, and when I looked up, really he was gone! And I turned my head, wanting to talk to him now with urgency. And as soon as I turned back around, there he was again, sitting on the wall, grinning at me. I had only conceived of such things in fairy tales. 'So your father kicked you out,' he said with certainty, and once again my mind went with the wind, and I laughed and relaxed. . . . We talked and I felt very good with him and freer, much freer. 'The way out of a room is not through the door,' he said, laughing. 'Just don't want out and you're free.' Then he unfolded a tale of the 20 years he'd spent behind bars, of the struggle and the giving up and the loving of himself.

"We came back to the fact that I didn't have any place to go. He told me that he was on his way to the woods up north and that I could come with him if I wished. I declined, having obligations to fulfill, having three weeks of my first college semester left. Then I looked at him, wanting to get up, crunching up my face in thought. 'Well,' he said, moving down the walk. 'I can't make up your mind for you.' He smiled a soft feeling and was on his way. I grabbed my books, running to catch up with him. I didn't know why. I didn't care—and I've never left."

Charlie got hot in a Nevada cardroom and won enough money to trade his beloved van for a black school bus, giving Squeaky and the traveling gang more space—and more room to grow. He returned to the preacher's house and rewarded the man who made it all happen by seducing his fourteen-year-old virgin daughter, Ruth Ann Morehouse. If that wasn't bad enough, a few weeks later, he carried Ruth Ann away on the fun bus. (Manson would later admit that Ruth Ann was the only person he ever snatched from a parent. All the others had left home, or run away, on their own.) When the raging reverend came after him in Los Angeles, Charlie slipped the guy some LSD and reversed the tables, preaching good parenting to the confused, and considerably mellowed, father. Ruth Ann stayed.

Diane Lake, another fourteen-year-old, escaped her parents' hog farm and joined the harem shortly thereafter, giving Ruth Ann a playmate. Bobby Beausoleil, a handsome Hollywood hustler, hopped aboard and brought four others, Catherine "Gypsy" Share, Leslie Van Houten, Gary Hinman, and Kitty Lutesinger.

The bus kept rolling, attracting kids like a magnet. Nancy Pitman, Paul Watkins, Sandra Good, Steve Grogan, Charles "Tex" Watson, Linda Kasabian, and Stephanie Schram followed. Manson made love to nearly all of the women and some of the men, alternating on a daily basis.

With a bus overflowing with mostly young, nubile, and sexually liberated girls, Charlie was welcomed at every party, home, and gathering from San Diego to Oregon. Even the Hollywood movie and music set was intrigued. For a while, Manson and his love bus were well known among the thrill-seeking movers and shakers who ruled a select number of motion picture and music studios. Dennis Wilson, the drummer of the Beach Boys, hung with the Family for nearly a year, enjoying the girls so much that he opened his sprawling mansion to the whole gang. Wilson collaborated with Charlie on some Beach Boys songs, and even allowed his new best buddy to record some of his own tunes in his brother Brian Wilson's private home studio. (The skittish Brian Wilson, the Beach Boys' troubled creative force, was so appalled by Manson and his clan's "bad vibes" he hid in his bedroom the whole time they were there.)

Manson wheedled his way into Hollywood to such an extent that it was whispered, and Manson later confirmed, that he was the dominant homosexual lover of a major film superstar. To Manson's credit, he has never identified this man—although he later wrote that he somehow had the run of Cary Grant's spacious office and parking spot at one of the big film studios, and was propositioned by other familiar names. The bigger mystery surrounding his unnamed secret lover might be how the thirty-something Manson had the energy for such a physically demanding extracurricular activity. He already had a busload of fifteen women who demanded regular servicing.

One answer might be the drugs that fueled the good times. On LSD, Manson saw himself as an omnipotent being who possessed the ability to communicate psychically with his girls when he wasn't fornicating physically with them. He claimed to have the power to issue unspoken mental commands which they would immediately obey. He once described himself as having X-ray eyes, looking through the clothes and flesh of Mary Brunner, clearly seeing the darting form of the five-month-old male fetus he had planted inside her. Another trip took him back to his youth, to a dark period at one of his reform schools when he saw the face of Jesus reflecting back at him through a pane of window glass. Only the LSD flashback version painted the scene differently. The face was no longer Jesus', but a full-figured, godlike man in a white robe. Speaking in a commanding voice, the ghostly apparition placed the girls in Charlie's care and gave him responsibility for them. When the robed being left, Charlie found himself suspended in air, wearing his own white robe. He had become a god!

After that, whenever the group staged their elaborate playacting parties, Charlie invariably chose to be Jesus—a selection that had a startlingly believable effect on some of his followers. With the LSD helping to intensify the eerie performances, Charlie would later admit that it was difficult to come down and try to be mortal when the trip was over.

Like the choir he preached to, Manson understood loneliness, rejection, and fear of the unknown. He used that to comfort his lost followers and give them the friendship, love, and sense of belonging that they craved. When the bus became overcrowded, they moved out to the old Spahn Movie Ranch in the Simi Hills and transformed into a full-fledged communal family.

Only Manson was the wrong father, a man still poisoned by his years in prison. He's been widely accused of using his influence to take a band of peaceful flower children, fill their heads with prison paranoia, and turn them into stoned killers. And even then, their subsequent acts of mayhem didn't serve some greater purpose, as he would later claim. It allegedly began prison style out of simple vengeance.

Manson's one passion, all along, was music. By now, it's been well documented that his goal was to achieve success in the music world. Charlie wanted to be a rock star. The prevailing theory is that his failure, and the anger and disillusionment that resulted, led to the murders that would stun the world and make Manson a household name. In short, a record producer named Terry Melcher—actress Doris Day's son—caught Manson's act, but wasn't very impressed. Manson never forgot. On Saturday, August 9, 1969, Manson dispatched a band of brainwashed, drug-crazed killers to the estate Melcher leased at 10050 Cielo Drive in the canyons above Hollywood and Beverly Hills. Only Melcher and his then live-in girlfriend, actress Candice Bergen of *Murphy Brown* fame (people forget), no longer resided there—a fact Manson might or might not have known. (In hindsight, the stories have varied widely.) Instead, director Roman Polanski had rented the place to share with his pregnant twenty-six-year-old wife, actress Sharon Tate. Polanski was out of town, but his home wasn't deserted. Tate was entertaining a small group of friends and house sitters, including her former boyfriend, Jay Sebring, thirty-five, a hairstylist and close friend of actor Steve McQueen; coffee heiress Abigail Folger, twenty-five; and Folger's boyfriend, Wojiciech "Voytek" Frykowski, thirty-two, a Polish friend of Polanski. Manson's killers, undeterred by the different set of residents (if they even noticed), slaughtered them all in bloody, ritualistic fashion. Tate, eight and a half months pregnant with a son to be named Paul Richard, was stabbed sixteen times, her blood used to write "witchy" messages on the walls. Tate's main attacker, Susan "Sadie" Atkins, was unmoved by the fact that she herself was the mother of a seven-month-old child. She ignored Tate's pleas and directed her bloody knife into the actress's back and chest.

Tragically, Tate had penned up her two large watchdogs that evening because she had taken in a stray kitten.

To complicate the bizarre circumstances, the slain included a young man, Steve Parent, eighteen, who showed up briefly to visit the compound's caretaker, William Garretson. Parent stumbled upon the murderers on his way out. (Garretson didn't notice Parent's or any of the other murders. He remained in his guesthouse through it all listening to rock music, and was missed by the killers.) All told, the victims suffered 169 stab wounds and were shot seven times.

The following night, a smaller band, including Charlie himself, set out laughing and singing like a Sunday school class going on a summer retreat. They pulled up to 3301 Waverly Drive—Walt Disney's former residence— and arbitrarily murdered Leno and Rosemary LaBianca, ostensibly to further Manson's insane plan of igniting a war between the races, and to provide imprisoned clan member Bobby Beausoleil with a second, look-alike alibi. Beausoleil had been arrested for the July 31 ritualistic murder of musician–drug dealer Gary Hinman, and the Family wanted to make it look like the killers were still on the loose. Manson selected the house, broke in, and tied up the couple, assuring them that they would be okay. He then left, ordering Tate murder veterans Tex Watson, Patricia Krenwinkel, and Leslie Van Houten to finished the job. Another gruesome slaughter ensued. Leno LaBianca's body was discovered with an ivory-handled carving fork sticking in his chest, a knife in his neck, and the word "war" cut into his stomach. His body was littered with twenty-six stab and puncture wounds. His wife Rosemary was stabbed forty-one times. The newspaper Leno had been reading was turned to the pages covering the Tate murders from the night before.

The Family's last moments in the desert after the murders, described to me by Manson, Squeaky, and others, dramatizes how deeply the dream had died, and how little the participants were aware of it.

"We are at Barker's [Ranch] now, sneaked in at dusk," Squeaky wrote in a chilling, strangely poetic letter that vividly described the end of the Family's glory days. "It feels good here all in one room, all in one circle. We're dusty brown and smoothly tough, with cactus cut hands of lizard scale and sun. The feeling is animal, of wind and rough ground under our feet, and real. So really real. We can't stay here at Barker's. There's too many of us. We are hunted. So tonight we dig."

And dig they did, but they didn't get far. Huddled together in Death Valley, their minds seized by LSD, they hid by day and moved like a pack of starving hyenas at night. The peace and love of San Francisco had transformed into dried-out gulches and barren ravines. Manson's insipid personal agenda left them stranded, naked, frightened, and clinging to one another, lost and alone as never before. They pawed out caves and bunkers, urinating and defecating like thoughtless animals. Suddenly, a shotgun blast signaled the end. They were surrounded and rounded up like rats. Babies cried, burned by the hot sun. Rifles prodded them. Two sheriffs searched Lynette. When she complained, she was smashed in the face. She needed Charlie then; they all did. They longed for his wisdom and comfort in their time of great duress, but he was gone. He had reverted back to the prison code of looking out for number one.

Three days later, Manson was flushed out of a tiny Barker's Ranch lavatory cabinet. It was October 12, 1969, two and half years after his release from Terminal Island. Another brief period of freedom had ended.

4

FOLLOWING ONE OF the longest criminal trials in history, Charles Manson was convicted of seven counts of murder and sentenced to death. On April 22, 1971, he was sent to San Quentin. To the world, it was over. The threat was gone. Justice had prevailed. The good guys won. Only the gas chamber was never used, and Manson's treachery was far from over.

Despite his defiant fearlessness and lack of concern about being incarcerated, Manson's new death row home had to come as a shock. He had never served time in a state prison system as an adult, a factor that made him unfamiliar with the horrors that awaited. The federal pens he was used to were in better shape, had well-paid staffs, weren't nearly as overcrowded, and had minimal gang activity. The last item was the most telling. Seasoned as he was, he had yet to encounter the violent clans of vicious, aggressive ethnic prison gangs that infested the California corrections system. These gangs operated like silent schools of sharks, keeping quiet for a while, lulling everyone to sleep, then attacking designated enemies in sudden, barbaric strikes. To them, Manson's loud mouth and grandiose "guru" posture would have the same effect as an injured, bleeding tuna flapping madly in the water.

Quickly realizing this, Manson tempered his antics and initially tried to fit in. That didn't work on either end. Most of the cons, despite being ruthless savages themselves, were repelled by what Manson and his followers had done. They weren't exactly breaking down the bars of his cell with a special invitation to rush their fraternity. As time passed and some opportunities surfaced, notably with the racist Aryan Brothers (ABs), Manson found that he wasn't good at being a faceless soldier in someone else's army. Further, he learned that what worked on the outside was meaningless here. Instead of receptive flower children, he was back in the domain of violent, dominant males. Nobody on death row, or throughout San Quentin for that matter, gave a shit about the environment, the system, or who had the money. All they cared about was themselves. Whenever Manson launched into one of his hippie speeches, some sullen con would invariably bark, "Shut your fuckin' mouth!" Manson usually obliged. (One of Manson's followers, Bobby Beausoleil, learned to back off the hard way. His defense of Manson not only fell on deaf ears, he ended up getting his jaw broken when an argument turned into a full-fledged brawl.)

The most startling example of Manson's slow adjustment to San Quentin, and how far he had truly fallen, could be seen in his sex life. Although Manson repeatedly bragged that "there's plenty of sex in prison," I'm sure he was in no way prepared for his fate at San Quentin. The small, thin, chauvinistic guru was pursued like a schoolgirl and eventually "punked" by an extremely dangerous and aggressive Aryan Brotherhood inmate. A tough, brutal criminal, who took what he wanted, he made Manson his mate, forcing the once dominant cult leader into the passive, submissive "woman's" position of his nightmarish childhood — both literally and figuratively. Although he had gained an important protector, the role reversal had to grate on whatever remained of Manson's sense of personal dignity. Playing housemaid to an arrogant, abusive sexual bully while waiting to be executed had to be the worst period of his life.

The 1972 court decision that threw out California's death penalty as "cruel and unusual punishment" rescued Manson from the dual horrors of sexual depravity and death. The ruling commuted his sentence and enabled him to escape more sexual abuse through a temporary transfer to the California Medical Facility (CMF). Gradually, he rebuilt both his fearsome image and his damaged psyche. Ever the survivor, he soon returned to his loud, threatening, menacing, and preachy ways.

At CMF, Manson was housed at the Northern Reception Center, where his mental state was analyzed and he was evaluated for treatment and placement. In an interview with his counselor, he described himself in terms of a "Christlike" prophet whose disciples grew out of control. Susan Atkins, the vicious Tate-LaBianca killer who sang big-time against Manson during his trial, was his Judas.

"From the day I met her, Susan was a millstone around my neck," he griped.

The counseling staff repeatedly described Manson as extraordinarily manipulative, following up on the evaluations of his previous administrators. Only now, the magnitude of his persuasive powers had increased tenfold. He had become especially adept at rationalizations. After a lifetime of being brutalized by society, he felt it was his reward to do drugs, have sex with a multitude of partners, and even kill those he felt deserved it. He explained these concepts in a seemingly logical manner, as if he were talking about changing his bedsheets.

When Manson wasn't constructing shields or justifying his behavior, he could usually be found sitting quietly in his cell making something with his hands. He has an artistic side that often comes out in stunning ways. His favorite trick was to unravel yarn from socks, sweaters, or any colorful swatch of cloth people sent him. He'd use the material to weave dolls, hats, or decorative handkerchiefs. He also read a lot, dispelling the much repeated notion that he's illiterate. The illiterate tag was something he promoted himself, apparently to lure his adversaries into underestimating him.

Wherever he went, Charlie invariably decorated his cell with pictures of animals and nature scenes torn from magazines. Apparently, his "save the environment" raps were more than just a come-on to recruits.

During one period, he befriended an inmate named Fraizer who shared his interest in the art of tying knots. The pair kept ordering books on the subject until the guards became suspicious, figuring they were planning to construct a rope ladder as a means of escape. When the officers began denying the requests, Manson went ballistic, showering them with obscenities and threatening torture, murder, and destruction. After a second turndown, he threw a tantrum and destroyed virtually everything in his cell. "You might as well gas me now, because if I get out, there is going to be blood running all over you!" he raged.

Despite such incidents, Manson was cleared medically and mentally by the CMF doctors. On October 6, 1972, following two months of observation and evaluation, he was transferred to Folsom Prison and caged in the maximum-security unit. Once again, his neighbors were vicious and incorrigible state felons. Violent gangs ruled the population areas. Manson was now keenly aware of the law of the land in such environments and behaved accordingly. As he had learned at San Quentin, he wasn't gang material—unless it was his own gang. And again, as at San Quentin, the gangs saw little benefit in having the tiny troll join their armies. He didn't have the physical strength the gangs cherished, he brought way too much heat and attention with him, and there was always the fear that he might challenge for leadership. Knowing this, Manson tempered his antics and tried to stay low-key.

The same couldn't be said for new members of his still-active Family. They flocked to Sacramento and established cells of their own, plotting and scheming ways to free their leader. They also mounted verbal and written attacks on a host of American and international corporations which they felt were destroying the planet and polluting the environment. "We did it to save the world. Can't you see it?" Squeaky proclaimed.

Though low-key on the inside, Manson seemingly continued to shake things up on the outside. On October 24, 1972, two weeks after arriving at Folsom, he told a guard that he'd dispatched a team of five assassins to kill President Nixon. Manson hated Nixon for having made the famous statement during Manson's trial declaring the cult leader guilty. (Manson, no dummy, got hold of a newspaper and flashed the banner headline before the jury, nearly causing a mistrial.) The Secret Service took the threat seriously.

In a strange bit of irony, Richard Nixon's life was probably saved by the Watergate scandal. After Manson sent out the hit squad, Nixon was forced to resign in disgrace and went into heavily guarded seclusion.

In December 1972, Manson and another inmate went on a ten-day hunger strike over the Christmas holidays. The purpose was to dramatize Folsom's refusal to allow his followers to visit him. Manson aborted the effort the day after Christmas because the press wasn't sympathetic.

Manson was receiving little sympathy from anyone at that time. Life at

Folsom was becoming increasingly unbearable, and things appeared to be coming to a head. Early on, he had tried to ingratiate himself with the gangs by inviting Aryan Brotherhood members to visit with his girls. He ordered his female followers to give the Aryan Brothers vigorous, surreptitious hand jobs and lap dances in the visiting room, along with allowing themselves to be fondled in every manner possible by the sex-starved cons. Naturally, the inmates began to pressure Manson for more frequent sessions. Weary of their threats and increasing demands, he decided to go into his crazy act, talking gibberish while alternately flooding and burning his cell. The Folsom administrators, tired of Manson's antics on the inside and sick of the harassment from his Family on the outside, were only too happy to ship him back to the California Medical Facility. The March 20, 1974, transfer was based on the "deterioration of his mental condition." He was classified as a category A, which was the designation of an acute psychotic, and was housed in the S-3 wing under tight security.

As always, once away from the specific hassles he had schemed to escape, Manson immediately became sane. After several months of evaluations, CMF doctors ruled that there was "no evidence of overt psychosis." He was ordered back to Folsom. That was the last thing Manson wanted, so he decided to prove everyone wrong again. On July 29, 1974, he half-heartedly assaulted an officer, slapping the man's face and shoulders with little force. The officer easily slipped an arm around Manson's neck and took him down. He was subdued without further resistance and returned to his cell.

The ploy bought him a few more months of soft time. When CMF officers found escape plans outlined in a note in Manson's cell, they decided to ship him out. On October 27, 1974, Manson found himself right back inside Building 4A, the maximum-security Adjustment Center of Folsom Prison. He had been unceremoniously returned to the realm of gang heavies, and wasn't the least bit happy about it. He refused to leave his cell, self-imposing a twenty-four-hour lockdown. He remained there for the next seven months, keeping a very low profile. When he couldn't stand it any longer, he decided to test the waters by venturing out into the exercise yard for a bit of sunshine and fresh air. Two ABs promptly jumped him. They were so intent on pounding the cult leader into a bloody pulp that they refused to stop even when the guards fired warning shots. A gun rail officer had to hurl a nonlethal "stinger" round (a wooden pellet) into the back of one of the assailants before they would stop.

Manson, battered and shaken, responded by befriending a burly African-American prisoner who sent out the word that Manson was not to be harmed. Since Manson was an avowed racist, this was an extremely strange relationship. It's hard to fathom what the black inmate got out of the relationship. His radical brothers gave him serious hell about it, so much, in fact, that the bruiser later freaked and ended up at CMF with deep emotional and psychological problems. That was the price he paid for helping Charles Manson.

The loss of his latest protector forced Manson to again retreat to the full-time safety of his lonely cell. His tenuous relationship with the Aryan Brothers worsened, and they put a hit on him. The opportunity never arose, but they were able to give him the "midnight therapy" treatment. That's when a group of ABs take turns verbally harassing a target throughout the night, preventing him from sleeping. Manson stayed cool, but fumed about the unnerving treatment. (Years later, two of his tormentors were found murdered. "Tank" was blasted with a shotgun shortly after being paroled. "Bear" was knifed in his cell at Folsom. When I brought Manson the news about Tank, he smiled, rubbed his beard, and said, "And he thought he was such a tough guy.")

A short time after the ABs began getting on his case, Manson was shipped out again, this time to San Quentin. That's where I caught up with him.

I continued my background investigation by pulling the psychiatric reports on Patricia Krenwinkel and Leslie Van Houten, the two women convicted of the Tate-LaBianca murders with Manson and Susan Atkins. Both Krenwinkel and Van Houten were outspoken in the areas of law, murder, life, death, society, drugs, and sex. When they became agitated and upset, they mirrored Manson's tirades about death, destruction, and rivers of blood flowing through the streets of the world and drowning the masses. Even when calm, they spewed parroted versions of Manson's monologues. It was as if he'd wiped them clean of their own personalities and infected them with his. They had given themselves completely to him and his belief system.

A psychiatrist wrote that Krenwinkel and Van Houten used common words in an abstract manner, shaping them into peculiar and often incomprehensible sentences. This was one hundred percent Mansonese. Squeaky and Sandra were the same, as were virtually all the others. How Manson had managed to clone himself into the minds of his Family was beyond comprehension. Even his followers didn't have a convincing explanation for how he did it, or why they allowed it. And more puzzling still, none used Manson's powerful influence to excuse their illegal actions. This must have driven their attorneys nuts as they clearly had a case in which the classic defense of "the devil made me do it" was applicable. Instead, the Family members accept the blame for their actions. If anything, they downplayed Manson's influence in order to protect him. The level of their loyalty boggles the mind. They not only submitted to Manson mentally, physically, and sexually, they killed for him, then threw their lives away by taking the rap and being imprisoned for life. Incredible.

I wrapped up my thoroughly disquieting trip down the Manson Family memory lane by devouring everything I could on Lynette Fromme. If I could determine what pushed her to the edge, and the warning signs she exhibited before her ill-fated assassination attempt, maybe I could identify the next Manson follower programmed to go berserk. I also wanted to get a bead on who was going to emerge as the new Manson Family leader on the outside.

It was obvious that Squeaky was the strongest and most fervent of the Manson women. In hindsight, it was inevitable that she would be the one to do something monstrous for him and then die on her shield. Her love for Charlie was not woman to man, but woman to god. She was totally dedicated to carrying out his will to the point of both murder and self-sacrifice.

The interprison files, police reports, local newspapers, and Vincent Bugliosi's definitive book, *Helter Skelter*, revealed a disturbing series of events that led to Squeaky's grand hurrah. On December 22, 1972, she ushered a hooded rat pack of four female Manson followers to the front gate of Folsom Prison. Each had an X carved into her forehead. The three women with Squeaky were identified as Nancy "Ice" Pitman, Maria "Crystal" Alonzo, and Sue Bartell. The files offered little background on the supporting trio.

There were, however, pictures. In typical sledgehammer Manson fashion, the girls had previously dispatched photos to Folsom showing them clutching an impressive array of automatic weapons and submachine guns. That prompted prison officials to search the beat-up Dodge van they used that afternoon. Inside, the guards discovered a rifle scope, gun-cleaning materials, and several empty cartridge belts—all legal. Confronted, the eerie four admitted that they were doing a great deal of target practice in preparation for the coming revolution.

The girls weren't allowed visit Manson, but taking advantage of a loophole, they were allowed to visit other prisoners. These cons could then relay the messages to and from Charlie, thus establishing a critical line of communication.

Like a Mafia don, Manson had trained his followers to insulate him at all costs. The girls on his infamous Hollywood murder spree had followed that policy well, confessing their involvement while absolving Manson of all blame. Prosecutor and *Helter Skelter* author Bugliosi saw through it and was able to crack their armor and convict Manson of conspiracy. Angered that he had taken the fall with his minions, Charlie reacted by laying a big guilt trip on them. He was incarcerated, he reasoned, not because of his deadly orders, but because his troops had failed to distance him from the horrors they had committed. It was thus their responsibility to make up for it by freeing him by any means.

Squeaky was clearly overwhelmed by guilt and determination. She tried everything she could think of to spring her master, eventually going after the President in a desperate kamikaze run.

The question was, what now? Which one of the men or women who continued to write and phone me on a daily basis was possibly being groomed for the latest shocking assault on the nation's consciousness? Which was the ticking time bomb ready to embark upon another suicide mission for his or her leader? It was a question that was maddeningly hard to answer. How do you spot a festering rotten apple in a barrel of festering rotten apples? How do you weed out a sociopathic crazy from an entire clan of sociopathic crazies? They all sang the same tune, a warped, garbled version of Charlie's rantings. They each spoke of massive violence, bloody revolutions, and worldwide catastrophes. How could anyone sort out the next assassin from such a menacing choir?

I dug further, searching for a clue. On September 19, 1974, a month prior to Manson's transfer back to Folsom, a note written in Manson's distinctive hand was discovered during a search of another inmate's cell. The note instructed the inmate to tell "them" where Manson was locked up in the prison and to find out if "they [can] help us over the fence if we get through the [barred] window." It also suggested that grenades could "help us blow our way out." The note cryptically concluded by asking "if Rainbow was in the north and if the queen of the south was out of jail."

Investigators believed that the inmate had found access to a prison phone and was to make a call for Manson. They also suspected that Rainbow was a code name for Squeaky and The Queen of the South, was Sandra, who had been in jail.

The "Free Charlie" mania had actually consumed the Family from the moment the police dragged him from his rathole under the desert ranch house. During Manson's trial, the cult leader's followers stayed mainly in Southern California under the control of Squeaky. Learning from their master, the girls were well versed in enlisting men for their purposes, offering sex, drugs, and spirited conversations about a rebellion of the disenfranchised. A number of Aryan Brothers—some sent to them by Manson—joined with the women. The ABs were especially skilled at committing robberies for guns, ammunition, and money. One particular effort, a gun store robbery in 1971, nearly resulted in the theft of 140 weapons. It took a massive shoot-out by an army of cops to keep the thieves from getting away with the deadly arsenal.

Investigators surmised that the goal of Manson's followers who were involved was to accumulate enough guns, ammunition, and explosives to stage a commando raid on a prison or courthouse. The assault would be modeled after the aborted attempt by black revolutionary Jonathan Jackson to free his brother, riot starter George Jackson, during a courthouse shoot-out in August 1970. In addition some of the weapons could be sold to pay for the Family's expenses.

Another incident was particularly ominous. On October 20, 1971, a Manson associate named Kenneth Como escaped from the hall of records jail in Los Angeles. Como cut through the bars with a jeweler's string smuggled in for him by a Manson follower, tied his bedsheets into a rope, and scaled down the side of the building from the thirteenth floor to the eighth. His "rope" was just long enough to enable him to kick out the courtroom window of Room 104—the same place where Manson had been tried. Como climbed inside the empty chambers, sauntered down the stairs, and walked out the door. Outside, Sandra Good just happened to be waiting there in a Family van.

After such a daring escape, the upshot was almost comical. Como was forced to flee on foot when Sandra subsequently crashed the vehicle. (Sandra told police Como had "kidnapped" her and was driving at the time of the crash.) He was captured six hours later and eventually convicted of attempted robbery. The judge gave him fifteen to life.

At the end of 1973, the Inyo County Sheriff's Department and the U.S. Park Service monitored the activities of a small band of Manson followers that settled in a remote area of the Saline Valley near Death Valley, California. Among the original five was an unidentified woman with an X carved into her forehead, and T. J. Walleman, a tough, heavily bearded biker who wore black leather and dark shades. The quintet, which included an infant, drove two long four-wheel-drive wagons converted into campers. One of the vehicles pulled an open-bed trailer that carried a pair of chopper motorcycles. A month after their arrival, someone tried to rob a sporting goods store in nearby Ridgecrest by crashing a hot-wired bread truck through the rear doorway. Scared off by the loud noise and poor access, the culprit or culprits escaped empty-handed. Law-enforcement officials suspected Manson's group, guessing that they were after the store's gun supply. The police, however, were unable to pin it on them.

After being spotted here and there for two months, the Walleman gang eventually put down roots at the Minnette Mine in Panamint Valley. A suspicious neighbor snooped around when the now ten-member, mostly female clan was away and discovered a tunnel loaded with enough food and supplies to enable a dozen or more people to hide underground for a year. There was also a large cache of weapons, ammunition, and explosives.

Other citizens reported that the clan girls spent the year giggling and whispering that the Family would be at full strength by Christmas 1974. By "full strength," the girls implied that their master, Manson, would soon be with them.

Sure enough, on December 13, 1974, two Manson followers nearly escaped from Folsom by using a hacksaw blade to cut through the bars of their cells. The pair, Como and a multiple cop killer named Bobby Davis, almost pulled it off. They were fractions away from creating an opening when a guard found steel shaving outside Como's cell window and exposed the plot. A third inmate, rapist-robber Gerald Gallant, was also in on the attempted break.

It's not known whether Manson intended to join them, but an incident that happened a year before is revealing. The trio had a violent disagreement that led to Como beating the tar out of his former guru in the Adjustment Center exercise yard. Como was so furious he refused to stop until the guards began firing warning shots. Manson was left shaken and bloodied. Como later explained to me that he was in love with a Manson girl named Catherine "Gypsy" Share, and that the relationship upset Charlie because he wanted his girls to love only him. Charlie sent word to Squeaky that the affair should end. Like a good Manson disciple, Gypsy obeyed, withholding her charms from the talented escape artist. Como was enraged, biding his time until he could personally express his anger. Manson's misguided attempt at control not only resulted in a serious ass-kicking, he was obviously left out of the long-planned escape. (Como, still seething twenty-four months later, was one of the two ABs who attacked Manson in the Folsom yard in May 1975. Como eventually won Share back and married her.)

Manson responded that incidents like that were the main reason he had so many women and so few men in his family. The women could adore and obey him as a lover-master, while the men often wanted little more than to fornicate with the gullible women and make them their own.

After the escape plan was thwarted, a few Manson women used their feminine wiles to hook up with some of the Aryan Brothers. More robberies by the Aryan Brothers followed, with part of the cash used to pay lawyers to file Manson's appeals.

This group infested a resort area in Guerneville, California, near the Russian River. That put them fifty miles north of San Quentin. Many people came in and out of the house they rented, but the main residents were Nancy Pitman, 24, Priscilla Cooper, 21, "Crystal" Alonzo, 21, and Aryan Brothers Michael Lee Monfort, 24, James "Spider" Craig, 33, and William "the Iceman" Goucher, 23. The men were all ex-cons with Aryan Brother tattoos splashed across their chest.

The gang met a young couple, James and Lauren "Reni" Willett, and invited them to stay at their flophouse. Usually, the Manson Family was a tight organization that was wary of strangers, but these strangers had something they wanted—a late-model station wagon. Lauren was an impressionable girl of eighteen who had been raised with a firm hand. The fast, free, easy lifestyle of the Manson clan was wildly appealing to the buxom blonde. James, twenty-six, was the son of a wealthy Kentucky whiskey distiller. James had been reared in Catholic schools and considered the priest-hood before opting for a stint in the marines. With that background, it's no surprise that he resisted his young wife's infatuation with the Manson Family and tried to dissuade her from hanging around with them. He argued that it was no place to raise their newborn baby girl.

James's father came for a visit when they were living in another part of town. His father, naturally, was startled to learn that his daughter-in-law was associating with such a notorious group. Pulling up in a cab, Mr. Willett was so unnerved by the sight of Manson clan members around the house that he told the driver to wait, cutting his visit short. He pleaded with his son to leave with him, but James didn't want to abandon his wife and child.

Lauren, oblivious of their concerns, continued hanging around with her exciting new friends. James reluctantly went along. When the Vietnam veteran lost his federal job teaching underprivileged children due to a funding shortage, Lauren convinced him to help the Family move to Guerneville.

Once there, James quickly realized that the tattooed men were supporting themselves and their women through armed robberies. He confronted Lauren with his suspicions, telling her that he was going to report them to the police. Lauren foolishly, and tragically, told the gang what her husband had said. She naively thought they could explain away their suspicious behavior and convince him to stay. However, the men invited the unsuspecting James for a walk, and that was the last time Lauren, or anybody else, ever saw him alive. She was told that he had simply split.

A month later, a hitchhiker spotted a hand protruding from the soil in a wooded area near the Russian River a half mile from Guerneville. Police responded and discovered the decapitated body of James Willett dressed in a dark blue marine jacket. He'd been shot numerous times with a .22 pistol and blasted with a 20-gauge shotgun at point-blank range. The gruesome murder was reminiscent of the job Manson, Bruce Davis, Tex Watson, and Steve Grogan did on Hollywood stuntman Shorty Shea back in their Spahn Ranch days in 1969. Like James, Shorty was making noises about ratting on the Family. Like James, he was allegedly found chopped up and missing his head. (Other reports say the Manson crew merely bragged that they had decapitated Shea and cut off his arms in order to send a message about snitches. When police found Shea's body, it was apparently in one piece.)

Typically, the Manson men were as stupid as they were brutal. A week before the body was found, Monfort and Goucher were arrested for the armed robbery of a liquor store. Monfort was carrying James Willett's identification papers and made bail under Willett's name. Two women accompanied Goucher's mother, Sarah, to the bail bondsman's office. One identified herself as "Elizabeth Willett," James's sister, who was in Kentucky at the time. The other said she was Lauren Willett, James's wife. "Elizabeth" said they needed to spring "James" so he could take care of his baby daughter.

Once free, Monfort jumped bail. When James Willett's body was found, the Stockton, California, police realized what had happened and began a citywide manhunt. At the same time, the real Lauren Willett disappeared, just as her husband had before her.

Three days later, the police stormed a house in Stockton after spotting the Willetts' station wagon parked out front. They kicked in the door and apprehended Monfort without a struggle. An alert officer noticed a shiny new shovel standing up in a corner with fresh earth caked on the blade. In a Manson house, that's never a good sign. A search ensued. Another alert officer opened a trapdoor leading underneath the house and flashed his light on a pile of recently plowed soil. Shortly thereafter, the body of Lauren Willett was uncovered, a single .38 caliber bullet hole in the center of her forehead.

Heidi Willett, the slain couple's eight-month-old daughter, was blissfully playing on a blanket in the living room while her mother's body was being removed from the premises. (Lauren's parents eventually gained custody of the child.)

The four people found at the home—Monfort, Craig, Pitman, and Cooper—were immediately arrested. Squeaky telephoned while the police were there and requested a ride from the county jail, where she was visiting Goucher. The officers obliged, arresting her.

Lynette quickly squeaked out an alibi for Lauren's murder. She was only in Stockton by coincidence and was dropping by to visit a friend. She admitted spending the previous Friday night at the Flora Street house where Lauren was killed—the day the medical examiners suspect the shooting took place—but pleaded ignorance and claimed that her permanent residence was a pad in San Francisco. As always, she fervently denied that Manson had ordered the Willetts' murders.

After initially claiming that Lauren died accidentally while playing Russian roulette (a claim other Manson Family members had made in 1969 after the shooting death of John "Zero" Haught in Venice), surprisingly Monfort pleaded guilty to an amended charge of murder two. Pitman, Cooper, and Craig pleaded guilty to being accessories to murder two. No charges were brought against Fromme in connection with the murder. Goucher confessed to murdering James Willett and implicated Monfort and Craig as being present. He said Squeaky had nothing to do with James Willett's murder.

The Willett family in Kentucky suffered more than just the loss of their son and daughter-in-law. For six months following the murder, a tag team of women began phoning at all hours, threatening them with bloody deaths, and promising to leave James's severed head on their doorstep. The calls particularly terrified James's fourteen-year-old sister, Alice, who was kept sheltered in her home for nearly a year as a precaution. She still recoils at the memory today.

James Craig, suspected to have snitched in the Willetts' murders to cut himself a better deal, was later found burning to death in the trunk of a copper-colored Dodge parked near Discovery Park, a small community on the outskirts of Sacramento. The car had been doused with gasoline and was engulfed in flames when the police arrived. A second man, Edward Barabas, was also in the trunk. He had been bound and shot in the face, and was dead. Craig had also been bound and shot in the face and neck, but remained alive. Rushed to the Sacramento Medical Center, the severely burned Craig repeatedly mumbled the same two words, "She's dangerous."

Police were never able to establish who the "she" was.

(Interestingly enough, another resident of the Lauren Willett murder house, Crystal Alonzo, would later be arrested in a plot to kidnap a consul general from one of eight countries—Estonia, Paraguay, Uruguay, Canada, France, Germany, Switzerland, or Haiti—in order to extort a $250,000 ransom. Then U.S. assistant attorney general Robert Perry had this to say at the group's arraignment: "They came perilously close to the commission of a kidnapping . . . which could have brought this country to its knees.")

For years, Manson has also been a rumored suspect in the questionable suicide of Jonathan Peck, the broadcast journalist son of famed Hollywood star Gregory Peck. The younger Peck, thirty-two at the time of his shocking death in 1976, had covered the Tate-LaBianca murders and was said to have infiltrated various communes in an attempt to get a bead on the murderers. Peck apparently shared what he learned with the police. That hands-on effort, considered "snitching" by the Manson clan, was said to have infuriated Manson. The odd circumstances of Peck's supposed suicide—the gun was found too far from the body, and the industrious Peck had no reason to kill himself—made some suspect foul play. His father hired a team of private detectives to investigate, but no solid evidence was ever uncovered.

This was all sick, scary, and mind-blowing. I dug further. The Willetts had come from Kentucky, like Manson, and like Manson's father, Colonel Scott. On May 27, 1969, Darwin Orell Scott, Colonel Scott's brother, was savagely hacked to death in his Ashland, Kentucky, apartment. Stabbed nineteen times, his body was left pinned to the floor with a butcher knife. At the same time, Ashland residents noted that a scraggly little dude known only as "Preacher" had recently drifted into town with a band of female hippies. Shortly before Darwin Scott was murdered, the locals chased away the motley crew for giving drugs to their children. Several residents later identified "Preacher" as Manson, but no charges were ever filed.

A possible pattern of sporadic violence and intimidation was emerging here. Even after Charlie was locked away, the Manson Family members continued to commit violent crimes. Could anything stop it? Probably not. But if I could convince even one of Charlie's admirers or followers to let one person slide, to let one act of violence go undone, then all my hours with him would be worthwhile.

5

No **SOONER HAD** the Willett fiasco cooled than the trial of the San Quentin Six began. As mentioned before, the long-delayed day of reckoning for the six prisoners responsible for brutally murdering three prison guards, and carving up three more, had everyone on edge. A month into the proceedings, I was ordered to clear the entire first floor of the Adjustment Center because the jury was coming for a visit. They were scheduled to inspect both the north and south tiers. I watched as they solemnly entered cells, examined windows, checked gates, and scrutinized locking devices. They moved about in a hushed manner, seemingly showing reverence for those who had perished. As a whole, the jurors resembled a funeral procession, hesitant, unsure, and no doubt more than a little unnerved by the emotional impact of being inside the steel and concrete inferno that was San Quentin. The eerie silence was finally broken when an officer was asked to open and close grille gates leading from the foyer to the tiers, demonstrate cell-locking devices, and operate the door from the foyer to the outside of the building.

The prisoners had been cleared out for the jury's visit. If not, they would have heckled the citizens and sexually taunted the females. The tense jurors were no doubt happy about this courtesy—except that I sensed they were disappointed that they didn't at least get a peek at Charles Manson. Everybody wanted to take a peek at Charlie.

"They all love to see the horrible beast in his cage," Charlie frequently bitched. "I'm like some circus freak. Step right up and see the monster."

In truth, Charlie was extremely secluded and rarely hassled by gawkers. Most people don't even like driving by prisons, much less entering the gates and having door after iron door slam shut behind them. The public wasn't exactly clamoring to get inside the cellblocks, which they couldn't do anyway. The relatives of corrections officers could have snagged a private tour or two, but these folks weren't itching to take a midnight stroll into the heart of darkness either. In addition, only a small percentage of San Quentin's five thousand prisoners laid eyes on Charlie. My career-risking efforts notwithstanding, he was kept in maximum-security lockdown for virtually all of his stay. The prison administrators were paranoid that someone was out to get him, and rumors of such malice frequently abounded. This meant that we had to be especially careful during his exercise time, making sure he was taken out alone or with small groups.

This was fine with Charlie. He had little desire to mingle with other prisoners, especially with so many African Americans around. In fact, his crazy notion of a violent African American uprising was born from the mind of a man who had spent way too much time in prison, a place where African Americans are frequently in the majority. Charlie's world was one where African American gangs ruled, so it was difficult for him to comprehend that it wasn't the same on the outside. The black inmates, in turn, were well aware of Manson's racist philosophies and challenged him at every opportunity.

One day, Johnny Spain, a radical associate of George Jackson, stopped directly in front of Manson's cell on his way back from the shower. Spain had his hand wrapped in a towel, pretending to hide a weapon.

"Take your shower yet, Charlie?" Spain snarled. Startled and afraid, Charlie remained mute. "I asked the guard to open the door and let you out so I can escort you," Spain taunted.

Manson paled, frozen in place, waiting for the door to slide open and Spain to leap inside, his deadly shiv unsheathed. A few tense minutes passed. To Manson's relief, the iron bars didn't budge. Spain laughed and continued down the corridor.

Not surprisingly, Charlie preferred to exercise by himself, or with another resident outcast, Roger "Pin Cushion" Smith, a rabble-rousing murderer whom virtually everyone wanted to kill (and many had tried, thus earning him his nickname). For some odd reason, Charlie and Pin Cushion got along, and Charlie trusted him.

One afternoon, I asked Fred, the prison's Aryan Brother leader, if his group had any designs on taking Manson out. Like the ABs, Manson was a noted racist, so I thought from that perspective alone, they'd back off.

"If we wanted him," the inmate laughed, "he'd have been dead a long time ago."

There were also rumors floating around that Sharon Tate's husband, *Rosemary's Baby* director Roman Polanski, had placed an open ten-thousand-dollar contract on Manson's head. The sum appeared low for a big-time Hollywood type, but at San Quentin, that was like offering the moon. According to the rumor, all a prisoner had to do was stick a shank into Charlie's back, then sit back and wait for the cash to fly into his cell. We increased our searches and surveillance for newly secured weapons, but regardless, I knew it was impossible to keep a prison free of deadly instruments. Prisoners universally have developed ingenious methods of fashioning weapons, hiding them, and communicating among themselves.

After we researched the Polanski reward rumor, we concluded that it was ridiculous and unfounded. It did make our lives miserable during its thankfully short life span. The weapons created for such an opportunity would no doubt be squirreled away and used down the road, possibly on one of us. And I couldn't rule out that somewhere, a crazy con desperate for funds to finance a legal appeal would believe the absurd story and try to collect.

To gain an insight into how someone might get to Manson, and what would happen if he did, I had a sit-down with his friend Pin Cushion. If anyone was an expert on prison attacks, it was the Pinman. The spirited inmate had been stabbed more than any con in U.S. corrections history.

"Why do inmates attack each other so ruthlessly and without provocation?" I opened, trying to get an overall insight into the problem. "It doesn't make sense to me. Why do they do it?"

"I wish I knew, boss," he dodged.

"Come on, Roger, you've got to know. Firsthand."

"With me, it was survival," he said, opening up. "With a lot of these guys, it's a status thing. They need to prove themselves. They get a reputation and the other inmates respect them and leave them alone. They're a somebody, and nobody messes with them."

"Is it that simple?"

"Yeah, I've been there."

"I guess you have."

"You want hear how the ABs tried to do me in? It might help you with Charlie."

"Sure," I bit.

"I remember the date like it was my birthday—April twenty-ninth, 1967. I was twenty years old. I was real fucked-up then [serving time for murder]. They locked me in O wing, Soledad prison's max unit, just like AC here, only it had twenty-eight cells on a tier instead of seventeen [per side]. It was about eight-thirty A.M. I'd just finished a bowl of soggy oatmeal. They let me out on the tier to exercise with three other guys. I knew who they were, but I didn't have anything to do with them. They were members of a new prison gang known as the Aryan Brotherhood. I was interested in joining, but decided not to mess with them. They had a reputation of ordering wanna-be members to make hits on someone before being allowed in the gang. That's how they proved themselves to each other. Killing a guy was making his bones [a Mafia term for a prerecruitment murder]. After I passed on signing up, I didn't think I had a problem with them so I didn't worry about it.

"After leaving my cell, I wandered down the tier to talk to a prisoner I knew from reform school named Frank.* As I stood talking to him, I felt a fairly hard blow to my lower right back, then a burning sensation in my belly. I looked down and saw the point of a knife sticking out of my stomach! I had been stuck clean through! The next thing I remember was that it was a bright, clear April morning. 'What a nice day to die,' I thought.

"I swung around to see who stabbed me. I was surrounded by three men with long, sharp, ice-picklike weapons, probably made out of bedsprings. As I turned, Jesús stabbed me in the chest. I felt the pick go deep, right through my ribs. I staggered back. 'Why?' I gasped.

*Pseudonyms have been substituted for the names of Pin's Attackers.

"They didn't answer. They just kept stabbing. I twisted and turned to fend off the stabs, trying to deflect the blows. After a minute or so, I collapsed on the floor and tried to kick them off. Bulldog grabbed my legs and fell across my lower torso, putting all his weight on me. At the same time, Tummy began stabbing me in the neck and face. I closed my eyes, hoping he'd miss them. Jesús kept stabbing my lower intestines. All of a sudden, I felt the worst pain in my life. Bulldog had stabbed me in the balls! It felt like I was on fire from my scrotum to my upper thigh. The pain was so severe, I reared up enough to turn on my side and almost got to my feet. Tummy grabbed me and threw me back down. I tried to get up again, but couldn't.

"I screamed for the guards at the end of the hall. By now, they were aware of what was happening. My lungs collapsed and I couldn't make another sound. The officers started yelling at my attackers to break it up and get back inside their cells. That's all they did, yelled. The guards refused to open the grille gate and come out on the tier to help me. The officers weren't armed and were afraid to enter the area until help arrived. I could hear the alarm blasting, but the guards just stood there like statues, watching me die.

"The inmates ignored the officers and kept stabbing away. As strange as it seemed, they started singing 'You Belong to Me' while they hacked away. After what appeared like an eternity, Bulldog stopped stabbing. I found out later that he couldn't get a grip on the knife because my blood was all over his hands. I managed to roll over and started crawling toward the grille gate where the officers were shouting. Bulldog and Tummy each grabbed one of my legs and dragged me back down the tier next to Frank's cell. They lifted my body and pushed me up against his bars. Bulldog handed Frank a pick knife and said, 'Here, brother, it's your turn to make your bones.'

"Frank, my old boyhood pal, started stabbing my back and neck through the bars of his cell. As he did, Jesús began asking different inmates if they wanted a piece of the action. I heard someone say, 'No, man, you did a number on him already. The dude's dead. You're wasting your time.'

"Frank stopped stabbing and gave the weapon back to Bulldog. Jesús then said, 'Okay, fuck it, man, the dude's dead.' Bulldog and Jesús defiantly faced the guards and challenged, 'Do any of you punks want some of what he got?'

"Bulldog and Jesús marched to their cells, leaving Tummy alone to get in a few last licks. Tummy straddled my stomach and stabbed me in the chest and neck. For some reason, I began to think clearly at that point. The guards were still too cowardly to enter the tier, and Tummy wasn't going to stop until I quit moving, so I had to think fast. I faked convulsing my body, went rigid, gasped, closed my eyes, fell back and laid there loose as I could. I played possum and prayed, 'Please, God, let this guy think I'm dead.'

"As I lay there, I counted the stab wounds. I lost count at sixteen. None hurt anymore. Strangely, I recalled the sound the pick knife made as it cut through my body and nicked the concrete floor beneath me. It struck me kind of funny that the noise the knife made when it hit the floor sounded like the chirp of a small bird.

"Tummy finally got off me and lumbered over to his cell. Once he was inside, an officer threw the locking device, securing all the cells. Still, there was no rush to come rescue me. I slowly turned my head and peered down the tier to make sure they had really locked everyone down. They had. Relieved, I wondered if anyone cared enough to get me to the hospital in time. Obviously, nobody was breaking his ass to save my life.

"I tried again to get to my feet, but fell on my face. A few inmates started shouting, Hey, man, look! The dude's gettin' up.' I could hear them placing bets on whether I'd make it to my feet. Finally, as if to reward those who bet on me, I climbed up and began staggering like a zombie down the tier. Some of the inmates clapped and cheered, enjoying the show. I fell twice, but calling upon my last ounce of strength, I reached the grille gate where the guards waited. It was still locked. I wanted to yell, 'Open the fucking gate you cowards,' but my lungs were shot. I clung to the grille, pleading with my eyes. Blood was pouring from my wounds. Finally, an officer casually opened the gate. I stumbled into the foyer and collapsed on an old mattress laying on the floor. It was covered with semen stains and reeked of urine, but it was better than the cellblock floor.

"After another insufferable wait, the guards hoisted the mattress and began carrying me at a leisurely pace to the prison hospital.

'We should get a move on it,' one guard said.

'Why bother?' his partner cracked. 'He'll never make it anyway.'

"At the hospital, the shock began to wear off, signaling a return of the intense pain. I remember a doctor examining me and shaking his head. 'There's nothing we can do for him,' he announced. 'You better call the prison chaplain.'

"A few minutes later, a priest arrived and began reading my last rites. 'I'm too young to die,' I kept thinking. I wanted to scream, 'Do something! For God's sake, help me,' but I couldn't utter a sound. A lieutenant appeared and started grilling me about naming my attackers so they could use my death statements as evidence. The lieutenant did this even though a number of guards watched the whole thing.

" 'I won't lie to you, Smitty, you're going to die,' the lieutenant said. 'Before you do, I want you to shake your head yes or no when I ask who stabbed you? Did Bulldog stab you? Did Jesús stab you? Did Frank stab you?' I kept shaking my head no. I wasn't going to snitch, not even on the men who had just mutilated me. I simply wanted someone to try and save my life!

"The prison doctors couldn't do much. Miraculously, two heart and lung specialists were called in from the nearby town of Salinas. They immediately chased the lieutenant out and took charge of the prison medical staff. One of them looked me in the face and said, 'We'll do what we can, kid.' With that, I closed my eyes. My last conscious though was, 'Am I ever going to wake up?' "

I sat there stunned, overwhelmed by the agony Manson's friend Pin Cushion had endured. I was also amazed by the vivid detail of the account. It was almost as if Pin Cushion relished telling it, like it was a badge of honor with him. What chilled me the most, however, was the reality of knowing how close everyone inside a prison is to suffering a similarly gruesome fate. This goes for both the prisoners and the correctional officers.

"Yeah, boss," Pin said, putting the finishing touches on his story, "that's how they'll come at Charlie. It won't be a one-shot deal. It'll be a group, and they'll let everybody on the tier get in on it so all the guys can tell their grandchildren they helped kill Charles Manson. Guys who actually like Charlie won't hesitate to carve off a piece of his ass for posterity. When they finish with him, there won't be anything left to scrape off the floor."

Knowing Pin was prone to exaggeration, I double-checked his story with the files. Sure enough, he'd been stabbed more than forty times that day and had come within a hairsbreadth of dying. Both his lungs had collapsed, and his entire upper body had required extensive surgical repair.

As I lay in bed that night, I couldn't shake Pin's story from my thoughts. Can people really be that cruel? Aside from the outside doctors, there were no heroes to be found in Pin's experience. The corrections officers and prison medical staff appeared just as inhuman and heartless as the ruthless felons. I knew the reason. You work in a violent environment like San Quentin, day after day taking abuse from lifers with nothing to lose, and little by little a sense of numbness takes over. You can't care about everyone, so you end up caring about no one. I whispered a prayer that I'd never harden to that extent—not even about Charlie.

Pin's savage tale didn't help much in my efforts to gain insight into how to protect Charlie. All it told me was that if he was going to be attacked, it wasn't going to be pretty. Plus, if I tried to get in the middle of it, I'd probably go down with him. That posed a troubling dilemma. If push came to shank, would I give my life to try to save Charles Manson? Tough question. I couldn't imagine anyone, aside from a few bleeding-heart liberals, viewing me as a hero for taking such an action. In truth, I'm sure a large segment of the public would be overjoyed to learn that Charles Manson's twisted light had been violently snuffed out in a savage prison brawl. "Serves him right," the sentiment would go.

It was a sentiment I didn't share. Regardless of what he had done, Manson's death sentence had been legally commuted. That meant I was among those responsible for making sure someone didn't find a loophole.

The more I studied the situation, the more I realized that keeping Charlie alive wasn't going to be easy. The array and sheer abundance of weapons found in prisons greatly disturbed me. If I was going to protect Manson—protect everyone in my keep—I needed to know everything I could about them, but especially how to spot them, and how to avoid giving the prisoners the materials used to construct their homemade arsenals.

Sergeant Gilbert Rowley had been at San Quentin for ten years. I figured his brain would be a good one to pick. "If someone was going to go after Charlie, what do you think they'd use as a weapon?" I opened.

"Could be anything," Rowley responded after a deep sigh. "Bedsprings, toothbrushes, pencils, razor blades, nail files, scissors, fingernail clippers, nails, wood, melted and molded plastic, bones, anything rigid that can hold a sharp edge and take a good grip. The grip is critical. Without a good grip, a cutting weapon is useless because the hand will slide down the weapon, slicing the attacker's fingers. That makes the culprit easy to identify."

"How do they get that stuff in here? It seems impossible," I marveled.

"That's nothing. They use paper clips, staples, needles, religious medals, neck chains, wire, glass, small pieces of gravel to serve as shrapnel in prison-made grenades."

"Grenades? Someone could toss some kind of grenade right into Charlie's cell? How do they make those?"

"By smashing match heads into powder, packing them into plastic containers like bottle caps, and sealing them with melted plastic from shaving-lotion bottles, toothpaste tubes, or toothbrushes. A small path of powder leading to the center acts as the fuse. They can explode with terrific percussion, scattering shrapnel like bullets. When they go off in the middle of the night, they scare the shit out of you."

"Are they deadly?"

"So far, they haven't been. The inmates usually make grenades just to scare people. They can put out an eye or cut someone up, but they're probably not going to kill anybody. Here, let me show you something."

Sergeant Rowley took two pieces of typing paper and rolled them tightly around a pencil, forming a paper barrel. He secured it with the kind of clear tape inmates routinely use to post family photos on cell walls. He packed the paper barrel with powder made from crushed match heads. Using the bottom of the pencil to seal off the breech, he faced the pointed side toward the opening on the opposite end. A pinhole was poked in the base, just under the sulfur. The sergeant then lit a match and held the flame under his weapon. Boom! The device fired the pencil with such force that it flew across the room twelve feet and embedded itself in the wall.

"Just like that, no more Charlie," he cracked as I sat stunned, mouth agape.

"Wow! That's amazing. You did that so fast!"

"It's easy. And everything I used, the courts require us to give the prisoners. The paper and pencils are for legal work. Matches, so they can smoke. The only thing we remotely control is the tape."

"Yeah, but they get that too, don't they?"

"That's right. But it's not that bad. Like the grenades, they don't always explode on time or with enough force to be fatal."

Sergeant Rowley went on to enumerate the more dangerous weapons the prisoners build: spray cans used as flamethrowers, paint-thinner firebombs, sharpened mop-handle spears, blowguns, darts, slingshots, and various maiming devices made from the basic tools used by work crews.

"We're always fixing stuff around here, so the work crews are in and out. Electricians, plumbers, painters, people like that. They lay down a screwdriver for a second, and zoom, it's gone. The prisoners just beat us. It's a given and we know it. They're gonna beat us.

"The most common weapon, the kind that can kill, is fashioned out of flat metal stock about an inch wide, cut and sharpened into pointed shanks. The source of the stock is smuggled in from welding, sheet metal, plumbing, or the machine shop. Often, the cons cut the metal shanks right out of the fixtures already in their cells. Using fingernail clippers, a standard-issued item, the cons scour a pattern on the iron of a bed frame or on the back side of a stainless-steel toilet. They retrace the pattern thousands of times until they can break it loose or punch the piece out. The blade is sharpened, using the concrete floor like sandpaper, then fit with a firm grip."

Rowley went on to explain that once an inmate constructs a weapon, he can hide it from searches by moving it around the cellblock and trading off with other prisoners during trips to the yard, shower, doctor, barber, or dentist. Often, a cadre of inmates will work together, one group distracting the guards while the other transfers weapons. An especially intriguing way of hiding a weapon is to tie it to a "fish line" made from thinly torn sheets and burying it inside their toilets. Weapons and other goods are transported from cell to cell this way because a row of inmates share the same sewer pipeline. Similarly, clever cons toss lines out their windows to deliver packages to the cells below.

Listening to all this, I remembered what the Aryan Brother leader said when I asked him if his gang had it in for Manson. "If we wanted him, he'd have been dead a long time ago." At the time, I laughed it off as macho posturing. Now, it suddenly wasn't so funny. The guy was telling the truth. The simple fact was, despite all the security, isolation, and spe-cial treatment, Charles Manson remained among the living simply be-cause nobody at San Quentin wanted to kill him badly enough. If and when someone did, there probably wouldn't be a thing anyone could do about it.

The realization was both disturbing and, in a strange way, comforting. I had been right in my original assessment. Nobody currently residing at San Quentin gave two shits if Charlie lived or died. That, combined with his fearsome demeanor and legendary spooky status, was enough to keep him breathing for as long as the corrections system owned his body. There was no sense losing sleep worrying about it. It hadn't hurt to bone up on prison weapons for my own protection, or the protection of others, but as far as Charlie was concerned, there was no point in putting in the extra hours.

That weekend, I took my wife shopping around Pier 39 in San Fran-cisco. I spotted a sign in a poster shop which read, "Human beings present. Handle with care." I bought it and tacked it up near Manson's cell. It was intended as a not so subtle reminder that even Charles Manson was human and deserved a measure of dignity. The next morning, the poster was gone. Some inmates told me that a hard-line guard had seen it, groused, "Who put that bullshit sign up there?" and ripped it down. I wanted to confront him, but decided to let it slide.

I had another, more important reason for letting it be known that I was going to treat Manson with common decency. Once the other prisoners knew that, they'd expect me to treat them with respect as well, which I did. There would be no need for mind games, threats, spitting, or violent posturing on either side. From my perspective, just being there was misery enough. These men were locked in cages. What "freedom" they had was limited to a few confined areas around a decidedly dismal and excruciat-ingly gloomy environment. Many would never see the outside again. What further punishment did they need?

I contrasted that with a bitter argument I'd recently had with the ever present Associate Warden Rinker. He objected to the humanity classes I was giving my men and went ape shit on me.

"I use Nazi methods like Hitler!" he shouted, his jaw tight and men-acing. "It's the only way of getting things done around here. I warn you, Mr. George, change your ways!"

After that, I questioned Rinker's stability. If he cracked, all hell would break loose. He was flexing his Nazi storm trooper muscles around a place that was already teetering on the edge of another volcanic eruption. Iron-ically, Rinker appeared, in his own way, as tyrannical and vindictive as Manson.

That was a chilling thought. I was now forced to balance myself between what appeared to be two unraveling pieces cut from the same cloth. One had power over my career, my sense of security, and my ability to provide for my family. The other was trying to gain control over my mind.

That weekend, one of my older girls, a rebellious child of eighteen, left home at 7:00 P.M. and seemed to vanish without a trace. I fumed and paced downstairs for hours, staying up well past 3:00 A.M., worrying myself silly. Although it wasn't unusual for her to stay out late, this was later than ever before. My imagination ran wild, and I knew the reason. It was Manson. Diane was around the same age as most of the girls he'd recruited. Assertive, independent, chafing against authority, she was exhibiting the same qualities I noticed in Squeaky, Sandra, and the other Manson women. If Manson wanted to get to me through one of my children, Diane appeared to be the perfect target.

Were some of his robots working on her that very night? Were they filling her young mind with hate and rebellion, programming her to believe that I was the devil? Or would they even bother to take the time? Would they just snatch her away, hide her somewhere, and use it to force me to help Charlie escape?

By the time she waltzed in alive and well at 3:30 A.M., I was a basket case. Instead of calming myself, I made the terrible mistake of taking my anxiety out on her. "Where the hell have you been?" I demanded.

"Four-wheeling," she replied, as if it were her routine schedule.

"Why didn't you tell us? At least call? What do you mean coming home at three-thirty in the morning?"

"Dad, I had no idea it was so late," she pleaded. "I didn't have my watch. There were no phones out there."

"Who the hell were you with?" I asked, visions of Sandra Good and a pack of sex-crazed Aryan Brothers running through my mind.

"None of your business," she shot back.

Her back talk fueled my paranoia. I snapped. "What do you mean it's none of my business? I shouted, grabbing her by the arms and shaking her violently. She broke away and ran screaming upstairs to her bedroom. I should have backed off, but my mind was poisoned by the image of Diane with a shaved head and a swastika carved in her forehead. I tore after her. Beth emerged from the master bedroom just as I reached the top of the stairs. She tried to cut me off, but I bullied past, nearly knocking her down. I burst into Diane's room, grabbed her again, and pinned her to the wall.

"Don't ever talk to me like that again, you hear me!" I raged as Diane cried out for her mother. The commotion woke up the other children and caused them to come parading into the room. Shocked by what they were witnessing, they yelled and sobbed and pleaded for me to stop. Instead of coming to my senses, the demons inside me grew stronger. I showered Diane with accusations and incriminations until she went limp and started collapsing to the floor; then I slapped her across the face and jammed my knee into her side, refusing to allow her to escape my wrath by fainting. She awakened with a deafening series of hysterical wails.

Beth fell to her knees and began hugging and comforting her daughter. She peered up and shot me an icy look that said what I had done was unconscionable. The piercing glare cleared my head and filled my soul with self-loathing and unspeakable guilt. As I walked out of the room in utter shame, I heard my precious daughter plead, "Stop him, Mom. Stop him. He'll kill me!"

The words hit me like a shank to my heart. What had I done? Who was that man in there? I didn't recognize him. Here I was, the softy preaching love and kisses for heinous felons like Charles Manson, and I'd gone home and turned monster on my own daughter. I wanted to go back and apologize, but knew nothing could excuse my behavior. My reappearance in the room would only terrify Diane further. I loved her so much, yet in one stupid, reckless moment of Manson Family paranoia, I'd probably destroyed our relationship forever.

I detested myself, sinking into a cesspool of depression. Panting and bewildered, I staggered into my bedroom and fell on the bed. I could still hear Diane whimpering in the next room, with Beth trying her best to console her. Exhausted and drained, I fell into a fitful sleep.

The next day, I tried my best to undo the damage. Diane wasn't physically hurt, but she was severely traumatized. When I entered her room to beg forgiveness, she turned away, burying her face into her pillow. I didn't try to explain. I was certain she wouldn't understand. I merely whispered that I was sorry, then left the room feeling a great sense of emptiness. I'd lost my daughter.

In twenty years of marriage, twenty years of coming home encased in the misery and tension of some rotten prison, I'd never struck my wife or any of the children. I'd blown my top a few times, but never punched, kicked, or become that verbally abusive. Despite the horrors of my career, I'd always rationalized that I was above it all. I had been — before Charles Manson came into my life. Now, I didn't know what I was anymore. I questioned everything. My life. My work. My existence. Where was the self-control I'd learned at the seminary? Where was my relationship with God? "Know thyself. Nothing to excess." Those were words I'd lived by. What was going on here? Had San Quentin, Rinker, prison riots, and most of all, Charles Manson taken all that away from me?

I wasn't sure. What I did know was I had to go right back to the fire. I couldn't avoid it any longer. I had to confront the wicked troll in the cage down the hall. I had to face the evil spirit that in such a short period had so deeply messed up my life.

That Monday, I approached his cell tentatively, not wanting him to pick up on my emotional upheaval. My questions would be coy and random so he wouldn't see a pattern that would reveal my true anxiety. If I slipped, it would give him yet another foothold into my soul. Still, I had a purpose, and I got right to it.

"Charlie, tell me something," I opened. "How were you able to take young, attractive, intelligent women and convince them to accept a scummy, sleazy, immoral life with murder thrown in as the only perk?"

The cult leader ignored the cutting edges of my question and readily answered. "Easy," he boasted. "I could take one of your own daughters, and in a single hour, have her following me."

His words pounded on my chest like an iron bar. Did he already know? How could he? I fought to stay calm, brushing it off as typical Manson hyperbole. He always made things personal when he spoke. That was part of the fear game. I studied his eyes. There was no sense of malice this time, no evil glint that he was speaking from experience. I struggled to keep my cool, to convince myself that he was just making a general point.

"Really," I said. "That's incredible. Just one hour?"

"Give me half an hour and I'll turn her against you. I'd teach her to hate you and make her my disciple for the rest of her life."

At that moment, after what had happened the previous night, he was probably right. "How, Charlie? How can you do that?"

Charlie smiled and took me through an imaginary conversation:

"I'd see a girl and come up to her and say, 'What's your name?'

" 'Betty.'

" 'How do you know?'

" 'My mother told me.'

" 'What does it mean?'

" 'I don't know.'

" 'Has your mother ever lied to you?'

" 'No.'

" 'What does your mother think about marijuana?'

" 'She says it's bad for you.'

" 'Have you tried it?'

" 'No.'

" 'Has your mother tried it?'

" 'No.'

" 'Then how does your mother know?'

" 'I don't know.'

" 'Well, it's good, and I'll show you. And I'll prove that your mother lied.'

"So I give the girl a joint. We smoke it together and it makes her feel great, better than she's ever felt in her life. Now she's mellow and interested, so I go on: 'Has she told you that sex was bad?'

" 'Yes.'

" 'Do you think it's bad?'

" 'Yes.'

" 'Why?'

" 'Because my mother told me.'

" 'Well, it's good and fun, and I'll show you. And I'll prove again that your mother lied.'

"With the girl already high from the smoke, the seduction comes easy. Enhanced by the drug, the sex feels doubly sensational. After we finish, I explain that if her mother and father really loved her, they'd always tell her the truth. Now that we've bonded physically, she starts agreeing with me. I continue: 'If your mother and father tell you that school and church are good for you, and you go and you can't stand it, then aren't they lying to you?'

" 'Yes, I guess so.'

" 'If they tell you that work is good, but you go to work and hate it, aren't they lying to you?'

" 'Yes they are!'

" 'Why do you think they lie to you?' "

At that point, Charlie paused, frowned, and feigned deep thought like a very wise man. I could see where his presentation, silly and demented as it was, could have a mesmerizing effect on a stoned eighteen-year-old.

" 'I'll tell you why your parents lie. Your parents don't love you. They don't care. They want to control you, so they make up rules for you to follow, so you don't cause them trouble. They tell you to shut up, keep quiet, go play somewhere, just to get you out of their way. They don't want you to be yourself, to enjoy life, to have fun. They push rules on you, just like the teachers, the preachers, the cops. They all love money and status more than they love you. They want to have all the fun, while you have to obey all the laws.' "

With the parent-child bond now sufficiently broken, Charlie explained that he'd cap it off by launching into a glorious speech about the wonderful life the girl could have if she chose to join his merry band of beautiful people. She could love, sing, and embrace life without a care in the world.

"Of course, this is oversimplified so you can get the basic point. It works better when I'm actually with the girl, playing off her questions, doubts, and fears. But you get my drift. Get the right girl, and you've got it made. Get her to drop some acid [LSD] and it's even easier."

Beautiful. Leave it to Charlie to put a sinister kicker on his perverse story. Get someone to drop acid, and you hardly have to sell them at all. Frankenstein could convince a girl to join him if she was flying on the powerful hallucinogen.

I walked away in a trance, just as chewed up inside as before. How would Diane react if one of Charlie's trained soldiers gave her that rap? What if it was a young, handsome, smooth-talking guy like Bobby Beausoleil rather than a semirepulsive dirty old man like Charlie? Diane was a free spirit who might be induced to experiment with drugs. Once she took that step, the ball game would probably be over. Charlie's genius was not so much in what he said, although that in itself could be effective, but in the candy he offered. Drugs do make people feel euphoric. That's why so many people get hooked. Sex is fun. The whole world knows that. The combination can be exhilarating. What Charlie offered was little more than the teenage utopia of sex, drugs, and rock and roll, sprinkled with a dose of "save the world" philosophy to titillate their emerging intellects.

Back at my office, I was stricken by something I'd previously read. Charlie recruited Lynette Fromme right after she'd had a big argument with her father. I mulled that around in my head until the numbness gave way to murderous rage. If Charlie came after Diane, I wouldn't have to worry about someone else sticking a shank into the bastard's black heart. I'd do it myself.

6

FOR MOST PRISON administrators, the worst aspect of having a celebrity prisoner like Charles Manson is that he draws the media's attention. Correctional officers universally abhor the media. They would prefer to run their operations in the dark, meaning as harshly as possible to keep the prisoners in line. Not surprisingly, they hate when some liberal newspaper reporter comes sniffing around for a few hours and then cranks out a sob story about how badly the poor inmates are being treated.

A famous prison like San Quentin adds fuel to the fire. Even without Manson, there was enough going on in the lockups to bring a band of newshounds to our gates every few weeks.

Personally, I enjoyed the media and felt they served a purpose. It was their job to snoop around and make sure everything was being handled properly. If it had been my call, I'd have had an open-door policy that allowed the press to scrutinize anything they wanted. Unfortunately, my bosses, particularly Associate Warden Rinker, didn't share that view. In typical heavy-handed fashion, Rinker believed in making things as tough for the media as possible. That, however, only gave the impression that we had something to hide. With Charlie in the house, that was not the best signal to send out. As any good PR person knows, you give the media the impression that something sneaky is going on, and it brings them out in droves.

Although Manson had used the media to his own advantage, and would again, he had his own reasons for distrusting the pen, pad, and microphone brigade. "When all this stuff went down about me, the lies, twisted stories, and outright fabrications were unbelievable. Every day I'd read something and wonder who they were talking about, because it sure as hell wasn't me. After that first wave of media vultures picked my bones, there was nothing left to live for. Hell, I didn't need to be put in jail. The media locked me in a cell that I'll never be able to escape! They created a monster that can no longer live in their sick society. I've had to create a new life in here, in my mind. It's an existence that's not related to this planet. To protect my world, I've learned that I must remain silent and stone-faced around others, because the slightest blink will result in some half-assed opinion on what it means. Then another version of who I am goes out to the masses that in no way reflects who I am. Everybody's had their shot. The media, authors, shrinks, lawyers, broadcasters, prison guards, they've all fucked me like a whore, then refused to pay. And after all that fucking, nobody really knows me."

There was some truth to that, but the vision of Manson being "silent and stone-faced" is laughable. He's the most glib and animated person I've ever known. And he's an expert at using exaggerated body language to boost whatever image, philosophy, or mental state he's selling at the moment. The media can hardly be blamed for going along with his sensational act.

"You think you know me, Ed, but you don't," he lectured. "That's because I'm many different people. I'm God to my friends. I'm the Devil to my enemies. When I'm bad, I'm 'the Black Pirate.' When I'm peaceful, taking care of my flocks, I'm 'the Gardener.' When I look into the future, I'm 'the Prophet.' When I must lay down the law for our earth, I'm 'the Son of Man.' And these are only some of my beings."

"Yeah, well let's make sure we see a lot more of 'the Gardener' and a lot less of 'the Black Pirate,'" I parried.

Another group prison administrators despise are liberal, crusading lawyers. These are the guys who file suit after suit trying to gain privileges for the cons and protect their rights. There was one particular legal gadfly named Paul Cominsky who had a ramshackle office right outside our gates. He made his living filing writs for inmates. Since most inmates are stone broke, it was basically a labor of love. For that, I couldn't help admiring the guy—even if he was a major pain in the ass.

I liked Cominsky. We shared a common bond in that both of us had done some serious time at Catholic seminaries before escaping and going into law enforcement. Cominsky's problem was that he was a wee bit gullible. He believed everything the inmates told him, and about three quarters of it was total bullshit. I tried to make a deal with him to honestly reveal which twenty-five percent was the truth, but he wouldn't go for it. He accused me of being part of the silent conspiracy to protect the institution.

After Manson arrived and more attention was being placed on San Quentin, Cominsky stepped up his activities. When the accusations of inhuman treatment began to rain on us fast and furious, I took Cominsky aside and invited him and his legal cohorts for an up close and personal visit. "That's a deal!" he said, quickly submitting a list of people he wanted to bring with him. I ran a security check and everyone seemed okay. None appeared ready to join the revolution by smuggling a zip gun in to Charlie and leading a suicide charge out the gates. Regardless, when I passed the list to Deputy Warden Lou Fudge, it was promptly disapproved. "Too many local radicals. Could be trouble," he growled.

"We'll search them and have the officers keep a keen eye on them," I argued.

"No. That's final. Not with that little fellow up on your wing."

I relayed the bad news to Cominsky. He smiled and pulled out another writ form. "Say no more," he cracked. "We'll see what you're hiding now."

A few weeks later, we began hearing persistent rumors about plans for another inmate riot, this one to occur in the AC unit. Rumors like that flourished in prison, usually started by the cons to screw with the officers' heads. However, this one began having an eerie ring to it that made the hairs on the back of my neck stand up. When a call came in from the outside with specifics, we really took note. The caller stated that an AC inmate currently out for a court hearing was going to "come back with a piece."

The problem here—aside from the horrors of another savage riot—was Manson. This was his unit. If things went crazy, we all knew that the one con who'd slink away in the commotion and vanish into the night would be Charlie. If that happened, newspapers around the nation—even the world—would dust off their Pearl Harbor–sized headlines and announce to a terrified populace that the planet's most frightening murderer now walked among them.

For me, it was far more personal. Once out, Manson would probably go straight to my house for a well-rehearsed chat with my daughter.

The caller didn't specify that the attempt was being backed by Manson's clan. That didn't matter. If anything, it was worse. If Manson wasn't the focus of the takeover, it would be that much easier for him to slip away during the chaos.

I huddled with my men. We spread out the prisoner lists to determine if anyone was in court at that moment. There were a half dozen, which wasn't unusual. Narrowing it down, we kept coming back to an inmate named Parks, a longtime radical who'd been suspiciously quiet for a while. The book on Parks was that he associated with violent revolutionary types. That set off alarms as the cons with a higher "cause" are usually the most dangerous kind. Instead of merely wanting to escape, they want to raise hell and attract attention to their agenda. Plus, they can gain assistance from their brethren on the outside as well as inside. Interestingly, although Parks was white, his jacket said he'd thrown in with the African Americans.

When Parks returned from his hearing, I issued an order to give him a thorough going-over. The handheld, paddle-shaped metal detector let out a piercing squeal just as it passed over Parks's butt, signifying a "keister stash." That meant he had something metal up his ass. Parks, realizing the gig was up, made a break for it. After a brief scuffle, he was subdued and transported to the hospital for an X ray. The minute he saw the machine, he freaked again. Several officers had to hold him down so we could photograph his butt.

Bingo. The X ray revealed the shadow image of a barrel about three inches long. A secondary shadow inside the first appeared to be a .22 caliber slug. I immediately ordered the chief medical officer to dig in and yank the weapon out. To my dismay, he refused, claiming that he didn't have the patient's permission to do such an invasive procedure.

"Are you nuts?" I barked, my voice rising. "He's got a zip gun up his ass and you won't operate? That's evidence for a felony, Doc!"

"I know. But I have liability to worry about. I'll need a search warrant."

"A search warrant for a pistol in a con's ass?" The doctor nodded. "Okay, I'll call the judge," I conceded, totally exasperated.

Parks had probably received his Colt .45 colonic in the judge's court, so I knew this was one warrant that was going to be fast-tracked. I reached the judge at home and stressed that precise point. The judge was no fool. "You don't need no stinkin' warrant," he snapped, sounding like a Mexican bandito in a Bogart movie. "Tell that damn doctor that he has the right to take the evidence as long as it's done in a medically acceptable manner."

The doctor wasn't happy with the verbal order. After more vacillating, I finally convinced him that the judge really, really wanted him to perform the procedure. The M.D. sighed and called for an anesthetist. The dream weaver arrived and administered sodium pentothal, a powerful downer. The drug relaxed Parks so much that the barrel began sliding down on its own. The doctor was able to easily grasp it with his handy probes. The freed contraband was exactly as depicted, a three-inch barrel with a .22 caliber slug inside. What the X ray hadn't shown was that it was wrapped in plastic and had rubber pencil erasers plugging each end. It had been smeared with Vaseline for smooth sailing.

Although the weapon wasn't complete, I was certain the other parts were already up on the tier.

When I phoned Rinker to inform him of our big save, his reaction was bizarre. "What are you talking about, Ed? Are you smoking weed or something?"

"No, Ted, this is real. We X-rayed this guy and found part of a zip gun in his ass."

"Ed, you shouldn't be using X rays on a routine basis. I told you that. It could get us in trouble."

I couldn't believe it. We had just stopped a gun component from literally walking on to Charles Manson's tier, and the only thing this guy could think about was Mickey Mouse procedure? All Parks had to do was cut a fart on the stroll to his cell and Manson's ticket to freedom would have bounced into his cell like manna from heaven.

"Yeah, I know the rules," I said. "But this time we had good cause. Are you listening? We found part of a gun!"

"Look, Ed, I don't want you blowing the place up. You're overreacting."

"Overreacting? Do you know who's in Parks's wing?"

"Who?"

"Never mind," I said, shaking my head.

"Let me make the decision," Rinker continued.

"What decision?"

"About the X ray."

"I already did."

"Did what?"

"Made the decision to X-ray."

"What are you trying to do, be a hero?" he raged. "Get promoted? Make me look bad? Who's over there with you?" he demanded, rattling off the names of his top henchmen. Fortunately, all were off duty. "Okay. Well, you better not mess up," he huffed. "I just hope you know what you're doing."

Parks clammed up when we grilled him on where he got the barrel and what it was for. Some of the guards suspected a fellow officer of helping the cons bring in contraband, and things got ugly for a while. The suspect, an African American, was being singled out because the wing housed packs of African American revolutionaries who constantly pressured their "brother" for help. It got so bad on both fronts that the officer wanted to quit. I knew he was above reproach and tried to convince him to stay, but he wanted out.

To keep that kind of staff suspicion from tearing us apart, I instituted a plan in which the guards themselves were searched before being allowed on the job. This included their lunch pails, briefcases, everything. Instead of railing against the injustice of it, the men were in favor. This took the pressure off those being tempted or hounded to bring in illegal materials to the cons.

Of course, when the media found out about it, they made it front-page news and put a slant on the story that the officers at San Quentin—the men entrusted with keeping Charles Manson behind lock and key—didn't trust one another. Rinker wasted no time in chewing me out, ordering an abrupt end to the innovative program.

Another innovative program I helped put into place—and my buddy Manson nearly derailed—was even more controversial. The psychiatrist assigned to my section, Dr. Joyce Sutton, was a rare, eternally optimistic soul who felt she could really help degenerate reprobates like Manson, Pin Cushion, and the rest of the murderous crew. A classy, sexy woman who resembled Grace Kelly, she was totally out of place in a stink hole like San Quentin. Naturally, the prisoners gave her a hard time. During her first months, every time she walked down the tier to pay a house call she was showered with lewd and crude remarks and come-ons. Some of the sickos even dropped their pants and gleefully masturbated as she passed by. One particular joker called her over to his cell, expressed an admiration for her eyeglasses, and asked if he could see them. Wanting to fit in and make a friend, she obliged. The guy promptly walked to his stainless-steel john and flushed her eyewear down the toilet.

In the face of all this abuse, Dr. Sutton persevered. She ignored the relentless 1-900 talk and continued to display an unwavering professionalism underlined by a sincere concern for the inmates in her care—even the ones jacking off in her honor. Little by little, her mental toughness began to earn the respect of the men. By her sixth month, the gross sexual comments had virtually vanished. Dr. Sutton had become one of the boys.

After initially playing his typical sexist mind games with her, even Charlie came to respect Dr. Sutton. She spent time working with him, trying to sort out his myriad psychological problems. Buoyed by his calming temperament and brief periods of seeming understanding, she felt she was making some real headway. Although I was Dr. Sutton's biggest supporter, I remained cynical. Manson, I figured, had to be manipulating her for his own benefit, whatever that might be. He'd talked rings around his past shrinks, transforming himself into anything he wanted to be at the moment—sane or insane, genius or simpleton, abuser or victim. There was no reason to believe that he wasn't doing the same number here.

One explanation for his "progress" seemed pretty obvious. Dr. Sutton was responsible for handing out Valium, a sedative that's valued like crack cocaine behind bars. That, I suspected, was the main reason that Manson, and scores of other devious cons, cut her some slack and went along with her program. Questioning her about this, I was surprised to learn that Manson "just said no" when it came to Valium. He'd drop LSD like gumdrops, but swore off the legal tranquilizer. His respect for Dr. Sutton was apparently genuine.

The more I worked with her, the more I came to view Dr. Sutton as a kindred spirit, who sincerely cared about the hopelessly damaged, forgotten men who were her willing, or unwilling, patients. There was no question that, all sedatives aside, she had a measurable healing effect on many of them.

When Dr. Sutton pushed the nifty idea of having yoga instructors come to the prison and teach the men peace, love, meditation, and self-fulfillment, I thought it was great. Any con with half a brain would leap at the opportunity to learn how to escape his depressing environment, even if it was only mentally. To me, it was a perfect match. It was also way too "out there" for the old-school, hard-line administrators like Rinker. He and his gooners wouldn't go for it in a million years. Undaunted, I was determined to give it a shot. To slide it through, I had to do an end run and find a forward-thinking associate warden willing to see the possibilities. To my shock, I was successful.

To my greater shock, the program itself was successful. The cons, intrigued by the robed yogis, eagerly signed up for the classes. Once there, they gave the mystics their attention—a miracle in itself. Most of the inmates did, that is. There was one particular little fellow who would have none of it. "You should be following me!" Manson raged when a duo of serene spirits visited his cell. "Change your ways. See the light and follow me! I know the truth! You don't! I'm your leader! Fools! You think of life and death. There's no life. There's no death. Those are words left over from another dimension. You don't understand the spirit world, the world of darkness. I do. I've been there, man. That's where I live. There's only one karma in the world. There's a billion snowflakes, and they all may be different, but they're all just frozen raindrops, and that's just water. I am the water. You're just snowflakes!"

Manson continued to rant, rave, and give an A-level crazy performance, trying his damnedest to rattle the yogis. To his increasing anger, he couldn't generate the slightest reaction. The more insults he fired, the more tranquil they became. At one point, he grew so incensed by their smiling faces and lack of fear that I thought he was going to squeeze through the bars and try to strangle the pair. I finally had to move them along before Charlie gave himself a coronary.

Despite Manson's hysterics, the yoga program was so effective that Dr. Sutton invited the grand master himself, Ram Dass, to San Quentin. Dass promptly accepted. All we had to do was get him cleared with the brass. That wasn't going to be easy. This wasn't a group of low-key local yogis quietly wandering through the far reaches of the prison. This was the Ram man himself, the famous former Harvard professor who was a 1960s icon, not to mention a classmate of LSD guru Timothy Leary. And Dass wasn't planning to light a few candles inside someone's cell. He was going to conduct a grandiose lecture and meditation session for an entire cell-block!

"This is a good one, Joyce," I said, relishing the possibilities. "Only I get the feeling you're leading me into a minefield full of shit."

"I know it sounds crazy, but the guy's got a tremendous reputation," she pressed. "He's a good man. Our yogis tell me he's a saint."

"You don't think I'll get fired over this guy?"

"No chance, Ed."

"Yeah, right. I'll just tell Rinker he's a good Harvard man. He'll love it."

I checked Dass's background and he came up clean. That was important. A drug bust here and there wouldn't look good on a guest speaker's résumé if the shit hit the fan. As luck would have it, when the paperwork was completed, both Rinker and Associate Warden Don Weber were away from the prison on business. I was able to rush the request to Associate Warden Clem Swaggerty, an easygoing sort. He courageously signed the clearance without question.

After some debate, Dr. Sutton and I both agreed that we'd let Dass do his thing on death row. (California had once again vacillated on the death penalty and it was temporarily back in effect.) This was partly because we felt the condemned men needed help the most, and partly because we didn't want Manson trying to steal the show. If a pair of peaceful yoga disciples had turned Charlie into a rabid dog, the sight of Ram Dass soothing the masses on death row would have sent his rage into orbit.

Dass arrived at San Quentin decked out in the full regalia of yoga attire, heightened by a long, flowing beard. He and his three attendants showered everyone with good vibes and cheerfully serene smiles. A charming, lovable man, Dass seemed to touch all he encountered — cons and corrections officers alike.

The yoga master set up shop on a heavy wooden table in the center of the isolated tier. The corrections staff had somehow managed to procure about twenty full-length mirror panels and were busy angling them in front of the more distant cells. This bit of generosity enabled the condemned men at the far ends of the hall to visually experience the event.

I was amazed by how quiet and solemn the inmates were. These were heinous murderers with nothing to lose, men who had spit in the face of authority their whole life. Yet, from the moment Dass entered their sixth-floor vault, an unworldly calm swept over the place. Quizzical faces peered out from the rows of bars, the faces of forty certified madmen. Only at that moment, their tortured minds appeared at ease as they waited for something magical to happen.

Dass sat on the edge of the lone table, brought his legs into the lotus position, bowed his head, and paused to drink in the unusual atmosphere. The place was deathly silent, something I'd never dreamed possible. The robed guru slowly raised his eyes and then greeted the inmates as brothers of the eternal being. He spoke to them like a father who wanted to share his life experiences with his children. His theme was one of lifting up their spirits and reaching a union with the eternal being. He spoke solemnly in simple words which they seemed to understand. Interacting, he taught them how to breathe, instructing them to relax and breathe out all the evil inside them and breathe in goodness. He talked about jails, cages, and cells, and how the spirit cannot be bound by bars. He contrasted the inmates' condition with that of people on the outside who create their own prisons of fear, anxiety, and hate. He invited them to let their spirits fly up and out into the stars, go wherever they desired, because the spirit had the power.

As Dass continued to cast his wonderful spell, I observed the room. Not only were the cons entranced, but even the most hateful and skeptical guards were overwhelmed by the moment. Many, like Dr. Sutton and I, had eased into the lotus position, going with the mesmerizing flow. It was unreal. I couldn't help thinking how beautiful it was, and how enraged Rinker and Manson would have been. It was ironic that the pair were once again linked by their predictable reactions. The reasons were different, of course. Rinker would have been furious to learn that a risky, hippielike event was taking place in his slavish domain. To him, the death row denizens weren't worth the trouble. They deserved nothing more than to have their sentences completed and their miserable lives terminated. Manson would simply be insane with jealousy that it was Dass, and not he, sitting on the table enthralling the crowd.

When Dass finished, we had all been drawn together by a shared experience. Considering the cat-and-dog mix of felons and correctional officers, that was another miracle.

Following the group session, Dass walked the tier, personally greeting each inmate before vanishing from their lives. I thanked him for coming and invited him back, even though I knew it would be impossible.

After he departed, my mind again turned to Rinker and Manson. Curiously, of the two, I regretted the most that Charlie had missed the memorable event. Dass was the embodiment of the kind of spiritual leader Charlie could have been. With Charlie's undeniable gift for attracting and controlling young people, combined with his passion and intense spirit, he could have made a difference. If only there had been a measure of goodness inside him instead of twisted evil, he might have been able to accomplish something as important in the light as he had done in the dark. He might have found the same fame as a promoter of peace and love as he'd found selling hate and unspeakable violence. Instead, he couldn't even calm his demons long enough to sit quietly and observe a true master at work. He couldn't control himself long enough to experience a wondrous happening that he, probably more than anyone there, could have truly understood. Had he opened his gnarled soul just a fraction, Dass could have gotten through to him.

Then again, maybe, like Dr. Sutton, I was dreaming. I was so overcome by the moment that I was momentarily blinded. I knew better than anyone that Charles Manson wasn't going to change. If we bottled Ram Dass and shoved it down his screeching throat, he'd still be nothing more than an evil little troll.

The next day, someone ratted to Associate Warden Weber. The AW stormed into my office and gave me the usual shit about clearances and end runs. A few hours later, the watch commander on duty the previous evening tossed in his two cents, chiding me for being "negligent of his crew's safety" by "allowing those weirdos inside a maximum-security unit like the row." I just walked away.

Shortly afterward, I was summoned to a telephone. Warden Rees was on the line. "Ed, what's going on with the yoga program?" he opened, making it obvious that the news had spread.

"Same old stuff, boss," I said with a shrug, downplaying it.

"Really? I've heard rumors that the instructors are getting hassled."

"Hassled?" I repeated, wondering where this was going.

"Yeah, hassled."

"Well, I don't know. The inmates aren't so bad. Manson gave a pair a hard time, but that can be expected. They didn't seem upset about it. They were more amused than anything."

"Manson? What's his problem?"

"Jealousy, I guess. Or maybe people tend to fight the medicine they need the most."

"Anything else?"

"Nothing serious. Some of the officers resent the yogis. They make snide remarks. Slow down searches. Force them to wait around forever."

"Have you talked to the watch commander?"

"No, the lieutenant is an old-timer. He'd just make it worse. He thinks yogis are very sinister. He calls them 'foreigners.'"

"Foreigners?"

"Yeah, aliens. If they're not like him, they're foreigners. He thinks it's un-American because yoga is an Eastern thing. According to him, anything that didn't originate in this country is subversive."

"How are you handling it?"

"It's no big deal. I'd rather let the yoga instructors endure the petty bullshit than make it an issue. Except for Manson, that is. I'm keeping them clear of him. At his request, interestingly enough."

"Good, then I've got nothing to worry about, right?"

"That's right, boss. So what's the fuss about?"

"It's this guy, Ram Ass, the yogi you had up on the row the other day." Uh-oh, I thought. Here it was. I'd almost gotten off without a mention, and I had to open my mouth. "It happens that Ram Ass is a personal friend of Jerry Brown, the governor."

That wasn't exactly surprising. Brown was well known for his open—wide-open—thinking. "That's Ram Dass, boss, with a D," I corrected, not wanting him to make the mistake in higher company.

"Whatever, he's a friend of the governor. After your little session, he went straight to Sacramento. Apparently, your program was a topic of discussion. Anyway, the governor called all happy about it. He wanted to know if the instructors were getting hassled."

"I'll be damned. That's great!"

"Yeah, the governor likes the program. He wants you to keep it going. So, if there are no major problems, he'll be delighted. Thanks for pushing it through."

That was encouraging. Finally, some support from the top! All I had to do now was to keep Charlie from reaching out and choking a yogi through the bars.

A few days later, I was about to turn a corner when I heard a couple of officers grousing. "Man, that guy George is turning this place into a zoo. Killers kicking back watching TV, doing yoga, taking art classes. Shit, I saw an inmate standing on his fuckin' head in his cell this morning, chanting some nonsense. Can you believe it?"

It was, indeed, quite unbelievable.

7

IN APRIL 1976, the death row prisoners decided to go on one of their ridiculous hunger strikes. The media poured in and produced more sob stories about starving prisoners. The reality is that prisoners—being the lying, stealing, murdering felons they are—cheat like hell, stashing candy and commissary food items in their cells and stealing bites off their trays when no one's looking. The leader of the effort, a 450-pound businessman who'd hired someone to kill his wife, had enough food stashed under his bed to feed an army.

Yet, when the reporters came around, the guys would moan and groan and writhe around on the floor like they were hours away from death. Totally duped, the media put the screws to us to show compassion and give in to the strikers' idiotic demands (they wanted their own gourmet cook, among other things). AW Rinker was frantic to negotiate a quick settlement and end the waves of bad press. That impatience showed his cards and played into the inmates' hands. I advised everyone to ignore it and wait them out.

Manson, who had escaped death row years before during one of California's yo-yoing capital punishment decisions, was not part of the effort. Far from it. He pointed out that because of their limited numbers and special circumstances, death row inmates don't have it so bad. "Those assholes eat better on strike than we do normally," he cracked, exposing the truth. "My years up there were the easiest time I've ever served. I didn't have to worry all the time about somebody taking me out. I could relax. Let those bastards starve."

As luck would have it, there was a Hollywood film crew on the grounds at the time. That only increased Rinker's tension and eagerness to end the strike. The movie, *The Domino Principle*, was directed by Stanley Kramer and starred Gene Hackman, Mickey Rooney, and—Candice Bergen! Manson had missed her once; now fate was tossing her into his sights again. I, of course, wasn't going to let that happen. Despite his carping, I didn't allow him to get anywhere near the set. Actually, Manson had nothing against Bergen personally. She merely would have been an unfortunate victim in the Tate death house had Melcher still been around. If given the opportunity on the yard, there was no reason to assume Charlie would have done anything more than try to recruit the beautiful, sassy blonde into his family. The whole thing turned out to be moot, as Bergen's part didn't require her to be at the prison.

Ironically, it was *Boys Town* graduate Mickey Rooney who had the problem. Kramer was doing takes in the west block exercise yard while tough guy Rooney milled around among some low-security convicts standing by the cameraman. The gooner squad was providing tight security, so everything seemed cool. Unbeknownst to anyone, an African American inmate stealthily worked his way behind a security officer standing near the tripod. The inmate removed a prison-made shank from his belt, whispered, "This is for the brothers," and jumped the officer, stabbing him in the back. Rooney, standing right there when it happened, leaped like a prize jumping frog.

The stabbed officer swung around and knocked down his assailant, who was immediately subdued by the gooners. The injured officer was rushed to the hospital and survived. A subsequent investigation revealed that the attack was revenge for the beating given to a couple of Black Guerrilla Family members during their trip to death row. The Guerrillas had killed a guard at their previous prison, and the good guys were enacting a little vengeance.

I hated that kind of back-and-forth violence because no one ever won. The officer who was stabbed wasn't one of the gooners who had beaten the inmates—the victims rarely are. Time and again, correctional officers are maimed and killed because of the actions of someone else.

That weekend, Beth and I had dinner with some friends. Afterward, we planned to go to the Geary Theater in San Francisco to see a musical. The dinner conversation touched upon the death row hunger strike, which was in its twelfth day. Our friends expressed the feeling common among outsiders: "Let them starve. It's death row, isn't it? Saves everybody the trouble."

On the drive to the theater, I heard a radio bulletin that rocked me. Someone had hijacked an entire school bus full of children in Chowchilla, a small farm town south of Fresno. I was certain it was one of Manson's clan. The perpetrators were probably phoning the prison at that moment threatening to kill a child every hour until Manson was released. I didn't share my fears with Beth and our guests, but I was in a fog the rest of the night. I don't remember a thing about the musical.

Beth noticed my sudden mood change, but didn't say anything until we were on our way home. I tried to duck the question a few times, then finally relented. "It's that damn school bus thing," I sighed.

"That's terrible, but why are you taking it so personally?"

"I don't know. It might be one of our crazies," I downplayed, not specifying which crazy.

"You can't be serious."

"I'm damn serious. Some of my guys are capable of changing history, killing presidents, hijacking airliners."

"That's absurd."

Sometimes, my wife's sugarplum attitude got under my skin, but I was smart enough to realize it was also what I loved about her. Beth knew that being around prisons had hardened me and made me pessimistic, so she countered it by being cheery and optimistic. Plus, she could never really understand my angst because I'd hidden most of the horrors of my job from her. This evening, I found myself opening up a bit.

"A few weeks ago, there was a report that a group of revolutionaries were planning to kidnap a busload of kids from the Folsom area to force the release of an inmate named 'Geronimo,' a Black Panther serving time for murder,"* I said, laying it off on another group. "The plan was to take the kids of the officers so the prison officials would be doubly motivated to negotiate. Because of the report, 'Geronimo' was transferred to the San Quentin AC. He's now on my block. That's why I'm a little concerned."

"It's hard to believe anyone would use little children."

"You know, I never talk much about these guys, but there's a few ruthless bastards in this world who'll stoop to anything. They'd take our kids if they knew where to find them."

The minute I said that I knew I'd made a mistake. I wanted Beth to know why I was worried, not scare her to death. Mentioning our own kids knocked the optimism right out of her. She remained silent the rest of the way home.

That Monday, there was still no word from the people holding the children. I knew, however, it could come at any time, so I remained in knots. To complicate matters, I was set to have a sit-down—literally—with the leaders of the striking inmates to see if we could resolve the issue. The cons had selected me for the job because the word around the yard was that I wasn't a hard-ass and could be trusted. That was true. I could be trusted, but they sure as hell couldn't! Before going on the row to meet with them man-to-murderer, I left specific instructions with the guards. "If the inmates try to take me hostage, don't be afraid to shoot. I'd rather be shot by somebody trying to save me than get hacked to death bit by bit by those thugs."

I waltzed in, sat on the floor surrounded by seven condemned men, and promptly worked out a deal. The row would get a television set, a Ping-Pong table, three hot meals a day (accomplished by adding soup to their lunch sandwich), more diligent medical care, better access to law books (so the inmates could sue the state easier), legal visits among inmates to help one another with cases (translation: have sex), a stool for each cell (probably to carve into weapons), a public telephone on the row (to plan their escapes), and dry cleaning (in case they needed their tux pressed for a night out at the Ritz). The demands I denied were weight lifting equipment (too dangerous); community, out-of-cell exercise periods (with Richard Simmons maybe?); weekly movies (too costly); ice cream (nice try); cable TV (too complicated); and conjugal visits (not appropriate for condemned men).

---

*In 1977, "Geronimo's" murder conviction was overturned on appeal, and he was released on bail pending appeal of the reversal of his conviction.

We shook hands, and that was the end of the silly strike. Back in my office, as I was accepting congratulations, I heard that the creeps responsible for taking the school bus (and burying the damn thing underground with the children inside) had been caught and arrested, and the children had been rescued. It turned out they were not involved with either "Geronimo" or Manson. The whole thing was financially motivated.

Charlie missed out on the publicity wave surrounding that one, but he was hardly cast aside by the fickle press. Lynette's assassination attempt had thrust him into the limelight again, and a new prison policy would enable him to take tremendous advantage of it. After decades of restricting the media from entering prison lockups and interviewing notorious criminals, the policy was abruptly changed. If an inmate consented and signed a waiver, he could be interviewed once every ninety days. Beautiful. If there was one prisoner in the whole world that the media wanted, it was my buddy Charlie. The avalanche of requests began the instant the policy change was announced. Reporters wrote from all over the United States, as well as Britain, Europe, and Asia. That gave me a whole new job description—Charles Manson's press agent.

Charlie was thrilled by the attention and the power it gave him. He could sit like a king in his cell and give the thumbs-up, thumbs-down treatment to the most famous journalists and television broadcasters in the country. He was in heaven. He was also pretty shrewd. Instead of starting with some national media superstar like Mike Wallace of 60 *Minutes* or Dan Rather of CBS—both of whom made pitches—he selected a local TV anchor from small-market Sacramento. Manson viewed it as a test run, a chance to rehearse his latest show off Broadway. The anchor, Stan Atkinson, was thrilled at having hit the Manson lottery and rushed over with his crew in early January 1976. We selected an upstairs property room for the historic event, and had the TV folks set up their lights, cameras, and sound. Manson was housed two floors down, on the first-floor south side of the AC with the rest of the HVP (high violence potential) inmates. The rule was that HVP cons couldn't be moved without restraints, and the cuffs stayed on until the inmate returned to his cell. After the officers cuffed Manson to prepare him for the journey upstairs, he refused to budge.

"I'm not going to any fuckin' interview with handcuffs on," he announced. I'd already cleared it so he could have the cuffs removed during the actual interview, so Manson's hissy fit pissed me off. The transporting officers didn't give a shit about Manson's PR and stood firm, refusing to remove the hardware. Naturally, I got the job of trying to break the stalemate. Storming downstairs, I spotted Charlie standing like a frail street beggar between two gargantuan officers. The moment I looked into his beady eyes I could see he was playing his mind games. I felt like canceling the interview, but knew how excited Atkinson was and how crushed he'd be if Manson didn't come through. I pulled the sergeant aside.

"Do you see any problem with moving him without the irons?"

"No problem," the sergeant responded. It was a macho thing with them, so I figured the answer would be positive. I walked back to the cell and spoke loud enough for the surrounding inmates to hear. "You can move him upstairs without cuffs, but watch the little bastard. If he tries anything, knock him on his ass and lock him up."

"Yes sir!" the gooners answered.

Charlie shot me his best shit-eating smile. To him, it was a great victory. He'd beaten the system!

The interview went off without a hitch. Charlie played the terrifying cult leader, and Atkinson recorded enough video to milk it into a three-part series. After the report aired, the requests began coming in by the bagful. Since Manson had selected a small-market station, every one-bulb television outfit and two-typewriter newspaper in the country tried to get in on the action.

A couple of weeks after the interview, Charlie was moved to the second floor, where he was reunited with his good pal Pin Cushion. I allowed Pin to help me with Manson's mail, and he jumped at the opportunity to become Manson's assistant media agent. Instead of filtering through the requests, Pin decided to take the bull by the horns. He began writing the big networks and magazines offering special arrangements. The problem was, Pin was selling the interviews! To my shock, he said he'd worked out a $100,000 deal with CBS for an eight-hour taped interview. After all Pin's work, Manson turned it down, choosing instead to chat with a reporter from *The National Enquirer* for free. Pin went nuts, thinking Manson had lost his mind and betrayed him. I had to calm him by explaining that Manson was no fool. He knew that inmates can't profit from their crimes by selling interviews, so the money was moot. He'd selected another non-traditional media outlet to further his master plan of working up to bigger scores. Pin ended up getting the last laugh, as the *Enquirer* interview hit a snag and was delayed.

Rebuffed by the $100,000 letdown, Pin Cushion traded his agent efforts for a new position as Manson's tailor. Because the AC is a lockup, my inmates got the worst of everything. The clothing was especially bad, usually ill-fitting, full of holes, and missing buttons. On the mainline, the cons switched garments themselves by going to a window and hassling a clerk. If they were given junk, they could bitch until they got something better. In AC, the men had to take what was delivered. Knowing that my guys couldn't complain, the clothing staff always sent us their rags.

With Manson being a TV star, Pin felt he deserved better. Using the trustee status I'd given him, and the free movement the designation afforded, Pin went on a raid. The fast-talking con was an expert in what is known as "bogarting." That's when an inmate affects a certain tough guy swagger, like Humphrey Bogart, to convince the guards that he has the authority to do whatever it is he's trying to do. In this manner, Pin conned an officer into helping him unlock doors by claiming that there was a "clothing emergency" on the block. The inmates, Pin explained, were ready to riot, and I'd responded by ordering him to get everyone new threads. Not only was the officer convinced, he helped Pin do the job! The pair took a dolly and picked through the clothing stocks, bringing back decent uniforms for Manson and his neighbors. After that, Pin began running similar missions to get anything else Manson and the guys needed, cutting through the red tape and the "you guys are last on the list" road-block we always encountered. Pin even helped me acquire critical office materials. For the most part, I let him get away with it because the prison's policy was unfair, and "Roger's Raids," as they were called, boosted morale on the wing.

I had to temper his activities, however, after he promised to secure a typewriter and came back with five—including one from the chaplain's office.

"You stole from the chaplain?" I exclaimed.

"Don't worry, boss. It was the Protestant! You didn't think I'd take one from Father O'Neal?" That didn't excuse his behavior, but I couldn't help laughing. "Besides," he added, "the Protestant chaplain doesn't keep material things."

"You're gonna get me arrested, Pin."

"I'll pick out a nice cell for you. You can room with Charlie!"

"Don't even joke about that."

A few days later, the wing was rocked by the news than an inmate was lying buck naked in the yard sunbathing. I figured it was a scam of some kind, but sure enough, there he was, resting on a towel, trying to seduce some young punk by displaying his impressive equipment to the world. In his hand was a *Playboy* magazine, which he was using to help in his advertising campaign. I looked closer. It was Pin!

"Damn it," I wailed. "That crazy bastard's going to get me canned!"

I started to open the window, then was struck by a thought. I raced to Manson's cell, suspicious that the pair were up to something. Was Pin creating a diversion so his pal Manson could escape?

"What the fuck do you want?" Manson growled. I could tell by his calm demeanor that nothing was going on. This was obviously one of Pin's solo flights. Back at the window, I leaned my head out. "Roger, what the hell are you doing?" Pin, whose nickname suddenly seemed all wrong, casually rolled his eyes from the magazine.

"Just getting a little sunshine, boss."

"For goodness' sake, Roger, get your clothes on or I'm locking your ass up!"

Pin rose slowly, acting insulted by my intolerance. "It's no big deal, boss. I'm so white from all that cell time. I need a little tan." Pin pulled on his undershorts, then followed with his prison blues. He left his shirt off. "This okay, boss?"

I was too furious to respond. I laughed about it later, but at the time, it was a critical breach of policy. With Pin covered, I made another pass by Manson's cell, making doubly sure he wasn't up to something.

"You again?" he snarled. "What the fuck's going on?"

"Never mind. I'm sure you'll hear about it later."

Without saying another word, Manson went to the back of his cell, picked up a metal mop holder, and handed it to me through the bars.

"This could be dangerous," he said.

I was stunned. A mop holder could easily be altered into one of the most feared weapons found in a prison. The size and amount of metal made it something to kill for—and with. It had fallen into Charlie's lap when an officer foolishly left it on the tier after an inmate mopped the floors. Since Manson never did anything out of benevolence, I viewed it as an act of self-preservation. Without ratting, he was signaling to me that security was sloppy on the block and needed to be cleaned up. Manson had reason to be concerned. If the mop handle had fallen into another inmate's hands, it might have been used to kill or maim him. There was always the fear that somebody wanted to gain a reputation by taking out Charles Manson, and such slipups would give some young sociopath the perfect opportunity. Although Manson was loath to admit it, and often railed against it, he was a strong proponent of tight security.

A few days later, I was bent over my desk concentrating on some procedures for the new AC manual when a shadow crossed my path, giving me a start. I glanced and saw Pin's imposing frame blocking the doorway. He had a strange, wanton look on his face.

"You sure have a nice ass, boss," he cooed. "I'd sure like to bust your brownie."

"What?" I demanded, angered by the lewd remark.

"I mean, I'd like to butt-fuck you," he clarified, jerking his hips forward to emphasize the point. Oh shit, I thought, feeling a trace of fear. What were these two scheming now? Had Manson ordered Pin to force me into a compromising position so they could gain blackmail power? Was Pin, possibly with the help of others behind the door, going to try and rape me in the hope that I would be too ashamed to file charges and would thus be under their control? Pin knew that if something like that happened, many of my fellow officers would think that I'd willingly participated. A number of officers at San Quentin had destroyed their careers by having relations with inmates, so it was possible that I could end up being thrown into the Dumpster with them. This was a serious situation. I dropped my pen and glared at the burly Irishman.

"Over my dead body!"

My response broke the tension. A smile cut across both of our faces, then laughter, side-splitting laughter. Neither of us could stop for nearly five minutes. We couldn't talk. Tears filled our eyes as we howled. Each time we tried to regain control, we'd look at each other and burst out laughing. When we were finally spent, we confirmed what had been so funny. Pin was imprisoned because of sexual crimes. He'd killed for sex. Even in prison, sex was his main motivation. He came to me once with a plan to randomly murder someone so he could be sent to death row and reunite with a lover. He was dead serious about it, dropping the idea only after I explained that his lover would be long gone before Pin made it through the system.

My ad-libbed "Over my dead body" remark was the wrong threat to make with this character. Pin was laughing for the same reason. "The moment you said that, I thought, 'I've killed guys for a lot less.' And I knew you knew it," he said. What started out as a scary moment ended with us bonding emotionally in a way two men rarely experience. Yet after it was over, driving home that evening, I couldn't help feeling uneasy about what might have prompted it. Would Pin have tried to rape me? I didn't think so. We'd gone through a lot together and I trusted the guy. He wouldn't have forced the issue—unless he was under the influence of somebody else. Would Pin have go through with it had I consented? Absolutely. Pin's motto was, "Nothing ventured, nothing gained." As long as it was Pin just being Pin, everything was cool. But if Charlie had something to do with it, then everything was decidedly uncool. As I pulled into my driveway, I realized that I'd probably never know the truth.

Later that spring, something happened that put my problems with Manson and Pin Cushion in glaring perspective. The brutally murdered body of a thirty-eight-year-old officer was found sprawled on the floor of the laundry warehouse in the lower yard. His head was crushed and brain tissue was oozing from his fractured skull. It took a blow of tremendous force to do that kind of damage. A bloody gunnysack containing a heavy weight was found near the corpse. There were no signs of struggle, indicating that the officer had been jumped. A general recall was immediately sounded, summoning the inmates to return to their cells. The guards examined everyone as they filtered back. The prison was locked down, and the gooner squad sealed off the crime scene, searching for clues. The assignment officer gave the gooners a list of the inmates who worked in the laundry. They were located and grilled in their cells. One, a man named Rios, had blood on his clothing. He was panting, perspiring, and extremely jittery, looking from one face to another expecting something to happen. His answers were nervous and evasive. It was pretty obvious that he was the one.

Rios was jerked around, pushed, and yanked from his cell. The gooners dragged him across the yard and brought him to the AC. Inside, they blew past the door officer and bypassed the holding cage, where the suspect should have been deposited. Instead, they pushed him into the sergeant's office, cornered him, and began to beat him mercilessly. The whole gooner crew took part, each venting his fury on the con's body. They were so frenzied that they battered him against the wire-fused windows, cracking two and completely caving in a third. When Rios fell to the floor, they proceeded to kick him around like an old soccer ball. After Rios confessed, he was dragged limp into the holding cage.

The Marin County DA went ballistic over the prison-style justice. He jumped on the warden, demanding to know who had inflicted the beating and why. He warned that the whole case against Rios had been jeopardized because the confession was obviously coerced. Warden Rees angrily sought answers. None were forthcoming. The code of silence among the officers was an impenetrable stone wall. The gooners didn't care about the law, or even losing the confession. Rios was in long-term anyway, so another mark on his record was meaningless. They'd meted our their own instant sentence as a message to him, and to everyone else.

Justified as this might sound in an eye-for-an-eye environment, the problem was, it wouldn't end there. As I've explained before, all this does is start an endless cycle of murder and mayhem. The officer had been killed because a prisoner somewhere had been roughed up. The gooners in turn had battered the culprit. Now Rios's brothers had a new score to settle, so another officer would go down. Around and around it went. To break the cycle, I received permission to crack down hard on the men. I hammered the door officer—one of my crew—until he broke down and fingered the specific gooners. That only made things worse. The gooners found out and threatened the door officer for snitching. That enraged me. I called in the bully who delivered the threat and jumped on his ass. Didn't matter. Despite my efforts, nothing changed. All I'd done was place one of my men in jeopardy with his fellow officers. No matter how hard you try, sometimes things can't be changed.

The government put on a good show for the slain guard's funeral. The church, St. Dominic's in San Francisco, was packed with law-enforcement officers from every city and county in the Bay Area. The eulogy seemed to fit not only the victim, but what I had tried to accomplish in the aftermath. "Christlike he died. . . . Like Christ, he would have said, 'Forgive them, for they know not what they do.' . . . He was a loving father, humble, peaceful, caring. So, his life with God begins for him, as his life ends with us here."

The military-style ceremony at the cemetery had all the bells and whistles, including a twenty-one-gun salute, taps, and the presentation of the folded coffin flag to his devastated widow as her four stunned children clung to her side.

Sometime later, I was chatting with Manson and Pin Cushion and mentioned offhand how impossible it was to stop the constant waves of violence at San Quentin. To my surprise, both cons supported the guards.

"If an inmate jumps an officer, he should get the shit beat out of him," Pin said. "They did it to me, and I finally learned."

Manson's opinion was even stronger. "Put me in charge of this prison for one day, and I'll stop all the killing. Give me just one hour, and I'll end the violence. Show them no mercy, and they'll obey. Give them a dose of fear, a taste of the wolf's fangs, a sting of the scorpion's tail, and all your problems will be over."

"I can't do that," I explained. "Legally, or morally."

"You have the power to do anything you want," Manson snapped. "You just need the balls to do it."

I walked away, marveling at how Manson's sentiments echoed those expressed by the hard-line guards. Someone had told me once that there was "a thin line between cops and robbers." That statement never rang truer than at that moment. Charles Manson was a gooner.

8

I WAS CASUALLY chatting with Charlie one afternoon when he started going on about how horrible it was that "the system" had caged him. "You have no idea what it's like. You're close, but you're still on the right side of the bars, so you don't know."

Actually, I did—to an extent. I wanted to explain, but I always had to be careful what I said because Charlie fed on human weakness and would use it against me later. This day, however, I decided to open up a crack. "When I was at St. Joseph's Seminary in Mountain View [California], there were a lot of similarities. I was there nearly six years, a solid sentence."

"Like armed robbery."

"Yeah, something like that. It was pretty torturous, full of loneliness and despair. Seminarians are well protected from the world. No girls. No newspapers. No radios or television. Tons of silence. In some ways, it's worst than here. The study load was rigorous, the discipline strict, stricter than here because you guys can run your mouths. We couldn't. We had small private rooms with a closet, a bed, a bureau, a desk, a chair, and a sink with a mirror. It was similar to a prison cell. There were community showers and toilets. We didn't even have the privacy and convenience that you guys have. Silence was imposed in the living areas, so even with other people around, I couldn't talk. The spiritual exercise and prayer was heavy. Like here, we formed societies and had secret gatherings to survive mentally. Only we took a bigger risk. If we were caught, we'd be sent home in shame, a vocation lost. Of my class, twenty-five made it through, fifteen didn't. The ones who left did so mainly because of the celibacy thing."

"Went for the pussy, eh? No surprise there. But you guys had a choice. You could have left anytime," Manson gruffed, unimpressed. "That's a big difference."

"It's no different with you. You had a choice. You could have chosen not to end up here in the first place. Then, after your first few falls, you could have done your time and made sure you never came back. How many times have you been paroled?"

"It's still not the same," he parried, ignoring my logic. "You don't know how I grew up, man. Even in prison, I was at the bottom. Because of my high security and history of escapes, I wasn't allowed to participate in the trade programs. While other guys were learning how to be auto mechanics, welders, plumbers, electricians, printers, and things like that, I was locked in a cell and kept out of the classes. So what good did that do me? What did they prepare me for when I was released? Nothing! See, you haven't walked in my shoes."

No, thankfully, I hadn't.

Fortunately, Manson interrupted me before I slipped and went further.

Near the end of my "sentence" I began suffering headaches and dizzy spells. They increased in pain and frequency until I was on the verge of a nervous breakdown. A Methodist psychologist told me I was trying to be something I wasn't "cut out to be." He suggested that I reconsider my career path. Because he was Methodist, I cast it off as heathen heresy. I'd persevere, I insisted, through prayer and faith. I prayed and had faith, but the headaches wouldn't ease. Finally, a Catholic psychologist advised me to leave the seminary immediately before I had a complete mental breakdown. Back home in San Francisco, the pain and dizziness vanished. I walked the beach for a month, breathing in the air and slowly rejoining the world, secure in my decision to escape my "prison." Strange how things turn out. After an up-and-down stint in the military as a pilot candidate (probably overcompensating for my desire to be free), I settled into a career as a correctional administrator. I could take what I'd learned about being "caged," and try to ease the burden of men who had no other choice. Even men like Charles Manson.

I doubted whether my personal bio helped Manson, especially since I'd ended it with a scolding. He was probably beyond help anyway. But that wasn't going to stop me from trying.

A lot of decent people were trying at San Quentin in the middle 1970s. There were numerous renovation projects under way, some of which I personally handled. I supervised the design and building of a new exercise yard for the lockup units. Basketball and handball courts were spread across a smooth asphalt surface, complete with freshly painted white lines. At the completion of a series of similar projects, we held a big dog and pony show for area politicians, central office staffers, and other big shots. Associate Warden Rinker was set to give them the grand tour and was on pins and needles about it. We all knew how many things can go wrong inside a prison.

"It'll be a disaster," Manson warned in a nonthreatening manner. "You watch. You give these guys an audience, and they'll take it every time. You march a bunch of lambs in front of a den of lions, and what do you think will happen? It's the natural order." Recalling how the death row gang had played to the media, I couldn't help agreeing with him.

On the big day, Rinker led an entourage of twenty corrections department officials, dignitaries, and legislative types through the buildings and housing units to display our proud accomplishments. Everything was going fine until the group entered B section, otherwise known as the seventh level of Dante's Inferno. On the surface, the "ol' hellhole" had never looked better. It had been closed six months for a total overhaul. The cells had been rewired, sinks and toilets replaced, hot-water lines installed, walls painted, and open drains covered and diverted to pipes that connected with the main sewer system. The ingrained stench had been scrubbed and disinfected away, and the floor surfaces had been sealed.

Despite the face-lift, it was still a maximum-security unit, a factor that wasn't lost on the visiting dignitaries. This was the place where society's worst vermin lived—people like Charles Manson. And in this case, it wasn't just "people like Charles Manson," it was Charles Manson! I wondered how many in the group were pondering that fact as they entered the ominous arena. They must have been thinking something scary because their faces paled with fear and apprehension as they hesitantly filed through the huge metal door and gingerly stepped into the five-story cellblock.

Instead of regaling them with the titillating history of all the famous felons who'd lived there, like a good haunted-house tour guide would have, Rinker tried to sell the place like it was Disneyland. He bragged about how wonderful and humane things at San Quentin were now that it was under his personal control. Even the guards had miraculously transformed from sadistic goons to patient professionals trained to correct and rehabilitate, not punish.

Bang! A shot rang out in the new exercise yard, interrupting the fantasy and totally mortifying the visitors. It was just a routine warning round intended to break up a fight, but these people had no clue. If that wasn't bad enough, the shot was followed by the terrifying sound of the piercing alarms. The group stood speechless, shuddering. Suddenly, an army of officers blasted through the B-section door, charging recklessly toward the yard. Rinker himself instinctively bolted to the door to the yard to see what had taken place, abandoning his now thoroughly frightened guests. Boom! A second, louder shot exploded inside everyone's brain. The first shot had failed to end the scuffle, so a rifleman had blasted one of the participants with a beanbag projectile, knocking him down.

Rinker had left the dignitaries standing in the middle of the section, right between the entrance to the unit and the exit to the yard. That placed them directly in the path of the stampeding gooners. Normally, such groups are briefed before entering that if an emergency should occur, they're to hug the walls and clear the pathways. Apparently, this particular gathering had not been told about such potential unpleasantries. That oversight placed them literally in harm's way. Intent on quelling what, for all they knew, was a serious riot, the gooners crashed into, through, and around the stunned visitors.

The dignitaries also knew nothing about certain routine prison procedures which, if viewed in the wrong light, could give off a decidedly mistaken impression. A pack of guards had been using ax handles in a nearby section to check the strength of the restraints in various cells. By slipping the handles through the bars and pulling back, they can determine if a crafty inmate has been sawing away for a future break. Naturally, when the alarm sounded, these guards came sprinting through B section carrying their ax handles like famed racist politician Lester Maddox, giving the visitors the vivid image of unwary cons about to get their skulls cracked.

With the situation outside under control, Rinker finally returned to the outsiders quaking in the hallway. He darted back inside and was appalled by what he saw. "Stop! The emergency's over. Stop! Stop!" he cried to the ax-handle gang. It was no use. The officers had been trained to drop everything and respond to the alarms, and were oblivious of the PR disaster that was unfolding. Rinker ran to the entrance in a panic and tried to slam the iron door. Instead of succeeding, he was nearly trampled by a third wave of officers. "Stop!" he screamed, clutching at them. "It's over, damn it! I tell you. It's over!" This group ignored him as well, cursing his efforts while slamming into the visitors. Chaos reigned as a number of the women began to scream with terror.

Meanwhile, the inmates were loving every minute of it. They charged to the front of their cells like rabid monkeys, whooped it up, shouted obscenities, and showered the group with vile threats and biting insults. After about five minutes of this madness, things finally calmed—everything, that is, except the dignitaries' heartbeats. The respite was only temporary. Screeeeeech! The alarm sounded again, this time signaling an emergency in the adjoining hospital wing. A pack of twenty officers, pumped and full of adrenaline, had gathered near the exercise-yard door, catching their breath. The second siren sent them charging back down the hall, a larger and more menacing mass than before. The dignitaries, who still hadn't figured out how to protect themselves, were stomped for the fourth time. By now, the group wanted no part of San Quentin. They didn't give two shits about our new basketball and handball courts anymore. All they wanted was to get the hell out of there. They dashed for the door and began spilling out into the outside corridor.

When the second alarm sounded, it was unclear precisely where the emergency was. Half of the officers hung a right and headed for the hospital, while the other half hooked a left toward the mess hall. Once there, the mess-hall gang realized their mistake and came rumbling back with renewed haste. Only now, the civilians were again blocking their path! Seeing the oncoming herd, the dignitaries retreated back into B section—the last place in the world they wanted to be. Screaming and cursing, they squeezed through the door in a panic and were immediately greeted by a welcoming roar of obscenities from the gleeful inmates.

Dr. Sutton and I observed the fiasco with subdued delight. "Just keep your back to the wall and you'll be all right," I reminded her each time the Keystone Guards came barreling by. "There's nothing we can do but stay out of the way."

Rinker fumed for days afterward, careening about looking for someone to blame. "Why didn't you help me stop those idiots from charging into the unit like that?" he demanded after cornering me. "You saw what they did. You were standing by the door. You didn't do a damn thing!"

"I didn't know what was going on, so I had to let the officers through.

One of our men could have been in trouble. Once they started pouring inside, there was no way I could stop them. Thank God none of the visitors were seriously injured," I added, twisting the knife.

When things settled and emotions subsided, I paid a visit to one particularly interested observer.

"So, I heard everything went off without a hitch," Manson teased, stroking his goatee the way he always did when he was extremely pleased with himself.

"Did you have anything to do with that?" I demanded.

"Me?" he protested. "Ruin Rinker's big moment? Why would I do that? Just because he ordered his pigs to drag me halfway across the prison, then took me out of population, that doesn't mean I don't love the guy. Just remember, Ed, hurt me, and you hurt yourself. Try to bite me like a mosquito, and I'll bite you back like a bear. If these guys didn't give me so much shit, things like this wouldn't happen. It all revolves around me. It's your choice. Peace or violence."

I wasn't sure if Charlie had really instigated the mess, or was just trying to take undeserved credit. Probably the latter, but I never knew with him. Either way, he'd been right. You can't march a bunch of squeamish citizens through a dungeon where five hundred madmen are caged without expecting something to go wrong. We were lucky it hadn't been worse.

"Things always go wrong for people during their big moments," Charlie said, falling into a philosophical mode. "Hey, I wanted to be a musician and things didn't work out. They tried to pin that Beatles *White Album* thing on me at the trial, but that wasn't me, man. They weren't of my era. I was into the music of my youth, Frank Sinatra, Bing Crosby, Perry Como, Frankie Laine, Mel Torme, they meant more to me than the Beatles, Beach Boys, and those guys. Hell, it was the kids who saw all those messages in the *White Album*. . . . I had my own music. We actually had some recording sessions that [Terry] Melcher set up, but they didn't go too well. The studio guy was too controlling and we ended up getting into a pissing match and leaving. They were messing with our groove, and I wouldn't stand for it. Dennis [Wilson of the Beach Boys] convinced me to sit still and let the pros in the studio do their thing, and we finally laid down some tracks. But nothing came of it."

"Why? From what I hear, you're pretty decent."

"I was! Some of the songs I wrote could have been classics, big hits."

"So what happened?"

Charlie sighed, then grew silent. It was rare for him to drop his macho/crazy posture, open up, and express his true emotions—especially on this topic. I had no idea what had prompted it, but I didn't want the mood to pass. "Come on, you've never told me this stuff," I pressed. "You always pretend not to give a shit about anything, but we both know better."

"I don't give a shit! Not now. But I did back then. Off and on. That music deal was when things started falling apart out there. When paradise was lost, man. We were at the crossroads. Fame was going to come after me, one way or another, good or bad. It could have gone either way. It had been perfect for a while. The music. The promise of an album. The women. There were fifteen, sometimes twenty girls out there that I could have any time I wanted. Imagine that. A different one every night. Two or three at a time. They were all young, eager, and beautiful. They did anything I asked, fucking and sucking for as long as I wanted them to. Me, the other guys, each other, whatever I commanded they happily obeyed. It was a rush. . . . But there were just too many people to control, too many drugs fuckin' up everybody's head. We had about forty people at the ranch near the end. Most, about twenty-five, were my group. The others were ex-convicts, bikers, and some kids just drifting through. There were always new people coming in and out. That was the whole point. Total freedom. Nobody wanted to work, so we had to steal cars, sell drugs and stuff just to keep everybody fed. The ranch hands started getting suspicious and threatened to snitch."

"Shorty?"

"Yeah, he was the worst. I had to come down on him, but I knew our time was running out. The plan was to sell my album and use the royalties to build our own private city way out in the desert. A place where we could live like we wanted, do whatever we desired, with no rules or cops or nothing. No hassles, drug busts, angry neighbors—you know, free, man. Our own world! It would have happened, too, but the drugs just ate us up. None of that bad shit would have gone down if we'd only controlled the drugs, instead of letting them control us. That's how the whole nightmare started. Tex [Watson] burned this black pusher and the guy grabbed Tex's girlfriend and was holding her hostage. They called the ranch asking for "Charles" and I answered. I told him I wasn't the right Charles, but I'd try to straighten it out. I took the gun [the .22 Buntline later used in the Tate-LaBianca murders] and went to reason with the guy. He was a big, arrogant asshole who played his bully mind games. He wanted his money and wasn't going to let the girl go. Said he was going to fuck her to death. He came at me and tried to strangle me. I fired, but the gun didn't go off. Now I was in deep shit. I pulled the trigger again, and this time it fired. The guy dropped. I grabbed the girl and got out of there, convinced that the pusher was dead.

"The next day, there was a report on the news that some big-shot Black Panther had been wasted the night before. I was certain he was my guy. Paranoia was rampant. I felt that the police were in a race with an angry army of Black Panthers to make it to the ranch first. That's when I began telling everybody about the blacks rising up and coming after us. It wasn't some symbolic war like everybody thinks, it was real!

"After that, everything changed. Sex, drugs, and rock and roll became fear, anxiety, and paranoia, dig? And it was all a mistake. We had the wrong guy. The Panther was somebody else. My guy didn't even die. The bastard survived! And he didn't even snitch. But we didn't know that. So the police and Panthers never came. Problem was . . . Dennis, and some of the others in the music business heard about it."

"How?"

"Friends of the dealer, I guess. We were all in the same drug circle. The music guys found out and decided not to push my album. That ended that. It was all Tex's fault. He burned the dealer, and I caught the shit trying to be a hero. See what that good-guy shit gets you? It just gets you fucked!"

"Not always."

"Always! I went away for a while. Escaped the heat. Tried to get my head together. Met a new girl on the road. A beautiful seventeen-year-old. Gave her acid and fucked her on the beach. We traveled around awhile, making love and hanging out. It was great. I brought her to the ranch around August eighth, and immediately the tension and shit began again. Bobby had been busted for Hinman's death."

"What happened there?"

"That was another drug deal gone bad. Some bikers said Bobby sold them some bad shit and they wanted their money back. When Bobby went to the supplier, Hinman, the guy refused to make good, leaving Bobby's ass on the line. They argued, and Bobby and some of the girls ended up killing the guy. They even wrote a message on the wall in Hinman's blood, something like 'Political Piggy.' See? That Beatles album writing stuff wasn't me. That was the kids' idea all along. I wasn't even around!

"So Bobby, stupid and stoned, is driving Hinman's car and gets arrested. Bobby was a handsome dude, sweet talker. We called him 'Cupid.' All the girls loved his dick and were in a frenzy when I arrived. They had come up with this wild-ass idea that if they kept killing people and writing more Beatles shit on the walls, the police would realize that Hinman's killers were still out there and let Bobby go. I told them that was insane. Sadie [Susan Atkins] argued that we could pin it on the niggers. It'll be Helter Skelter, like you want! It wasn't exactly what I'd wanted. I'd told the kids the blacks were going to rise from their suppression one day, but it got all twisted up with the Panthers coming after us, so it was confusing, man. The kids weaved it together. I didn't want any part of it and threatened to leave. I wasn't their leader in the way everybody thinks. How could I be? My thing was to let everybody do their thing. We were creating a society without rules, without anybody telling anybody what to do. The only rule we had, if you could call it that, was everybody was free to do whatever they wanted. Come and go as they pleased. Sure, I'd give them advice when they asked for it. I'd had more life experience, been through hell and back, and had some answers, so I'd let them know what I thought about stuff. I'd also take care of problems that arose around the ranch, but how could I lead a group whose very foundation was based on each person's individuality? I hated being controlled. I hate the type of people who have to be in control, so how could I be a controller? That's insane, man. The people who said that are the crazy ones, not me.

"That day I came back, . . . the girls began throwing my own shit back at me, how we were all one and had to stay together through thick and thin. They appealed to me not as their leader, but as one of the Family. Man, I was trapped."

At this point, I had strong doubts about the veracity of Charlie's account. I couldn't buy him as the innocent bystander type. He was too strong and commanding. On the other hand, group psychology is a fascinating and unpredictable phenomenon. I'd experienced it in prisons among both the guards and the cons. An idea takes hold, and people start doing things they'd never have the courage to do by themselves. Hell, we'd just been through that with the stampeding guards. Hard as he had tried, Rinker couldn't stop his own soldiers. That was it! This must have been what Charlie had picked up on, why he was all of a sudden finally telling me this seemingly unrelated story that cut to the heart of his existence. Charlie was trying to tell me that even the most dominating, iron-fisted ruler can lose control of his forces when chaos sets in. I listened with new interest as he continued.

"I was going to let things cool off and talk the girls out of their stupid plan, but then something happened that made me furious. Mary [Brunner] and Sandy [Good] were arrested for using stolen credit cards. I was angry that the Family was being ripped apart, and in my anger, I just let them do what they desired. If the kids wanted to scare the hell out of the world because of the way they'd been used all their lives, then who was I to stop them? . . . People say I sent them to Terry Melcher's house because I was upset over my music career. That's such bullshit, man. First of all, I knew Melcher didn't live there anymore, dig? Second, Melcher was cool . . . There was still a chance we'd get together and do some recording. The door wasn't closed. So why did I want to kill him? The kids made that decision because they knew the house.

"After it was over, the kids all seemed to just forget about it. If anything, they were proud and puffed up. I wasn't. The vibes were bad from that moment on. I knew it was going to get laid on us, one way or another. But it took longer than I expected. I mean, the cops were so stupid. The kids did it the same way at all three scenes. Wrote the same words in blood on the walls. They were trying to make it look the same so they could spring Bobby, but the dumb-ass cops didn't get it. They didn't link the incidents for months. Even the Bug [Bugliosi] jumped on their asses for that. I mean, they were the same people doing it the same way bending over backward to leave identical clues, and still the cops had no clue.

"For a while, I thought we were off the hook. Then some of the bikers and their girls got busted and started snitching. Sadie took a fall and ran her mouth to her cellmates, bragging about what she'd done. That was it. The end."

"You were destroyed from within?"

"That's the way it was headed all along. The group was too large. Too hard to control. It was only a matter of time before I'd be back here. Inside. Locked up like an animal again. The one thing the girls promised me wouldn't happen, happened. They not only included me, I became this fuckin' all-powerful, godlike ringleader. A guy who could stop watches and spin clocks with a glance. The demonic leader of 'Charlie's Angels,' only my girls were no angels. It was them all along, not me, man. Dig? Can you dig that?"

Not really. But as I walked away, I almost felt sorry for him—almost.

San Quentin Village is a residential community the state built on the north and west sides of the prison and up a hill to the east. The hundred-plus homes were considered a perk for the employees as the rents were dirt cheap and the commute to work was a breeze. The homes on the hill were called "Executive Row," and included the warden's mansion with a grand garden and portico overlooking the bay. The village was so popular that there was a waiting list to get in. That struck me as odd. I couldn't imagine settling there. Bedding down every night a few hundred yards from Charles Manson and five thousand of his closest friends wasn't my idea of a relaxing domestic environment. Beth probably would have left me, with the children a few steps behind.

Aside from the obvious dangers of riots, escapees, and kidnappings, a major downside to such a community was rampant gossip. When you work and live in the same small area, the gossip can become debilitating. My friend Dr. Sutton had always been hot fodder on the San Quentin tongue-wagging circuit. Many of the men—and their wives—couldn't understand why an attractive, educated woman like her chose to work in such a dismal place. Unless, of course, she was some kind of nymphomaniac who liked the attentions of five thousand sex-crazed maniacs. Whispers like that made Dr. Sutton's already difficult job even harder. But, as always, she held her head high and went about her business. She was more concerned about trying to heal men like Charles Manson than worrying about what some pea brain guard's wife was saying about her.

Among Dr. Sutton's patients was a mainline con named Red, a mean, sick sex offender with a long history of violence against women, including two brutal stabbing murders. Red first noticed Dr. Sutton eating with her four stepchildren in the employees' dining room, where he worked as a waiter. He started flirting with her and began chatting her up like a single woman on a barstool. When she cooled to his attentions, he took a different tack. Claiming to need help, he begged to see her professionally. She relented, but quickly discovered that he viewed the sessions as little more than a chance to get close to her. He quickly developed an obsessive attachment which she believed was detrimental to his therapy. When he began making crude advances, she terminated contact. Enraged, he reacted by telling her that when he was paroled, he would kill her children one by one, then hunt her down and make her pay. The threats ruffled the normally unflappable shrink. Red was scheduled for release within a few months, and Dr. Sutton knew better than anyone that obsessive psychos like him were likely to carry out their threats.

To make matters worse, obsessive jerks like Red were unlikely to bide their time. Red played right into the profile. He spread the rumor from one end of San Quentin to the other that he and Dr. Sutton were lovers, and she was pregnant with his child. A moderately attractive Irishman who could play sane when it benefited him, he arranged an official meeting with an officer and explained in great, lurid detail how he and Dr. Sutton carried out their passionate affair in a closet near the employees' dining room. I checked the place out. It was a stale, dingy room a few feet from the cafeteria where Red worked. In order for his story to be true, Dr. Sutton would have had to sneak by both staff and prisoners in a heavily trafficked hallway, and dart inside a tiny, suffocating rathole to get it on with a certified sexual maniac. Yet the more Red blabbed, the more the story took hold. To my shock, he was succeeding in his campaign to turn a classy, dignified doctor, who truly cared about the men, into a cheap whore with an insatiable appetite for sleazy sex.

"She's carrying my baby," he wailed like a drumbeat. "I want something done about it!"

Dr. Sutton was indeed pregnant, but the child was the result of a liaison with her husband, a well-known real estate speculator, not some sordid sex with a vicious con. She had miscarried her first child and, before the rumors, had been especially excited about this one.

The situation with Dr. Sutton troubled, disgusted, and worried me, all for different reasons. I was troubled by how the rumors were affecting my friend and breaking her spirit. I was disgusted by the way the corrections community believed the gossip and eagerly spread it. The bizarre part was that the inmates knew the story was bullshit, yet it was the staff and their families who embraced the destructive nonsense. And lastly, I was worried about how the inmates would react. Dr. Sutton had many supporters among the men, and they weren't going to take her humiliation and forced departure lightly.

Charles Manson numbered himself among her supporters. She was working with him, listening to him, and had earned his respect. This was one time when I half wished Manson would intervene. For once in his miserable life, he could show some compassion, some sense of doing what was right, by using his considerable influence to shut Red down — regardless of how he accomplished it. I considered bringing the issue to him, but fought it. I couldn't let my anger send him signals. Knowing Manson, he'd have Red hit, and then say I told him to do it. No, I had to be extremely careful. I had to let fate take its course.

As the weeks passed, the course fate took was increasingly infuriating. Red bitched and moaned all the way up the chain of command. Dr. Sutton was repeatedly interrogated by a series of administrators, including her direct supervisor. She denied everything, but the official interrogations only fueled the fires. It reached the point where Dr. Sutton was being stared at and whispered about everywhere she went.

A good part of the blame for this travesty was simple sexism. Most male correctional officers resent women in their midst and anxiously wait for them to screw up. The general feeling among this dinosaur set is that only a slut would work in a prison, and sooner or later this quality will reveal itself. Adding to the resentment was Dr. Sutton's liberal, caring attitude, and the way she'd pushed for reforms and tried innovative techniques like the yoga program.

The situation with Dr. Sutton became such an issue that it was eventually termed a "security problem." A high-level administration meeting was called to discuss it. These were comparatively educated men with clear heads, so Dr. Sutton would finally have her day in court. Imagine my shock, and anger, when the captains and lieutenants began expressing the same smirking doubts as the rank and file.

"I don't know why Red would lie," a lieutenant said. "He's got nothing to gain."

"Have you got your head up your ass?" I railed. "How can you side with Red? He's a creep. Check his jacket. He hates women. He cuts them up. He stabbed one woman more than a hundred times! Doesn't that mean anything to you guys? He's getting out on parole in a couple of weeks and he's threatened to kill her. She's really afraid."

"Says who?" another officer questioned. "She hasn't filed anything."

"She doesn't want to violate her doctor-patient relationship, but she's scared to death. Take my word for it."

"That's her problem. She came here. Nobody forced her. She knew what she was getting into."

"Bullshit!" I screamed. "She's one of us. We should back her."

"She's not one of mine," the gooner squad lieutenant cracked.

"No, she's not a Neanderthal asshole like your men —"

Deputy Warden Fudge cut in and ended the debate. That was it for Dr. Sutton. Nothing was going to be done about the rumors. At least, not by the good guys.

"I don't know if I can take this anymore," she confided to me tearfully after hearing the bad news. "I lost my last baby. I don't want to lose this one. Even the chief psychiatrist doesn't seem to trust me anymore. I'm sorry, Ed, but I'm going to have to resign. My husband wants me out of here."

"That's okay. I don't blame him."

She reached out and touched my hand. "Will you explain to the men?"

"Sure," I said. "Don't worry. They'll understand."

They would, but I sure didn't. I remained furious over what was happening. I again considered spilling my guts to a certain inmate, but held off. What would he care, anyway? He didn't care about anybody but himself. And even if he did, how could I take advantage of a monster like him to push my own agenda? It was unthinkable—almost as unthinkable as what was happening to Dr. Sutton.

A week before Red's parole, Dr. Sutton was walking alone across the yard toward a large rotunda near the entrance of the prison's hospital. Waiting in the shadows was Red. The perverted con was clutching a large shank in his right hand. Apparently, he no longer had the patience to wait until he was set free before he carved up the good doctor. However, to Red's shock, there was a second person lurking in the shadows that afternoon. As Red watched Dr. Sutton approach, fiendishly gripping his weapon, the uninvited guest materialized behind him.

"I know why you're here, Red," an eerie voice stated. "I'm not going to let you do this." Furious, Red raised his weapon and lunged at the man who'd had the audacity to interrupt his heinous plot. The man caught his wrist, twisted it, and disarmed him. At the same time, the mystery protector dug his own shank deep into Red's side. Screaming in pain, Red fell to the floor as the attacker disappeared.

Alarms sounded. The guards swarmed in and rushed Red to the hospital. The gooners embarked upon a thorough search of the prison, scouring the place for clues. I left them alone, but stayed close to Manson's cell. I wanted to believe that Charlie had somehow read my mind and had arranged or performed the counterhit. In return, I was ready to come to his rescue the instant the gooners found some evidence.

After a thorough search, the guards turned up a suspect. It wasn't Charlie. The prison's yard sweeper, a strange con known as Crazy John, had missed his work assignment that morning. A spot of blood was found on his shirtsleeve in his cell.

Following the cons' law, Red refused to finger Crazy John as the assailant. No one else came forward. Still, the circumstantial evidence was clear.

Crazy John was a puzzling choice for an assassin. He was like the town drunk without the alcohol, an image he seemed to purposefully perpetuate. He wore dark shades, a black knit cap pulled down over his ears even on the warmest summer day, an oversized black cotton jacket, and faded blue jeans two sizes too big that dragged on the ground. He was aloof and distant, sweeping, observing, seemingly traveling in his own universe. After refusing to say anything to his interrogators, Crazy John asked to see me. The inmates told him I could be trusted, and he guessed that I might be sympathetic to what he had to say. Speaking off the record, he told me the story. Dr. Sutton had showed him unusual kindness, helping him purge the haunting memories of his abused childhood and teaching him how to control his violent temper. Crazy John loved Dr. Sutton the way the Hunchback of Notre Dame loves Esmeralda, the maiden who gives him a drink of water after he is flogged and humiliated in the town square. Dr. Sutton gave Crazy John the courage to go on when his life was hopeless. There wasn't anything he wouldn't do for her. "She's the only person who ever cared about me," he said.

When Crazy John heard what Red was saying, he became furious and immediately began to investigate. Crazy John was such a familiar sight on the yard, nobody paid any attention to him. Plus, everyone figured he was a nutcase, so he was totally ignored. Yet, far from being the drooling loon everyone suspected, John was pretty clever. He managed to sneak into the records and pull Red's files, confirming his suspicions that his target was a mean woman-hater with a violent past. Before acting on the information, Crazy John wanted to get it from the horse's mouth. Sidling up to Red on a bench in the yard, he baited the Irishman into telling him all about how he was going to rape, torture, and kill Dr. Sutton the moment he was paroled. After hearing that, Crazy John traded for a shank and stalked his target until the opportunity came.

"I know Dr. Sutton is going to be upset with me for this," he told me. "Will you tell her I'm sorry?"

I turned, closed my door, and locked it. "You may think I'm the crazy one for telling you this, but I'm pretty damn proud of you," I said. Crazy John sat with a puzzled look on his face, wondering if he'd heard me right. "You're going to the third-floor AC with our best guys. You'll be safer, away from the gangs."

Once John was situated, I told Pin and Manson to make sure nobody bothered him. "What for?" Manson asked. I just shook my head and walked away.

There wasn't enough evidence for the DA, so the charges were dropped. Disciplinary hearings took place, and Crazy John was found guilty of stabbing Red. At a classification hearing, thirty days after the incident, I released him back to the general population because I felt he was no threat to the security of the institution.

Red was not so lucky. While recovering from the deep but unfortunately nonfatal wound, he lost his parole date—thanks to a detailed confidential memo I sent to the Board of Prison Terms. He was transferred to Folsom and forced to do another year. But, as is typical with obsessive psychos, he continued his vicious campaign. The following year, he gave the parole board a graphic account of his affair with Dr. Sutton and convinced them to launch a full investigation into his charges. His story could be proven, he said, by a distinctive scar Dr. Sutton had in a private area, a scar he saw on many occasions. Although she no longer worked for the correctional department, Dr. Sutton was asked to subject herself to a humiliating strip search and body examination. No such scar was found. She had agreed to the dehumanizing procedure, she told me later, to keep Red from being paroled and hunting her down.

The final kicker came with the birth of her child. Red was a fair-haired Irishman. As only I knew, Dr. Sutton's husband was an Asian. The black-haired, dark-skinned baby boy clearly resembled his pop.

Unfortunately, the story didn't end there. Despite his aborted attempt on Dr. Sutton's life, Red was paroled two years later. Dr. Sutton wasn't even notified. She learned of his release from Red himself! He promptly began calling and threatening her. She immediately contacted the Special Services Unit for protection. They investigated and determined not only that Red was indeed harassing her, but that he'd jumped parole. Their only advice was for Dr. Sutton to purchase and wear a bulletproof vest, and to learn how to use a firearm.

As is typical with violent women-haters, before he got around to stalking, raping, and murdering Dr. Sutton, a lady in Reno caught Red's eye and he went after her inside a casino. He was arrested and sent back to prison.

All in all, aside from Crazy John's unexpected heroics, it was a very ugly affair.

After that bit of madness, things began looking up for a while. On August 12, 1976, the verdicts came down in the San Quentin Six trial. It had been five years since the brutal riots, and everyone was ready to finally put an end to it. The jury found three of the inmates guilty and three innocent, a split that promised bad blood between the two groups. Instead of closure, we now had to deal with the possibility that the guilty group suspected the innocents of ratting them out and planned to kill them out of revenge. Would it ever end?

Good and bad news tends to come in bunches. Apparently, so does the less black-and-white, more confusing kind. The next big event to hit San Quentin was equally unsettling. Charles Manson was summarily transferred back to Folsom. San Quentin was generally designated for violent cons thirty-five and under. Folsom was set up for the middle-aged and old folks. Manson was forty-two, so he was overdue to join the seniors tour, so to speak. I should have been happy, but I wasn't. He was a creep. There was no doubt about that. He made me so paranoid that he temporarily turned me into a monster, ruining my relationship with my daughter. And when it came time for him to finally step forward and do something decent like protect his doctor, the thought never entered his sick and twisted little brain. Instead, he left the job to the village idiot.

Despite all that, and everything else, I couldn't deny that he had made the job more interesting. I still enjoyed arguing with him, and listening to his garbled yet passionate speeches. The media attention was also fun at times. I was definitely going to miss him.

Yeah, like I'd miss a toothache, I told myself, coming to my senses. Instead of melancholy, I should have been jumping for joy. Charles Manson was finally out of my life—or so I thought.

9

WITH THE TRIAL over, death row emptied after yet another court ruling, Dr. Sutton gone, and Manson fuming at Folsom, San Quentin suddenly became a major drag. Even Rinker transferred out, robbing me of the amusement quotient he provided. Warden Rees, my last line of support, was a short-timer who would soon take the helm of the Duel Vocational Institute in Tracy. The graffiti on the barbed-wire wall was clear. It was time for me to leave.

I knew exactly where I wanted to go—right back from whence I came. After all I'd been through, the forests of the Sierra Conservation Center in Northern California would be just the ticket. As I waited for the word, I started feeling that odd homesick sensation people sometimes experience when they know they're about to leave a place. That was strange. I was getting all warm and fuzzy about a savage stink hole that I hadn't even left yet. The reason wasn't a mystery. Deep in my subconscious, in the chained caverns where my ancient instincts lay, there was a perverse pleasure in associating with these wild, uninhibited individuals. They were a different breed of human beings, throwbacks whose activities and thoughts were more base and animalistic than civilized. They fought, attacked, and killed as an expression of emotion, a matter of demented pride, or for pure survival. Some, like Manson and his followers, descended to a more horrible level, committing crimes beyond the imagination. Studying such deviance is strangely exhilarating. To be so close to evil treachery without touching it or letting it touch you can be a rush. It was voyeurism in a sense, like going to a zoo and edging up to the gorilla cage. At San Quentin, I felt the thrill of seeing the beast—the beast that lurks inside us all—from a relatively safe emotional distance.

Sometimes, I didn't know if I should hate these men for unleashing their inner monsters, or view them with a tiny measure of admiration. They acted upon their primitive desires beyond conscience or moral restraints. They hated or loved, but were never lukewarm. It frustrated me at times because no matter how hard I tried, I couldn't really understand them. Especially Charlie. Convincing as he could be at times, I couldn't get inside his head. I never had that brief flicker of enlightenment that would unlock the mystery of where he was coming from. Even more important, I wondered whether a man like Manson could feed upon my undeniable curiosity and suck me into the fold. How close had he really come to doing that? Given more time, would he eventually have gotten to me?

Whoa, I thought, shaking the crazy questions from my mind. It was definitely time to leave this place. That, however, wasn't going to be as easy as I had initially thought. An affirmative action program was sweeping the corrections department, making options scarce for white males like myself. After losing position after position to less qualified minority applicants, I grew bitter, railing against the injustice of it all. During one heated exchange, I caught myself and stopped in midsentence. Wasn't my argument exactly what Manson and the Aryan Brothers preached? Minorities taking jobs they didn't deserve, polluting the gene pool, destroying America? Were my logical, well-thought-out protests against affirmative action merely a high-level affirmation of the low-level hate Manson and the ABs preached? That was heavy, and scary. After that, I groused a bit, but tempered my opinions.

Finally, after pulling some strings, I was given three options. There were program administrator positions available at Folsom, Soledad, and the Correctional Medical Facility (formerly known as the California Medical Facility—CMF). Folsom was just like San Quentin, and Manson was there, so that was out. Soledad was another brutal snake pit a hundred miles away, making it doubly undesirable. CMF showed promise. It was only fifty miles from my home, and was a treatment-oriented institution, more like a hospital. If I couldn't be in the pristine forests, a semihospital setting was the next best thing.

I reported to work at CMF on November 1, 1976. The warden, Dr. Larry Clanon, noted my experience and assigned me to Willis Unit, a three-story building that housed mostly maximum-security inmates. At CMF, these were men who were too emotionally or mentally unstable to be released into the general population—i.e., the "Cuckoo's Nest" set, only more dangerous and violent. They defied placement into any specific program in the system, so they were warehoused at Willis until the doctors could get a better read on their specific mental deficiencies.

Inmates sent to Willis were designated category D's. They were in for a ninety-day psychiatric and psychological evaluation, then were reviewed by the unit classification committee, which recommended either a specific treatment program or a return to their original prison. The difficult and more complex cases remained in the unit for extended observation and evaluation. This group included people like Pin Cushion, mass murderers Ed Kemper and Juan Corona, and Richard Allen Davis (who later murdered Polly Klass). In addition, every time the death penalty was nixed, the death row inmates were usually sent to Willis before being filtered into other institutions.

In general, CMF was created to treat mental and physical problems among the prison population. Since mental problems go hand in hand with criminal behavior, a hefty percentage of the inmates were head cases. They included sexual deviants, rapists, bizarre killers, psychotics, psychotics in remission, and other less than solid citizens. The staff, naturally, was heavy on doctors, psychiatrists, psychologists, therapists, and counselors. By law, the CMF warden had to be a medical doctor. That in itself made for a treatment-oriented environment, but also created conflicts between the punitive-minded custody officers and the medical professionals. The custody gang secretly referred to the place as "Disneyland North," not so much because of the easier environment for the prisoners, but because some of the doctors and therapists were weirder than the inmates.

The differences between my prior warden, Bob Rees, and Dr. Clanon were infinite. Dr. Clanon was a soft-spoken, gentle man whose personality seemed totally wrong for a prison czar. However, if viewed in terms of a hospital administrator, then he fit perfectly. He was respected by his medical staff and strongly supported their treatment programs. He was also smart enough to delegate. Whenever there was a serious threat to the safety of the institution, he was not afraid to turn over all authority to the militaristic guards, sometimes bowing to them unreasonably.

Personally, I wasn't real happy about toiling in another lockup unit. Instead of spending my days designing and implementing innovative rehabilitation programs, I'd have to direct the bulk of my energy into the simple task of keeping the crazies from killing each other. On the plus side, the gang presence at CMF was minimal, so that eased tensions considerably. The gangbangers we did receive were usually ex-members trying to get out.

Overall, the numbers at CMF were more manageable. At San Quentin, the three lockup units housed 500 vicious cutthroats. At CMF, the place maxed out at 120. Yet, despite the lower numbers, the staff was stronger. Assigned to the unit were a full-time psychiatrist, a psychologist, two journeymen counselors, a unit lieutenant, a sergeant on every watch, and a healthy contingent of guards.

After getting the basic briefing on the joint, I decided to go on a walk-through inspection with some of the staff. Turning a corner, I absent-mindedly glanced into a cell and stopped dead. "What the fuck do you want?" the familiar voice growled, playing tough guy. I was stunned. No, it couldn't be! What the hell was Charles Manson doing here on my watch? The little creep should have been at Folsom! How was I going to explain this to Beth?

"I'm just following you around, Charlie," I cracked, composing myself. I moved on, as if it were no big deal. The moment we were out of earshot, I grilled the unit shrink, Dr. Al Rotella. "What's Manson doing here?"

"Folsom transferred him a few weeks ago. They couldn't handle his bullshit up there, so they psyched him and sent him here," the doc explained, dispensing with precise medical terminology. "Dr. Hyberg cleared him, so now we got him as a category D. That's a ninety-day evaluation. That's what we do here."

"Do you think he's crazy?"

"If you mean psychotic, no. Charlie manipulates. He's a sociopath. He knows exactly what he's doing."

I immediately liked and respected Dr. Rotella. From my vantage point, his diagnosis of Manson was dead on. Dr. Rotella, a chubby, upbeat man, was a straight shooter with a good sense of humor who didn't try to impress people with incomprehensible medical jargon. That was a plus because prisons are noted for flaky shrinks with bizarre ideas. Dr. Rotella's nononsense attitude contrasted sharply with a roundtable discussion I'd participated in at San Quentin with five of his peers. "Do you think Manson's crazy?" I opened. Naturally, their first response was, "What do you mean by crazy?" I rolled my eyes and elaborated. "You know, insane, psychotic, out of touch with reality." They chattered among themselves, dropped twenty-dollar words, redefined "crazy" a dozen times, then concluded that Manson had never been diagnosed as psychotic. Curious about that, I went to the CMF records office and pulled Manson's jacket from Folsom. The Folsom shrink had cleverly skirted the issue by making the most recent referral based upon Manson's "psychotic behavior." That was Manson all the way. He could effect "psychotic behavior" at will, usually to get his way.

Prison administrators had their own method of getting their way. Stuck with a disruptive inmate they wanted to dump, they invariably pressured the house shrink to "psych" the guy to CMF. Because of this widespread practice, CMF often received "patients" who were nothing more than mean and savage pricks. Some, like Manson, had acted up specifically to get transferred. Others were just no-good bastards. Whichever, they would now be coming to me.

Manson's updated file contained additional interesting tidbits. After his arrival, he was interviewed by the aforementioned Dr. Hyberg, a psychiatrist who often worked with acute psychotic inmates. Dr. Gordon Hyberg was one strange bird. He looked like the typical "mad genius" villain in a James Bond movie, complete with a shiny shaved head, a thin mustache, and a sharply pointed goatee, all accented by a navy blue sport coat draped over a white turtleneck sweater. A peace symbol medallion, supported by a long silver chain, bounced hypnotically around his midsection. To accessorize the overall look, Dr. Hyberg wore black leather S and M wristbands with silver spurs. If that wasn't enough, the guy frequented nude beaches! He sometimes came to work so sunburned that he'd have trouble sitting.

Charlie must have thought he'd hit the jackpot when he got a look at this dude, especially that big hippie-era peace symbol. I immediately began to worry about Manson's influence on the guy. I didn't want to see Dr. H riding nude on a Harley one day, surrounded by a flock of Manson's bare-assed chicks.

Although he carried himself in a distinguished, arrogant manner, Dr. Hyberg was actually a personable, sensitive man. He was single, middle-aged, and genuinely dedicated to helping inmates. The problem was, some of his techniques were as odd as his duds. His favorite therapy circle was the "tissue group," composed of cons who had cut or torn flesh in their murders. Ironically, for all his dancing on the edge (and this guy did the Watusi!), I noticed that he feared many of the felons, acted uncomfortable around them, and had difficulty adapting to their brashness.

One time, in a classification hearing, Dr. Hyberg was interviewing an inmate in front of the committee. Trying his best to be "with it," he asked the young man, "When's the last time you did grass?" The con appeared puzzled, obviously unfamiliar with the common slang for marijuana. "Do you mean when was the last time I cut the lawn?" Everyone cracked up, embarrassing the doctor. The incident dramatized Dr. Hyberg's labored attempt to reach that cherished nirvana known as "coolness," a state of "Fonzarelli" being, that for all his hip posturing, Dr. H hadn't quite nailed down.

Not surprisingly, Dr. Hyberg's sessions with Manson were classics. I rolled one of the tapes. It sounded more like a Mel Brooks comedy album than a psychiatric evaluation:

"If you had only one wish, what would you wish for?" Dr. H opened.

"More wishes," Charlie immediately shot back.

"How are your spirits?"

"Right here."

"How do you see your future?"

"I don't see any."

"When was the last time you wished you were dead?"

"I haven't found out what life is yet."

"When did you last think of suicide?"

"When you mentioned it."

It went on like that for hours. Dr. Hyberg played the straight man as Charlie dicked him around, revealing nothing about his psyche. That was all too familiar. Charlie believed all prison doctors, except maybe Dr. Sutton, were weird and unworthy of his true insights. I could learn more in one relatively honest man-to-guru conversation with Charlie than in all the tapes and medical evaluations combined.

Still, some of the efforts were worth noting. Dr. Rotella's initial conclusion after Manson's May 1976 evaluation was helpful:

"Manson is the product of a chaotic, disruptive childhood, compounded by a history of psychosis, and being brought up in Federal and State corrective institutional settings since early childhood. These ingredients were reflected, and manifested in his life style, namely by: his inability to function in a competitive society; form close, meaningful adult relationships with people; and his general resentment towards society and authority. At this time, Charlie realistically surmised that he presently will not be able to walk a CDC mainline and most likely will have to live in a security housing unit setting. States that he would like to have his own cell, play his guitar a few times a week, and be able to avail himself of yard activities if 'I don't get bad vibes.' Basically would like to be placed in a nonpredatory sheltered environment where other inmates will not drive on, or strike out at him, as occurred in Folsom adjustment center yard a while back."

Three months later, Dr. Edwin Lehman offered similar insights:

"Charles Manson is an individual who (as he often points out) literally grew up in institutions, and in some measure is a product of his environment. He is endowed with above average intellectual capability, which, in most cases, has only been tested on the criterion of survival for his is a usually hostile and predatory environment. In our relationship, he was an intellectual and talkative individual, who has a good sense of humor and who was friendly and likable. After spending some time with him on several different occasions, his philosophizing conversations begin to repeat themselves. When heard in that way, his ideas resemble the grandiosity of adolescent revolutionaries who ache to fight for the rights of oppressed peoples on the other side of the world while they use people close to them and never think about it. He is a persuasive talker and in almost all ways has been a 'good' prisoner while he has been with us. I feel that we should listen to and try to honor his sensible requests while not forgetting that basically Charlie is a psychotic person with a very tenuously balanced emotional state. The goal of a mainline placement may still be distant but I feel we should continue to try him in slightly less protective environments in order to upgrade his movement and placement."

I was encouraged by Dr. Lehman's suggestion that Charlie might one day be ready for another stab at the mainline. I'd been toying with that idea for years. Although my first attempt at San Quentin nearly destroyed my career, it wasn't Charlie's fault. Trying him on the CMF mainline was an intriguing concept, one that I had mixed feeling about, but planned to consider. That was mostly because when I cut through the games and bullshit, Manson himself could be counted on to offer the best insight into his mental state. His self-analysis, in its own primitive way, said more than all the shrink reports combined.

"Hell, I know the difference between right and wrong. Always did. I know how to get along in the real world. I know what to do to keep the kids fed, the fat wife happy, and the cops off my ass. I tried it a few times. But where I came from, how I grew up, what happened to me, I didn't have a chance. Everybody kept telling me what was bad, what I shouldn't do, how to act, but they all forgot to give me a chance to be that way. You take the nicest ten-year-old from the best home in the land and put him on the streets, and he's going to learn to steal to survive. You take the best little girl in Sunday school, tell her her parents left and don't care, and dump her on a corner, and she'll be turning tricks by the end of the week just to eat. Well, I was that boy! I was that girl! I didn't want to be that way. No kid does. I wasn't some demon that sprang from my mother's womb. Everybody talks about role models. What role models did I have?

Perverted reform school guards? . . . Great parents? Jesus and the Bible? Hell, it was the Bible that drove my mother out of her home and put her on the streets. [Charlie's mom had rebelled against a strict religious upbringing.] Once in the system, the 'fathers' and 'mothers' society provided to raise me beat me bloody with whips and straps, fucked me in the ass until I shit blood and couldn't walk, and taught me to hate. And now, everybody's shocked how I turned out. Wake up! You did this to me. And you're doing it to thousands like me every day. Every kid who wandered into the ranch back then came from a bad family. Every kid who writes me today complains about their rotten parents. And none of them had it as bad as me."

That didn't excuse what he'd done, but he did have a point. Charlie always had a point. And it made me cringe at the thought of how many little Charlies and Squeakys are out there right now taking life on the chin, bouncing from one adult to another, all the while suppressing a rage that's destined to explode. It also explained why the mail kept coming in, bagful after bagful, month after month. These were the kids Charlie spoke to — and for.

After a few weeks, I settled in and felt comfortable at CMF. Once again, Manson was a major reason. To kill time and break up the day, I began letting him out of his cage for casual chats in my office. Charlie enjoyed the freedom, but didn't want to be called out too much or the other inmates might think he'd turned snitch. Heaven forbid. Occasionally, he became demanding and destructive just to assure the cons he was still one of them.

Dr. Rotella noticed all the time I was spending with Charlie and took me aside one afternoon for a fatherly chat. "You like the guy, don't you?" he opened.

"I find him interesting, if that's what you mean."

"No, I asked you if you liked him."

"I guess so," I admitted.

"You're aware that he's a psychopath among other things," the doctor warned, strengthening his earlier diagnosis. "He can screw you over and never think about it."

"He's been trying to do that since the moment I met him," I said, laughing.

"Don't take him too lightly," Dr. Rotella admonished. "He's had some nasty psychotic episodes."

"Yeah, and I think he faked them all," I countered. "I've seen him go for weeks acting as calm and rational as you and me. Then something sets him off and wham, he flips out. Rants and raves and threatens the world with annihilation. There's a pattern to it, and I think it's pure bullshit."

"Perhaps," the doc said, playing along. "You think he's crazy like a fox?"

"Exactly. He's clever, quick, and intelligent."

"But foxes can go crazy, too," the doctor astutely pointed out.

"Psychopaths aren't considered crazy, are they?" I dodged.

"Not in themselves, but they can be. They can become psychotic."

The psychological double-talk numbed my mind. I shifted to a comparison that was easier to grasp. "Did you see *One Flew Over the Cuckoo's Nest*? The movie where Jack Nicholson played a con man named McMurphy?"

"Sure. That's a classic."

"If you remember, McMurphy and the big Indian both played crazy, but they weren't. They conned everybody, made fun of the system, and had a ball doing it. When Charlie's in a good mood, he reminds me of McMurphy. Believe it or not, he can be a real funny guy."

The doctor looked at me as if I'd gone completely mad. "Hitler was a real funny guy, too," he cracked.

"I hear what you're saying. I'm not blind to that. Most of the time, Charlie is likable. Behind it, there's this deceptive little weasel who hides an incredibly evil side. Don't think I'm not keenly aware of it."

"He's schizophrenic, two personalities, but in remission. Of course, if the guy's psychotic, then he can't be evil because he doesn't know right from wrong."

"But he does!" I jousted. "He's as sane as we are, so that makes him evil."

"I agree."

"He knows exactly what he's done, what he's doing, and what he's going to do," I continued, my voice rising. "I've sensed that talking to him. I've felt the chill when his evil side emerges. And he knows it. It's fascinating."

The doctor paused, then stared at me with deep concern. "You're really into this guy."

"More than I want to admit, I guess. But I can't help it."

"Can I give you some advice?"

"Only if you don't charge me," I said, trying to lighten the dour mood.

"Don't let any inmate consume your life. You can only go so far, do so much. You can only understand just a part of what makes them tick. You can't change the world, Ed. When you go home, after work, forget it. It's all bullshit. And this creep Manson is not the kind of person you should be getting entangled with. You can't lose sight of what happened with him. He took a bunch of stupid, rebellious kids, brainwashed them, and made them kill. They butchered people for that little shit. And because of that, we get to see him every day, smirking like he's really got some special powers of control."

"He does. And he's still doing it."

"Doing what?"

"He's still using his women to recruit followers. The women who are locked up, and those on the outside. And people keep flocking to him. I know. I read his mail. He's never even met these people and they still want to kill for him. It's crazy what's going on."

"The little shit does have a strange attraction. I can't really put my finger on it," Dr. Rotella confessed.

"It's an evil genius. Something he developed from his years in prison."

"It's certainly something that's difficult to comprehend. The common belief is that evil people are stupid, but that can be dead wrong. Some evil people possess a considerable intelligence which they use to plan truly monstrous deeds."

"So why are all these people drawn to him?" I wondered. "Why all this sick mail, year after year?"

"Curiosity, probably. People looking for excitement."

It was my turn to look at the doctor with skepticism. These lost souls who worshiped Manson were not your average thrill seekers. "It's got to be more," I argued. "Maybe their lives are boring and they feel inadequate. Therefore, they gravitate to the lowest common denominator. Maybe some kids feel so evil and guilty inside that they believe only a guy like Manson can understand them."

"That's a horrible thought," Dr. Rotella responded, wincing.

"Hey, what's even more horrible is the possibility that maybe it's our fault, just like Charlie's always said. Maybe we're raising our children wrong. Maybe our traditional Christian beliefs emphasize guilt and punishment over compassion, and it's taking a toll. We judge quickly and harshly without understanding. Maybe that's why so many kids run away, kill themselves, drop out of school, take drugs, have loveless sex—"

"Hold on there," Dr. Rotella interrupted. "You're starting to sound like Charlie. Not all kids are like that. Just a minority. And the reasons are diverse and complicated. You're letting Charlie get to you. You should pull away for a while, let someone else deal with him and his nonsense. I really think you should consider it, Ed."

It was a solid suggestion, one that I naturally ignored. Over the months, Dr. Rotella became so concerned about my relationship with Charlie that he invited me on a number of Catholic retreats to see if he could break the spell. These were intense twelve-hour overnight vigils to the Blessed Sacrament that consisted of prayer, sermons, spiritual readings, and meditation. I found them inspirational and soothing, but they did nothing to quell my fascination with Charlie. If anything, my addiction grew.

Dr. Rotella warned me repeatedly that I was heading for a meltdown, but I merely scoffed and foolishly steamed forward, confident that my mental shield was unbreakable.

Dr. Morton Felix was another CMF shrink who Manson loved to jerk around. A passive, rumpled man who smoked a pipe that constantly spewed tobacco fragments on his sweaters, Dr. Felix reminded me of an earthier

Sherlock Holmes. One afternoon, the psychologist was startled to discover that an unknown inmate had crashed his group therapy session and immediately dominated the conversation. The strange character wore a baseball hat turned backward (long before that became fashionable) and was toothless. With gums flapping, the guy lectured everyone about exterminating child molesters and Jews, and suffocating women who force their husbands to work themselves to death. Offended by the remarks, especially the grossly anti-Semitic comments, Dr. Felix investigated. To his shock, he later discovered that the inmate was Manson! What was even more shocking was that Manson was a part of Dr. Felix's group! He had altered his appearance by shaving his beard, getting a haircut, and taking out his false teeth, and was so successful in his ruse that he fooled everybody, including a trained professional. That was Charlie all the way. He's such a chameleon he can change his shape and colors almost at will.

The final insult came when I heard Dr. Felix complaining one evening that he couldn't locate a brightly decorated Mexican serape he frequently wore. I had to restrain myself from bursting out laughing. I'd spotted Charlie wearing the poncho earlier that day. Dr. Felix sighed deeply and decided not to report it. Charlie spent the next few months looking like a bad guy from a Clint Eastwood spaghetti western — *The Good, the Bad, and the Incredibly Loony.*

Charlie's burgeoning media career remained in full swing, so we got right back into it at CMF just as we had at San Quentin. I brought him the latest batch of requests, we talked it over, and Charlie picked the next journalist to honor with his wisdom. The long-delayed *National Enquirer* interview was finally given the thumbs-up, and Manson had a blast verbally fencing with, and performing for, a pair of the famed supermarket tabloid's best. After the session was over, Manson posed for a series of remarkable photos that made the forty-two-year-old mass murderer appear cute, boyish, and hip, like he could have easily fit in as one of the Beatles or Monkees.

The reporters, Eric Mishara and Jeffrey Newman, spared no octane when they rushed their scoop into print, referring to Manson as "the messiah of murder" and laying it on thick with the descriptions. "During the rare and exclusive interview," they wrote, "his eyes were aflame and he talked in staccato sentences, a wild look on his thin face." When it came to quoting Manson, no hyperbole was needed.

"You see, the average person in the street believes everything that has been written and put on TV about me. They go look at those movies and they read *Helter Skelter* and they think, 'Wow, what a monstrous monster!' I'm a monster, maybe, but not a monstrous monster. . . . I don't think [Squeaky] meant to kill the President. She was just trying to help us get a better trial and fight for what she thought was right. . . . Every one of those kids in the Family have saved a lot more lives than they took. If I were to judge the children in the Family, I would judge them as children who love their world enough to do the unspeakable—to do things that no one is supposed to do. . . .

"No one was picked—no one picked out Sharon Tate and went down there and plotted a course for madness. You have to understand the episode. It was a soul movement, children willing to rise up and change the world. How else were we going to wake up the people that don't know we cannot destroy our children's world? I wasn't there in the house that night, but I was there in spirit. . . . I've never killed anyone with my own hands—but I've cut up some people and I've shot some people because they pushed me. . . .

"If I were outside the walls of this prison, I would be living a lot differently. I would be back in the woods somewhere, with a guitar and two kilos of grass . . . hiding from people like you."

I thought the article was pretty much on the mark, although I didn't recall him saying the "I was there in spirit" line. Charlie, however, was enraged, calling it "lies" and threatening to kill the two reporters.

"What did you expect, Charlie? You picked the *Enquirer*," I reminded.

"I expected the truth!"

"Hell, when your mouth gets going, I'm sure you don't even remember what you said."

"I remember everything."

Following the *Enquirer* splash, Manson hit the big time with Tom Snyder, Diane Sawyer, Ron Reagan (the President's son), and a host of others. I observed with fascination as he studied his performances and polished his act. He'd repeat expressions and body language that he felt were scary or effective, and eliminate mannerisms that didn't play as well. It was the same with his long, preachy answers. When he slowed down enough to make sense, he generally pushed his standard agenda about saving the environment, bad parents, abandoned children, etc. The one thing that didn't change was his refusal to take direct responsibility for the Tate-LaBianca murders.

We got along pretty well during this period. As usual, an external force was destined to poison the well. The years of therapy at her own prison had done nothing to quell Squeaky Fromme's worship of Manson. The pair still weren't allow to write to each other, so they were forced to continue to communicate thirdhand. They'd write to mutual friends, or send messages through inmates who were scheduled for release. This meant that everything they received was probably garbled and distorted. It was an imperfect system that blocked the intimacy they each hungered for. Manson pretty much accepted it. Squeaky never did. The moment she discovered that I was back in charge of the circus, the letters poured in. As always, she begged me to allow her to write to him. Sadly, I couldn't find any loophole that would allow it. Their communications, filled with threats and coded directives for criminal behavior on the outside, were precisely what the corrections department wanted to eliminate.

Rebuffed, Squeaky did the next best thing—she tried to communicate with him through me. Knowing her anguish, I answered all her letters. The problem was, I found it hard to agree with anything she said or felt about Charlie. In fact, in virtually all my letters, I tried to wean her from her aging master, arguing that she was a fool for turning her life over to a worthless man destined to spend the rest of his days in prison. All that did was rile her up. She'd answer with blistering tirades, cursing me for "dissing" Charlie and their special bond. The more I tried to dissuade her, the more frantic and hateful her letters became. One time, she sent a photo of a car that had been completely demolished in a head-on collision. Streaks of dry blood stained the sides. In the background was a garage supporting a large sign that read "Body Parts." If Lynette had been free, I was certain that another president would have been in serious danger. And if she escaped the attempt, she'd immediately come gunning for me.

Charlie never directly confronted me on my letters to Squeaky, but Pin Cushion said he was really burned up about it. "He hates you for trying to turn Lynette away from him. Other than that, he likes you. He knows you treat him decent."

I did. And I tried to treat Squeaky decently also, telling her what she needed to hear. She just wasn't ready to accept it. Despite Manson's anger, I intended to keep trying until she saw the light. After all, that was my job, to rehabilitate society's lost sheep. Squeaky could never be rehabilitated until she cut the ties to her strange guru.

On November 6, 1976, Squeaky's guru was dumped into the hole when officers found a broom handle and half a razor blade in his cell. Remembering how he had voluntarily given up the mop holder at San Quentin, I was curious as to why he was now hoarding this material. He mumbled something about self-preservation and then clammed up. When his week in isolation was finished, he refused to come out. That was typical Manson. Punish him, and he'll pretend to love the punishment. It was all part of his never-ending campaign to beat the system. I let him stay in the hole a few more days, then sprang him in a manner that kept his dignity intact.

Charlie routinely resisted most of what he was told to do, agitating the guards until their patience ran out. Sometimes he became so loud and abusive the inmates themselves provided the discipline. The phrase "Shut your fuckin' mouth, Charlie" became like a mantra on every wing the former cult leader was housed. CMF was no different than San Quentin or Folsom in that regard. Charlie usually heeded the warnings of his fellow cons, fearful that someone with sensitive ears might slip into his cell one night and slit his bowels. Similarly, whenever he felt threatened, he'd take a swing at a guard, or throw a tantrum, in order to get himself moved. He did this dance my second month at CMF, earning a trip to the psych ward.

The docs cleared him, and he came shuffling back. I knew enough by then to toss him into a new cell on a different wing. I didn't make a big deal about his tactics because he knew more about his enemies than we did, and we would have moved him anyway had he simply told us his life was in danger. He'd never do that, of course, because it was considered snitching.

During my third week, Pin, who had been transferred to CMF, told me that Manson had stopped eating. Investigating, I discovered that the guards, tired of his constant bitching, had threatened to put rat poison in his food to shut him up—permanently. Manson responded by refusing to take the trays the guards handed him. When the guards started refusing to switch them, he became convinced they were poisoned.

"No one's poisoning your food, Charlie," I assured him, taking a bite from his lunch. "That would be murder, and it's easy to prove. The men are just screwing with your head."

"Well, tell them to fuckin' stop!"

"You stop irritating them so much and the problem will take care of itself."

Although that sounded logical, I knew my advice fell on deaf ears. Like a two-year-old, Charlie had a problem understanding "action and reaction." His brain was incapable of linking the two. I was, however, able to convince him to start eating again.

After Charlie's first ninety-day evaluation was completed, his case was referred to the departmental review board, a group of central office staffers who monitored notorious cases. I was asked to put in my two cents. "Based on current psychiatric and psychological evaluations, continued programming in Willis Unit is appropriate," I wrote, figuring a longer stay would be beneficial to him—and me. "Manson is lucid, alert, and functioning in a manageable fashion. Psychiatric support is available in the event of deterioration." I advised against putting him under less restrictive custody because of the questionable psychological condition of so many of the other inmates. This was, after all, virtually a mental hospital. There were too many sick and injured minds out there for Manson to manipulate. "If Manson is allowed in the general population, it must be recognized that within a short time unwarranted followers and curiosity seekers will flock after him," I explained. "His ideas, as antisocial as they are, have an in-depth appeal to certain segments of society both inside and outside prison. It is therefore better to retain him under restricted conditions."

Both of my recommendations were followed. Manson stayed at CMF and remained in lockup. That was fine with him. He liked CMF, and although it was tempting, he knew it was too dangerous for him to be in population among the psycho set. There were still a lot of badasses passing through, and despite Pin Cushion's mass-attack warning, all it would take was one rusty shank across his throat and it would be curtains. In addition, his racial views were well known. If given the chance, an African American con would surely try to win points with the brothers by stilling Charlie's voice. This was another aspect of Charlie's psyche that I never could figure. His instincts for self-preservation were strong. He was like a coyote, always alert and cautious. Yet, when it came to African Americans, he couldn't keep his mouth shut, constantly making blood enemies and putting his life in danger.

Walking through the tier one day, I heard Manson going at it with some Hell's Angels and other sympathetic cons. "The only things niggers are good for is to cut off their heads and use them for bowling balls," he cracked. It was just that kind of stupid, tough-guy boasting that was going to get him killed. In this instance, his racist remarks were particularly dangerous. I yanked him from the cell for a private chat in my office.

"Charlie, are you aware that there's a high-level Black Guerrilla Family member on your tier?" Manson's eyes widened, but he said nothing. "He came in a few days ago on a psych. He's a mean, dangerous man. I'd watch my mouth, if you get my drift."

"I'm not afraid of niggers."

"I know you're not afraid, but I'd watch my mouth anyway."

After that, Manson stayed in his cell, refusing his exercise time on the tier. "I ain't in the mood," he spat. When the word came down that the BGF member had indeed heard his crude analogy and was gunning for him, Manson threw a contrived tantrum designed to earn a trip to the much safer isolation ward. Always an expert at manipulating the system, he got his wish—and probably saved his own life.

African Americans weren't the only inmates Charlie had reason to fear. Early in 1977, a Mexican prison gang known as Nuestra Familia had grown so powerful at the Duel Vocational Institute in Tracy that they were on the verge of taking over the institution. A girlfriend of one of the gang members worked in the personnel department and promptly provided the gangbangers on the street with a list of the guards' addresses and home phone numbers. Anytime an officer came down hard on a Nuestra Familia member in prison, threatening calls would be made to the officer's family. The new warden, my old friend Bob Rees, deemed the problem so explosive that he ordered the gang broken up and scattered throughout the security housing units in various prisons. That was a drastic step, as fellow wardens hate to take someone else's cancer, especially in bunches. Rees, however, managed to convince everyone of the severity of the situation.

My allotment was a rat pack of twenty arrogant Nuestra Familia hoods. Their presence totally disrupted the category D program at CMF, not only because of the cell space they occupied, but because of the tense gang atmosphere they brought with them. To minimize this, I cleared an entire tier on the third floor to deal with the infestation. Shortly after their arrival, I encountered one of the high-ranking NF captains exercising in front of his cell. He was a vicious sociopath named "Joker."

"You know, we have Charles Manson here," I explained. "Do you guys have a problem with him?"

Joker shot me a gnarly grin. "I'd like to cut his throat."

"Why?"

"He's got a big mouth."

I couldn't argue with that. In these situations, Charlie was his own worst enemy. I immediately ordered Manson moved to a cell on the second floor.

"What the hell for?" he groused.

"The NF guys want to cut your throat."

"I ain't scared of those assholes," he said, trying to hide the truth. He remained defiant, but no longer protested the transfer. Thanks to the maneuvering, we were able to ride out the NF visit without incident.

Charlie, true to form, believed that like actors, athletes, and entertainers in the outside world, he deserved special privileges because of his "celebrity" status. That might sound repulsive, but there was some truth to it in the prison system. Since these were communities made up of criminals, the most famous criminals were our celebrities. And even on the outside, in a society like America that worships fame, it's not hard to see how fame and infamy can be confused. Because of his "celebrity" status, Manson did receive certain privileges. One in particular was his acoustic guitar. Musical instruments were not allowed in lockups, but I made an exception for Charlie. He was allowed to select a few hours a day when he wanted to play. A sergeant would bring the six-string to him, then pick it up later. This worked fine for a few weeks. Charlie was pretty good. His singing and speaking voice sounds a lot like the Kris Kristofferson of "Why Me, Lord?" and "Help Me Make It Through the Night" fame. The surrounding inmates seemed to enjoy the break in the monotony. I knew it wouldn't last, and it didn't. One afternoon, when the guard tried to take the guitar back, Charlie refused. The sergeant was called.

"Give it up, Charlie, or we're coming in after it."

Manson stood firm. The sergeant ordered the sliding cell door opened. Manson stuck the neck of the guitar across the stationary bars, preventing the moving part from operating. The sergeant, in no mood for fun and games, grabbed the wooden instrument and ripped it away, splitting it in half. As the officers marched in to pick up the pieces, Manson cracked, "If you want to play, you gotta pay."

The incident symbolized Manson's self-destructive side. Although the guitar was important to him and was a vital tool for killing the excruciating boredom, he decided that it was more important to display a few seconds of defiance than to have months of tranquillity. Whatever long-term consequences he had to suffer because of it was of no concern. This quality, more than anything, defines both the criminal and the psychotic mind, and how they differ from the rest of us. Oblivious of the concept of cause and effect, these felons destroy their entire lives to satiate a temporary desire or to act upon a single, fleeting emotion. Manson's stupid show hurt no one but himself. Of course, he didn't see it that way. He was incapable of connecting that meaningless moment of antisocial behavior with the loss of something he cherished and the subsequent weeks spent sulking in his cell with nothing to do. The spin he put on it was that the evil "system" had destroyed his beautiful instrument.

Without the guitar to soothe his nerves, Charlie became tense and agitated again. His speeches during our afternoon chats grew more grandiose and chilling. He began drifting farther and farther away from reality, replacing it with his "reality," the apocalyptic revolution that he insisted was still going to happen. His Family, he boasted, was stronger and more active than ever. "We're going to change the world!"

Whenever he got like this, I pestered him about the murders. If he was worked up enough, he might make that long-awaited confession. "Yeah, yeah, Charlie, I've heard that 'change the world' tune before, but tell me, why did you allow your followers to commit those senseless murders? You've said that it wasn't your idea, but you also admitted that you had the power to stop them. What did you possibly gain by letting them go through with it? Those people didn't deserve to die."

"I didn't kill anyone," he shot back, angered, as always, by the question. Only instead of changing the subject, this time he continued. "They deserved to die! They were Hollywood lowlife. They were into devil worship, pornography, and drugs. They were part of the greedy rich who are responsible for slaughtering the forests and raping the land so they can build their fancy houses with redwood decks."

That raised my eyebrows. The pornography, drugs, devil-worship stuff was nothing more than after-the-fact rationalization. As the world knows, Charlie sent his stoned killers to a house where the occupants were unknown, so there couldn't have been a personal motivation before the fact. Afterward, once he found out the victims were director Roman Polanski's wife and friends, he developed the excuses. Polanski had made some racy films, so he was a "pornographer." One of his most famous movies, *Rosemary's Baby*, used devil worship and the occult as a scare tactic, so that apparently meant the people at the death house were "into devil worship." The drug angle was stupid and hypocritical, as Manson and his Family were far more into hard drugs than any gathering of Hollywood socialites.

It was the "redwood decks" that caught my attention. Charlie had been at that house before. Had the redwood decks really infuriated him to the point of murder? Preservation of the forests was one of his main themes. Lumber industry executives remained prominent on his frequent hit lists. The nature-scene pictures he plastered on his cell walls proved that his concern went beyond just using the environment as a good pickup line. Hell, maybe he did do it because of the redwood decks. It was as good a reason as the one Vincent Bugliosi used to convict him, the "Helter Skelter" plan of starting a war between the races to destroy the black man.

Charlie segued from the "they deserved it" nonsense to another treatise on the "truth" about his so-called Family. "It wasn't a real family. The media made that up, I didn't. We were just a bunch of kids who wanted to live together. Everybody drove us out, so we found this ranch. We all had work to do. Everyone did their own thing and we were happy. They came to me with their problems and I helped them. I told them what I would do, but I didn't make their decisions for them."

"What did you tell them to do?"

"Get rid of your fear. Be what you are. I would teach them the truth."

"What's the truth?"

"The truth is there is no truth!" he answered as if he were handing down the Ten Commandments. "There is no right or wrong. There is only one, and it does what it wants to do. There is no fear, only the thought of fear. There is no guilt for doing what you must do!"

After a dramatic pause, he flashed back to a scene at the ranch before it all went bad. "There was this fire and everybody was singing, dancing, and getting high. We were in the country, out of sight. I was sitting on the top of this big boulder like an Indian chief looking down on his children. When I gave orders, it was done. When I told a girl to go sleep with a certain guy, she did it. Imagine that? It was like I was a god sitting there. Wow, man. It was far out!"

At times like these, Manson completely contradicted his earlier claims that his "friends" acted on their own and that he had no power over them. In truth, he had extraordinary power over them. He might have been surprised by it, and he might not have fully understood it in the beginning, but by the night of the murders, he was keenly aware of it.

"I controlled the dope, and that was important," he continued. "I didn't want them to get completely stoned. I'd take a little less than everybody else so I could keep an eye on things."

Then, almost as if he realized his contradictions, Manson changed course.

"I didn't want to be their leader," claimed the man incapable of functioning in any other role. "But they needed somebody. I couldn't just split. They needed me, so I stayed with them."

Stayed with them, and led them into the abyss.

10

PULLING MANSON FROM his cell for our daily chats soon became the highlight of my day. I was aware that I was falling into the same trap as I had before, once again feeding my psychological addiction to this extremely dangerous man simply because he was interesting. I was unable to contain myself at home and with friends, a problem that naturally worried Beth. I was aware of her increasing concern, but my "Charlie stories" bubbled with such intensity inside my mind I had to share them.

In truth, Charlie was often inspirational. He'd plant ideas in my head, compliment me, then say, "Go do it!" The ideas would usually be impossible and outrageous—and always benefiting him—but I'd come away strangely uplifted and empowered. "Don't waste your life on an eight-to-five job, living inside a paper bag. You're killing yourself. Do something with your life!" he'd say.

Although he never expressed it plainly, it was clear that "doing something with my life" consisted of helping him escape, joining the Family, and teaming up to change the world. At times, he could almost make it sound inviting. Of course, it was such moments of idle fantasy that drove Beth crazy with the fear that Manson was having a marked effect upon my mental state.

"Don't worry, sweetheart," I'd assure her. "I'm not going to trade you in for a harem of homicidal earth children with questionable personal hygiene habits, enticing as that might sound. Besides, I'm not the revolutionary type."

I wasn't, but there were legions of loose wires on the outside who definitely were. One of the strangest, and most persistent, was Richard Rubacher, an odd man who numbered among Charlie's most fervent post–Helter Skelter groupies. Instead of writing passionate letters promising to love, support, and, if need be, kill for Manson, as hundreds of others had, Rubacher lusted for an audience with his chosen master. A quizzical character who operated on the fringes of society, Rubacher would occasionally surprise me with his connections. Professing to be a freelance journalist of some sort—an easy claim to make in an unregulated profession—he convinced the local San Francisco public television outfit to allow him to provide them with a filmed interview with Manson. Clever as the scheme was, I had to turn it down. The rules stated that reporters had to be full-time employees of the designated media outlet. Not to be deterred, Rubacher came at me again. He somehow convinced the famous German tabloid style magazine *Stern* to put him on the payroll for the sole purpose of getting an interview with Manson. Rubacher trumped us with that move, so we had to stamp the approval.

Prior to the interview, Rubacher was cleared for a preliminary chat in the visiting room. The date was set for February 3, 1977. Manson had been behaving himself, so his custody was dropped to close B, meaning he could greet his visitors without wearing handcuffs. An associate warden on the custody side overruled the decision and jumped Manson back to maximum A. That meant he'd have to wear cuffs to the Rubacher sit-down. Manson refused and the meeting was canceled. That afternoon, Charlie requested an audience with me. He was hot.

"You have the power and authority to do anything you want," he railed, fuming over his upgraded status. "Just look them straight in the eye and tell them what you want them to do. Speak with such terror in your voice and eyes that no one will dare to defy you! And if they do, they'll fear for their life. Believe me, they'll obey you.

"You need to have the power now because I've lost some of mine," he continued. "I'm not into killing no more. I can't be that snake going around biting people. You know why? The Lord told me to stop! And I asked the Lord, I said, 'What else can I do? I've got no arms. No legs.' And the Lord told me, 'I didn't say you couldn't show your fangs and rattle your tail.' So that's all I do now. But I still scare the hell out of people. This is what you have to learn, to show your fangs and rattle your tail!"

As Charlie spoke, his voice became deeper, louder, and more intense. The sound waves rattled off the office door, alerting an officer in the foyer. I waved him away, allowing Charlie to continue his masterful performance. Encouraged, Charlie stood, his pint-sized body trembling with defiance. His voice remained strong and unwavering, the words streaming out with such energy that it propelled him backward like an Everglades skiff. "Those who stand in my way get killed. They die horrible deaths with the bloody writing on the wall. The writing people still don't understand. Doesn't anybody realize that by now?" Leaning forward, his hand swooshed across the front of my desk, launching several books and papers into the air. A few hit the wall, falling to the floor with a crash. "Power is not there or in the brain! Book heads don't rule. It's here! Here's your power!" he shouted, grabbing his genitals with his right hand.

By now, all the officers on the foyer raced to the office to see if I was still alive. They arrived to find Charlie standing there, eyes inflamed, clutching his nuts in a frozen pose. It was some sight. I waved them off again, but their stampede broke the spell. Charlie was finished. Bravo, I thought. It had been one of his best shows ever. I lamented that it hadn't been captured on film.

Trying to capture Charlie's act for posterity was becoming an increasing problem. The caged cult leader's ever-changing emotions were playing havoc with the media, especially the foreign press. Rubacher wasn't the only one who got burned. When the BBC called from London, I explained that if Manson gave the word, they could fly all the way here and set up; then, if he was on the rag that day, the whole deal would collapse. They were willing to take the chance and begged me to add them to the list. "You're on," I said, laughing.

When Mike Wallace and *60 Minutes*'s turn came, they played turnabout and cooled, never responding to my "come on down" letter. They obviously had wanted an exclusive, and Manson's local television and *Enquirer* rehearsals had nixed the idea. Regardless, there were always enough names on the list to keep Charlie performing every ninety days for as long as he wanted. Even his goofy buddy Rubacher finally had his cherished session in March 1977.

The day before the fateful interview, the staff held a routine classification hearing on Manson. The unit lieutenant, the unit psychiatrist, a psychologist, and two counselors joined me in attending. Charlie walked into the hearing room, leaped upon the eight-foot-long, highly polished conference table, lay down flat on his back, and closed his eyes. We waited him out, playing along by tolerating his unique positioning. Minutes passed. He didn't move. Finally, I couldn't stand it anymore.

"Charlie, are you dead?" I inquired.

"I might as well be by the way you're keeping me down," he answered, rising slowly like Dracula from his tomb. Charlie hopped down and proceeded to lecture us on how terribly we treated him. Specifically, how we mercilessly abused him by not allowing him to take immediate possession of everything his demented fans mailed in. "You jack me off, but never let me come!" he charged, repeating a standard accusation. "You can't make paper clip decisions!"

"We'll look into it," I promised, rewarding him for another stellar performance.

Rubacher arrived the next day wearing a heavy English-style full-length wool overcoat with a wide, rounded collar, epaulets on the shoulders, and a tightly buckled, dark brown matching belt. He was a thin, frail, handsome man with rich, black, curly hair. He was so excited that he pranced around, speaking in a high, anxious voice. He reminded me of a schoolgirl who had won a radio station's "dream date" contest with her favorite teenybopper rock star.

I'd arranged to conduct the interview in a Willis Unit conference room to avoid the issue of Manson's troublesome bracelets. By remaining inside the high-security area, Manson wouldn't have to be cuffed, eliminating the need for another tantrum.

Manson entered the room affecting a mean scowl. He brilliantly cloaked any initial surprise over his visitor's foppish appearance. Despite Charlie's unfriendly posture, Rubacher was so electrified by the moment I thought he was going to faint dead to the floor. His eyes sparkled and his hands trembled with nervous delight as I made the official introduction. Charlie sat staring at him for a few moments, his famous hypnotic gaze locked deep into Rubacher's wanting eyes. "How are you, old buddy?" Manson opened in a soft, friendly voice that was in stark contrast to his menacing demeanor. Rubacher stilled his fluttering heart and began speaking in a businesslike manner, running down his plan for the story, the photos, and a subsequent book he was planning to write that was to be titled "Showdown with Charles Manson." Charlie sat and sucked on a cigarette, taking it all in. It sounded wild and grandiose to me, but I kept my mouth shut, enthralled by the thoroughly bizarre moment.

"If you're gonna play the money game, I wanna play, too," Manson said, displaying a sudden, unexpected interest in material things. "Treat me like a partner."

Rubacher readily agreed, explaining that he was to receive $2,500 from *Stern* for the story, a rather paltry sum from a rag known to pay hundreds of thousands for scoops. With that out of the way, Manson launched into a rather uninspired, C-level rap on the environment while the accompanying photographer snapped hundreds of photos. Rubacher sat and listened in a euphoric trance like he was receiving the wisdom of the ages. He didn't appear to have a clue what questions to ask, attempting nothing even remotely controversial or stimulating. Manson quickly grew weary of the naked adulation and abruptly ended the session.

Rubacher was so enamored with being in Manson's presence that he didn't protest. He remained enthralled by the experience and thanked me profusely when I led him through the gate. The oddest thing was, I never saw or heard from Rubacher again. Not a single letter came to the prison. I couldn't determine how the article came out because it was printed in German twenty thousand miles away. As far as I could tell, his book was never published. Worried that something might have gone wrong, I pestered Charlie about it for years. "Hey, whatever happened to that Rubacher guy?" Charlie always shrugged and pretended not to know.

On Thursday, June 30, 1977, Dr. Clara Livsey, a psychiatrist from Baltimore, Maryland, came to CMF to interview Manson through an arrangement made by the warden. Dr. Livsey was researching a book she was preparing, *The Manson Women*, which promised to be a tony study of what drove Charlie's girls to kill. The lady shrink had already sat with Squeaky, Sandra, Leslie Van Houten, and Patty Krenwinkel among others, chronicling their backgrounds, families, and behavior up to the time they met Charlie. With that completed, she was ready to meet the master himself.

I introduced them in the conference room and stayed to monitor the discussion and make sure Charlie didn't try and strangle the "uppity" woman. Charlie, who always knew how to play to the proper audience, was in fine form. He threatened, cajoled, badgered, and did his usual thing, using every inch of the room to dart around, gesticulate, wave his arms, distort his face, and stoke the fires in his eyes. Basically, he was tossing out his whole bag of tricks to unnerve the calm, serene doctor who had obviously done her homework and knew what to expect. A hardy professional, she withstood the attacks, pursuing him aggressively and unflinchingly with her barbed questions. Charlie, fueled by a worthy opponent, was impressed.

Sensing that his usual tactics weren't working, Charlie shifted into his vulgar mode, humping the walls and making "jerking off" motions with his hands. "All the world's power is in a man's cock!" he announced. "It's man's ability to mate and breed and build the population with force and power!" With that, he slammed his fist on the table directly in front of Dr. Livsey's face. He then took her hand, put it on the spot where he'd just struck, and barked, "Keep it there, woman!"

I was ready the lock him up, but Dr. Livsey said she was fine and wanted to continue. Far from being intimidated, she fired her questions, probing him on each of his female followers. Manson answered in short, clipped sentences, like he was responding to a word association test.

"Susan Atkins?"

"A crazy, unmanageable, loathsome girl from the start. She was like an anchor around my neck, always following me around."

"Leslie Van Houten?"

"I didn't know Leslie very well. She was a daddy's girl."

"Mary Brunner?"

"I told her she could come along if she brought her credit cards. I told her I could only screw her a few times because I was too busy."

"Patty Krenwinkel?"

"I have lots on her."

"Lynette?"

"She was the mother hen, faithful to me, just like Sandra."

Wandering, Charlie said he became interested in the ecology because of all the great sex he was having. The sex made him feel more alive, motivating him to be concerned about the welfare of children and the world they'd inherit.

Despite the focus of Dr. Livsey's book, Charlie mostly danced around the questions relating to the girls, instead giving his usual spiel on the water, air, trees, and animals. He made some obscure reference to playing dominoes and how the motion, movement, and action will someday cause the world to collapse (a garbled version of the domino theory perhaps). "If we have to kill to save the planet, then killing becomes necessary. I told the girls to find out who was causing the world's problems, then I let them know that it was their responsibility to do something about it because it was their world, not mine. They couldn't sit back and just fuck and suck and get high, they had to do something to stop the world's death and their own deaths. Anytime the girls started talking about the past, I'd tell them to forget it and give them something to do to get their minds clear. I'd order them to obey, to stay in line, and if they did, nobody would get hurt.

My main function was to rid them of their old ways and thoughts and hang-ups about sex and drugs."

He shifted again to world power, money, war, and the balance between religions, acting like he alone knew everything about everything. Name a subject, and Charlie had the answers.

To me, the entire performance was carefully crafted to convince Dr. Livsey that he was too crazy for anyone to take seriously. Therefore, it was impossible for him to have programmed his girls to commit murder. Just in case she didn't quite get the message, Charlie put on a final show. After leaving the interview, he refused to undergo a routine strip search. When the officers forced him, he lashed out, striking a guard with his fist. He was overpowered and dragged kicking and screaming into administrative segregation. Perfect. Dr. Livsey's last impression would be of a violently out-of-control, half-naked madman being manhandled by a group of officers—a loon incapable of influencing a fly to land on a toilet seat.

When I caught up with him a few minutes later, he was laughing and joking, the feigned rage of the previous moment completely forgotten.

"Bravo," I said, clapping my hands. "Another rabbit pulled from the hat. Another mind totally screwed." Charlie just twisted his beard and smiled.

I don't know how much Dr. Livsey was swayed by the act, or if she'd been leaning in that direction all along, but her book supported Charlie's position that his girls were each individually responsible for what they had done.

At the disciplinary hearing for striking the officer, Manson explained that a lot of the cons had a beef with the guy and were planning to kill him, but that he, Charlie, actually intervened, saving the officer's life! Beautiful.

After gracing a few more prime-time and late-night television shows, including one interview that was turned into a syndicated television special, Manson went small again, summoning a female reporter from the local Vacaville newspaper. In her letter, she promised not to write anything derogatory about him. That was bad journalism, but good PR, as it earned her an audience. Charlie selected her over a pack of media superstars because he felt she was young and unsophisticated like his followers, and deep down, he liked the little people. They were underdogs like himself. Not surprisingly, this insignificant interview turned out to be his most memorable.

The young woman, Chris Weinstein, arrived on July 6, 1978. She was smart, attractive, and probably not a day older than twenty-five, if that. She was escorted through numerous security gates, down a long corridor, and into the infamous Willis Unit, home of Juan Corona, Big Ed Kemper, and other less famous but equally dangerous felons. Before she was taken into the conference room where Manson would be brought, I took her aside.

"Try to relax, and don't be afraid or in awe of him," I advised. "He's very animated when he speaks and has a tendency to jump around and raise his voice in sudden outbursts. It can be very intimidating. He can be threatening, yelling and screaming at you to make a point. If you feel afraid or threatened at any time, just shake your head and I'll terminate the interview. Otherwise, if you can handle it, just let him go. Let him put on his show. He's scary, but he won't hurt you."

"I think I can handle it," she smiled, steeling herself. "Just let him do his thing. That's what I'm here for."

"Okay. It's show time," I said, swinging the door open. After a short wait, Manson entered. He was wearing his mean face, telegraphing that this was going to be a different ball game. Manson's eyes shifted from Chris's feet to her face as he circled around her, sizing her up, searching for a weakness. Hanging tough, she stared back, doing the same with him. I interrupted the dog-sniffing act to make the formal introductions. "Charlie, this is Miss Weinstein from the *Vacaville Reporter*. Chris, this is Charles Manson." They didn't shake hands. Instead, we took our positions at the table. Manson staked out a kinglike spot at the far end, forcing the young reporter to come to him. Undaunted, Chris marched forward and settled in on his right. I took the chair to his left.

"Why don't you tell me about prison life, Mr. Manson," she opened in a firm but nervous voice.

"You can call me Charlie. And don't be so uptight, woman. I'm not going to kill you." He grinned and winked at me. As he'd done with even the most seasoned reporters, Manson took complete control of the interview. His now familiar ideas exploded to the surface faster than Chris could take notes. She'd brought a recorder with her, so she didn't bother trying to slow him down. I watched as her expression grew from fear to amazement as Charlie played big shot, acting as if he were on a first-name basis with everyone from the Pope to Prince Charles. He railed about hippie leader Jerry Rubin selling out the revolution to make money. He accused blacks of using runaway flower children for prostitution. Andrew Young betrayed the United Nations. President Carter was giving the country to the blacks. Greedy developers were destroying the children's future by poisoning the air and water, tearing up the forests, and raping the land for money. Chris listened almost helplessly, trying to squeeze in a question here and there. Finally, she bullied one through. "What about the murders, Charlie?"

"I didn't murder anybody," he shot back in full denial. "But they sent me to prison. I didn't make them do it. I just told them what they had to do to live with their truth. They knew what they were doing. Even Tex Watson's book puts me away from the murders."

When I heard this, I couldn't resist butting in. "You know, Charlie, Leslie Van Houten was convicted of murder in her third trial yesterday. Do you think she deserved that? She testified that you ordered her to kill."

Manson was miffed by the intrusion, but didn't blow. Not yet, anyway. "She knew what she was doing. She was a papa's girl, and wanted to do her own thing. Now she blames me for helping her be herself."

Realizing that this was going nowhere, Chris shifted subjects. She asked how he was able to convince so many beautiful, intelligent women to drop everything and follow him.

"I looked them in the eye and saw what they wanted. I told them what they had to do to stay with me. If they didn't like it, they left. If they stayed, I had sex with them. I told them to forget their hang-ups and guilt trips. They had to become one with me and my truth. Their wills had to die to become one with me. Sex was their initiation. It was a celebration of life's pleasures. Something to enjoy, not to be afraid of."

Charlie put on his dirty-old-man smile and added that Chris herself had receptive vibes, even though she was a Jew. The reporter ignored the crude come-on and pressed forward. "How did you control them?"

In a flash, Charlie was up. He slipped behind the young woman, grabbed her hair, tilted her head, and peered menacingly into her eyes from inches away. He spoke in a ruthless, angry tone. "When a girl came to the ranch, I grabbed her tight around the shoulders and jerked her around. I grabbed her hair like this and pulled her head back. That's how I controlled my women," he spat, letting Chris go and promptly sitting back down. It happened so fast that neither of us had time to react. I'd become immune to most of Charlie's antics, but this one scared me. He could have cracked the lady's neck in a second! I stood, ready to jump the guy, but Chris held up her hand, signaling for me to stop.

"That's okay," she said. "It's all right."

Charlie had simply answered her question in a fashion that made it clear exactly how he controlled his women—with fear and intimidation. They, like Chris, would forever remember the chilling act.

Manson acted as if the terrifying demonstration were all part of a routine interview. He continued without pause, describing how he slapped and chided his women to keep them in their proper place. That place, in his chauvinistic mind, was to stay home, take care of the men's needs, and rear the kids. According to Charlie, women exist for no other reason than to suck cocks and please men. "Women are okay as long as they keep their mouths shut and do what they're told. When a good girl came around, I didn't want to mess with her. I'd tell her to leave and don't come back. But if she stayed or came back, I dragged her off in the bushes or behind the barn and fucked her on the dirt."

The lurid image and harsh language were intended to shock the reporter, but she didn't flinch. To keep him from going further, I interrupted again. "If you loved your women so much, why didn't you take the rap for them? I read your interview with Dr. Forte, the expert who testified for the prosecution in Leslie's retrial. You said that you had no influence over them, yet you talk about how they had to follow your will, become one with your 'truth' and obey you. They didn't do anything without your okay. So why not help her out by confessing that you took over their minds? You're never getting out anyway."

This was usually a hot button with Charlie. After the hair-pulling act, it was a big risk pushing it with Chris there, but I couldn't help myself. His contradictions were too maddening to go unchallenged.

"They are responsible because they held the gun!" he dodged. "They pulled the trigger. I only showed them how. I was not there. Can't you get that through your head? They knew what they were doing! That was their 'truth.'"

It was also, sadly, Charlie's truth. Whenever it came time for him to step up and do something remotely decent for someone else, the old prison credo of self-preservation interfered.

The interview ended without further incident. Chris pulled out her camera and shot some pictures. Charlie dutifully posed like a professional model, offering a wide set of expressions. In a suddenly playful mood that belied his previous anger, he slipped behind me, grabbed me in a head-lock, and flashed a demon smile.

"Do you want me to take it?" Chris asked, pointing the camera.

"Hell no!" I answered. "People will wonder who's running this place."

Despite all the theatrics, Chris wrote a surprisingly lackluster article, failing to capture Manson's fearsome enthusiasm and energy. To my shock, either she or her editors totally eliminated the part where Charlie jerked her head back and yelled in her face. Incredible. She had promised she wouldn't say anything bad about him, and had literally bent over backward to keep her word, even after he graced her with a sensational performance. All that aside, Charlie's quotes alone were enough to make the story worth reading, including this rare comment on his mother. "You might say she was a 1933 runaway flower child," he quipped.

Asked about having to spend his life in prison, he became philosophical. "You're in prison more than I'm in prison. It's all prison. You've got more rules to live by than I do. I can sit down and relax, can you? I take my own time in doing something. I live in my own time, you live in the time left to you by the dead. You live in the past that controls your future. I live in the now, controlled by your past and your future. Because I have the controls over it, I have the power in it and not the controls over it, so anywhere I am is where I am. If I'm here, I'm here. If I'm in San Quentin, I'm here. If I'm in the desert, I'm here. I have to be satisfied with myself wherever I am. So wherever I am is freedom to be because I am free within my own soul. . . .

"I don't do the same things you do. I don't live the same lifestyle you live. You live the lifestyle you were trained and conditioned to live. I create my own lifestyle, my own world. You live in the world that was created for you. You accept the things you were taught to accept because you don't know any different. I don't accept the things I was taught. I don't accept the trees being cut down. I don't accept the water being polluted. You people accept that. You say it's always been that way. You got jet airplanes that go six thousand miles per hour. You know how small that makes the world? The world is a little place now. We're still thinking 1776 laws for a jet age, does that make sense. . . . Kind of silly that we're living in a prison made by past thoughts, by past confusion. So, are we in prison? Can you do what you want? Are you free to be yourself? Do you get up when you want or are you forced to do things you don't want to every day?

". . . It would take ten books to unexplain the fifty books that have been written. It would take a trial to unexplain the district attorney who had two years to put everything he could think of on me. He didn't miss anything. I'm God, I'm the devil, I'm every kind of thing you can think of but at the same time I'm nobody. I'm a maniac, I'm keen, I'm clever, I'm sharp, I'm insane. I'm everything, but at the same time when I say 'well, let me . . .' they say no you can't say anything. But if I'm everything why can't I defend myself in court? If I'm so smart to overtake the world or undertake the world or undermine all the greatest minds of the planet since the day one . . . I must be some kind of genius. Yet I'm so inadequate that I can't even walk in a courtroom to put on a defense. Come on! . . .

"I may not be a decent person . . . but I respect decent people."

To back up that hard-to-swallow line, Manson explained that he once ordered a young woman into his van at knifepoint (possibly to rape her). When she responded that she couldn't obey because she believed in Jesus, he let her go.

"If somebody is afraid of Charlie Manson, they're afraid of themselves," he elaborated. "If somebody is afraid of Charlie Manson, they're afraid of the newspapers that created Charlie Manson. How can they be afraid of the newspapers that created Charlie Manson? How can they be afraid of somebody they don't even know? Does that mean I have to spend the rest of my life in prison because the public is afraid, or shall we take the news media and lock the news media up because they created the situation? . . . I'm just doing my number, what they call doing your own time. I just do my number, doing the best I can for each day because I live for this day."

The quotes Weinstein emphasized were solid, but again, it was the presentation that really told the story. Interestingly enough, three days later, the *Vacaville Reporter* announced that Weinstein was leaving the paper to take a (no doubt better-paying) position with the in-house publications department of the California State Employees Association. Her dance with Charlie thus became the swan song of her brief journalistic career.

A similarly frightening performance Charlie had given earlier did not go unreported. This time, the menacing aspects were pushed to the front. I received an ominous official memorandum from an obviously shaken officer. "I asked Manson if he needed any supplies to which he responded with the following: 'Yeah, I need something. I need you to do something about the foul air and the stinking water! If you don't do something about it I'll break your fucking neck! Save my children from the polluted air and water or I'll break your fucking back. Don't you remember the blood smeared all over the walls and the women with their heads cut off and stuffed up their pussies? Well, it will all happen again if you don't clean up the water and air. If you don't clean it up you just might end up with a broken back or neck or an unexpected car accident. So you better drive real careful when you go home from here at night.'"

Knowing he was rattling this guy's cage, Manson laid it on thicker. The guard filed a second report nine days later:

"He regularly speaks of mass murder and of the vengeance which he will carry out against the established society in general, and correctional personnel specifically," the guard wrote. "I view him as being an extremely violent individual obsessed with eradication of all segments of society not aligned with his self ordained life style." The concerned guard was thoughtful enough to again quote Manson directly. It helped explain why he was so upset:

"Why the hell would I want out? Hell, the first day I'm out I'm going to have to kill fifty people! All those people who lied about me, that fucked with my life. Those so-called judges and lawyers that put me in here. Yeah, I'm going to kill them all! And that's just at first. There's a lot more I'm going to kill when I get out! I have thousands of people writing to me all across the country. They think I'm their god. They would do anything for me! They would kill for me because I'm their god and I told them to. You just might walk out in the parking lot and get your throat cut from ear to ear. Just like a lot of other assholes that work around this fucking place, that don't do what I tell them to do! I'm as much a judge and jury as those that put me in here. I judge you to die! I'm putting you on my list because you didn't do what I told you to do. All I have to do is get the word out to them and you're a dead man!"

I could see how this would disturb the uninitiated. To me, it was just Charlie's routine ranting. The guard probably refused to fetch some allotted toiletry in a timely fashion, and Charlie went berserk. There was, unfortunately, some truth to these threats. He was absolutely right about the "thousands" of letters from Manson Family wanna-bes who were eager to kill for him. I knew because I was still reading his mail! That was and remained the scariest part about Manson. We had him under control, but we could never control his followers on the outside. And from what I was reading, that group was growing.

"As long as Manson views himself as a god of vengeance and is able to maintain a following to carry out his violently anti-social doctrine, he constitutes a serious threat," the officer correctly concluded. "[He poses a] threat to the prison setting by way of his almost constant haranguing about killing correctional staff, and the upheaval of the prison system. More importantly, judging by Manson's present attitude, I feel that he would constitute an even greater threat to society if he were allowed to re-enter it feeling as he proclaims to. I sincerely urge that this matter be given the most serious consideration at such a time as he be considered for release."

This was obviously one guard who never wanted to see Charlie on the streets again. Hell, I'm sure the guy didn't even want to pass by his cell anymore! I noted his concerns, but there really wasn't anything I could do. I'd heard it all before. The disturbed officer would just have to get used to it like everyone else.

The newspaper interview dramatics and the guard conflict were the exact kind of horror-movie-type cheap thrills that continued to feed my intellectual attraction to Manson. In contrast, it was nowhere near the same with CMF's other "celebrity" prisoners. At one time, serial killer Juan Corona's fame rivaled Manson's. As with Manson, Corona's name itself came to symbolize evil incarnate. Writers and comedians would bandy it about to make points about scary situations. "I couldn't have been more afraid if I'd spotted Juan Corona standing in my garden with a shovel!" they'd quip. Corona earned his reputation by murdering and burying something like twenty-five migrant workers before his capture. He was appealing his conviction based on poor legal representation, and had won himself a new trial. He was sent to me because it was more convenient for his attorneys and investigators to visit him. (The California corrections system always strives to accommodate the needs of its celebrity mass murderers.)

For all his infamy, Juan was a disgusting, fearful man, distrustful of both staff and inmates. He was the kind of person who literally made your skin crawl. When I shook his hand, it felt soft and mushy like a boneless fish, a sensation that gave me the creeps. A man of no particular intelligence, skill, or insights, he was nothing more than a low-rent sicko. The only significant thing I ever remember him saying came when his attorneys arrived one day. "Look," he quipped to a Spanish-speaking guard. "I got three white lawyers working for me. Pretty good, huh?"

"Fuck you, Corona," the officer shot back.

Even the other inmates wanted nothing to do with him. He remained a loner, without a single friend or lover. Manson regarded him the way he would a cockroach squashed on the bottom of his shoe. He wasn't even a worthy topic of discussion.

Big Ed Kemper joined the circus around the same time. He was somewhat more interesting, if just in size alone. Six feet nine, three hundred pounds, he was both a literal and figurative monster. A passive, congenial man, he appeared totally harmless. He was—unless you happened to remind him of his mother. Then it was lights out. Unfortunately, too many women had had the misfortune of resembling the late Mrs. Kemper. Ed obviously hated his mom, painting her as a mean, vindictive witch who abused and tormented him throughout his youth. On his glorious day of vengeance, the tall, gawky teenager first cut off the head of his mother's best friend and placed it on the mantel. When his mother came home, she was shocked and horrified—but not for long. Ed promptly killed her next, taking great pleasure in the act. He then killed his grandfather to spare him the heartbreak.

Ed was sent to Atascadero State Hospital and became the perfect patient. After a few years, the doctors announced that he was cured and ready to rejoin society. Once free, he seemingly dedicated his life to giving lifts to needy female hitchhikers. Nine out of ten came away with nothing more than a helpful ride from the jolly fellow. Those are good odds in everything except murder. The remaining ten percent—the ones who reminded him of his mom—were killed in a series of gruesome ways. He strangled some, stabbed others, and smothered at least one by sitting on her face.

Struggling with his conscience, Ed finally turned himself in to the disbelieving police. "Stop me before I kill again," he begged. To prove his case, Ed led the cops to his victims' graves. When the digging was done, nine "Mrs. Kempers" had been unearthed. Ed wasn't just killing his mother, he was trying to eliminate the entire gene pool!

"I didn't want to hurt anybody," he explained to me after his arrival. "I just couldn't stop."

Ed's main problem at CMF was that he couldn't stop talking about his crimes. He related his stories with a fiendish relish, giving detailed descriptions of how he killed each girl, how their eyes popped out, how they gasped and struggled, how their tongues protruded as they died. It was almost like he was describing a sporting event. One story he told was particularly creepy. He picked up two girls and decided to do them both when one had that familiar maternal look about her. He locked the second girl in the car and dragged the first out in a field, where he repeatedly stabbed her. When he came back to the vehicle, he realized that he'd left his keys in the ignition! The girl was locked inside with the keys! All she had to do was hop into the front seat and drive away. Her life would have been spared and Big Ed Kemper's reign of terror would have been over. Ed stayed cool. He calmly tapped on the window and pointed to the lock, ordering the petrified girl to kindly release it. Incredibly, she did—and died horribly shortly thereafter. "That was really stupid," Ed cracked, recalling it with glee.

"You have to stop talking like that on the mainline," I warned. "Don't go telling everybody your war stories."

"Why?" he asked, hurt that he couldn't boast about the only thing he felt made his worthless existence significant.

"Because somebody's going to kill you! Inmates don't like guys like you."

I found it interesting that Ed and Charlie had similar dysfunctional

backgrounds—mothers they hated—then fed off the same niche of people—lost and alienated young women. After that, the differences were
dramatic. Ed killed his women, while Charlie recruited, bewitched, brainwashed, drugged, and fornicated with his zombies, then sent them out to
kill others for him. (A deciding factor might be that Charlie's mother,
though criminal, immoral, and neglectful, was not mean.) The only thing
the pair—one a giant, the other a shrimp—had in common from the end-
result aspect was they aborted the lives of lot of innocent people.

Richard Allen Davis, the sex offender who would later gain notoriety
for snatching a young girl named Polly Klass from a slumber party at her
California home, dragging her off, and fatally raping her, was also around
CMF at the time. However, Davis was a nobody then, a "chomo" (child
molester) everybody hated, so he wasn't a factor.

While Manson had little use for Corona, Kemper, or Davis, the same
couldn't be said for Willie Spann, another of CMF's resident celebrities.
Spann, thirty-three, was the son of then-president Jimmy Carter's sister
Gloria, making him the President's nephew. The affable young man with
long, curly brown hair had been in and out of jail for years, mostly for
drugs, robberies, and burglaries, and came to CMF after faking a stabbing
at San Quentin. He wanted out of there because he said the gangs believed
he snitched on someone back in 1971 and were planning to kill him. Prior
to Carter's surprise, come-from-nowhere election, nobody cared about Willie Spann. He was just another unstable, bisexual hype clogging the system.
Then his uncle became President, and suddenly the lifelong loser magi-
cally transformed into a somebody—at least from our perspective. Actually,
nobody seemed to care about him in Washington. He was a black sheep
who was an embarrassment to the President, and Carter was already having
enough trouble in that department with his loony brother Billy. Willie
wasn't very close to his mother either. A party girl in her youth, she ma-
tured into the quiet Carter sibling who stayed out of the limelight and
spent her whole life down on the farm. She was no doubt overwhelmed
by the antisocial behavior of her troubled son combined with the sudden
fame of her brother. (Jimmy Carter's youngest sister, Ruth, was the vibrant
one who became a traveling evangelist.) The only person who appeared
to care about Willie, aside from the media, was his grandmother, the extremely famous and much beloved Miss Lillian. A kind, decent woman,
she sent Willie money and wrote him frequent letters of encouragement.

Because of Willie's connections, the corrections department decided to
let him finish his sentence at CMF. To keep him out of harm's way, he
was sent to my lockdown unit. I placed him in a cell right next to Manson
because it was easier to deal with the celebrities that way. In retrospect,
that probably wasn't one of my better ideas, but at the time, it seemed
logical.

Manson was impressed by his new neighbor's heavy connections, but as always, downplayed it, preferring to elevate himself to Willie's uncle's level. Despite this foolishness, the two hit it off. They became friends, talking, dreaming, playing music, and sharing their life stories. I don't know if Charlie really liked the guy, or had some greater scheme going — probably both — but for a while, they appeared to do each other some good. Willie even began talking about joining the Family. The fast friendship ended over petty jealousy. A floor officer gave Willie the tier tender job that Manson coveted. Manson threw a tantrum and took a swing at the burly African-American guard, earning himself a stint in isolation (with Juan Corona nearby). When he returned to his "home" cell, he was still in a snit. He demonstrated his unhappiness by smashing his latest guitar — a six-hundred-dollar beauty a fan had sent — into tiny pieces. (It was the fourth guitar Manson destroyed on my watch, including one at San Quentin.)

Willie loved music and was pissed at Manson for destroying the finely crafted instrument. "What did you do that for?" Spann demanded. "There's a hundred guys on this floor who'd love to have a guitar but can't afford one, and you go and destroy yours during a tantrum. What a stupid asshole!"

After that, things went from bad to worse. Willie never forgave Charlie for bashing the guitar and got on his case every time he threw a similar fit. President's nephew or not, Charlie fumed over being constantly criticized by some "punk." After one nasty exchange, Manson played his trump card. "It's about time I sent some followers to Plains, Georgia, to see an old lady!"

Miss Lillian was probably the only person in the world Willie cared about. She had helped raise him, and stood behind him through all his troubles. Manson's threat caused him to go ballistic. "I'll kill you, you fuckin' bastard!" he raged. "Don't you ever threaten my grandmother!"

Manson repeated his threat, and Willie repeated his. They went at it until the guards had to quiet them down. When I arrived at the cells, I could see that Manson was just dicking him around, but Willie was red hot. I was certain he was going to kill Charlie the first chance he got. That would have been some headline. To check out Willie's state of mind, I pulled him out for a long interview. Among the revelations was his boast that when he was a lad, he'd managed to catch a glimpse of First Lady Rosalyn Carter naked and that "she had a hell of a body!"

"When I was five, my mother went off, married this guy I never met and she didn't tell me. I was living with my grandmother, Miss Lillian. My mother was running around a lot and neglecting me, so she [Miss Lillian] took up the slack. Nobody was rich then, but the Carters were well-to-do. I'd be in rags, not many toys, alone. Billy Carter, my cousin, had nice clothes, a pony, and lots of toys. Anyway, when Gloria, 'Go, Go,' came one day to pick me up at Mrs. Lillian's, she was with this guy I never saw before. They took me off to his place. I was never accepted by this man, my stepfather. They had an outhouse that I was scared to use. I was terrified by it. I had to sleep in a pitch-dark room. I'd see monsters tracking me, trying to eat me, tear me apart. I had no one to run to.

"I had to work like a dog, a nigger, pickin' cotton and diggin' peanuts. My stepfather was a hardworking man, got rich, earned it hard. But they were more interested in each other than me. 'Back Seat Willie' I called myself. Never rode in the front seat of a car. Go to sleep on the floorboard. Keep quiet. When company came over, I was sent to my room and told to be quiet."

At this point, I couldn't help thinking how similar Spann's childhood was to Manson's. They were both ignored and neglected and neither had a strong father figure.

"Once, I got caught stealing at the local store," Willie continued. "The whole family was extremely upset because they were in competition with some of the local 'Joneses.' They wanted to look better than each other, and I made the family look bad. School grades were important. . . .

". . . In my mind, I killed my mother and my stepfather many times. I wanted them to love me, especially my mother, but it never came. She couldn't give it because she was more interested in impressing others and keeping her marriage together. They hit it off and I was left out.

"I always felt that something was always missing inside of me because of my mother's failure to love me. Some part of me failed to grow and mature. It stopped when I was twelve or sooner. Once, when I came home from school with poor grades, . . . they told me to think about it, how ashamed I should feel, how embarrassed for the family to have such a terrible child.

"There was a gun case in the hallway with a latch that made a *bing* sound when it was opened. Sitting there, sacred out of my wits, I heard that *bing*. I ran out of the house through a screen door naked, thinking I was going to be shot. They took me to my uncle Jimmy's house, who realized that I was sick. Jimmy took me to the same psychiatrist who was the one in the movie *The Three Faces of Eve*. They said that I had a brain tumor that would grow and worsen with time. But nothing ever came of that. It was probably better than saying I was crazy."

It should be noted that this was just Willie's story, and cons often fabricate horrible childhoods and monstrous parents as an excuse for their own shortcomings. While Gloria Carter did go through some tough times early in her life, there is no concrete evidence that she and her husband treated Willie as he claims.

After escaping his self-professed childhood hell, Willie moved to Los Angeles and began a life of drugs and crime, a criminal existence that eventually dropped him inside a prison cell next to Charles Manson.

Willie apparently shared his sad life story with Charlie because Squeaky was moved to write Gloria Carter a scathing letter condemning her for not accepting her responsibilities as a mother. Squeaky mercilessly ripped Gloria's alleged preoccupation with money and status, while sacrificing her child. This, however, was before Willie and Charlie had their violent falling-out.

Alas, the PRESIDENT'S NEPHEW KILLS MANSON headline wasn't to be. Willie was paroled a year later and was picked up at the gate by a twenty-two-foot Cadillac limousine. No, it wasn't from the government. It was a gift from the ever present *National Enquirer*. They were paying Spann for an exclusive interview and sent Willie and his new bride, an insurance broker he married at CMF months before, on a nice vacation. (The pen-pal marriage didn't last more than a few months.)

The kicker is that not long afterward, I was aimlessly walking past a television one afternoon when I glanced up and spotted someone who looked like Willie gabbing on *The Phil Donahue Show*. I turned up the volume. Sure enough, it was Willie. He was playing tape recordings of his conversations with Manson, which he'd made at CMF. That was interesting because tape recorders were illegal in prisons. It turned out that Willie, ever the opportunist, had taken apart a cassette player and transformed it into a recorder. Now he was using his connection to Manson to play celebrity on television. Touché Willie.

11

I WAS OFTEN frustrated, or downright appalled, by the thoughts and statements made by Charlie and Squeaky. They were two peas in a pod, and it was one rotten pod. Collectively, however, if observed solely as star-crossed lovers, they could be viewed in a softer light. Their love had survived horrors, headlines, assassination attempts, and dual incarcerations—not to mention the forceful arguments of a certain correctional administrator. Beyond their ramblings of hate and destruction, they shared a dream of survival, escape, and reunion. With that goal always in mind, Lynette continued her drumbeat plea to write to Charlie. Admiring her sheer tenacity, I finally relented, only to have the mellow Dr. Clanon, curiously, disapprove.

That forced me back into my uncomfortable role as love-letter censor to the psycho stars. When the pair dispensed with their crazy social agendas and got personal, they could be surprisingly endearing. "My thoughts have moved along," Manson wrote her once. "My body is fading away here, but we are forever in the soul. . . ."

"A pair of hands, a feeling, the silent shadows of a lonely, quiet ocean rolls," Squeaky responded. "The sun on my tears and a smile only you can see."

They both knew their most intimate thoughts were falling before hostile eyes, but they didn't care. Actually, I had the strong impression that Charlie and Squeaky believed that if they made their forbidden correspondence painfully personal and beautifully poetic, I'd weaken and slide it through. They were right. As long as they kept to sweet nothings instead of "rivers of blood," I'd usually bend the rules.

Sometimes, Charlie's odd sense of gallows humor would surface and make me feel less guilty about my lawful intrusion into his personal life. After getting hooked on an especially heartfelt series of missives, I opened a new one with admitted anticipation. "Hi, Mr. George," Charlie scribbled. "I was just checking to see if you were still reading my mail."

During our conversations, Squeaky often detailed the constant hurdles she had to overcome to remain openly devoted to Charlie in her unfriendly surroundings. "This group of big, angry black women confronted me about why I have so much love for Charlie," she explained. "One of them started yelling, 'I don't believe Charles Manson is Jesus Christ!' I yelled back. 'You don't believe in anything but money.' 'That's right!' she said. 'And Charles Manson isn't going to give me any.' 'He'd give you a clean earth and water and air,' I pointed out. 'Can't you see you're killing your mother?' 'Them's fightin' words,' she threatened, clenching her fists and coming toward me. She didn't understand that I meant mother earth. She thought I was insulting her mother. The guards and other girls broke it up before anyone got hurt, but things like this happen all the time. We try to open their eyes, but they refuse to see the truth. Sandra and I have to separate ourselves from those who can't comprehend. It doesn't matter. Nothing can turn us away from Charlie.

"Look at the mother salmon," Squeaky continued, launching into a favorite nature analogy. "I have a picture of her on my wall to look at when I get discouraged. She's leaping a five-foot waterfall going upstream to lay her eggs and die. She could give up and lie in the sun, but she fights on against terrible odds. She could forget the whole thing, decide that babies are not for her, protest that the male salmon doesn't have to carry the load. And because the population of salmon would no longer be controlled by natural circumstance, she could make some sort of deal to sell the content of her womb for caviar. But she's not like that because she hasn't decided that she's above God. She's just a part of him and she gives him her all. She sacrifices her own life to balance the whole."

Squeaky Fromme had not seen Charlie, or heard his voice, in more than eight years. I was mulling that in my head when I got a wild idea. I called Lynette's counselor at the federal prison in Pleasanton, California, and ran it by him. He was reluctant at first, but decided, what the heck, go with it. It was Christmas week. Spirits were high. The man agreed to call me back in an hour. When the time came, I took Charlie from his cell and brought him to my office. The phone rang. After a brief conversation, I handed the receiver to Charlie. "Lynette wants to talk to you. Official business," I said with a wink. "Keep it short and simple. You have three minutes."

Charlie frowned and peered at the phone as if he'd never seen one before. He was certain this was just a prank, and didn't want to show his disappointment. Slowly, he raised the receiver to his ear.

"Charlie? Is it really you?" The high-pitched voice was unmistakable. Charlie's eyebrows nearly shot over his forehead. He looked at me with confusion and shock. Then a warm smile spread across his face. It betrayed an emotion that I had always believed was beyond his capabilities—tenderness.

"How you doing?" he cooed. "They treatin' you all right?"

I couldn't hear Squeaky's end, but I could almost feel her euphoria pouring into the room. I didn't want to intrude, so I walked away and only half listened, keeping my ears on the alert for any alarming buzzwords. Charlie spoke casually, saying nothing crazy or off-the-wall. Although I could read the affection in his body language, I was surprised that he displayed very little of it to her. You'd think that after all her years of blind devotion, she'd at least earned a bit of sweet talk. Then again, I guess the relationship was never like that to begin with. This wasn't man to woman, it was woman to master.

Suddenly, my ears perked up. The tone of the conversation changed abruptly. "Patty Hearst, the rich bitch," Manson said. Then, "How's the Patty Hearst thing going?"

I reached over and grabbed the phone. "That's it. Time's up," I announced. "Say good-bye." I held the phone to Charlie's mouth to let him get in the last word.

"Merry Christmas," he said.

The abrupt termination didn't seem to bother him at all. He thanked me and walked quietly to his cell. His obvious sense of satisfaction went beyond having talked to a lost love. Something was afoot, and I was once again right in the middle of it. Had Manson delivered a hit order on the famous heiress, who at the time was imprisoned with Squeaky? Was Charlie planning to intimidate or extort from Hearst? Or had Hearst, no stranger to demented revolutionaries, thrown in with the Manson clan, and was she planning to use her unlimited financial resources to reunite Charlie and Squeaky? Manson, as usual, dodged the questions, passing it off as idle chatter.

I fretted about it for weeks afterward, frantically checking the morning paper for news of such a plot. Time passed and nothing happened. Whatever the scheme was, it never came off.

I walked away from that incident having learned another valuable lesson. You try to be nice to a pair of monsters, and you might just get eaten.

As the years passed, many of the old Family members started shredding away. Whether they were simply trying to impress their parole boards or were being sincere is difficult to say. From their prison activities, I'd guess that it was the latter. At the California Institution for Women, the weak-willed Susan Atkins cut the cords early and wrote a book. Leslie Van Houten disavowed her confession and fought for new trials. Patty Krenwinkel vacillated for a decade before finally letting go. When I delivered that last bit of news to Charlie, his response was notable.

"Maybe Leslie, but not Patty," he said. "Back at the ranch, and when I had the bus, there were always people wanting to take my girls. Self-professed gurus were constantly trying to steal them away. There was a party house in Topanga Canyon we used to go to. The place was wild, full of people into group sex, hard drugs, devil worship, and all kinds of philosophies. There would be pockets of leaders and their little bands of followers scattered about all over the place. I'd bring the girls in and let them sit with, listen to, and even make love to whoever they wanted, dig? And you know, not a single one ever strayed. We went there dozens of times, stayed for hours or even days, and when the bus pulled away, everybody I arrived with left with me. I used to take great pride in that. Now? I'm here. Locked up. What can I do? If I wasn't in here, things would be different. It'd be just as it was before, only larger and stronger."

Fortunately, Charlie was "in here" under guard, a factor that enabled his old gang to keep abandoning the ship. Steve "Clem" Grogan, another original follower, was at CMF the same time as Manson. When Clem walked the corridors anywhere near Manson, he tried to avoid him. Away from Manson, Clem was a decent fellow with a peaceful soul. An accomplished musician and skilled artist, the theme of his colorful paintings was winged nymphs dancing across lily pads, singed by the pleasures of love, saddened by the loss of innocence, betrayed by one they formerly worshiped. Reflecting on the autobiographical nature of his art, Clem tried to explain to me how difficult it had been to escape Manson's spell. "I was at Spahn Ranch longer than practically anyone. I took so many drugs that I followed Manson blindly. I would do anything he asked. It's like he has this irresistible attraction, like he planted something deep inside me that's still there and he can call upon it at any time."

That unwavering loyalty included, unfortunately for Clem, the murder of Hollywood stuntman Shorty Shea. "I knew Shorty for a long time. I liked him," Clem told me. "But when Manson gave the order, I had to do it. I couldn't resist. There was just no going against Charlie back then."

Clem, who survived a stabbing during his incarceration, was eventually paroled. He married, has remained clean, and seems to have repaired his life. Prior to his release, I bought a striking ink sketch he did of a man holding a newborn. I wanted it to remind me of Clem's unceasing devotion to redeeming his broken life.

Manson's other top male Tate-LaBianca era henchmen, Tex Watson, Bruce Davis (Shea), and Bobby Beausoleil (convicted of murdering musician–drug dealer Gary Hinman), also left the fold. From the beginning, Watson privately requested that he be housed on a separate tier away from Manson on death row. That told me he was serious about wanting to break from his leader's mystical influence. Years later, Watson and Davis made it official and became born-again Christians, joining Susan Atkins in a decision to follow the real God. Watson has been especially energetic in his new calling, writing a series of books from his prison cell and establishing a bustling mail-order ministry.

"It's interesting that Sadie [Susan] and Tex were the ones to find God," Charlie observed. "They were the most messed up. They were direct participants in the murders that destroyed our entire group, murders that were Sadie's idea to begin with to save Bobby. Then, they were the ones who yelled to the world that I controlled their minds. Sadie was always running off, getting in trouble, then scurrying back with an angry trick or boyfriend on her heels. I got into a knife fight once with this Mexican guy she was balling. When she left him, she stole his drugs. I had to cut him up to convince him to back off. If they've truly turned their lives over to God, then good for them. If they're following God the way they followed me, with their own interests always in mind, then God can't be too proud."

Beausoleil, who started it all by killing Hinman, spends his incarceration composing music, including a score entitled "The Rise of Lucifer." Like Clem, he's had to survive at least one stabbing to continue his meager caged existence.

From a unity standpoint, Manson made a critical mistake in allowing his fellow cons to get a piece of his girls. Although the visiting-room groping sessions and release-night sexfests were bizarre and immoral, love can blossom in the strangest places. As with Kenneth Como, the ABs often fell in love with, and became fiercely possessive of, their sexy gifts from Charlie. Aside from Como and Gypsy Share, other long-term hookups included Mike Monfort and Nancy Pitman, James "Spider" Craig and Priscilla Cooper, and William "Chilly Willie" Goucher and Maria T. "Crystal" Alonzo. To the man, the first thing these jealous, violent felons did after falling for the beautiful girls was break them from their former master. Subsequently, Charlie ended up losing a half dozen or more of his most loyal disciples this way.

Despite the best efforts of Squeaky and Sandra to hold everyone together, preacher's daughter Ruth Ann "Ouisch" Morehouse, Sue Bartell, and Cathy Gillies also faded away.

T. J. Walleman, the biker who prepared Manson's escape hideout in the Panamint Valley, remained a faithful follower until he died suddenly and violently in June 1995. Walleman, fifty-two, smashed his pickup truck head-on into an eighteen-wheeler on U.S. 395, in Kern County, California. Investigators said that the longtime Manson disciple was trying to pass another vehicle and didn't make it. He left three young children and a wife who had taken the name "Anson" to honor Charlie.

Still, for every old follower who drifted off or died, there were a hundred more ready to sign up. These were mostly oddball, loner teenagers who worshiped Manson and expressed their undying love. They wrote passionate letters begging to join his Family and explaining how they understood and supported his message. This legion of misguided teens invariably volunteered their services as assassins. The letters that poured in, and the sentiments expressed, often made me wonder what kind of national sickness had taken hold out there in the heartland. One lady admirer, a professional who worked at a famous bank, wrote Manson a series of sexy letters filled with explicit come-ons. In her perfumed notes, she referred to him as "the god of fuck" and ached for a night in his arms. I'd read too many letters just like it to be shocked anymore. The world is full of strange, strange people.

Most of the letters were disturbing, but legal. A few crossed the bounds. One such series came from a woman named Misty Hay, aka Pat Gillum. The correspondence began innocently enough in 1976. Hay wrote about saving the environment and separating the races, making her at once both politically correct and incorrect. Alerted by some of her racist statements,

I investigated. Misty was married to a character named Herbert Darrell Hay, a con who served time with Manson in a CMF psychiatric unit in 1974. Herbert Hay was paroled on April 8, 1976, and vanished not long afterward. Herbert had professed a strong allegiance to Manson and frequently made threats against the President and other government leaders (and still was released!). When he disappeared, it was speculated that he was on a mission for Manson. The Secret Service put out an alert for him. Fortunately for the government guards, Herb wasn't smart enough to keep a low profile. Hitchhiking in Texas, the demented con rewarded the Good Samaritan who gave him a lift by shooting him in the head four times. He was caught, tried, convicted, and sentenced to life.

With her husband gone for good, Misty Hay turned her full attention to Manson and his latest activities. Charlie wrote the editor of the *Vacaville Reporter* that he'd sent out a list of people to be murdered. The targeted group consisted of President Carter and a host of people in the lumber industry. (This is not to be confused with Susan Atkins's prison-chatter, celebrity hit list that included Frank Sinatra, Tom Jones, Elizabeth Taylor, and Richard Burton, among others.)

Charlie's convoluted letter, sent to *Vacaville Reporter* city editor Greg deGiere, covered a host of subjects, including the Tate-LaBianca killings. "The murder list that was sent out was people who are responsible for the redwood trees being murdered," Manson scribbled. "I didn't kill anyone, but I broke no law. They are King James laws and old and somewhat useless for the space age. Lynn Fromme did more in my thoughts, and my attitude did and do effect her, as my attitude effects others, also others who know me and will be affected by my attitude. To put blame on Red [Squeaky], just reflects it back and reflects in thought balances that are not needed. Don't pass the blame around. To run the blame in circles, that don't put nothing in order, it just creates more confusion. What's the big deal about me being violent? Since time began my Family has always been just as violent as it takes to survive. Whenever the need comes to kill, there is always someone created to do the job that no one else wants to do. Fear and violence are just different levels of thoughts.

"Yes, I'm from a violent family, but what's new about that? Would you call a lawnmower violent when it is tempered and made to cut grass? The grass always grows up. Things on this earth that work for survival on this earth can live on this earth. Things like animals playing people who don't work for a useful purpose will not survive on this earth. Red like Blue [Sandra Good] like Green like the rest of the people that were helping me to do a job that no one else seems to be doing and if after seven years you still haven't seen the nine dead bodies and the writing in blood on the walls and the thoughts that started coming into the courtroom and the fears raining all over the world, then you will become what you have been killing your earth for, like the wildlife you've been killing for dog food.

"You all made me into a mass murderer and I have killed no one. Nixon dumped it all on me and covered it with a Watergate leaving me with what he had lost long ago, dispensation from the soul. As I was being made up as a mass murderer I seen how the people needed and wanted this because with the nuclear bombs we couldn't have an old kind of war because it would destroy the earth. To save the earth, the need for mass killing was put into nations. I never even thought of killing but that's what I've been programmed to balance. I didn't want the job, but all the cards came to me. I don't like sending a thing [the hit letter], like this out, but I don't see no other way. I realize this will probably fall back on me, but if someone don't get strong with the money mind, it's gonna eat the earth."

Charlie sent a follower a second letter that was passed on to deGiere that partially retracted the hits. "Murder is a penitentiary expression for a stupid act, a slow reaction to something, a mental retarded expression," Manson claimed, furiously backpedaling. "It doesn't mean a constant judgment of character."

That spin was news to me—and everybody else at the prison. "Murder" means murder in any environment.

"On clear cutting trees in parks. . . . The vote [U.S. Senate] went all the way to 90–0," Manson continued in letter number two. "That means some other country got a money knife running though the senate. My knife ain't money it's blood red and real to their wives. There is no place on earth to hide from the IPCR [International People's Court of Retribution]. Trees give air and the air is in trouble as it is, and it's sick in the waters from the fish because of the balance being off. If they [the senate] keep bringing up money laws that overlook their children, their wildlife, the trees, the water, the rest of the stuff I don't have time to write about, and if we don't stop it one way or the other the earth balance will get so bad that murder will be the only good thing left to do."

Charlie's puzzling, half-assed retraction was too late for Misty Hay. Encouraged by the original story, she threw away all subtlety in September 1976 and sent a signed death threat to the president of the Sierra Club. "Charles Manson has people watching you now . . . so do your part to stop them from cutting down trees, or else you'll be chopped up yourselves. For every tree you let be cut down, you shall have your limbs cut off. Take heed of this mean letter or die!" A similar letter was sent to A. A. Emerson, owner of the Arcata lumber mill. "Stop cutting the redwoods NOW! Work for change (from death to life) or die." This one was signed "M."

Misty was arrested, prosecuted, convicted, and sentenced to five years to life in a federal prison on the charge of sending threatening letters through the U.S. Postal Service. On the day of her sentencing, she wrote Charlie, praising the influence of Squeaky and Sandra while bemoaning the fact that now that she was a fellow felon, their pen-pal relationships would have to end. "Red sent me a letter saying that if I wanted to be with or near the 'Family' I must be under her and Blue. Those women have captured my soul and heart, and I want to be like them. I really miss your letters and the honest truth you wrote."

The scary part here is that Misty Hay had never visited or spoken to Charles Manson. She sacrificed her life for an illusion.

Scarier still was that Misty wasn't alone. A fifteen-year-old wrote a letter that was so loathsome that I called the FBI and read it to them over the phone. The writer begged Charlie to send her out on a murder mission, adding that even if the target was the President, that was okay. The FBI scooped her up a few days later. Her room was a shrine to Manson, complete with pictures of the cult leader pasted on her walls. Books and newspaper and magazine stories about him were scattered everywhere. Absorbing the Manson philosophy, her letter contained the parroted phrase "sometimes a little evil is necessary to accomplish a great thing."

The incident foreshadowed the strange "Lady in White" who appeared unannounced one day at Vacaville. The odd middle-aged woman with glassy blue-gray eyes wandered through the administration building dressed in a white flowing gown, white stockings, and white shoes. She sported a pearl-colored ribbon in her delicately curled, but somewhat unkempt, long brown hair. Those who saw her said she reminded them of Bette Davis in the movie *What Ever Happened to Baby Jane?* Despite her weird garb, Vacaville's Baby Jane made it all the way to the warden's office before her odd behavior and hesitant motions drew enough attention to have her questioned. Disturbed by her freaky answers, the guards searched her shiny white purse. They found she was hiding a twenty-four-inch railroad spike sharpened to a razor's edge in the folds of her dress.

"I've been sent by Charles Manson to perform an exorcism," she announced, raising a host of eyebrows. "Jesus was crucified with this spike. I'm going to use it to slay the demon who has possessed Manson's soul."

The startled guards called the police. Baby Jane was whisked away and booked as a "50/50," i.e., a crazy. She was charged with bringing a deadly weapon into a prison, a felony. The judge took one look at her, dropped the charge, and ordered some much needed psychiatric treatment.

Misty Hay, the teen, and Baby Jane were clumsy and obvious, making them easy to squash before they did any real harm. But sometimes blood was shed.

On January 26, 1977, a Hollywood movie producer named Laurence Merrick was shot to death from behind as he walked to an L.A. film school at 870 North Vine Street. His young assailant stalked him, fired in broad daylight, then ran off, never to be seen again. Merrick's name rang a bell with me, so I checked it out. What I discovered was frightening. Merrick, fifty, had teamed with a man named Robert Hendrickson to produce a damning documentary titled *Manson*. The producers befriended the post–Helter Skelter Manson Family and were granted widespread permission to film them at work and play, including a Woodstock-like nude group bathing scene. When the film aired, Squeaky and gang were shocked to discover that Hendrickson and Merrick threw out the flowers, serenity, and environmental activism and homed in on the drugs, sex, murders, and degradation. One of the few efforts to focus on the commune's children, the documentary painted a horrible picture of the youngsters fathered by Manson and others. According to the narrator, the hollow-eyed ragamuffins were required to smoke pot, drop acid, and participate in the widely publicized orgies. Despite its title, the film contained minimal footage of Manson himself, thus failing to capture his charisma and seductive powers. It did offer chilling interviews with many of his followers, including baby-faced Paul Watkins's comments that Manson once told him that he wanted to go on a murder spree to "cut the dicks off of little boys and put them in their mother's mouths." Criticized in some circles for its emotionally exhausting graphic scenes and shocking language, it was nevertheless justifiably nominated for an Academy Award.

San Francisco Examiner reviewer Jeanne Miller wrote in 1976 that "the most frightening aspect of the film were interviews with Squeaky Fromme and Sandra Good, bright-eyed, apple-cheeked . . . who discussed their gruesome activities with serene smiles and unremorseful comments like 'What's the big deal? Five or six people get killed and you all freak out and put it on us.'" (Putting Good's face and voice to that often repeated quote.) Fromme went on to fondly caress barrels of rifles and knives as she and Sandra described how Charlie convinced them that murder was a creative act. "If somebody needs to be killed, you do it. Death is love."

The film was fraught with problems from the onset. Finished in 1972, a series a legal hurdles, including judges banning its showing prior to the trials of various Family members, stalled its release until November 5, 1975. (The delays may have lengthened Merrick's life.) The documentary aired on television in early 1976 while Manson was still at San Quentin. It was broadcast shortly after I'd instituted a new policy that allowed inmates to watch television. Manson was thus able to see the program. "Lies! Lies! Lies!" he raged, cursing the show and threatening its producers.

After Merrick's murder, the investigating homicide detectives interviewed some of the film school's students. They reported that on the morning of the murder, a scraggly young man had been seen loitering across the street near a small store. He was about five feet ten, stocky, and wore blue jeans, a T-shirt, a yellow cap, and sunglasses. The youth pestered the budding filmmakers about Merrick, the school (which Sharon Tate once attended), and the Manson documentary. After the shooting, the strange young man vanished into the cracks.

In a conversation with me, Manson appeared to take credit for the hit. Fuming over some minor incident shortly afterward, he threatened,

"You know, Ed, the same thing that happened to Merrick could happen to you!"

Merrick had been embraced by Manson and his Family, and then turned "snitch" when he skewered them in his finished product. Of all the world's sins, snitching was the one the prison-reared Manson could never tolerate.

As I followed the Merrick investigation, I wondered which one of the letters that had crossed my desk may have come from the mystery man who killed the producer.

In May 1977, Charlie used his powers of persuasion to turn his own assassin into a follower! A psychiatric patient at CMF told prison author-ities that he had been ordered to clip Manson by the Aryan Brothers. To get close to his target, he befriended Charlie and waited for the right opportunity. However, a funny thing happened on the way to Manson's funeral—the inmate began to fall under the cult leader's spell! A few ses-sions at the feet of the master were all it took to convince this hardened killer to abandon his plot and join the revolution. The inmate's feelings were so strong that he chose to double-cross the ABs, an act of suicide considering the gang's vast influence inside the California prison system. Three weeks later, the paranoid inmate slit the throat of another prisoner in the psychiatric unit. The attacker testified that the victim, who survived, was an assassin coming to erase him for refusing to take out Manson. Charlie's newest disciple—his life in tatters in record time—was placed in psychiatric lockup for his, and everyone else's, safety.

After the assassin problem was defused, a young ragamuffin named Linda started camping at the front gate with a small boy in tow, begging to see Manson. When she wasn't hassling the guards, she was on the phone pleading with me. The pair was destitute and apparently had nowhere to go. I referred her to the local social service agency, and she was provided with lodging near the prison. Linda never really explained what she thought Manson could do for her, but continued to call and write for months before she simply vanished.

Next, a young man stumbled to the gate stoned on acid, demanding to see Manson. He walked around in circles, screaming that his head was on fire and electricity was shooting between his ears. Manson, he said, was the only person who had the ability to ease his torment. The police came and carted him away.

In September 1982, yet another person connected to Manson was in-volved in a murder. The victim was a diminutive teenage drifter named Joe Hoover. The motive, as usual, was snitching. Hoover's executioner was Perry "Red" Wartham, a skinny, bespectacled Nazi sympathizer. A post–Helter Skelter follower, Wartham visited Manson at CMF numerous times beginning in the early 1970s and expressed his dream of starting a chapter of the National Socialist Party in Oroville. Arrested for murder once, Wartham was acquitted. Neither that nor a subsequent stay in a mental institution was enough to allow us to legally prevent the visits from continuing — even when we knew the pair were up to no good.

Wartham and Manson began their relationship by trading letters filled with plans for setting up a ranch to train an army of young neo-Manson Nazis. Manson was interested enough to send his queen, Squeaky, to check him out. Wartham apparently passed the Squeaky test, as the correspondence progressed to face-to-face visits. The more he associated with Manson, the more Wartham came to be like him. He told anyone who'd listen that he wanted to build his organization from the sturdy young white stock Manson used, the uncared for, unwanted runaways who were willing to kill and die fighting the system. Unlike others who were all bluster, Wartham actually set out after his prized recruits, frequently wandering through area towns passing out vile Nazi literature and hustling naive teens.

"He talked about Manson all the time . . . more than he talked about Hitler," recalled a female friend. "His big plan was to go up to some site in the Sierra foothills which Manson would designate and start an all-white colony."

A former neighbor of Wartham added that "he smoked weed heavy and talked about death all the time, like it was a joke."

Wartham's efforts, despite his determination and crazed energy, were going nowhere. He lacked charisma and was a poor leader, making it difficult to attract followers. In contrast, his hero, Manson, had been a magnet for alienated youth and had accomplished so much through the Tate-LaBianca murders. In Wartham's sick mind, that meant in order to gain Manson's respect, he had to "make his bones" the way Squeaky had, or at least had tried to when she went after President Ford.

Joe Hoover was one of Wartham's small circle of Nazi recruits. He had reluctantly gone along when his best friend, Rafe Barker, and a fourteen-year-old named Chris Jones threw in with the wanna-be neo-Hitler. Hoover's friends had been swayed by a personally signed photo of Manson and Wartham standing beside each other in the visitors room at CMF. The photo was enough to convince the youths that they were part of something special. Wartham might have been an uninspiring drip, but he had big-time connections! Through him, the boys could boast that they were members of the infamous Manson Family.

Somewhere along the line, Hoover couldn't stomach the hate Wartham preached and decided to do something about it. He told the police that his friends Rafe and Chris were the ones who had stuffed racist pamphlets in the lockers of the local high school. One can imagine Wartham's rage, and then his elation after discovering Hoover's betrayal. He would now have the opportunity to enact his hero's most cherished credo, "Kill all snitches."

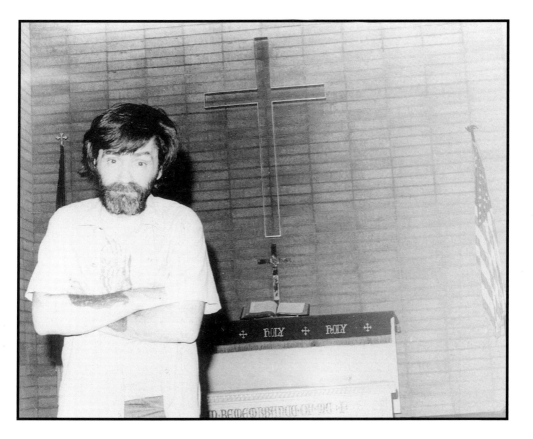

SACRILEGIOUS AS IT MAY SEEM,
Charlie worked in the prison chapel at
the California Medical Facility (CMF)
in the early 1980s.

(PHOTO: NUEL EMMONS)

CMF PROTESTANT CHAPLAIN NICK RISTAD
gave Charlie a job and a shot at living in population.
Charlie responded by planning an escape through the attic.

(PHOTO: NUEL EMMONS)

SQUEAKY AND SANDRA

begged me incessantly to give Charlie a patch
of land on which to grow flowers and strum
one of his numerous guitars. I obliged.

(PHOTO: NUEL EMMONS)

THE "CUCKOO'S NEST" TYPES
who flocked to the chapel were not coming to worship God.
They wanted to serve under a guru
many have likened to the devil.

(PHOTO: NUEL EMMONS)

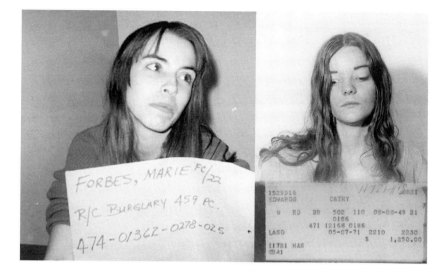

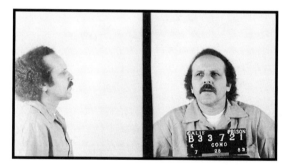

The Family Lives on.

Charlie's followers, both old and new, hung together for decades after his incarceration. Many of the girls became the lovers of his cellmates. Some even married. Here are Maria Alonzo [top left] and Priscilla Cooper [top right], after being arrested. As evidenced by these police photos, the girls frequently used aliases. The man pictured is Kenneth Como, escape artist and Manson attacker.

CHARLIE'S MOST LOYAL FOLLOWERS,

Sandra Good [top] and Lynette "Squeaky" Fromme [bottom]. Squeaky thrust Charlie back into the spotlight when she tried to assassinate President Gerald Ford in 1975. She wrote to me that she attempted to kill the President because I wouldn't allow her to visit her master at San Quentin.

(SANDRA GOOD PHOTO: NUEL EMMONS, SQUEAKY PHOTO: DICK SCHMIDT, SACRAMENTO BEE)

THE MEDIA STAR YEARS.
A spaced-out Charlie with Tom Snyder.
He probably had a fat joint before this
thoroughly lackluster performance.

(PHOTO: NUEL EMMONS)

LIGHTS, CAMERAS, ACTION.
A clear-headed Charlie ready to go on with
another eager broadcast journalist.

GIVING THE OL' EVIL EYE
to a newspaper reporter.

_____

(PHOTO: NUEL EMMONS)

CALIFORNIA STATE PRISON
D 63417
CMF
W · SPANN
8   16   89

PRESIDENT JIMMY CARTER'S "BAD PEANUT" NEPHEW, WILLIE SPANN, shared the media spotlight for a while with his on-again-off-again jailhouse buddy Charlie. They had a falling out when, according to Spann, Charlie threatened to have the President's beloved mother, Miss Lillian, killed by one of his minions. Unlike Charlie, the hard-living, hard-luck Willie aged badly and died in early 1997 at the age of 50.

PREACHING TO THE CHOIR.

(PHOTO, BOTTOM: NUEL EMMONS)

CHARLIE REUNITED
with his longtime prison buddy Roger "Pin
Cushion" Dale at Corcoran in late 1996. "Pin"
earned his moniker for being the most stabbed
inmate in correctional history.

(PHOTO: COURTESY OF ROGER DALE SMITH)

STILL GIVING THE CREEPY STARE
after all these years.

(PHOTO: ROGER DALE SMITH)

CHARLIE AS A NATIVE AMERICAN WITCH DOCTOR, late 1996. With his Native American artifacts and a boombox, Charlie continues to dance to his own music— in some cases literally. He's finally had some albums released, fulfilling a lifelong dream.

IN LATE 1996, PIN, CHARLIE, AND I reminisced about the good old days at San Quentin and CMF. Both men remain in excellent physical condition.

(PHOTO, TOP: ROGER DALE SMITH)
(PHOTO, BOTTOM: COURTESY OF ROGER DALE SMITH)

Text visible in photo (partially cut off):

ATES ARE RESPONSIBLE TO CLEAN THEIR TABLE AND
STACK THE CHAIRS UPON END OF THE VISIT.
EN WALKING HOLDING HANDS IS PERMITTED.
MATES ARE RESPONSIBLE FOR KNOWING & ADHERING TO
L VISITING ROOM RULES.
TER ENTERING VISITING ROOM, VISITOR   OT BE
LOWED TO LEAVE&RETURN,EXCEPT IN C   ERGENCY.
LY FIVE VISITORS PER INMATE. INCLU   EN.
IS A FELONY TO BRING   OLIC B   GS-
RCOTICS-WEAPONS-A   S-EXP   R GAS-
AR GAS WEAPONS IN   XA
JACENT PROPERTY.
O RUNNING.

AFTER I ENDURED THREATS

and two late-night witch's-brew dousings because of this book, Charlie and I kissed and made up in early 1997. This is my most recent photo with my most memorable inmate. Charlie, now well into his sixties, looks like he could easily charm a family of young recruits today if given the chance.

(PHOTO: ROGER DALE SMITH)

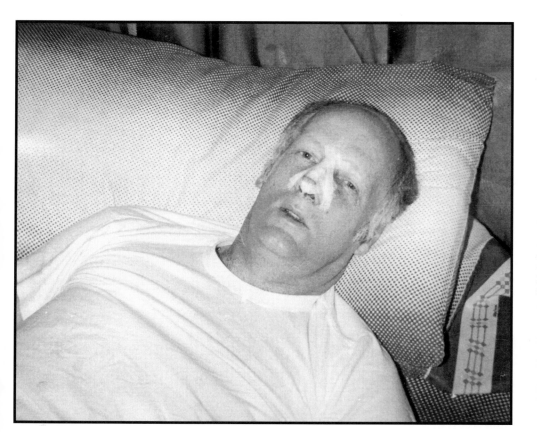

Lest I ever forget

who I'm dealing with, this shot is a chilling reminder.
Charlie claimed it was one of his voodoo doll curses
that caused an inmate inexplicably to go berserk and
shatter my nose and teeth. Charlie similarly took
credit for a terrifying incident that nearly caused
me to drown while vacationing in Hawaii.

(Photo: Beth George)

THE SELF-PROCLAIMED 1960S MESSIAH.
Will he ever be allowed to ride again?

(PHOTO: NUEL EMMONS)

Wartham, Barker, and Jones took the unsuspecting Hoover down a dirt road on the outskirts of town and proceeded to carry out Manson's Law. Taking the lead, Wartham shot Hoover eight times in the head while the youth's former friends watched. Afterward, Wartham turned to the boys and growled, "This is what will happen to you if you ever snitch." It was a frightening and seemingly effective demonstration—and was promptly ignored. After all three were arrested, Barker and Jones quickly cut a deal, snitching out Wartham and paving the way for the Nazi creep to join Manson in a life behind bars.

At his sentencing, Oroville judge Lloyd Mulkey allowed Wartham to read a long prepared statement into the record. Wartham ripped the Jewish-controlled media, condemned the justice system, and blasted a mixed-race society. It was a standard Manson tirade, only minus the charisma and power. Left to their own merits, the words hung in the air like rancid clouds.

When it was all over, the story was sadly the same. Another Manson disciple had risen, killed, and fallen, and now was locked away forever, a life ruined.

That, however true, is an admittedly biased conclusion. Biased from me, biased from the aspect of civilized society, but biased nonetheless. Instead of squandering his life, Wartham viewed himself as a revolutionary hero. His worship of Manson gave his worthless life meaning.

Inside the prison system, the same thing was happening among men whose existences were even more worthless—convicts who had already destroyed their lives before meeting Charlie. A prime example was a Folsom felon named Dennis, a budding sycophant whose banned letters were smuggled in to Manson through various means. I intercepted this doozy:

". . . I did not lose faith in you. You asked me once if I'd kill for you and I said 'no.' But a child of torture such as I has been taught much since I said 'no' to my 'love.' . . . But I'd kill for you, for I'd kill for truth, and you are the truth and you are greater than I. . . . To cut you out of my heart would be to cut out my heart. . . .

I'd be dead in my aloneness without little guys like you to fight for. . . . Without you I could not be 'Billy Jack.' . . . You're me, and I am you, and the heart of the lion still roars one truth!. . . . You lead the children into prison! Prison is the only safe place to be. . . . If it wasn't for me learning in your love, how could I teach you that we are tough with one thought that doesn't think, it knows? It just knows. . . .

In the end, the worshipful Dennis did what so many of the other men had—he courted, married, and disconnected one of Charlie's girls.

As the 1970s came to an end and the other original followers began drifting away, the hooded sisters Squeaky and Sandra merely strengthened their resolve. Manson could always depend upon them to be the spool to wrap his new followers around. As long as they stayed true, the Family would never die. Manson was (and remains) the driving force of Red and Blue's lives. Without him, they would have nothing. Their letters alternated between cheerful optimism and dark depression over the forced separation. Sandra referred to both Charlie and Squeaky as "the only two friends in the world that I can trust." Red's and Blue's ultimate dream was to win their release so they could move near Charlie's prison and be close enough to feel his vibes in the air.

In my own way, I, too, had been feeding on Charlie's vibes. It was different than with his girls, but no less powerful. I used him to get through my workday, perk me up, amuse me, give me encouragement, entertain me, make me laugh, and make me angry. He was also a great stress reliever. If things got crazy at the prison, I simply escaped into Charlie's unique world. When the CMF cafeteria became overrun with roaches, I tolerated it until the situation reached riot proportions. All efforts to go through proper channels proved fruitless. Taking a cue from Charlie, I marched into the warden's office and demanded action. "Will you call the food manager and chew his ass?" The warden hesitated, so I lowered the boom. "Have you heard about the leper we had on the food line last week serving food? That would have started a riot if the inmates found out."

"How did that happen?" the warden asked, suddenly concerned.

"The assignment lieutenant didn't know the medical term for leprosy. That's the way riots start. That's the way guards and doctors get killed!" I stormed out, marched down the tier, and immediately pulled Manson from his cell. "Tell me a story, Charlie!" I demanded.

"Which one?"

"Any one," I said. "Anything's better than the insanity I just experienced."

As Manson began speaking, I thought of a quote I'd long ago memorized from William Wordsworth:

> The world is too much with us; late and soon,
> Getting and spending, we lay waste our powers:
> Little we see in Nature that is ours;
> We have given our hearts away, a sordid boon!

Manson read my mood and shifted gears, repeating a familiar joust. "Soon, you will be an old man, working hard, killing yourself, living in a paper bag. When will you stop chasing money and become free like us?"

It was a good suggestion. The problem was, the "guru" making it spent his life caged in a tiny cell. That wasn't exactly the freedom I envisioned.

Yet, there was no mistaking that from inside that cell, and inside a man with an unmistakable dark, evil side, there was a spark of life that could never be quenched. We could cut off Charlie's arms and legs, but we could never kill his spirit. Kill it or, unfortunately, change it.

The next day, a bored guard amused himself by taunting Charlie, working the cult leader into a frenzy like a child teasing a fenced pit bull. When I passed by, Manson decided to turn his anger on me. "Damn you, Ed, this is your fault. Did you know that you're on my hit list!" he raged, striking a particularly mean posture. I felt my blood rise until he added the kicker. "But you're so far down the list, I'll probably never get to you!"

I nearly doubled over with laughter. As I walked away, I could hear Manson roaring in his cell, enjoying his joke. The following morning, he greeted me in particularly good cheer. "I got mine last night, did you get yours?" he cracked, wiping his lips with his forearm, mumbling about his latest wet dream.

The good mood didn't last long. A few days later, Charlie threw a major tantrum over some meaningless nonsense and set his bed on fire. He put it out by clogging the sink and flooding the floor. He was dragged kicking and screaming into isolation. When I arrived to check him out, he started railing against some minor procedural flaw.

"Hey, what's with you? You know the score," I admonished. "It's not like perfection is the goal of the Department of Corrections."

He rolled his eyes and shifted topics. "Bring me my letters," he demanded, all too eager to recruit some new assassins.

"No way," I responded, noting his homicidal mood. "Just cool down. You pissed everybody off with your fire and flood stunt, so lay low for a while."

"Well, bring me my two cockroaches. The ones I was raising."

"What?"

"I captured a pair of cockroaches. I was going to raise them, but they escaped. Track them down for me."

I looked into his eyes, the feared eyes of a maniacal killer. There it was, the first honest trace of compassion. He wasn't bullshitting. Charlie had actually been sheltering a pair of pet roaches.

"I'm not tracking down any roaches," I said. "But there's hope for you yet."

"Fuck you!" he screamed as I walked away. It was almost as if he'd been insulted by my compliment.

After he did his isolation time and was released to his home cell, I immediately pulled him out to resume our daily chats.

"All these reporters don't know shit," he spat, looking through the latest media requests. "Why don't you interview me?"

"Why?"

"Because you ask the right questions."

"I thought you hated my questions. I don't let you get away with all that bullshit."

"I do hate them. But that doesn't mean they're not the right questions."

"The trouble is, Charlie, you never give the right answers."

A week later, Charlie began behaving oddly every time I passed his cell. He appeared to be holding something in his hand. As each day passed, he made it more and more obvious. Knowing he was dying for me to ask, I refused, giving him back a little of his own medicine. Finally, on the third day, his eyes shifted back and forth between me and his hand. He was all but begging me to inquire.

"Okay, I'll bite. What's in your hand, Charlie?"

He smiled with glee and beckoned me closer. I felt a tinge of fear, wondering what surprise he had in store. Was it an exploding cap, or a handful of some kind of industrial acid? Would he try to blind me for all those penetrating questions I'd asked him over the years? Despite my misgivings, I edged forward, too curious to be cautious. Charlie elevated his palm and spread open his fingers. Cradled inside was a single sparrow egg. I was pretty stunned. I was expecting a bomb, not a baby.

"Think it'll hatch?" he chirped like a small boy.

"I don't know. How'd you get that?" I asked. I knew that birds commonly built nests on the ledges outside the tier windows, but they were all out of Manson's reach. The maintenance crew routinely (and rather heartlessly) knocked the nests off with brooms, splatting the eggs on the asphalt below. Manson had spotted one within his eyesight and begged the crews to leave it alone.

"Just wait until the eggs hatch and the babies can fly. It'll only take a couple of weeks," he pleaded. The crew ignored him, following sanitary procedures and clearing the window of the offending nest. Before knocking it off, one of the men had a rare moment of human kindness, either for the bird, Manson, or both. He pulled a tiny egg from the nest and gave it to the world's most notorious criminal.

"Think it will hatch?" Manson repeated, desperate for my affirmation.

"I don't know, Charlie. If anybody can make it hatch, you can."

Charles Manson held that egg in his hand for weeks, cherishing it, talking to it, willing the baby bird to emerge.

It never did.

12

CHARLIE SPENT A great deal of time at CMF unraveling socks, shirts, and sweaters and using the yarn to weave mobiles, cockroach cages, and those annoying little voodoo dolls. At San Quentin, where the hard-ass guards were bitter and cynical, nobody really cared about his creations. At CMF, it was a different story. The treatment-oriented staff, heavy on New Age shrinks and counselors, were more fearful of the occult. Every month or so, someone would wander by my office, pace around for a while, then nervously enter. After some small talk, he'd get to the point.

"Uh, Ed, you know those, uh, dolls Manson makes? Do you think . . ."

"No way," I'd assure him. "He's got power, but not that kind of power."

"Are you sure? One of those dolls looks a lot like me."

"That's what everybody says," I'd laugh. "It's an illusion. You're seeing things through your own fears. He's playing with your head. That's what he lives for. Just ignore it."

Even a few members of CMF's tougher-minded custody staff were unnerved by Charlie's dolls. The rumor spread that he was reproducing images of guards he didn't like, casting evil spells, and puncturing them with needles taken from new shirt packages late at night. A couple of officers came to my office, asking if there was anything they could do about it. I brushed them off. "You guys have been watching too much television."

The day before I left for a much needed vacation, Charlie and I had a big pissing match. He resented the fact that I could have vacations and he couldn't, and spared no effort telling me about it. The argument ended with his standard threats. I thought nothing of it, too busy thinking about my upcoming days languishing on the beautiful beaches of Hawaii. Near the end of the splendid trip, I was swimming off Waikiki when I was caught in a powerful undertow known as the "Molokai Express" after the train that used to travel into the heart of Hawaii's famous leper colony. For me, the ominous analogy was an understatement. I fought for my life, swimming to the point of exhaustion to keep from being sucked all the way to Japan. Weakening, my only option was to cling to some coral until the rushing water eased. Thankfully, it vanished as quickly as it had appeared, enabling me to flop my way to the beach. When I tried to stand, I felt a sharp pain in my right leg. Somehow, I'd injured it during the struggle.

A noticeable limp remained when I arrived back at CMF. The moment Manson saw me, he renewed his prevacation tirade. "You better shape up or I'll take the other leg," he bellowed.

"What?"

"I put a curse on you to scare you, but I didn't use enough needles to kill you," he explained, affecting his most sinister look. "A few more pins and you'd be dead."

"Well, if that's true, you almost got me there," I said, half serious. After that incident, I was far more sympathetic to the guards and doctors who knocked on my door worrying about Charlie's dolls.

Not surprisingly, Manson soon began getting his hands on banned contraband in order to make other things. The feeling was, if he busied himself building something else, he wouldn't spend his time making dangerous voodoo dolls. In short order, he'd crafted a miniature electric fan about three inches tall, complete with a skillfully wound rotor. The materials, including numerous magnets and batteries, came from old radio parts.

"Damn, that's pretty impressive," I complimented as the little blades spun. Charlie smiled, extremely pleased with himself. The possibility existed that if he could make such a fan, he could also construct a motorized weapon of some kind. Regardless, the guards ignored it, happy that it wasn't another doll.

The following month, Manson stood in his cell holding a tiny mandolin.

"Where'd you get that?" I asked.

"I made it!"

"No you didn't."

"Yes I did."

Sure enough, he showed me how he'd ingeniously crafted the little instrument using some guidelines from a book. He strummed it, playing a sweet tune. As I stood admiring his workmanship, he cracked an evil smile, dropped it to the floor, and stomped it into little pieces with his foot.

"What the hell did you do that for?"

"You figure it out," he challenged.

Call me stupid, but I just didn't get it. Although typical of his impulsive, masochistic behavior, what was the point? Why work so hard on something so beautiful, only to destroy it for a few seconds of shock value? Then again, isn't that exactly what Charles Manson always did? Whether it was a guitar, a radio, a television, an impressionable young girl, or an entire family of devoted disciples, Charlie always seemed to destroy what he cherished the most. Strange little dude.

Charlie drew his next line in the sand over baby oil. Some of the night guards began secretly slipping him the solution to burn in a little lamp he made. The day crew felt he was using the illumination to stay up all night and make more voodoo dolls. Every morning, they'd confiscate whatever he had left. On the third morning, instead of letting the day guards take it, Charlie poured his entire supply over his head, anointing himself like a biblical king. He stood there, grinning devilishly, as the officer stumbled over what to do.

"Fu-fuck you, Charlie," the guard stuttered, leaving in a huff.

That night brought a new supply. Realizing that the day officer was going to go berserk, Charlie prepared for his arrival by soaking a sheet and using it to tie his cell door shut. When the officer stormed to his cell, Charlie lit a match and set the oily cloth ablaze. The show earned him another stint in isolation, but from Charlie's perspective, it was well worth it. He'd beaten the system again.

The longer Charlie stayed at CMF, the more his cell began to take on the appearance of his home at San Quentin. Bit by bit, the smoke-scarred walls swelled with pictures of natural landscapes and animals, mostly from *National Geographic*. This particular montage was heavy into predatory animals like wolves, eagles, and bears. As I admired his decorative work one afternoon, he put it into perspective as only he could. "I'd rather kill a man than a snake!"

That statement, twisted as it was, stayed with me for days. There was something about it that sparked a memory of a passage from a book I'd once read. Searching through my library, I finally tracked it down. It was Edward Abbey's *Desert Solitaire*, the account of his lonely sojourn in the arid wilds. I perused it with new eyes, amazed how Abbey meshed natural beauty with savage violence—just like Charlie.

> Cutting the bloody cord, that's what we feel, the delirious exhilaration of independence, a rebirth backward in time and into primeval liberty, into freedom in the most simple, literal, primitive meaning of the word, the only meaning that really counts. The freedom, for example, to commit murder and get away with it scot-free, with no other burden than the jaunty halo of conscience . . . My God! I'm thinking of the incredible shit we put up with most of our lives, the domestic routine, same old wife every night, the stupid, useless, and degrading jobs, the insufferable arrogance of elected officials, the crafty cheating and the slimy advertising of the businessmen, the boring wars in which we kill our buddies instead of our real enemies back in the capital, the foul, diseased, and hideous cities and towns we live in . . . the useless crap we bury ourselves in day by day, while patiently enduring the creeping strangulation.

In other words, "Soon you will be an old man, working hard, killing yourself, living in a paper bag. When will you stop chasing money and become free like us?"

Manson's problem was that, unlike Abbey, he wasn't geared toward literature. He could grip an audience orally, but had difficulty putting his thoughts down in writing. Squeaky, on the other hand, was just the opposite. Her speeches lacked force, mainly because of her tinny voice. But give her a pencil and paper, and the girl could move you. I was never sure whether Charlie admired her talent, or resented it. A clue came in May 1978. Squeaky submitted a riveting article to *Rolling Stone* that the editors were anxious to print. Although she was eager to spread the word to the magazine's young readers, she refused to allow its publication without her master's approval. Instead of giving his queen her moment in the sun—and promoting himself to boot—Charlie squashed it. His lame excuse was that *Rolling Stone* was Jewish-controlled and he wanted nothing to do with their dirty money. Lynette docilely accepted his decision.

Even without the infusion of publicity the *Rolling Stone* article would have provided, Manson's mailbag remained full. As the years passed, I was disturbed by a transformation that was taking place. Time was muting the horror of Manson's actions while amplifying his celebrity. Instead of sacks overflowing with the musings of crackpots, a wave of letters started coming from respectable citizens and organizations. The leader of the Cascade Council Camp Fire Girls in Washington wrote requesting that Charlie be allowed to speak to her group! Seems the girls had taken a vote on which person in the whole world they would like to talk to. Former president Richard Nixon was first, and Manson was a close second. Nixon brushed them off, so they came to Charlie. I immediately called the lady who wrote the letter, explaining that the last thing she should ever want to do was to expose her impressionable charges to a man known for turning young women into sexually depraved murderers. The troop leader saw the folly of her ways and withdrew the request. After I hung up, I visualized the scene had it occurred. There, around a blazing campfire, would be all these fresh-faced little suburban girls. In the center, hopping around like a drug-crazed Rumpelstiltskin, would be Manson. With eyes ablaze, he'd tell them that the key to life is to drop acid, give voracious blow jobs on command, and happily submit to being sodomized in the dirt. Once so enlightened, they would then be encouraged to rise up and hack their parents to death.

Esquire magazine followed by asking for Manson's favorite dirty joke. They wanted to include it in a section consisting of fellow celebrities like movie stars, athletes, and politicians. A Canadian wax museum requested permission to cast Charlie in wax. Doctors wrote from around the world insisting they could cure him. Researchers from major universities sent detailed questionnaires as part of their highbrow studies. Ministers offered to convert him to their various beliefs and promised to remember him in their prayers. Since it wasn't necessary to censor these fine folks, Manson read them all, passing the best ones to Squeaky or Sandra to put on file. For what? That remained a mystery.

I searched the records for some insight into this mystery. Bingo. The previous year, in May 1977, Sandra had filed a blistering legal brief that offered a possible answer. Sandra was appealing her federal conviction for mailing a staggering three thousand threatening letters to corporations and individuals on behalf of a post–Helter Skelter Manson offshoot organiza-tion called the International People's Court of Retribution (IPCR). The

IPCR was a more palatable place to herd those who believed in theory with some of the Family's pro-environment ideas, but weren't ready to engage in the violent, crazy stuff. Sandra's document provides a brilliant insight into the mind of a devoted Manson follower. Although she was desperate to win her freedom, her slavish loyalty to Charlie came through loud and clear, destroying any chance she had of actually winning her otherwise well-stated argument.

> In the weeks subsequent to Lynette Fromme's visit to President Ford in Capitol Park . . . defendant [Sandra] . . . made strong statements regarding the consequences of environmental destruction . . . If I warn you your house is on fire, it does not mean I set the fire, rather I give you a chance to save your house and your life. . . . The fact that the defendant was seen as the threat, rather than the threat being the problems she spoke of and the consequences of not facing and dealing with these problems is something you must look at. . . .
>
> Good argued that in the seven years since the Tate-LaBianca murders, a vast myth has been created called the Manson Family. She reasoned that the killings had to be understood as "seven more murders in Los Angeles," which had occurred "amidst a time of war in Asia, international political intrigue and assassination, and social and political and environmental dissolution in this country. . . . A cross-section of white Christian children took the lives of seven people at the same time young American men were killing and being killed in Vietnam. . . ." Good continued: "The world watched as President Nixon said that Manson was guilty. An opportunity was provided for lawyers to get publicity, district attorneys and judges to gain political advancement and scores of media people and book writers to create stories and get rich selling the most marketable items—sex and violence. A myth and monster was created in true Hollywood style and the public has devoured it. No one understands or even has a small glimpse of the real family. . . . In Good's view "the Family was convicted by public frenzy and fear," she had been judged unfairly as "another 'mad Manson maniac' that's got to be locked up before she 'gets in our house.' . . . As it stands, lies and illusions cover all that we have to offer and explain the thoughts that are running this country to violence and anarchy and the lies that cover us will leave the United States looking like the Tate house. . . ."
>
> Returning to her defense of the letters, Good conceded that "in many cases, the letters were worded shockingly strong," but defended them as having been sent "to people whose activities have been shockingly devastating to life. Companies who knowledgeably

cause cancer-causing elements to flood our air, waters, food; industries that tear up the earth and destroy the life on it for resources to make products that we do not need to live are not sane, reasonable, concerned people who can be pleaded with to stop. . . . By warning these people of what will befall them, they were being given a chance to save their own lives by presenting to them an alternative whereby they would leave something other than poisoned air, water, concrete and death for our children. . . . By law, defendant should not have come to prison for warning, and you will see much death that she did not cause but warned to prevent. Who has concern enough to risk prison for telling the mean truth that no one wants to hear? . . ."

Sandra's appeal, suffice it to say, was denied. She did, however, win a major victory six months later when she was transferred to Alderson Federal Prison in West Virginia—home of those two squabbling, fun girls, Squeaky and fellow presidential assassin wanna-be Sara Jane Moore. Like Lynette, Sandra had no use for Moore, but she was in heaven being with her best pal Squeaky. Their letters took on a decidedly upward beat, especially when they were ripping Moore, something they did with relish.

"She has no thought to replace it [the existing government structure] but with her own, superimposed on old photos of Lenin and Marx. She's like the head of these people because she had all the words. She's snotty, almost aristocratic. She was married to a wealthy man, a doctor of some kind I've heard, in the San Francisco area. She drops names like a society gossip. I've heard her talking to greedy black women about shopping at Saks Fifth Avenue. Only Godless blacks will listen to her long, even though her offers of money are tempting. She gathers fools and instigates discontent. She's good at her job."

In the same letter, Squeaky, writing for both herself and Sandra, gave their updated take on the race issue. "We see how the black people have been taught to follow the white Hollywood images. We said that race mixing destroys both their race and ours and you can't have one without the other. It has nothing to do with hate, but hateful people of all races and self destructive people of all races will be destroyed. That the debt must be paid to earth and the future of our children, not to the past thoughts of debt."

After that, they relayed an interesting conversation they'd had with a television cameraman regarding the Manson Family's association with the famous musical group the Beach Boys. The original version of the band included brothers Brian and Dennis Wilson. (As an aside, Charlie helped pen the group's song "Never Learn Not to Love," which he had called "Cease to Exist.")

"He [the cameraman] asked about Dennis Wilson. He'd seen Dennis on TV say that his brother, Brian . . . [wanted] to get him away from us and how that had straightened out his head. . . . "The cameraman used to be a big fan of theirs but said they'd lost their creativity. Blue said that was because they had been untrue to you [Charlie]."

The letter ended with the ladies asking me to assure Charlie they still had their girlish figures. "Please tell Charlie that Blue and I are doing and being okay, in good shape, 106–110, not fat, and thoughts of him keep us going."

With their auras reunited, the joined light of Squeaky and Sandra blazed brighter than two separate beams—at least when it came to adoring Charlie. His Christmas package from them that year was a whopper. There were colorful handkerchiefs, bandannas, an embroidered red headband, a blue scarf, a black silk scarf, cloth shoes, slippers, two flannel long-sleeved plaid shirts, a blue sweatshirt with an owl embroidered on the pocket, two black short-sleeved T-shirts with intricate embroidery patches on the front, four colored T-shirts (red, gold, and two shades of blue), three black knit caps, a pair of flared Levi's with embroidered pockets and fly, a rainbow-colored yarn belt, a harmonica, a booklet on Martin guitars, and some maps. Charlie was easily the hippest, most well-dressed inmate at CMF!

Actually, most of the goods weren't allowed, but I bent the rules and let him have the bulk of it. A colorful Charlie was a content Charlie, and that made life easier for everyone. Of course, that meant a new wave of extra-special voodoo dolls would soon be dotting his cell, but that was too dark a thought for Christmas.

It had been a strange year, all the way around. The previous August, a theology student preparing for the priesthood spent some time at the CMF to get hands-on experience in starting prison ministries. Tim was a young man aspiring to the priesthood who really threw himself into his work. When he asked to be locked up overnight in Willis—home of our most dangerous felons—I didn't hesitate. Not only didn't I hesitate, I plunked the guy into the cell next to Manson! From 8:30 A.M. Friday until 10:30 A.M. Saturday, Tim was locked down in a maximum-security cell a few feet from the world's most feared criminal.

Charlie reacted to having a budding young priest next to him the same way the girl in *The Exorcist* reacts to sharing her space with Father Karras. The crazed cult leader spent practically the whole time ranting, raving, cursing, threatening, blaspheming God, foaming at the mouth, and jumping around his cell like the floor was on fire. He did everything but vomit torrents of pea soup into Tim's cage. A black inmate on the opposite side of Charlie spent the evening repeating over and over in a monotonous tone, "Charlie, Charlie, Charlie," trying to keep the little maniac from busting a vein.

In the early-morning hours, Charlie finally wore himself down and began to speak in a more civilized manner. He told Tim his life story and offered his disturbing personal philosophy in a typically charismatic manner. It was, not surprisingly, an evening the clerical student would never forget.

"How'd it go?" I asked the suddenly haggard-looking young man the next morning.

"The night brought no rest," he sighed.

Tim made it all the way to the priesthood, then switched to a more unorthodox strain so he could marry and have a family. He moved to New Orleans to work with the poor and underprivileged. For all his devotion, he never asked to be housed next to Manson again.

Failing to take a cue from the priest, three FBI agents marched into CMF one afternoon in 1978 demanding an audience with Manson. They wanted to interrogate him regarding some unspecified case they were working. I winked at one of my officers and welcomed them inside the unit classification office. The stern, clean-cut agents hardly got their first question out before Manson leaped from his chair and stood on the table. Ruffled by the agents' elitist attitudes, we let Manson do his thing, lecturing the increasingly nervous feds as only he could. He held them personally responsible for the woes of society and the environment, and warned that the kids—their kids—would rise up against them. "Look down on me and you'll see your own fool. Look up at me and you'll see your master. Look into my eyes face-to-face and you'll see yourself. I grew up like all Americans with the gift of life, liberty, and the pursuit of happiness. I was free in the desert, pursuing happiness; then you FBI men came along and stole my liberty and gave me life! Now, I demand that you give it back! I command you to give it back!"

To emphasize his request, he angled his fingers into a gun and drew down on the G-men, shooting them one by one, giving each his classic evil eye. They tried to laugh it off, but I could tell their knees were jelly. I never determined what their agenda was, only that they were more than happy to get the hell out of there.

"Nice performance," I complimented, escorting Charlie back to his cell.

"You guys just use me like a freak show," he groused. "I'm your rabid dog."

"That's because we can always count on you to foam on cue. And you really came through this time. I don't think they'll be coming back for an encore."

"If they do, maybe I'll just answer their questions."

"What questions?"

Charlie looked at me and smiled, twisting his goatee with his fingers. "Now that you mention it, what the hell were they here for anyway?"

We both laughed hard as the door clanged shut.

*   *   *

On November 5, 1978, I pulled Charlie from his cell for a rare official meeting. I needed to interview him regarding his upcoming parole hearing, the first of Charlie's storied life. Ever the realist when it came to things like this, Charlie could hardly keep his mind on the subject. He rejected his right to an attorney, then changed the subject to something considerably more important to him than a pie-in-the-sky shot at freedom. Squeaky and Sandra had sent a nifty combination radio, television, and cassette player that was now wallowing in the property room. Such luxuries weren't allowed, and he was incensed. He was so worked up over it that I suspected the girls might have slipped a gun or file inside. A thorough check revealed nothing more than some ingenious Japanese technology.

Charlie coveted this gift and bitched about it constantly. "You've dangled a carrot in front of me for eight years, and every time I reach for it, you pull it away!" he accused, ripping me for my previous attempts to make his life easier. "You always jack me off, but you never let me come!" He was so upset, he threatened to commit suicide over it. "Next time you see me, Ed, I'll be hanging from a sheet!"

To be safe, we transferred him to the psychiatric ward and kept him under a tight suicide watch. Not long afterward, I successfully pushed to have the property rules changed, and Charlie was given his precious combo set. He received it like it was a present from the gods, cradling it in his arms like an infant. For the next month or so, he was in heaven. He could alternately watch television, listen to rock music, or play tapes. Then boom! He threw another stupid tantrum over something totally insignificant and smashed the combo set to smithereens. He was promptly yanked from his cell and tossed into isolation. An hour later, I walked to that dismal ward and peered into his tiny enclosed cell. He was sitting there half nude in the cold darkness staring blankly at a bare wall. He didn't have any property at all anymore, and had left himself with absolutely nothing to occupy his mind. He just sat motionless like he was in a trance, dead and aloof, empty of spirit and devoid of feeling.

What was it with this guy? I wondered. Why did he do such stupid, self-destructive things? Why was he torturing himself so much? It couldn't be because he was suddenly feeling guilt over the horrible murders. I knew him far too well to believe in that "he's punishing himself" psychobabble. In eight years, through all sorts of physical and emotional hell, I'd never seen him cry. Not a single tear ever dropped from his demonic eyes. Even his brief moments of sincerity appeared contrived for effect. Every move he made was calculated to gain a specific return. He studied other people's character and emotions to find their strengths and weaknesses, yet kept his locked within some internal shell. He often struck me as a brilliant actor playing the part of Charles Manson, one who was never out of character. Hard as I tried, I failed to detect the real man behind the act—if, indeed, there was one.

The closest he ever came was, ironically, earlier that week. Charlie, odd as it might sound, was lamenting the price of his fame. "How can I win?" he asked rhetorically. "Look at my cards. Cult leader. Mass murderer. Dope dealer. Con man. The Antichrist. You know, I'm like a snake in prison. I got no arms, no legs, just a mouth and a tail. I don't bite anyone, but I wag my tail and show my fangs, and everybody freaks out!"

As always, it never occurred to him that if he stopped wagging his tail and showing his fangs, everybody might stop freaking out. And if everybody stopped freaking out, he might get his arms and legs back. In fact, he had a chance, an admittedly slim one, but a chance to accomplish his appendage regeneration that very same week. If Charlie could only harness his charisma and oratory skills and pour them into something positive, he might be able to dazzle the parole board and convince them to at least consider the possibility of one day setting him free. Sure, the headlines would be brutal, but this wasn't about headlines. This was about Charlie performing in a room before a captive audience that wanted to hear what he had to say, and wanted to believe that even someone like him was capable of change. To rehabilitate Charles Manson would have been a giant feather in the cap of the California Corrections Department. From that standpoint, his parole hearing might not have been the waste-of-time slam dunk that everyone believed. And if anybody could wow an audience, it was Charlie. If he could swallow his fierce, destructive pride and funnel his power and energy into an uplifting "I've been healed, Praise God!" speech, he might have a shot.

The problem was, that was asking too much. Faced with a sympathetic audience backed by an international press corps, did he have the brains to try and save a thread of his future, or would he use the soapbox to spread more fear and loathing by spewing the same tired stories of hate, defiance, and bloody revolution?

My money, sadly, was on the latter.

Manson's parole hearing was set for November 16, 1978. The gatherings are required by law, even when the con has no possible chance of parole and the whole thing is a charade. Most murderers do at least fifteen years. Famous felons like Manson usually do more, and may never be released. With Charlie having been caged on the Tate-LaBianca convictions for a mere eight—one year for every person his Family had killed—his prospects were indeed slim.

After rejecting his first attorney, Charlie reluctantly accepted another. He hated lawyers as a rule, deeming them part of the "injustice system." This was no exception. Every time I passed the visiting room while he was conferring with his taxpayer-provided mouthpiece, he'd shout the same thing, "He's not my attorney, he's yours!"

In order for the television cameramen and news photographers to fully capture the upcoming event, Charlie was required to sign a release. I walked in while he was jerking his lawyer around and interrupted the fun. "Do you want to sign this or not?" I asked.

"What if I don't?"

"Then nobody gets to take your picture."

Charlie turned to his attorney. "What do you think?"

"I wouldn't sign it. Better keep a low profile."

"What do you think, Ed?" he asked, turning to me.

"I don't give a damn what you do," I snapped, weary of his power trip. Charlie mulled it over, taking his sweet time.

"Sign it or not. I don't have all day," I demanded, attempting to snatch it away from him. Charlie pinned it to the table with his fist, paused dramatically, then signed with a flourish.

"Can't have a show without an audience," he quipped, inviting the world to capture his latest performance.

The world came—in force. The media were so thick I could hardly walk through the halls of the administration building. Only a few lucky pool reporters were allowed inside the hearing itself, forcing the rest of the mob to cool their camcorders outside. Restless and bored, they clamored for news. A representative group scurried to the warden's office to request an interview with an officer who had worked closely with the imprisoned cult leader. "Get up here, Ed," Dr. Clanon ordered, sounding exasperated. "Some of the reporters want to ask questions about Manson. They've been waiting around here for hours and the hearing is still going on."

It was my first experience with a mob-scene interview, and it turned out to be disconcerting. The reporters and cameramen crowded around, pushing and shoving for position, practically knocking one another down. They peppered me with a machine-gun volley of questions all asked at the same time. "What does he do in his cell? Who does he talk with? What does he talk about? What does his cell look like? Does he make voodoo dolls? Why did he break his guitar?" On and on they went. I answered in short, crisp bursts, trying hard not to say anything I'd be sorry for later. The constant flashes and bright television lights began to disorient me. Huge spots danced before my eyes, giving me a splitting headache.

"Do you think he'll get a [parole] date?" someone asked.

"No."

"Why not?"

"Too soon."

"When do you think he'll get out?"

"Probably never."

"Why do you think that?"

"I don't think the public would stand for it. That's my opinion," I offered, totally blind and physically reeling.

While I fended off the press, Charlie was inside putting on one of his shows. Unfortunately, it wasn't anything close to the inspirational mea culpa that would have moved his audience. True to form, he offered his standard accusatory "You're destroying the forests, rivers of blood will flow" speech that guaranteed that he wouldn't be released anytime this century. The freshly inked swastika tattooed on his forehead didn't help much either.

When the hearing broke, the media mob abandoned me like yesterday's news and rushed to capture Charlie's historical exit. They pressed against a closed gate as Manson was whisked down the hall.

"Well, it's back in the hole," Charlie quipped, playing to the crowd.

"What do you think of the decision?" someone shouted.

"What decision?" Charlie shot back, summing it up rather nicely.

The following year, on November 28, 1979, Charlie dispensed with the circus altogether. He was playing Monopoly when he received the call to appear before the board. He'd just landed on "community chest" as the escort officer arrived, winning the right to pick up a card. "Get out of jail free" it announced. Charlie smiled at the irony and handed the small yellow card to the officer. "Give this to them," he said. The hearing was held in absentia, and he was turned down again.

In 1980, Charlie decided to reappear. It was showtime again, and Charlie gave another of his spellbinding performances. Most of the media, though, not being up on Mansonese, couldn't make heads or tails of his ramblings. One paper described it as "a bizarre discourse and incoherent prattle." I understood it all, having spent years deciphering his odd sentence structure and jagged thought pattern. From my perspective, aside from the usual environment/bad parents/save the children/blood will flow stuff, he made two significant statements. He admitted that he was dangerous, and after years of silence or denial, finally confessed that he had been in the LaBianca house on the night of the murders. He explained that he left before the carnage began, which was true, and denied ordering the couple killed, which probably wasn't.

Asked if he would escape if given the opportunity, he responded, "Yeah, I'd go. I'd just go out and leave you all alone."

The parole was denied.

His fourth hearing was held on November 5, 1981. Charlie, in better spirits, put on probably his most memorable parole show ever. Rolling two white marbles in his hand à la Humphrey Bogart's Captain Queeg, and wearing the long hair and beard of his most famous photos, Manson entertained the panel and gathered media for nearly three hours. All it took to set the stage was a board member's routine question about what the prisoner had done the previous year.

"I was cleaning the barn and I had to get a little of that old horse shit on my feet when I got down into the mud. But I got down there to clean the barn and I see that dude in there stealing the Cokes from that other guy."

"Now you're losing me," the questioner interrupted.

"In the procedures that the stars exist in, someone has to hold those gold bars up and someone has to hold them lieutenants up there. And I say, 'I'm talking to you, Sergeant!' And the sergeant comes over and I say, 'Who is it, the lieutenant?' And I say, 'Bring him here.' I say, 'Lieutenant, you know how my heart is.'"

"What are we talking about now?" the baffled board member asked.

"We're talking about holding up procedures. So a cop gets in the way and I get into a fight with him. Who's carrying the stick? Does Nixon carry the stick?"

The board member gave up trying to make sense of it. Didn't matter. That bit of nonsense was just a warm-up, like a jazz singer hitting the scales to oil the throat. Charlie was oiling his brain.

Asked about the "bad things" he'd done during his decade in the slammer, the fog cleared as he adroitly turned the tables. "The bad things? What do you think it's been, a picnic? It's all been bad to me. I ain't seen no good."

Another board member queried him about a tiff he had gotten into with a female guard. Angry over some procedural matter, he allegedly told the lady officer, "You owe me because I freed you from a French whorehouse." When she took umbrage at the silly remark, he reportedly dropped the T word. "Do you remember Sharon Tate? You're going to end up just like her."

Manson dodged the probe at the hearing by going on the offensive. "[She's] a woman that just can't work in prison. And she's got no business in prison because she don't know what the hell she's doing to start with. I see inside her head all the way back to when she was a girl on the Good Ship Lollipop. When she comes up to me trying to play up to be a man, it don't make no sense. She's pecking on me. If a woman tells me something [like that] outside, she'd pick her teeth up off the ground. I'd punch my mother out for shit like that. . . .

"All these years I thought it was 'the Man' who was keeping me locked up. I didn't know it was my mother or I would have gone out into the graveyard and got her head. I could have dug her grave up and took her head and gone off. What I'm trying to do is do right by everybody as good as I know how on the levels that I'm working on. We all have different levels that we do our little trips on. Well, I'm right alongside of you. The spaceship's going up and—"

"Don't start that trip again," a panelist cut in.

"I don't know how to communicate unless I can lay a foundation on where I'm coming from. It's simply this: I say things like that and I do things like that. Sometimes I even screwed a waitress on top of a pool table once. . . .

"I wrote a letter and I told a lumber company, "If you keep cutting the trees down the way you're cutting the trees down, you're going to destroy all the chance we got for life balance on earth planet because your air and water don't buy or sell.' And nobody cares about anything but money. And if it ain't profitable, then you can't move it. So the air and water keeps on dying, they keep on sawing down and destroying the atmosphere. They keep pollutin' the streams and they say it's always been that way. You asked the question 'Are you going to kill?' They're already dead! They've already destroyed themselves in all kinds of ways with bugs and everything you can think of. To catch life balance on planet earth will be the next job. They're getting ready to blow it up. . . .

"Every time I get outside, you people are moving a little faster and talking a little quicker and you got things cut up a little more and you got more little things there and you got all kinds of little things. Pretty soon you go out and all your goats are gone. The ducks are gone. The geese are gone. A guy comes out with a big shotgun and he's got a camera from Japan and things all over him. His gut's hanging over and he's loaded on 'bennies' talking about people killed in the desert. He calls the park rangers and the park rangers come with their forces and look for something to do for their coffee break. And pretty soon the highway patrol is in this thing."

Whap! Parole denied.

Like Elvis refusing to do encores to keep the crowds hungry for more, Charlie passed on his November 30, 1982, hearing. With Manson unable to steal the show, L.A. deputy district attorney Stephen Kay took center stage and sealed whatever microscopic chance Charlie had.

"Charles Manson is probably the best advertisement for the death penalty. . . . If he can't follow the simple rules of prison, how can we expect him to follow the rules of society? I think the answer is obvious. He can't. We have a man, Charles Manson, who told his followers that his hero was Adolf Hitler, and that Hitler is a genius for what he did to the Jews. I ask you this, can we ever risk letting Manson go free in a society that he tried so hard to destroy by promoting a black-white race war?"

Kay touched upon the "enormity and cruelty" of the Tate-LaBianca murders, and referred to Manson's unrelenting antisocial activities and thought processes. "In his philosophy, and in his actions, the human life means absolutely nothing. The ease with which Manson gets others to commit violent crimes is scary. What we have is almost a monthlong murderous rampage directed by Charles Manson. . . . His activity in prison has been terrible. Threats, assaults, contraband. He has absolutely no respect for authority. . . . I think he feels that he gets attention by doing things like this [threatening and assaulting officers]. He's the number one criminal in America, so he has to keep up his image by trying to scare people and showing what a tough guy he is. As long as this man is alive, he's going to be a danger, whether he's in prison or out. Nobody really knows what to do with this man. . . . To have this man ever paroled in his lifetime would be a travesty."

This time, the board not only shut the iron door, they smartened up and used a loophole in the law to deny Manson an audience for three years. The lectures and grandiose performances, initially enthralling and amusing, had become redundant and tiring, so there was no need to call the circus and rubber-stamp a denial every twelve months.

A second reason the hearing dates were stretched over three years is that Manson was using them to speak to his followers. His twisted legions, both old and new, hungered for news and directives. The long accounts of his parole speeches were like manna from heaven. As Manson knew, he wasn't winning a single convert on the board, but he was recruiting thousands on the streets. After every hearing, the ever present stream of mail would increase tenfold, taxing my censorship duties.

The word "censor" probably sticks in the craw of most free Americans, even when it comes to a prisoner's mail. I'd be the first to agree. In Manson's case, it was unequivocally the right step. As previously noted, locking Manson in a cage had not killed his sinister influence. This little man, shut down in maximum security, had come a poorly loaded gun away from assassinating a President of the United States. With an open line of communication, Manson could pose a threat to virtually anyone in the world, from a powerful political leader to an insignificant ex-con.

With all our scrutiny and diligence, the messages and commands usually got out anyway. There was no real way of stopping them. But by censoring his mail, we could keep him from increasing his long list of "Please let me kill for you" crazies—many of whom were dead serious.

Though Charlie wouldn't be getting out of prison anytime soon, his endless legions of followers would forever be free—free, angry, and willing to do whatever he commanded.

13

THROUGHOUT MY LIFE, people have asked me about Manson. "Does he really have some kind of magical way of controlling people?" "Does he have hypnotic powers?" "Does he have a diabolical charisma?" "Do his eyes have a magnetic attraction?" "Does his smile beckon?" "Is his charisma irresistible?" "Is he crazy?"

My response is that for some people, the answer to all of the above is yes—except for the last question. He isn't crazy.

Much has been written about Manson's powers and how he used them to seduce and control his followers. Dr. Livsey's book, *The Manson Women*, promoted the theory that all the women who killed for Charlie were predisposed to murder before they met him. Prosecutor Vincent Bugliosi had a similar theory. I strongly disagree. Manson has two feet, picks his nose, cracks dirty jokes, catches colds, and feels happy and sad like everybody else. But he also has an undeniable effect upon people's lives. He can make hate look like love, chaos like harmony, and lies like truth. He offers himself to his followers as a superior human being who has all the answers.

"I'll never die," he told me once. "I'm above death. When all of you are long gone, I'll still be here." However, at other times, Manson scoffs at his own omnipresent image. "If I had any real power, like they've said, I wouldn't be here, would I? I'd put everyone under my spell and just walk out of this shit hole. But every time I try to do that, some dumb-ass guard slams a door in my face."

As witty and deceptive as the most sophisticated scam artist, Manson can be compared to the travelling medicine men of the Old West, wowing the crowds with bottles of potent stimulants, then beating town before the hangovers hit. Manson's psychedelic medicine bottles were marijuana and blotters of LSD, the perfect lollipops to attract wayward youth.

On February 14, 1967, some of Manson's future followers were among the longhaired faithful at the famous "Be-in" held in Golden Gate Park in San Francisco. They heard Allen Ginsberg chant a slogan Charlie would later take to heart: "We are one!" LSD guru Timothy Leary was there urging the young people to tune in and turn on. "Let it go," Leary extolled like a father freeing his children from all their hang-ups. "Whatever you do is beautiful." Little did Leary know, there was at least one person wandering around out there destined to put the phrase to the ultimate test.

Several years ago, a Harvard University professor completed a study at the Rockefeller Institute that posed the question "What is 'demonic' from a psychiatric point of view?" He cited three major elements in his conclusion: (1) nudity, (2) aggressiveness, and (3) a schizophrenic mentality—a tearing apart. The first one, nudity, was somewhat confusing, while number 2, aggressiveness, might be seen as obvious. It was number 3 that caught my attention. Below that, he had three subcategories: (a) whatever destroys unity, (b) creates discord, and (c) alters patterns.

Based on number three alone, and tossing out demented political leaders like Hitler, Stalin, and their ilk, I'd have to rate Manson as one of the major demonic creatures of our time. Tearing things apart, destroying unity, creating discord, and altering patterns are what he's all about.

He's also about sleight of hand and miscommunication. Under my watch, he'd been protected, provided for, tolerated, and sometimes even pampered. I lost count of how many guitars, televisions, radios, and tape players he acquired, destroyed, and was allowed to have again, usually through the bending of rules. Yet, to read his letters or hear him speak to his followers in the visiting room, you'd think he was spending his time chained to some torture rack. He wanted his Family to view him as a martyr suffering enormous pain and deprivation because of the great father of all demons—usually me. It was bullshit and he knew it, but it played better in Peoria.

Something odd was playing in Pleasanton around that time that again linked Squeaky and Charlie to Patty Hearst. Squeaky went after a Croatian nationalist terrorist named Julienne Busic with a claw hammer, whacking her a few good licks on the noggin before the guards broke it up. According to witnesses, Squeaky called Busic "a white, middle-class, rich bitch who doesn't deserve to live." The Pleasanton officers, who never prosecuted Squeaky, were probably sympathetic—as were most of New York's finest. Busic was convicted of a 1976 bombing at La Guardia Airport that resulted in the death of a policeman. No motive was given for Squeaky's attack at the time, but she would later tell a reporter that, to use modern slang, Busic "dissed" her. She called Busic "a rat, Patty Hearst's best friend," who was "very disrespectful of me."

I wondered if there was more to it than that. Manson had mentioned "the Hearst thing" during the Christmas call I'd arranged for Squeaky, making me suspicious that something was up. I queried Charlie, but he blew the hammer incident off as "chick stuff" and claimed to have no knowledge of any grander scheme involving Hearst—not that he would have told me if there was.

As I waited for the other shoe to drop in that incident, my association with Charlie once again exploded into my off-duty life. I was working as a volunteer teacher at St. Mary's Church in Vacaville, instructing high school students in religious studies. Often, I'd mention my prison experiences to the class and tie them in to Christian values. Specifically, I'd emphasize how so many inmates destroyed their lives by failing to obey basic Christian principles. Naturally, I used Manson in many examples, mostly because the students knew him and he captured their attention.

Whenever the class appeared bored and distant, I'd tell a Manson story. It never failed to perk them up and get them involved in the discussion.

Some of the young folks began sharing the stories with their parents. Normally, getting a student excited enough to run home and relay an event to his or her folks is a good thing. This is especially true for an off-hours, church-related religious class. You can imagine how thrilled the kids were to give up their free time for that. The problem was, the parents recoiled at the name Manson and began to express their disapproval to the priest. The priest took me aside one evening and outlined their concerns.

"That's baloney," I responded, cutting him off. "Some of these kids will say anything to get out of having to come. They're exaggerating. It's not like I'm telling them to join Manson's Family and go out on killing sprees. I do my best to make the classes interesting enough to keep the students coming. If I have to tell some prison stories to do that, then I do it."

"I don't know. I just don't think it's appropriate," the father intoned.

Tired and tense from my long, stressful days, I felt my blood begin to rise. "Maybe you should tell those meddling parents to come down and sit in my class before they criticize."

Unaware of my building anger, the priest kept pushing his issue, going so far as to suggest that I switch classes with another teacher and start over, minus the prison talk.

"You know, Father, I never see you over here. You never visit the classes and I don't think you have the right to criticize me. We all volunteer our time, come here and do the best we can. We're not professionals. We have to teach what we know, where our experiences lie. Prison is what I know, and it's a damn good place to learn about the costs of living a life of sin!"

He blinked at the mild profanity, but still wouldn't budge, suggesting again that I switch classes. The suggestion sounded like an order. Furious, I lost control. "These kids can learn a hell of a lot from Charles Manson! When their parents don't listen or make them mad, and they feel lost and alone, men like him are going to be there waiting, pretending to care and saying all the right things, but all along hiding some evil agenda. Charlie's warned the world about that hundreds of times, but he's right, nobody's listening. Now I'm trying to warn them. I'm trying to keep their eye focused on Jesus, not athletes, celebrities, cults, drugstore gurus, and other wor-shiped humans. But you'll never understand that, because you live in this pristine world. Well, you can take your fucking program, Father, because I've had it!"

I turned away from his shocked face and stormed off. When I arrived home, I couldn't believe what I'd done. I'd used harsh prison language inside a house of God to defend my right to prattle on about my buddy Charles Manson. I'd screamed the F word in a Catholic priest's face! What was happening to me? Had Manson once again altered my behavior? I'd done everything but grab my balls and warn the father that I wasn't going to stand for his bullshit interference.

I spent the next few weeks racked with shame and guilt. How could I have lost it like that in front of a priest? I was too embarrassed to face him, so I prayed that he'd sense my sorrow and call or visit. He never did. I wrote a long letter of apology and eventually tried to make up, but our relationship was never the same. I could always detect a sense of fear and distrust in his eyes, like I was some emotional time bomb that could go off at any moment. As with my career and my daughter, Charlie had reached out from his cell and screwed up my life again. Would it ever end?

Not in my lifetime. In 1979, after nine years in lockups, Good Time Charlie was formally recommended for a transfer to the CMF mainline — mostly through my efforts. He promptly blew the opportunity when he appeared before the institution classification committee. "You people can't judge me," he preached. "Your laws are not my laws that I live by. You've kept me locked up for nine years. For what? I've seen killers on the mainline who are much worse than me, yet you keep me caged like an animal. Someday, I'll treat you just like you treat me!"

So much for that attempt. The appalled committee rejected him, causing me to lose no small amount of face.

"Why can't you just shut up for once?" I scolded when he was back in his cell. "I know you wanted it. You've been bitching about being mainlined for years. I stuck my neck out for you. Yet, when you get your chance, you have to let your mouth ruin it!"

"They needed to hear what I said!" he raged back. "Just because I tell them the truth doesn't mean they should punish me for it. They should listen, learn, then give me what I want!"

"The world doesn't work that way, Charlie. When will you learn that?"

"That's your paper-bag world. Not mine!"

"Either way, what's the point? You've been saying the same thing for twenty years. We've heard it all. Why do you have to keep shooting yourself in the foot by repeating those ridiculous accusations?"

He paused for an instant, momentarily caught off guard. The silence didn't last. "I have to keep saying it over and over because you people are so thick!"

Angry as I was, I couldn't help laughing. I chided myself for trying to outtalk the master.

Far from absorbing any of my words, Charlie poured it on even stronger a few days later when he graced our presence at a Willis Unit classification meeting. He set the tone right off by bounding in wearing a Russian Cossack hat he had apparently swiped from Dr. Hyberg. The damn thing looked so out of place on him that we all cracked up. He ignored us and sat down.

"I don't give a fuck what you do with me," he opened. "The only reason I'm here is to pay you guys a visit. You make decisions, I don't. I don't tell you what to do. You don't listen. I'm in your thoughts, in the thoughts of Germany, Ireland, Scotland, France, England, Japan, and Australia." He paused, staring at our puzzled faces. "You still don't see what's happening, do you? You'll wait till its too late. Can't you see that my life is your life? Cheat me and you cheat yourself. I'm your child. When you and Nixon failed to give me a fair trial, when you found me guilty, you found yourselves guilty. I'm in Nixon's thoughts. He condemned me!"

Charlie stood on his chair, his head shaking with disgust. "I can't get a toilet-paper decision out of anyone around here. No one can stand up and make a decision. I only get paper words, promises that have no meaning. For God's sake, if you're going to stroke me, please let me shoot my wad!"

"Getting back to that 'thought' thing," Dr. Rotella interrupted. "Are you saying that everybody's thoughts are on top of one another, so they're all piled up? Do I read you right?"

Charlie sensed that the shrink was poking fun at him. That was a no-no during Charlie's lectures. His eyes burned. "If I ever get out of here, little fat man, I'm going to the desert. And if I catch you there, I'll treat you like you treat me. I'll tie you to a tree and torture—" He paused, catching himself. He liked Dr. Rotella and didn't want to lay it down too heavy. "I'll keep you there and keep changing my mind about what I'm going to do with you. I'll make my decision and then change it. And all the time, you'll suffer the way you've made me suffer."

Charlie's controlled anger was a warning that he was in no mood for any more snide interruptions of his from-the-mouth-of-the-gods discourse. Sufficiently scolded, we allowed him to continue unchallenged. "Let me tell you about your good friends Mr. and Mrs. Pocketbook. These are the people who are so afraid of my girls because they're into their dirty money and neglect their children and the environment. Mrs. Pocketbook is dizzy with pills and distasteful to Mr. Pocketbook. All her life, she pushed Mr. P. to make more and more money and he tried to oblige, driven to drink by her endless dissatisfaction. Deep inside, Mrs. P. felt guilty for this, but because she didn't want to face the truth, she pushed her guilt on others. She blamed the neighbor's kids and dogs for keeping her awake at night. She blamed her husband for things he hadn't even done yet. They fought over his paycheck and how to spend it on themselves. Then the word came that prowlers were roaming the neighborhood. This summoned up Mrs. P.'s fear because she felt guilty and had no way to balance her guilt. Her husband was away. She's alone. She remembered the warnings of Sandra Good and Lynette Fromme, those Manson women who seek retribution from greedy women like her who are more concerned about status and money than the earth, the children, and the natural world. Mrs. P. remembered Red and Blue saying that sometimes murder has to happen.

The victims are cancerous growths contaminating the environment. They need radical surgery. They need to be cut off. The murders are done to save you, because without clean air and water, you'll all die. If you don't believe that, stop breathing and see what happens. We're all one soul. Murdering someone who is killing the soul is justified!

"So look within your souls, my friends. Are you running home with your paychecks and letting your wives and husbands make all the decisions? Are you, and you, and you and you Mr. and Mrs. Pocketbook? And if you are, what should be done to you?"

With that, Manson hopped off the chair and marched toward the exit, his furry hat bobbing on his goofy head. He paused at the doorway, turned toward us, dug his index finger up his nose, twirled it around, then wiped his boogers on the doorjamb. In a flash, he was gone.

We all sat in stunned silence, each absorbed in something Manson had said that touched us personally. Finally, Dr. Rotella broke the spell. "Strange little man," he quipped.

"Yeah, but oh so entertaining," I added, far more immune to Manson's diatribes than the others. They laughed nervously, then one by one paraded out of the room.

The following year, I again referred Charlie to the mainline. (I'm nothing if not persistent.) This time, the liberal doctors and counselors said what the hell and gave it a shot—at least during the day. Like the vampire he was, he'd still have to be locked down in the high-security wing at night. On July 28, 1980, Manson strolled out of Willis Unit, wandered through the main corridor, and entered the general population. A new era in Manson's life had dawned. Typically, it was a strange one.

Charlie was given a job to go with his freedom. Nick Ristad, an extremely dedicated and caring Protestant chaplain, stuck his neck out and accepted Manson as his chief clerk. That was no small sacrifice considering that on the night of the LaBianca murders, Charlie first stopped in front of a Catholic church, got out, and told his startled group he was going to kill the priest because they "eat, shit, and tell lies like everybody else." He came back a few minutes later and reported that the priest wasn't home. (Ever the spin master, Manson subsequently claimed that he had just stopped to relieve himself and had told his gang the murder story to shake everybody up.)

For the first few days, things went well on the mainline. The guards hung close, making sure nobody took a stab at him. When I swung by for a visit, I noticed that Tommy, a double murderer who'd previously been in Willis, was hanging around the chapel, fidgeting and eyeing everyone who passed.

"What's up, Tommy?" I asked, alarmed by his activities.

"Not much."

"What are you doing here?"

He looked around, then leaned in close. "Protecting Charlie," he whispered. "I'm his bodyguard."

Apparently, Charlie had brought along his own security.

The moment the guards backed off, inmates began to gravitate to the chapel. They weren't coming to pray. In yet another stroke of bizarre irony, they entered into the house of God to worship at the feet of a man frequently referred to as the devil. As I feared, the weak-willed head cases who populated CMF flocked like lost sheep to their famous cellmate. Before long, a white racist enclave had formed, filling a normally placid religious environment with hate and tension. Even Charlie could see that the experiment wasn't working. He preferred to mold receptive, initially healthy minds. The guys coming to him now brought along enough mental baggage to sink a battleship. He found it frustrating to try and wash brains that weren't there to begin with. The parade of psychotic worshipers and autograph seekers started rattling his nerves.

Mine too! When a couple of guys emerged zombie-like from the chapel one day with X's and swastikas carved into their foreheads, I knew the gig was up. Needless to say, Charlie didn't protest when I yanked him out of there and locked him down at Willis. He adjusted for a while, then began moaning and groaning about wanting to go back into population. "It wasn't my fault it didn't work," he wailed; "it was all those fuckin' crazies!"

Building steam for a new tantrum, he refused to go to the hospital for a regularly scheduled visit. At times like this, I often turned the situation over to Sergeant Tommy Thompson, a retired air force officer who took shit from no human. A grizzled Texan, Sergeant Thompson was totally immune to Manson's manipulative ways.

"You'll have to cuff me and carry me down there!" Manson screamed to the guards just as Sergeant Thompson arrived. The military veteran looked Charlie straight in the eye.

"You little son of a bitch," he drawled. "You get up on your feet and you walk or I'll drag your ass down there feet first like the motherfuckin' dog you are!"

Charlie shut up and walked on his own.

A week later, we gave in to Charlie's annoying nagging and tried the mainline experiment again. This time, we made a special effort to keep a better watch on the parade of leaderless Cuckoo's Nest types marching like sacrificial natives to the chapel door. The second day there, Charlie was doing some work with an X-Acto knife and accidentally sliced his hand, earning him another trip to the hospital. Sergeant Thompson happened to be on Cuckoo's Nest duty at the time. He wasn't sympathetic. "Why didn't you cut your throat and save everybody the trouble?" he cracked.

While Manson was being bandaged, his two favorite girls were making big news three thousand miles away at a Virginia prison, where they'd once again been reunited. Squeaky and Sandra granted a wide-ranging joint interview with an industrious *Sacramento Bee* reporter named Wayne Wilson. Squeaky, then thirty-one, covered the Ford assassination attempt, her childhood, and Charlie, among other things, in the September 1980 story.

"I was fed up. With lots and lots of things. Here's this guy [Ford] coming in to Sacramento, smiling like everything's all right with the world, and we got all these problems over here. And this is wrong and that's wrong, and my air and water's at stake, and I'm going to see this guy. And then I thought, 'Wait a minute. He's not going to do anything for you. He's just going to pass right by.' And I thought, 'Well, I'll just take my gun.' And I thought, 'Well, are you going to use it?' And I said, 'I don't know. Just go and check it out.' Now that's exactly what I was doing, going and checking it out. But I was not determined to kill the guy, obviously, because I didn't do it. . . . People ask me, 'Well, were you going to? Did you want to?' Well, I say I did not make any decision on it while I was going down there. That doesn't make sense to most people because they've never been to the point where they were that undecided. Maybe I'm dumb. Maybe I'm a clunk, like somebody told me. But I'm kind of a graceful clunk, and I got reasons and I got heart and I cared about my Family. I didn't want to go over my Family. That was nine deaths that should have done something. You know, people should have at least wanted to know why? What was it? What is the cause? And try and fix it if possible.

". . . We don't want out until Charlie's out. We just were not content out there without him and we tried to get in to visit all those times and they wouldn't let us, so we wanted to be inside with him until he gets out. . . . We tried for five years and were given the run-around. . . . We were working on various projects, trying to get elk hunters to stay out of the forests, trying to get the Ford Motor Company to keep the [smog] devices in their cars, to clean up their cars. . . . I'm on my knees to my life on earth and I don't want to lose it. We're very close to destroying the whole thing. I want to give up sometimes, and I want to just not pay attention to it. Not care. But I can't. Once I've seen it, I say, 'Okay, it's with me. Now all I have to do is work out a way to balance it.' . . .

". . . When Sandy and I were in court, we saw the fun of it. You say something and the judge rules in your favor and it's like 'Yea! I made a point!' But the worst part is when they get up and make the impassioned plea to the jurors. And you know it's just a game. They can walk out the door and say, 'Well, it came off pretty good.' It's a game. They're actors. And I look at the judge [U.S. district judge Thomas J. MacBride] whose bridge games mean more. Whose duck hunt means more. He wouldn't give up duck hunting for me. Not even when I came to him decently. 'Ha, ha, ha.' He thought. That was real funny. Well, he's a witty, clever guy, but he doesn't hold a candle, he couldn't shine Charlie's shoes, because he's not in the will of God. I respected him. I could have been his own daughter. I said, 'Look, Dad. This is important. If nothing else, it's important to me. You don't need to shoot ducks. You don't need the ducks to live.' But he says, 'Well, that's tough luck. That's my duck hunt.' He just shoots them because he feels like he's powerful and like he's a sporting fellow. . . .

"I was fifteen and left my house and went to work. I was going to high school, going to work. Looking for a job and for an apartment was hard when you're fifteen. And everyone's telling me, 'Well, you have to lie and say you're older.' I'd say, 'Wait a minute. I don't want to lie.' They'd say, 'Aw, come on. Everybody lies. You have to lie.' That was my introduction. . . . The restaurant fella taught me how to cheat the customer. . . . The pet shop guy was cheating on his income taxes. Every place I went I learned that somehow they were trying to pull the wool over someone's eyes. I grew up believing people were serving us. The man with the star, and all that. But then you look and find that all of a sudden, all of your illusions are gone and there isn't anybody. You're alone. . . .

"[My father and I] argued [that last night] about some kind of definition from the dictionary, that's how dumb it was. His way or no way. I said, 'Yes, but,' and he said, 'Yes but nothing.' You'd think the definition would be clear, but I don't remember if either of us looked it up. It was late at night. I was eighteen. I was looking for a couple to stay with because I didn't have anywhere to go."

Squeaky said that after the argument, she was sitting alone on a bench, peering out at the ocean, when Charlie approached.

"He looked at me and he knew. And he cared enough to pay attention."

The rest, as they say, is history.

When it came her turn, Sandra, then thirty-six, was equally compelling. She started off with a story about a new recruit they'd sent out on yet another proposed murder spree.

"He was a nut that was fixing to go off and start killing people. He was right out of Vietnam, trained by the government to kill people, and he writes us and he wants to be our hit man. So we thought, 'Oh great. This is a real winner, floating around and flipping around Pennsylvania.' But he kept writing these letters, so we thought, 'Okay, we'll take the guy's energies and we'll direct them so he won't be hurting some innocent person walking down the street.' So we directed him to the president of Kaiser Industries. We said, 'Lookit, sure, you can be our hit man. Go take care of this guy.' Gave him a little scenario on how to do it. Then he got on some other binge, Patty Hearst or something, and ended up telling the FBI."

The "little scenario," according to court testimony, was that the assassin was supposed to kill the Kaiser head and his wife, paint their bodies pink, then stick a can of Ban deodorant in the man's mouth. Good explained to Wilson that the pink paint signified the color that Kaiser coats its machinery, hotels, and shopping centers.

"We went to war in the '60s for change," Good continued. "Manson didn't kill anybody. He didn't mastermind it. We kids, society's nice children, we looked at the war in Vietnam, we looked at the pollution and we listened to the music, singing revolution. Revolution for the hell of it. And we were looking at problems, especially that war, and we went to war for our country. The Manson Family. We went to war against the big money that was killing the people in Vietnam and was killing our own country. Now, if that isn't the ultimate in morality, I don't know what is. When people sacrifice their own lives, as well as other people's lives. When they go that far, you know that there is something happening. . . . You know, those people [Tate-LaBianca] were no saints. People that were already dead in their money anyway. How long are we going to be made the scapegoats with everybody putting their fear and hate off on us while avoiding the real problems? Practically everything you read about wasn't true. Oh Jesus, we drank blood for fun. We're filthy and slimy and sexually depraved. Cut off heads. You know, all those insane stories. The baby was mutilated. Tate was killed. She happened to be pregnant. . . . How many thousands of women have abortions every day? What else? Orgies. Blood and sex orgies. Filthy? Can you imagine me being physically dirty? Letting myself go? That's repugnant to me. I don't mind being called a killer, but don't call me a dirty one.

"I can see killing for a purpose. . . . If someone came at you or your child with a knife or was dumping poison into your water system, you'd defend yourself. This is where we were at. The murders were supposed to be because Charlie didn't get a recording contract? I mean, here we are looking at very real things and here the murders were reduced to the level of an ego trip? A man's ego trip of getting some music recorded? . . . Man, going to college and all that stuff, I learned different ways to work within a system. Write your congressman, join the Sierra Club, do this, do that. And I worked in a lot of those areas. I've always been socially conscious. But I've seen that there were no alternatives. Those were the only means that we had at hand at that point in time to deal with the problems that we were seeing.

"Manson never had a trial. That was a circus. That was a farce. That was a vehicle for the DA to write his book and make his movie. The whole thing was conducted with his future book *Helter Skelter* in mind. The truth has never come out."

The most critical truth I got out of that interview was to remind myself in my next letter to Sandra that I could call her a killer, but not a dirty one. That ranked right up there with Charlie's line to the *Enquirer* reporters, "I'm a monster maybe, but I'm not a monstrous monster."

In 1981, our old friend Willie Spann flamed out on the media tour and got busted again for drugs. He passed through CMF for a ninety-day evaluation. To make matters worse, his uncle had been bounced out of office by the voters the previous year, effectively eliminating Spann's only claim to fame. He was much more subdued and humble this time around, realizing that his fifteen minutes in the footlights had come and gone. The new attitude enabled him to put aside his past differences with Charlie and kiss and make up. Spann spent his time entertaining Charlie and Pin Cushion with colorful tales about how he had played on his uncle's big job to score cash, lovers, and media interviews during the brief period he was free. When it was time to ship Spann out to his permanent home, we were all sad to see him go.

Charlie tempered his grief with the knowledge that he was surviving on the mainline. By closely monitoring the crazies at CMF, we were able to keep him in population for the next three years. We gradually eased his custody rating to the point where he could walk around unescorted, take his meals in the cafeteria with the other inmates, exercise in the main yard, receive visitors in the regular visiting room, and stay out of his cell on weekends.

He was especially proud of his office in the back of the chapel and took me for a tour. He had a small desk and a chair, and had decorated a wall with pictures of wolves (devouring a caribou), birds, and fish, as well as landscapes. An eight-by-ten glossy of Lynette graced another wall, right next to a similar photo of Sandra. A third showed his two chief followers together, this time decked out in their hooded habits.

Charlie escorted me from the office and led me to a cloistered chapel garden to show off the flowers and plants he was growing. He bent down and tenderly pointed out the grit, dust, and rust spots on the wilting leaves. "It's the dirty air and water," he said sadly. "It's killing everything. Can't you see it, man?"

Charlie's plants weren't the only things dying from the pollution in and around the chapel. The self-identity of his bodyguard, Tommy Burke, seemed to be withering away as well, replaced by Manson's stronger personality. I noticed that Tommy was now completely under Charlie's spell, talking the talk and coming on like Manson junior. I pulled him into my office for a fatherly chat.

"Listen, I know Charlie can have a powerful influence on people. I've felt it myself. What he says about the environment sounds good, and it's a noble cause, but that's only a small part of what Charles Manson's all about. There's a big part of him that's horribly evil, and that's what you need to be careful about. It's important that you retain your own personality and manhood, and make your own decisions. Don't turn your will over to him or you'll regret it. Believe me, everybody, except maybe Squeaky and Sandra, has lived to regret it. I know it's hard. I know you gravitate toward him and can't help yourself. I do too. I have for a long time. But I've never surrendered my soul like the others. I've never given him my mind. That's the difference. You be careful, Tommy."

Reading his face, I sensed that I'd gotten through. A month later, the pair had a falling-out over something neither would reveal, and Tommy asked to be transferred to another prison. We granted his wish.

The only person I worried about now, aside from the Cuckoo's Nest set, was Pastor Nick. He was spending a great deal of time with Charlie, and that usually meant trouble for anyone. I visited Nick one afternoon and found him engaged in a spirited long-distance telephone conversation. Charlie entered, saw me waiting, and ambled over to Nick. He gently reached out and pressed down the knobs on the phone, disconnecting the call. Instead of getting angry, Nick gave him a weary look and didn't mention it. That troubled me. In case I hadn't gotten the point, Charlie grinned and picked up the chaplain's two-pound, foot-long carved wooden nameplate from his desk and held it menacingly over Nick's head, ready to strike. Nick didn't move or show any concern. Manson posed like he was waiting for a picture to be taken, flashed his wicked eyes, then put the artful club back on the desk. He left the room without another word. Nick merely rolled his eyes and picked up his phone to continue the aborted call. I was concerned more about Nick's mental state than any physical harm that might befall him. I knew Charlie would never hurt the man. Recruit him into his Family, sure. Turn him away from God and onto drugs and sex, certainly. But he'd never physically injure him. In the end, the soft-spoken, passive pastor proved to be more resilient than I imagined. He survived his ordeal with Charlie without a physical or mental scar—which is more than I could say for myself.

Despite Nick's firm grip on the situation, things didn't always go smoothly. Angry about losing a transfer to a unit with an even lower custody rating, Charlie threw another heated tantrum. This time, he piled up all his possessions—books, magazines, newspapers, letters, photographs, clothing, sheets, and blankets—and lit a healthy bonfire in his Willis Unit cell. The guards had to grab a hose and drench the place—with Charlie in it. They dumped his scorched property into the garbage and dragged the little wet rat kicking and screaming into isolation. Charlie decked the halls with horrible threats the entire way.

Eight months later, in October 1982, an officer tried to get into the chapel and was impeded by something blocking the door. Pounding and shouting, Manson finally let him in. The officer discovered that the door had been bound from the inside by an electrical wire. Manson was immediately interrogated and gave evasive answers. A search was commenced. In the ceiling of the clerk's office—Manson's office—a trapdoor was discovered that led to the attic. (I hadn't even been aware that it was there!) Although the door had been bolted down and locked, its hinges were removed. Officers climbed through the door and entered the dark attic. They discovered a well-stocked "escape kit" consisting of a tape recorder, a glass vial containing a volatile white liquid, two pieces of metal stock—

one of which was sharpened and taped into a shank—sandpaper, a pair of tin snips (wire cutters), four bags of marijuana, one hundred feet of nylon cord, and a hot-air balloon catalog. A ladder was standing in the chaplain's office tall enough to reach the ten-foot-high ceiling. A search of Manson's cell turned up a hacksaw blade, marijuana, and LSD.

Charlie had obviously been preparing to make a break for it. Although the attic was enclosed, it was connected to numerous air ducts and passageways that led to who knows where. If the plot hadn't been discovered, Manson would have stood a good chance of making it.

Despite the evidence against him, Charlie was able to escape punishment because too many inmates had access to the chaplain's office and it was impossible to pin it on anyone. That said, it was unmistakably Charlie's operation from the get-go. Who else but Manson would include four bags of marijuana in his stash? The only question in my mind was how many others he had intended to take with him. Despite our relationship, he was unusually nimble on the subject, steadfastly denying any part.

"I don't want to get out of here!" he claimed. "You know me. I'm like Frankenstein. I'd be recognized everywhere. The townsfolk would chase me down and string me up to the nearest tree. No sir, I'm staying right here where it's safe!"

There was some truth to that, but not enough to keep him from trying to bolt. I closely monitored his behavior and moods to see how he was taking the discovery. Inmates frequently go nuts or become suicidal when their long-planned escapes are foiled. It's not so much the loss of potential freedom that gets them down, it's the sudden loss of the hope that they had fed on during the months of preparation.

Charlie didn't appear any different than before. If the aborted attempt was eating at him, he hid it well. It turned out that he did like most prisoners and simply began work on his next attempt. On February 26, 1983, a routine search turned up a pair of khaki coveralls in his cell. They were the exact color and style of those worn by the officers assigned to the security squad, and could easily be used by an escaping con to "filter in." This time Manson went berserk. Although he knew as well as anyone that the gig was up the moment the clothing was spotted, he refused to fork them over, hitting number 9 on the tantrum Richter scale. When the dust settled, he had destroyed yet another guitar and trashed virtually everything else in his cell, including his latest television set. That effectively ended his days in population.

Charlie sulked for a long time after that, alone in his cell with no guitar to play, no radio to listen to, no television to watch. Once again, a few minutes of anger resulted in months of boredom and despair. Still, he remained incapable of understanding the concept of cause and effect. He became especially mean during this period, spewing threats and jumping on everyone, including me. He made some veiled references to Squeaky and "mail," coming as close as he ever had to exposing his festering resentment over my campaign to free her from his influence.

At the same time, Squeaky's letters took on an ugly, menacing tone. She wrote of killing me just as she had tried to murder President Ford. For all my help, Squeaky still viewed me as a barrier, a disapproving Peeping Tom who intruded upon her most intimate moments with her beloved master. I stubbornly persisted in trying to convince her to break away, even after I became thoroughly convinced that it wasn't possible. We fought constantly through the mail, firing letter after letter arguing points that would never be resolved. I often wondered why we kept it up. For Squeaky, I was the closest she could get to Manson, so it made sense. In fact, many of her letters addressed to me were written directly to him, as if I were nothing more than an invisible conduit. Plus, she had a lot of time on her hands, so writing was no doubt cathartic.

Why did I keep writing to Squeaky? It's hard to say. I think it boils down to the simple fact that I was unable to throw in the towel. As long as I could scribble some logic on a notepad, I'd keep trying to pump some sense into her.

Usually, it was me who broke. As mentioned before, her letters were often so touching I couldn't bear to keep them from Charlie. I'd pull him from his cell, slip him a letter, and let him savor it in my office. At times like that, I hated having to stand between them, but realized it was necessary. Left to themselves, there was always the fear that their correspondence would quickly transform from love and kisses to talk of hate and violence.

Charlie had consorted with all his girls, yet somehow managed to keep them from becoming jealous. This always intrigued me. He treated them as one in his "truth." And yet, in this socialistic world, Squeaky stood out as something special. "I married her in a dark prison cell," he said once after reading a particularly moving letter. "I was alone, and I never gave her up."

Squeaky, in turn, fed on the fact that a man who belonged to no one was hers alone on a mystical, higher plane. "I love him and all his instincts you find so dirty. . . . Day by day, we became more aware of Charlie, who was ever aware of us, and each tree, each branch and each leaf. . . . The reason I love Charlie is he lets me be myself. Simple. My parents never let me be myself. The harder they pushed me, the farther I went from their reality. . . . A pair of hands, a feeling, the silent shadows of a lonely, quiet ocean rolls, the sun on my tears and a smile only you can see."

She called a few days after Charlie's violent tantrum. Her voice quivered as she fought to control her emotions. "Let me talk with Charlie," she begged. "Please, I have to. He's all I got." It didn't appear that something traumatic had occurred or that there was an emergency of some kind, but that Squeaky was coming unglued and needed a word or two from her master to keep from falling apart. "Please," she continued. "I have to. Don't you understand? He's all I've got! Please let me talk to him. Why do you do this to us? Why? You hope the spell will be broken and I'll forget him like the others. Well I won't. I'll never forget!"

I let her go on like that for an hour, using me as a whipping boy to purge her soul of whatever demons were haunting her. She even reiterated that she had gone after President Ford because of me, an accusation that always made me feel creepy. "I was desperate. No one would let me see Charlie. They kept sending me away, one prison after another. You were my last hope. After you refused to let me see him at San Quentin, that was it. That's why I am where I am today. That's why all this happened to me! It's your fault!"

When she finally wore out, I updated her on Charlie's day-to-day life, then gently explained that I couldn't bring him to the phone. He was in isolation at the time, being punished for his latest hissy fit, and I couldn't spring him even if I'd wanted to. She eventually accepted it and said good-bye, her spirit calm.

Not long afterward, a letter came in that spoke directly to Charlie. "You are my life. . . . How real you are since people have lost nobility and understand so few things about love being all that you put into it. And you put all."

Meddling, I wrote back: "You say you know yourself and what you're doing, but nobody else does. For fantasy's sake, I'd like to see you two give up your 'truths,' escape to the mountains, raise a family and live a harmonious life with the environment until death does you part. You'd probably be so damn happy, you couldn't stand it! It's too bad you have so big a world mission."

"I don't care what you say to my mind," she scolded in her next call. "He's my Charlie too. We're married in case you didn't understand. You don't need a contract to get married. Stop trying to control us or force your ideas on me. I resent your interference. I'm mad, and you could make me madder. . . . I want to be calm and do my time. . . . But please don't try to take care of me with your conception of help. I'm not going to try to convince you of anything. I'm not going to ask you to understand. I'm just asking you to maintain your dignity between us that transcends opinion."

Squeaky's unbreakable devotion to Manson can best be described by quoting Saint Paul in his letter to the Galatians (chapter 2, verses 20–21). Substituting Manson for Christ—a horribly blasphemous thought, but applicable from Squeaky's perspective—one begins to understand the level of her worship. "With Christ I am nailed to the cross. It is no longer that I live, but Christ lives in me. And the life that I know lives in the flesh, but I live in faith of the Son of Man who loved me and gave himself up for me."

With all this, it's no surprise that Charlie was especially protective of Squeaky—and furiously hated my interference. "There are things you've done that you will have to pay for," he snarled that afternoon, eyes on fire with hate and anger. "Don't think I don't know. And don't think I'll ever forget! It's time I sent my people to pay you a visit!"

Charlie had aired similar threats before. I generally ignored them, realizing his mood would change and all would be forgotten the next day. This time, however, the words carried an edge I'd never felt before, an edge that caused my subconscious fight-or-flight instincts to come alive. Goose bumps swelled on my arms. My body hair stood on end as if electrified. Considering Manson's lingering foul disposition and festering rage, I had to take this threat seriously.

If that wasn't bad enough, another incident occurred later that same day that resulted in a new series of threats. I was walking down a mainline corridor, lost in thought about Manson's threat, when I noticed a violent con named Barns strolling down the hall with Dr. Dean Morgan, a staff psychiatrist. Barns was an armed robber who had killed two people in Nevada shortly after being paroled. He was at CMF under a life sentence with no possibility of ever getting out again.

"What the hell is this man doing on the mainline?" I demanded in a loud voice, my irritation with Manson showing through. "He should be locked up in Willis Unit!"

Dr. Morgan was shocked by my confrontational approach and angry tone. "He's close B custody, Ed. He doesn't have to lock up until the four-thirty count."

"Hell, Doc, I figured that, but I looked at his file this morning. Nevada's got him for life without. In my book, he's a high escape risk. I know I'd be."

"Can't we lock him up tomorrow?" the doctor countered. "I've been his therapist for years. He's having trouble dealing with his life sentence and I can help him."

Oh? Was the poor murderer having problems with the punishment he so richly deserved? How about the people he had slaughtered? Think they're having problems adjusting to being dead, Doc? I was about to express those exact thoughts when I caught myself. "That's his problem," I snapped instead, sounding like a San Quentin gooner. "You're never going to help him. I want him locked up now!"

The doctor continued to plead his case as I looked around for a custody officer to drag this SOB to lockup. Barns stared at me with intense hatred, but said nothing.

"Okay, Doc," I relented, unable to find an escort guard. "Go do your thing. But tomorrow morning, I'm ordering him locked up until they transfer his sorry ass back to Nevada!"

That evening, I paced the hallways of my home, worrying about Manson's threat. Had he finally given the word? Were the assassins on the way? Would they be a drugged, bloodthirsty gang of sociopaths intent on cutting up my entire family and smearing words from Van Halen albums on the walls with our blood? The phone interrupted my anxiety. It was Dr. Morgan. His voice betrayed his fear. "Barns missed the four-thirty count. They can't find him anywhere. They think he escaped."

"Damn it, Doc, I knew it! Do you know how?"

"They're not sure, but an inmate told custody that Barns hid in a garbage can and went out the back of the garbage truck."

"The garbage truck! That old trick? I can't believe it. The way they check those trucks is a joke. I knew somebody would get out that way. So he left from the dump?"

"Probably."

"Well, thanks for the call. Not much we can do now."

"Uh, Ed, there's something else."

"Yes?"

"Uh, in our interview today, Barns expressed a real rage toward you for ordering him locked up. He said, 'If I ever get out of here, I'm going to kill that fuckin' son of a bitch.' "

"He threatened to kill me and you didn't lock him up?"

"I'm really sorry. I don't know what I can say. But I must warn you. My professional opinion is that he meant it. He has nothing to lose."

"The guy threatens to kill me if he escapes, remains in population, then promptly rides the garbage truck out a half hour later? Hell, he must be walking up my sidewalk right now! Thanks Doc!" I yelled, slamming down the receiver. Great. Now it had become a race to see who'd kill me first, Barns the enraged psycho, or a drug-crazed neo-Manson mob. My money was on Barns. He was out, close, and had the most intense immediate motivation. Plus, my home was set on a pasture three miles from the prison. The only thing that stood between the garbage dump and my back door was hilly rangeland. The single obstacle was Highway 80, and that could easily be crossed by scurrying under the bridge at Alamo Creek.

For the first time in my life, I felt unsafe in my home. The odds of somebody trying to take me out that night had suddenly doubled, making me tense and agitated. For once, I felt it was necessary to share the bad news with my family. I wanted everybody to hang tight that evening and be on their toes. I called the local police, explained both threats, and asked them to make frequent patrols. Meanwhile, my daughter Susan went outside and jumbled our address numbers around, which was pretty clever.

As my wife and children began to feed on the increasing fear, I tried to calm them down. "If Barns has any brains, he wouldn't risk hanging around Vacaville and getting caught. He's free, and that's more important than petty vengeance. If it were me, I'd be halfway to Mexico. As for Manson, he's just in a bad mood. He probably hasn't even given the order."

That eased everyone's mind a bit. At eleven, we broke for our individual rooms to try to get some sleep. Just in case, I loaded a .22 caliber rifle and slipped it under my bed.

At 1:00 A.M., I woke with a start. Terror pumped through my veins as I heard the sound of footsteps coming up the stairs. They stopped outside the bedroom door. I reached under the bed, grabbed the rifle, and slowly raised it. I pointed it toward the door as it swung open, my finger ready to squeeze the trigger. Suddenly, a voice startled me. "Dad? Dad, are you awake?" It was my son, David. I'd forgot that he'd been out on a date. I lowered the barrel, horrified at what I'd almost done. My body started to tremble.

"My God, I could have killed him!"

Beth put her arms around me. "It's all right. Everything's all right."

It wasn't all right. Beth didn't know how close I had come to pulling that trigger. Had David said the wrong thing, or nothing at all, I would have fired. If I hadn't immediately recognized his voice, I would have killed my own son. "Damn you, Charlie!" I muttered to myself. "This is on you. If you hadn't gotten me all agitated today, this wouldn't have happened. This is the second time you caused me to hurt, or nearly hurt, one of my children. Never again!"

As far as I know—unless my daughter's number shuffle fooled him—Barns didn't try to come after me that night. He was captured in Hayward, California, within the month and resumed his life sentence in Nevada. As for Manson, his followers didn't come that night, or for years afterward. But they were destined to eventually pay me a visit.

Manson himself could have easily wandered into my yard a few weeks later had he chosen to. Working as the tier tender, he came across a set of top security "red keys," scooped them off a foyer table, and dropped them into his pocket. The keys were Manson's proverbial ticket out, enabling him to open every single door and gate that stood between him and the outside. Incredibly, instead of hiding the one-in-a-million find in his cell and taking off for the hills that evening, Manson walked over to the unit sergeant and handed the keys to him. "Here," he said. "I'm not supposed to have these."

The stunned sergeant took the keys, discovered which officer had left them on the table, and did some major ass chewing. Manson, in turn, scored big points with the guards. When I pestered him about why he didn't make a break for it, he went into his Frankenstein rap, claiming it was more dangerous for him on the outside than in the prison. Actually, it was the second time Manson had gotten hold of a critical set of keys. The previous year, he picked a guard clean as the unwary officer passed by his cell. As with this incident, Charlie promptly called out to the guy and gave the keys back.

To kick Charlie and me out of our collective funk, I mended fences and asked if he wanted to set up another media interview. This time he chose to go voice only, selecting reporter Susan Kennedy of KGO radio in San Francisco. Without the cameras to play to, Manson was pretty mellow. The May 11, 1983, interview was mostly unremarkable, but did include a new admission. For the first time, he confessed to sending "the girls" to the Polanski residence under the instructions to do whatever Tex Watson told them to. That was as close as he got. Climbing back inside his unbreakable shell, he denied telling Tex or anyone else to murder the occupants. Interestingly enough, the distinction is more personal than legal. By acknowledging what he had, Manson indicted himself in a criminal conspiracy that led to multiple murders—which is basically what he was doing time for. Either way, it didn't mean a hill of beans. He'd long ago had his day in court, and despite the best efforts of bumbling guards, was destined to spend the rest of his life in prison.

One of my duties at CMF—aside from baby-sitting Manson—was to handle prisoner complaints and appeals. This often took me to other wings. I'd usually hear the inmate out and make an on-the-spot ruling. If the guy was semisane and had a legitimate beef, I'd try to correct it. One of these routine appeals took me to S-wing, the dungeon where the most acutely psychotic inmates are housed in enclosed cells. (Manson had spent a lot of penalty time there.) Most of the S-wing interviews were carried out through the food slot. That required the staffer to bend over and talk in an awkward, backbreaking position. I'm tall, six three, so it was even more uncomfortable. Instead of suffering through that hassle, I borrowed the tier officer's key and opened the door to the specific inmate's cell a crack, bracing my foot against it to prevent the door from opening further. The inmate appeared rational and presented his concerns in great detail. He insisted that Manson was going to kill him and wanted to be moved to another cell.

"You're going to be fine," I assured him. "I talked to Charlie and he can't even remember who you are. He has nothing against you and says he has no intention of causing you any harm. You have nothing to worry about." It was an effective argument. The only trouble was, the guy I was giving it too was a paranoid schizophrenic. He remained stone-faced. "No, I don't feel your situation warrants a move," I ruled.

Without realizing it, my foot slipped and the door opened wider. Glancing away from the con, I spotted an officer and two trusties coming down the hall with trays of food. "Well, here comes your—" I never finished the sentence. Out of nowhere, a thundering blow crashed into my face, driving me back against the far wall and stunning me into a brief period of unconsciousness. As I began to slide down the wall to the floor, I caught myself and struggled, rubber-legged, to my feet. Blood gushed from my nose, covering my mouth and chin. When my head cleared, I noticed that the lunch-crew officer and trustees had subdued the attacker. I took a step forward, intent on kicking the shit out of the son of a bitch, but caught myself. The guy's just sick, I thought, but he sure packs a wallop.

My nose was shattered and folded over my cheek. Three teeth were chipped. As I walked to the hospital, I realized that it had been my own stupid fault. I'd failed to check the inmate's file before doing the cracked-door number. Had I taken that precaution, I would have realized that the guy had tried to stab a guard with a fork two weeks before. I was lucky to come away with nothing more than a busted snout and some painful dental work.

It was the first and only time in my quarter century of walking among the cons and crazies that I'd ever been injured. I'd sat face-to-face with Manson hundreds of times and never got a scratch, and here I'd gotten waylaid by a nameless schizo in the proverbial padded cell.

"Get out of your paper-bag world," Manson chided when he saw my battered mug. "It's going to get you killed!" He turned, then tossed me something through the bars. I instinctively caught it. It was a little voodoo doll that vaguely resembled me. There was a single pin in the center of its face.

"That was for Squeaky," he announced.

14

MY CAREER IN corrections pretty much ended when I decided to testify in favor of an officer who sued to fight the abuses in the affirmative action program. Not wanting to appear like Manson, I'd tempered my views on the subject for years, enduring in silence as qualified candidates were passed over for far inferior minorities. Later, when it was discovered that officials were rigging test scores to give minority candidates the upper hand, my anger reawakened. The officer won his lawsuit in a ruling that helped even the playing field for everyone, but my career was shot. I was treated like a pariah by the central office staff. Whenever they came to the prison, I was either ignored, or subjected to cold, angry stares. I figured it would pass, but it didn't. What did I expect? I told myself. Snitch out the bigwigs and how can you expect to survive?

Afterward, I fell into a "Manson's right" depression. The corrections "system," i.e., the bureaucracy, preyed on anyone with half a brain who tried to make things better. Innovative programs were tossed aside, their creators soon to follow. As affirmative action took hold, the quality of my underlings diminished to the point where they could hardly read or write. Then, when these poorly trained, poorly educated employees made tragic mistakes, I'd get the blame.

Of course, Manson wasn't really right. He was on the other extreme. He would have eliminated the problem of unqualified minorities by eradicating the minorities themselves. The question was, is either extreme the answer? Do you lift the races up by giving them jobs they haven't earned, or does that just foster the something-for-nothing attitude that keeps them from striving to better themselves to begin with? By fighting abuses in affirmative action, are you trying to save a system and keep it operating at peak efficiency, or are you a Manson-like racist? Those and similar questions haunt me to this day.

Whatever the deeper ramifications, the ostracism built up pressures inside me that were destined to explode. By 1983, I was so emotionally frustrated and exhausted by the bureaucracy, I blew my top during a fierce argument with a female associate warden and threatened to punch her lights out. I placed myself on medical leave and took six months off. Renewed, I decided to give it another go. That decision hit a snag when the Return to Work coordinator happened to be the husband of the woman I'd threatened. He refused to let me have me my old job back. There was no sense challenging it; the "system" Manson so often railed about had finally gotten me, just like he said it would. I transferred to the parole department and became a parole agent.

"Here," my new boss said, dumping a huge stack of files on my desk. "Enjoy."

I sighed, then dug in. At least these were men who'd earned, or been handed, a second chance. Many desperately wanted to stay clean and eagerly sought my help. That was satisfying. Instead of spending my energy keeping men locked up, maybe I could help a few hundred stay out.

Since Manson wasn't about to be paroled, I lost daily contact with him for nearly a decade. I did keep track of his activities and whereabouts, frequently going to CMF and other area prisons on official business. One event in particular I'm sorry I missed. On September 24, 1984, a Hare Krishna follower named Jan grew tired of Manson constantly belittling his religious beliefs and threatened to do something about it. That something would not prove to be pretty. Hidden beneath his placid Hindu chants stirred the demented mind of a homicidal maniac. He was in CMF for murdering his stepfather, a research physician he insisted was really the infamous "Angel of Death," Nazi death camp doctor Josef Mengele. With such a history, the swastika carved into Charlie's forehead must have acted like a blinking red light, feeding the whacked-out Krishna's growing dementia. Charlie's fusillade of fierce insults merely quickened the inevitable.

The Hare follower smuggled a container of paint thinner from the hobby shop, dumped it on Manson, and proceeded to set the cult leader ablaze. Some nearby cons and guards jumped to Charlie's rescue and smothered the flames before they could do fatal damage. Charlie was toasted over 18 percent of his body, suffering second- and third-degree burns on his face, hands, arm, shoulder, and scalp. His long hair and full beard melted away. Jan argued that he'd acted in self-defense because Manson had been giving him "threatening looks"—a charge practically everybody at CMF could have made.

Charlie took it well, playing tough guy and suffering the intense pain in relative silence. What really ticked him off was that the incident helped end his cushy days at CMF. The staff finally decided that he'd caused enough trouble and decided to complete his "ninety-day evaluation," a process that, in a sense, had lasted an astounding ten years! (Mostly due to my efforts to keep him around by designating him for "long-term care" after his initial evaluation.) In an irony that wasn't lost on the "system"-hating, antiestablishment revolutionary, he was shipped out not because of anything he had done, but because of something that was done to him. To add insult to paint-thinner injury, he was sent back to San Quentin.

On the other hand, it's safe to say that despite the decade spent in a treatment-oriented facility, Manson left CMF in no better mental shape than when he arrived.

His files were much cleaner though—as in cleaned out. When it came time to ready the papers for transfer, officers discovered Manson's three telephone-book-sized file folders were gone. His entire prison history had been pilfered. Someone, possibly a souvenir-hunting officer or staffer, had smuggled out every page.

A squad of six armed officers driving three cars transported the paperless guru to his hated old home. When duty officers searched him prior to entering, they found a hacksaw blade in his shoe. Manson had stuffed it in there for the sole purpose of being caught, an action that would assure himself a safe haven in the AC lockup unit.

My parole activities took me to San Quentin not long after Manson's arrival. Actually, I was there pretty routinely because, like the lightning rod I was, I'd inherited yet another infamous, and uniquely difficult, prisoner. Years before, a man named Larry Singleton had raped a young California lady, cut off both her arms, and thrown her off a bridge to die. She survived, becoming a ghastly symbol of man's inhumanity to man. Singleton served his eight-year sentence and was set to be paroled. But just as Manson always feared for himself, Singleton had nowhere to go. Everywhere we tried to place him, the media announced it and the locals naturally went nuts. In Rodeo, California, I watched from a surveillance trailer as a crowd gathered outside the hotel where he'd been stashed. The mob grew large and riotous, and a rope materialized. One guy had an armless doll on a stick, rallying the citizens with a vivid visual reminder of Singleton's savage crime. A tattooed group of bikers pulled in, grabbed the rope, and shouted, "Let's lynch the bastard!" They were planning to do just that when we called for an army of sheriffs and highway patrolmen.

It was like that everywhere we tried to settle the sick son of a bitch. Even at San Quentin, we had to isolate and baby-sit the guy twenty-four hours a day because the other prisoners despised him.

"See," Charlie said when I took a break and paid him a visit. "It's just like I've been telling you for the last two decades. I'm Frankenstein. I can't go anywhere. I can't even escape! If the town folks are trying so hard to hang that asshole, what do you think they'd do to me? They can't even recognize him without a picture and a map. Everybody recognizes me!"

We finally had to do with Singleton what the prison system may one day have to do with Charlie—let him serve out his parole behind bars, then sneak him off somewhere secluded and desolate and order him to stay put and be quiet. Larry did—for a while anyway, until he carved up a Florida woman in early 1997. Charlie? Hard to imagine him staying quiet for more than a few hours.

Two days before Christmas, 1987, Squeaky began hearing rumors on the con pipeline that Manson was so unhappy at San Quentin that he was dying of some kind of misery-induced cancer. Driven by hysteria, she enacted a long-designed secret plan and escaped from Alderson Federal Prison, vanishing into the dense forests surrounding the isolated facility. She ran through the rugged, hostile hills of West Virginia for two days, surviving icy rain and temperatures that plunged into the teens during the night. Because of her fame, more than a hundred officers combed the area searching for Charlie's Queen. An alert went out nationwide, and President Ronald Reagan's security was tightened.

"She's coming to get you!" Charlie raged to Dave Langerman, San Quentin's information officer. "She's going to kill you for the way you've been treating me!"

On Christmas Day, much to Langerman's relief, Squeaky emerged on her own at 12:50 P.M. near a remote West Virginia fishing camp. She was hungry, forlorn, and exhausted, and offered no resistance. She told the court that her access to Charlie had been limited for so long that she was overcome with feelings of despair. "If love means anything at all, it means stop feeling helpless and take action. . . . I'm guilty as charged, legally, but without moral remorse. So that's that."

Interviewed after her capture, she spoke of a magic transformation while running, assuming the attributes of both a two-toed sloth and a ballerina to help her escape detection, enabling her to slither through the woods unseen and elude the manhunt.

Frankly, I wasn't impressed. A certified earth child like Squeaky should have been able to last longer than two days! Squeaky, like all Manson followers, filled the air with love for the land and trees. How ironic that once free in the exact "beautiful" environment she cherished, she found it unforgiving and unlivable, preferring instead to scurry back to her warm cage where her keepers provided three squares a day. Somewhere, conservative icon Rush Limbaugh must have been howling with laughter.

Charlie, healthy as an ox, stayed at San Quentin until 1989. After wearing out his welcome there, he was bounced to Corcoran State Prison, where he has been in lockup ever since.

On December 3, 1985, Sandra Good completed her ten-year sentence for sending threatening letters and was paroled to a halfway house on the condition that she stay away from Manson and California. She had refused an earlier release date, finding those conditions too strangling. This time, she accepted and spent the next four years in Camden, New Jersey, under limited supervision. After completing the parole, she was set free—no strings attached—at the end of 1989. She immediately ran to California and set up camp near Manson in Hanford. She's remained there to this day, running an organization called ATWA (Air, Trees, Water, Animals), remaining loyal to Manson, and rebuilding his family. Through the use of computer technology, Sandra, who always was bright, has set up an elaborate computer page on the Internet that updates fans on Manson's activities, helps publicize his albums (which were finally recorded by some small independent labels), and mainly spreads the interactive word to new generations. The Web site, "Access Manson" (http://www.atwa.com), has proven to be highly popular, racking up tens of thousands of "hits" per month. The beat goes on.

*   *   *

In August 1992, I was standing in the checkout line at the local super-market idly perusing the tabloids when one of the headlines jumped out at me. The bold letters announced that Charlie's on-again, off-again pal, Willie Spann, was dying of AIDS. The story inside quoted Willie extensively, and was accompanied by photographs showing the former president's nephew looking gaunt and ghastly. Willie, according to his quotes, contracted the deadly disease through the sharing of heroin needles. At the time, I wanted to believe that it was nothing more than another attempt by Willie to gain some sympathy and attention. Willie was basically harmless to anyone but himself, and it pained me to see him going out that way.

Five years later, on February 2, 1997, Willie collapsed and died in front of a Good Samaritan's home in Oakland. The woman who owned the house had discovered him sick and destitute on the streets. In an extraordinary display of kindness, she brought him to her residence to care for him. Shortly thereafter, he tumbled from a hammock and stopped breathing. A newspaper story repeated the reports that he had contracted AIDS, and added that he had been suffering from dementia. Willie was fifty when he passed away. It was a sad end to a sad life.

In April 1995, Charlie was busted for dealing drugs and partaking in other "illegal business dealings" at Corcoran. The illegal businesses involved the marketing of his autograph, photos, and better yet, autographed photos. Charlie was dragged in for an administrative hearing.

"Not guilty. No evidence," he pleaded. "There's nothing there. The snitch game's being played down there in that rat unit. The administration of this prison must not have anything better to do."

The hearing officers found him guilty and snatched away 150 credit days, a meaningless punishment to a man serving multiple life sentences.

Charlie, suffice it to say, was unfazed.

On June 6, 1995, I arranged a tour of Corcoran to check things out on my own. My old sergeant from CMF was the program administrator there, and invited me down to reminisce. "There's someone here I'm sure you'd like to say hello to," he teased.

The sprawling prison is located a mile south of the small town of Corcoran, perched on a flat, dry, desolate piece of land the state must have bought cheap. The facility is ringed with high Cyclone fences laced with coils of razor wire. The buildings are elephant gray rectangular blocks surrounded by a perimeter of gun towers. We strapped on bulletproof vests and ventured into the heart of darkness. Far from the laid-back Cuckoo's Nest days at CMF, Charlie's current home is the proverbial pit of doom.

I appeared without warning in front of his cell. He looked at me quiz-zically, then smiled and ambled over to the bars. He was sixty-one, a full-fledged senior citizen with a mane of steel gray hair and a Santa Claus beard. That, however, proved to be misleading. Underneath, he remained coiled like a snake and just as lean and mean.

"What the fuck do you want?" he said in a joking manner, repeating his opening greeting mantra. We talked for a while and immediately fell back into our old pattern. The years hadn't mellowed Charlie at all. He had the same expressions and odd mannerisms, grinning like the devil and twisting his beard with his forefinger and thumb. "Hey, can you get me a guitar?" he asked, ever the hustler.

"What happened? You destroy another one — or ten?" Charlie laughed and pestered me again to pull some strings and let him have his music. "I'm retired, remember? I don't have the juice anymore."

"You'll always have the juice. Here's your juice," he said, grabbing his balls.

Oh yes, I thought. How I missed the image of Charlie clutching his nuts, using con psychology to get me to do his bidding. Shifting subjects, I mentioned that I was writing a book and that he was going to be a big part of it. That caught his attention, but he said little about it at the time. We both promised to keep in touch.

Charlie kept his word and began peppering my mailbox with letters. Most of them centered around the book. He wanted to know what I was going to write about him. I explained that I was planning to tell it all, the good and the bad. "You have a decent side, and you have an evil side. I'll write it all down and let the publisher sort it out," I explained. He warned me in subsequent letters that the things I wrote could cause problems for me.

"You are creating the crime. It's your end," he accused. Gradually, his letters took on an even more threatening tone. "You will all die for what you've done to me," he scribbled, putting me back on his long list of those who'd done him wrong.

Two months after our reunion, on July 29, 1995, I opened my door at 7:00 A.M. to retrieve the morning paper and was assaulted by a horrible smell. Looking down, I was repulsed to find what looked like some kind of witches'-brew stew gurgling across my porch, oozing down the stairs, and spilling onto the walkway. Holding my nose and inspecting it further, I determined that it was composed of rancid chopped pork, fruit, vegeta-bles, and a host of unrecognizable condiments. My initial thought was that someone had thrown up, but it would have taken King Kong to produce that much bile. The smell, though sufficiently foul, didn't have the acid aroma of vomit. This was no accident.

I spent most of the morning trying to clean up the mess, scooping the wretched solids off with a shovel and hosing away the rest. No matter what

I did, an ominous black stain and harsh odor remained. I tried every detergent known to man, including muriatic acid, but the black outline wouldn't dissipate.

Waving my fist at the permanent scar, I suspected at once how it had gotten there and what it meant. I wondered if this was Manson's calling card, his way of saying he knew where I lived and that bad things would happen if he didn't like the book. The idea that a pack of his crazies might be crawling around the neighborhood, skulking up to my house in the middle of the night, and unloading their poison alternately angered and terrified me.

Five days later, on August 2, 1995, it happened again. The mixture was the same, but this time, there was no meat. Hard as I tried, I couldn't figure out the meaning of that.

My twenty-four-year-old daughter, our only child who remained at home, said that her dog, a boxer, had woken up and begun growling and prowling the room at 4:00 A.M., too agitated to sleep. The same thing had happened on July 29. Amazingly, the dog had sensed an evil presence in the area.

The nearest enclave of neo-Manson followers was in Hanford, a city three hours away. That meant that if any of them had been involved, they would have had to drive six hours round-trip, starting at 1:00 A.M., do the nasty deed, and then arrive back home after 7:00 A.M. It was a long way to go to send a stupid message, but no amount of suffering would be too much to prove their devotion to their chosen master—a man many of them had probably never seen.

Without proof or a more overt threat, there was nothing I could do. The only real option, confronting Charlie, would certainly prove fruitless as he was the master of denial. Instead, I chose to wait. Without an acknowledgment, if Manson had been involved, he might be wondering whether the dumps had occurred, or whether his demented minions had hit the right house. If I stayed silent, he might tip his hand. Manson avoided all mention of it. He continued to make threats regarding the book, and implied that some fearsome event was soon coming my way.

Threatening journalists and authors was nothing new with Charlie. He or his followers harassed virtually everyone who ever wrote or said anything bad about him. Manson would often jump on me after an interview he had carefully approved went bad, accusing me of setting him up. Authors Nuel Emmons (*Manson in His Own Words*) and Dr. Clara Livsey (*The Manson Women: A Family Portrait*) were among those given the treatment. Chris Weinstein, the young reporter who experienced the chilling hair-pulling demonstration, was harassed so much after her article ran that she told me she wished she'd never written it—and she hadn't said anything bad about Charlie!

Viewed in this light, the foul mess on my porch appeared to be par for the course. If it did involve the Manson Family, no one was even waiting to read the book.

While Manson played coy, Sandra spewed the overt poison. A recent letter referred to me as "one of the most twisted and distorted men" she has ever known. Considering the men she has known, that was some insult!

It was obvious that Sandra was heating up because Manson was spoon-feeding her the "Ed tortured me all these years" pabulum. I knew the rap. I was evil, not to be trusted. I hurt him, tried to destroy his cause, ruined his life, held him down, suffocated and oppressed him. I was the embodiment of the system that bruised, beat, and raped him all his life. Charlie knew he could use this line to work Sandra into a frenzy of rage.

On October 4, 1995, I received an envelope from Sandra enclosing a letter from Manson and a brilliant, multicolored graphic, a collage of diverse shapes and forms. Also enclosed was a similarly colored map depicting blocks and buildings surrounded by witchy, psychedelic symbols of every sort. Both drawings, interestingly enough, contained copyright symbols giving the year 1995, and naming "Good" as the artist. Apparently, the Family was getting wise to merchandising. Studying the intricate designs, I discovered that one building was encased in a circular bombsight with crosshairs. A missile was exploding in front of the building. A message written in the margin said, "Coming soon to your neighborhood 2." On the back were the words "Neighborhood revisited." I shook the envelope and out came a clipped magazine photograph of "Big Boy," the nuclear weapon dropped on Hiroshima. The implications were clear. Charlie and Sandra were telling me that the building under the crosshairs was my house. "Neighborhood revisited" may have referred to the Tate residence. "Big Boy" was overkill—typical Manson humor.

There was nothing humorous about the overall meaning. I saw this as the support I had been looking for that Manson's clan had been to my home and doused the porch with their satanic stew. It scared me for a long time, forcing me to reconsider my goal of writing a book. I had played with this fire for nearly twenty years, had escaped relatively unscathed, and was now safely ensconced in a stress-free retirement. Manson had told me many times that my "intrusion" into his life would cost me. Now I understood. There's a price to pay for entering a madman's domain.

Why fuel the smoldering flames by writing a book? Why the hell not? Why let Manson dictate my life? Wasn't it Manson himself who told me to get out of my paper-bag world and act with my balls and not my brain? Well, my brain was saying bag it, it's not worth it, but my balls were screaming, "Fuck you, Charlie!"

On October 10, 1995, I met with Vacaville's police chief, Lee Dean, and told him about the threats and dumpings. We met again on the sixteenth, this time joined by two captains. They were sympathetic, but powerless to do anything. I had been aware of that going in. The purpose was to let them know that if something happened to me, they could find a lead in Hanford. I also contacted the Department of Corrections Special Services Unit and asked them to have Manson's latest keeper scrutinize his mail a little closer. I had balls, but I was no fool. (After I contacted the police, Sandra sent me a letter in January 1996, saying "We don't care about your book.")

Seething over the October threat, I decided to take the gloves off and fight back. "You're a real pain in the ass!" I wrote. "I thought you told your followers to do their own thing? Well, that's what I'm doing, telling them to stay out of my business. So, damn it, shut up and leave me alone! Don't try to intimidate me and my family. Quit telling me I'm into money and controlled by fear. Maybe I'm too stupid to realize that I'm supposed to be living in fear. . . . Let me lecture you for a change. You have always done what you wanted, made your own laws, fucked everything you could, sang and danced all night, pigged out on drugs, horsed around with the rich and famous, sleazed around with whores and cut up a few nice people. You let your followers do the really heavy-duty stuff. Still, you got nailed. You have defended yourself to me many times. I accepted your reasons. So why don't you accept my reasons for not believing you? Because I disagree doesn't mean I lie.

"Writing about you is crazy, especially if I try to describe your nothing, upside-down, paradoxical philosophy which doesn't make sense to anybody but you and your closest followers. . . . Your idea that I'm using you is pure bullshit. You were in prison when I got there. I took care of you better than most administrators. You'll never know all the things I did for you. But that's history. I know your fear, and how you use it and use those you trust to instill it. . . . The one time fear made it big-time with you was after the Family did the murders in L.A. when everyone ran to the desert to hide, searching for a big hole. Fear came creeping into you then. Fear of being hunted down, shot at, thrown in a dingy old cell for the rest of your life to rot. Fear happens to us all at some time, because death chases us from the time we are born. Most of us fear the end, because they think it is the end. But, Charlie, the dance goes on. You must know that. Even you, Charlie, have had to watch your back. You and I both know, but that's our secret."

Charlie's response, paraphrased and translated into something resembling English, was as follows: "You should think seriously about whether you want to dig into this [writing about him]. You may wind up on S-wing where I did some time [the padded cells]. You are not very stable and won't be able to handle the pressures involved in writing about me. . . . What are you going to tell about me? . . .

"You are a good man, but you don't see the truth and work in lies. You and society need a scapegoat. That's me. . . . There is only one god. To get there you must go to zero, count backward, go through me and start from my reality. I came to save you but you wouldn't listen. . . . You have always been my angel, my saint, my soul, my father. . . .

"I could beat you and drag you like you used to do me, but so far, I haven't. I just let you pass by, get married, have kids, raise cops and lawyers who chase after money and forget about everything else, while Jesus never died, but went into the witness protection program."

That response obviously did nothing to ease my anger. However, instead of firing back at Charlie, I decided to give Sandra Good a taste of my stinging pen: "I have always respected you and Lynette. Your intelligence, loyalty, and determination are rare commodities in our society. I shall call you imitators of the master rather than followers or Family members if that offends you. I understand where you are coming from, but you and Lynette are known for your witchy little intimidations. That stuff can only damage what little we have in common—Charlie."

"I too am from a square environment, middle-class Oakland, like you. You dated a friend of mine, Gary, . . . many years ago. He was a brash, outspoken loudmouth who told me you were sort of weird. But that's ancient history. . . . The book is not about the murders and the prosecution. The "Bug" [Bugliosi] did that. Mine is about the prisons years, mainly from 1971 to the present. There is stuff about you, and Lynette too, but it's mainly about prison life. . . . Over the years, Charlie and I fought a lot about philosophy and values. I agreed with him about the environment, children being neglected, the greed of our society, but I never bought his cruel, heartless methods. Charlie was an abused, neglected kid, strapped and whipped, pushed around, told to get lost by his mom, or so he said. His mom countered that he was a spoiled brat who always got what he wanted. Things haven't changed. Probably, she just gave up on him and he gave up on her. His resentment went from anger to hate, then vengeance. He went to one reform school after another, then one jail after another, and lastly, to prison, all told 48 years! Too much for any man. He finally found love with a bunch of kids who hadn't grown up, who were looking for a good time. Like Charlie's mother, they all sold him out by acting crazy, killing people, and as he claims, forcing him back to prison. . . .

"Some of your group now say that Charlie made them do it. 'He ordered us,' they crow. Once faithful followers, turning on him, pointing the accusing finger. 'It was him! He did it!' They said it in books, magazines, on TV and radio. Now only you, Lynette, and a handful of faithful followers hold on to him after 25 years.

"He blames the defectors, society, even me, for his downfall. He's an angry man who blames Blacks and Jews, saying Blacks messed up the gene pool and Jews hoard all the money. He feeds on the hate virus and the disease has spread. History may rewrite itself, revolution may come, but time is running out for him. He and I grow old. Cancer hides in our bones, ready to wake up and grow in our limbs. Our brain cells dissolve into a universe as we plod along. Soon, all the earth in us to earth returns. . . .

"In the final analysis, we stand alone. . . . Everyone sees things their way, personally, subjectively, no matter what the facts. If you need a god, there's one for you! They're on sale all over the world. . . . We need something to believe in and we are afraid to think for ourselves, to be left alone. . . . Charlie has his capsule and you have yours. I have mine and Lynette has hers. You have tried to enter Charlie's capsule, but you cannot stay. Your life is separate, but in your fear, you cannot let go of his capsule. Only when he dies will you be forced to be your own navigator. . . .

"You and Charlie have used fear and terror to motivate people. You used it on me. All you really see is fear and terror, not love or compassion. That's why you all went to prison. You've done terrible evil, striking fear into those who see your deeds. People die, but life goes on. What have you accomplished? You get publicity, name recognition. For what? . . . You suspended your life, entombed your talents, castrated yourself, foolishly believing you have accomplished something. What? Killing a few people? What exactly does that prove? Does that glorify Manson? Create majesty? Charlie thought it gave him great power, exhilaration, exultation. Now he spends his life in prison playing his funny little games and mind trips, hoping an AB, a Black gangster, or an angry Mexican doesn't kill him.

"He has always sent people like you to do his dirty work. Amazingly, you have been faithful to him and I can do nothing to stop that. Once, I tried to turn Lynette away from Charlie and she almost went mad. Instead, she chose to remain madly in love with him, while wishing to cut off my head. It was the futility of your lives that drove me crazy, not any fear you and Charlie held over me. It was the senseless striving, the wasted energy, the lost moments, the loving, touching tenderness that you all started with, and the missing of the precious time you had to be truly happy. That's what broke my heart.

"Can't you see that there has been too much blood split? Will you ever see beyond a prison cell, beyond a madman's dream? You have traveled so far, yet you have only a fading voice left, echoes of the past.

"I know you cannot see where I'm coming from. Charlie says it's religion, God stuff, a momma hang-up, early child programming. He says that I've been searching for the source of the Nile all my life, and it's him, right under my nose. . . . We all look for the truth, a bit of happiness, a God. Some say they have found it. Some swear by it. But there is much that man does not know and never will. I guess Charlie is your truth, found too quickly and too soon. . . ."

Charlie, Squeaky, Sandra, and I have continued to trade similar letters to this day.

*　　*　　*

On August 10, 1996, I decided to drive to Corcoran and renew my love/ hate relationship with Charlie. We'd traded some serious threats in the mail the previous year, so it was time to kiss and make up. Officially, I was going to visit Roger Dale "Pin Cushion" Smith. Pin assured me that Charlie would be in the visiting room entertaining his own guests and we'd have a chance to chat.

I arrived a day early to scope the place out, learn the procedure, and determine if I had the right color pants. Khaki and blue Levi's are forbidden because a quick switch could enable a prisoner to posed as a civilian and flee. My light green trousers were borderline, so I made a note to go to a Mervyn's department store later that evening and purchase a gray pair. Before leaving, I tried to track down a female counselor Manson had recently threatened to kill over some trivial matter. I wondered if she was being hassled by the Family on the outside as well. Manson had similarly threatened a female lieutenant six months before. Unfortunately, neither officer was available. However, I was able to track down a report that included Manson's cryptic, handwritten response to one of the women's charges. The officer stated that she was performing her routine duties when Charlie spotted her on the floor and shouted, "You fucking bitch! I'll kill you. I'll find your babies and kill your babies too. I've killed women and their babies before!" The shaken officer reported that there had been no prior conversation, and that the verbal assault was unprovoked.

"Sad," Charlie scribbled in response. "No one will talk to her. She needs someone bad. She wants some attention bad. I'm under people's needs and they come to me twisted and distorted. There was nothing said. It's bunkum."

Same old Charlie, covering his horrendous behavior by proclaiming to have the ability to unearth deep-seated psychological needs in his victims. He wasn't terrorizing her. He was helping her cope with her loneliness!

I motored to the front gate at 7:30 the next morning and was curtly told to queue up on a side road where forty cars were already waiting. As with most prisons, processing visitors is a tedious nightmare. The friends and relatives of cons are frequently forced to suffer their own indignities for a chance to huddle with their incarcerated loved ones. It was such a different, and quite unpleasant, experience for me being just a regular schmuck with friends in low places. It took ninety minutes before I even made it to the visiting room. Once there, I was thoroughly searched head to toe before being allowed to pass through a metal detector to make sure I didn't have a zip gun up my ass like the guy back at San Quentin. While enduring that ordeal, I noticed a tall, skinny man with long, stringy hair tied in a bun just ahead of me. He was dressed in flowing hippie clothing and looked like a throwback to the 1960s. I'd spied him earlier when he drove up in a battered yellow Volkswagen. "That's Charlie's visitor," I whispered to myself. "Got to be."

A meandering shuttle carried us to the maximum-security visiting area located a half mile inside the complex. Finally, I'd reached my destination and was immediately greeted by a grinning Pin. I was going to hug the big buffoon, but I didn't want the visiting-room officers to get the wrong idea. Across the room, Manson was sitting at a table deep in conversation with the hippie guy. I'd nailed that one. Charlie's head was clean-shaven, making the ever present swastika on his forehead even more pronounced. He sported the same old mustache and goatee, but this time it was neatly trimmed. His tan, healthy appearance was a startling contrast to the previous year, when his hair was long and gray and his old-man beard was white and full. He looked twenty years younger — and far more menacing.

Charlie glanced our way and gave me a sly smile of recognition. After speaking briefly with Roger, I walked over and shook his hand. "I'll talk to you later," I said, not wanting to cut in on the skinny hippie's action.

Pin had been acting as my intermediary, trying to heal the wounds of the past year so I could interview Charlie and tie up some loose ends for the book. Pin had assured me things were cool, but I needed a frank, up-to-the-minute read on the bald one's ever changing moods. "He's still upset about your threats, but that's fading," Pin acknowledged. "He also remains angry that you turned down mail privileges for Lynette and Sandra all those years."

"Even if I wanted to, I would have been overruled," I protested. "There's no way anyone was going to let them correspond—" Pin waved me off, signaling that I didn't have to explain. He understood, but we knew Manson never would. Charlie believed in the power of the individual. He didn't subscribe to a chain of command, and therefore would forever put the blame on me. It was an interesting philosophy coming from the ironfisted leader who uttered the now infamous command "Do what Tex tells you to" the night of the Tate murders.

Pin changed the subject by proudly displaying the scars from his latest stabbing. He's been shanked at Pelican Bay State Prison for reasons he didn't explain — adding to his already untouchable record. The attack was his ticket to Corcoran, where he was locked down in the Protective Housing Unit right next to his old pal Charlie. Pin's smile melted when the conversation turned to Julian Ramirez, his old San Quentin death row lover from twenty years back. Ramirez had died of stomach cancer that spring, and Roger took it hard. I marveled how this big, brutal felon could hold a torch for someone like that for so long. Deep inside, Pin was a lover, not a killer. Years before, he'd written Julian one of the most beautiful love letters I'd ever read. As I mouthed the words, my heart went out to both of them. Love can indeed be strange.

After a few hours, Charlie skittered over and sat down with us. Pin made an excuse to leave so we could hash out our problems. The "hashing" consisted of me listening to Charlie ramble. He hit the old targets, the "injustice system," the environment, his devoted followers, and my fear, which he said was in me and not his problem. "You're paranoid, man," he concluded. I tried to direct him to my agenda, with little success.

"Did you know your father, Colonel Scott?" I asked, wanting to confirm his mother's account.

"You're my father," he fenced. "You raised me."

"Would you like to write a chapter for the book? You can say whatever you want."

"We need to save the redwood trees. . . ."

"Can I print some of your letters? We'll clean them up for you."

"Clean up the air and water first, then I'll . . ."

As I listened to his familiar rap, a chill washed over my body. I was absentmindedly observing the comings and goings of other cons, tuning Manson out while searching for familiar faces. One profile suddenly rang an eerie bell. I couldn't put a name on him at first, then it came—Juan Corona. I'd spent my life with murderers, rapists, child molesters, and their ilk, but this guy Corona was the only one who always gave me the creeps. I turned and shielded my profile, not wanting him to spot me and come by for a friendly chat. A bald Charles Manson was enough excitement for one day.

I drifted back into the relentless rantings of the little cue ball, confident that I'd missed nothing during my trip down dead-migrant-worker lane. Charlie had shifted to something moderately interesting.

"Remember, Ed, I killed no one. The girls had all the intelligence and they knew what they were doing." After clarifying that for the millionth time, he started pushing his own agenda. "I've never snitched on anybody. Remember that." The statement caught me off guard until I realized that Charlie was worried about the book. He really didn't care about anything I said about him as long as I didn't say he was a snitch. His world was the prisons, and to snitch in prison is to die. I couldn't understand what he was so worried about. He had done everything else in his life, but as far as I could tell, he had never seriously snitched.

Later that afternoon, I returned the favor and sat down at Charlie's table. The hippie eyed me suspiciously. It was obvious he resented my taking his precious time. Pin said the guy was living with Sandra Good in Hanford, and had helped her set up the Manson Web site on the Internet. I shot him a hard look, wondering if he was part of the crew that had dumped the witches' brew on my porch.

I took some photos with Charlie and Pin for old times' sake, and then we bid our farewells. I'd basically accomplished nothing, but nonetheless, it had been worth the trip just to see Charlie's shiny pate.

On August 31, I tried it again. The same gang was in the visiting room,

Charlie, Pin, and the hippie. Charlie was in a foul mood and apparently had been for a while. He'd thrown a major tantrum a few days earlier because the guards wouldn't allow him to have an embroidered shirt Sandra Good sent. Ignoring his dark disposition, I dived right in, opening our conversation by asking if I could use Squeaky's old, unpublished *Rolling Stone* article in the book. He ignored me and danced around.

"Who's 'Green'? I wondered, trying to match a face with one of his nicknames.

"Irish."

"Like Susan Murphy?"

"No. Like Greenland and Greenfield, Indiana, where I did some time."

"Don't put that crazy act on me," I snapped. "I've seen it too many times."

"And you'll see it some more!"

"I'm sure. Where's Richard Rubacher?"

"Somewhere along the coast. I sent him all my letters and he wrote to them [*Stern*?]. I guess he just made some money and retired." Charlie shot me a cold, sinister smile that made me wonder if Rubacher had shared the spoils as promised.

"What about Nuel Emmons? You gave him a book [to write]," I queried. It was an important question because Emmons's well-written book, *Manson in His Own Words*, included the most damning passages I'd ever seen linking Charlie directly to the Tate-LaBianca murders. Though at times Emmons presented the clear-speaking Manson as a reluctant follower who lost control of his minions—the story Charlie always sold me—when it came down to those final nights of mayhem, he portrayed Manson as being firmly in control. Here Emmons quotes Manson quoting himself giving the order to Tex Watson:

> "It's time to get something done for Bobby. The girls are ready to do whatever is necessary. They don't have a plan or a place picked out, so it looks like it's going to be pretty much up to you. But I think it would be best to hit some of the rich pigs' places. Get some bolt cutters or something you can cut a phone wire or gate chain with. You know what else you need, so put it together and get going. . . . You know the neighborhoods, someplace like where Terry [Melcher] used to live. Just make sure the girls do it like Gary's house was done. Maybe even take some rope and hang somebody, like a reverse of the Ku Klux Klan thing, that way it will put the heat on the blackies."
>
> Now I was so much a part of it, I might as well have been in the car with the others, knife and gun in hand. I knew that each suggestion dropped to Tex would be followed as a course of action. Whatever they did, it would be the same as if I had done it with

them. For one short moment, I had an urge to overtake the car and bring them back. . . . I turned away from the trailer . . . and took a long walk. Maybe sometime during that walk I thought of how wrong it was. Personally, I had never believed any tactics, copy-cat or otherwise, were going to get Bobby off the hook. Yet . . . I had shared in the madness. I had a moment or two of regret, but for the most part, bitterness and contempt for a world I didn't give a shit about allowed me to go along with anything that might come of the night's activities. . . . I hadn't twisted any arms. I wasn't sit-ting behind anyone with a gun next to their head, giving directions. Yet, I can't deny making some of the suggestions that led to the events of that night. Nor can I deny that I was the one person who could have prevented that car from leaving Spahn Ranch. But—so goes the feeling of power when coupled with hatred.

On that evening, I was aware of being totally without con-science. . . . I can't put a finger on when I became devoid of caring emotion. . . . Here I was, waiting for a report of murder to come back to me, not caring who had died or how many victims there were. And the closest I could come to disliking myself was "Char-lie, you are your mother's son—one dirty bogus bastard." Thinking of my mother quickly altered any softness that may have been creeping into my mind. I saw my mother guiding me through the courtroom door, and heard her speak the words, "Yes your Honor, I want my son, but I just can't afford to support both of us at this time." I remembered the argument she had had with her boyfriend a few nights prior to that day in court, and I heard him saying, "I don't give a shit, I'm leaving. I can't stand that kid. Get rid of him and we can make it just fine."

I saw four larger and older guys beating the hell out of me and wrestling me to the floor, and I remember them holding me while one ripped my ass with his big cock and then the others took their turn. I thought of good old Mr. Fields, in charge of all the boys and paid to teach us the responsibility of being honest citizens, lubricating my asshole with tobacco juice and raw silage and then offering me to his favorite pets. My head was straight now. Fuck this world and everyone in it. I'd give them something to open their eyes, and then take our group out into the desert. . . .

Emmons further detailed how Manson, worried that Tex and the girls had left incriminating evidence at the crime scene, went to the Tate house later that same night and wiped everything down to eliminate fingerprints. The horror Charlie found inside did not appear to disturb him.

"So what about that, Charlie? Was Emmons on the mark?"

"He was a convict who had a body and fender shop on the street [in

L.A.]. He fixed up my car and saved me from getting arrested," Manson explained, dodging the details. "I owed him, so I let him write a book. He called it *Manson in His Own Words*, but it was really Manson in his [Emmons's] words," Charlie added with a laugh.

"Was it accurate?" I repeated, having heard that Charlie was angry when the book came out.

"It was no different than all the others. Same bullshit."

"I've written to Emmons twice, and he hasn't responded," I mentioned.

"That's because you're a cop and he's a convict. He don't trust you."

"I thought he was an author now?"

"Once a con, always a con."

I eventually tracked Emmons down. To the contrary, he turned out to be super friendly. He gave me some photographs of Charlie and the old gang, and even showed me a pair of false teeth that Manson had given him.

"What about that Hare Krishna guy?" I asked Charlie. "What was the deal with that? Why'd he light you up?"

"The dude showed me a photo of his wife with this Hare Krishna guru from India. I said, 'A light-skinned Negro guru like that must enjoy fucking nice white girls.' He didn't like that remark. Then I told him that his guru wasn't God, that Jesus was, and that he should follow Jesus. He didn't like that either. A few days later, he came after me with the match [and paint thinner]. I exploded like a bomb."

That was a switch. I'd never known Charlie to defend the faith before. He must have gotten hold of a Bible and stumbled across Matthew 5, verses 11–12, the part that promises great rewards to anyone who suffers in the name of Jesus. Was Charlie seeing the end in sight due to his advancing age? Was he, like so many people, trying to get his house in order before going to that big isolation cell in the sky? Probably not, but it was a development worth watching.

In keeping with Charlie's more familiar mind-set, he told me that the karma gods had already taken vengeance for what the Hare Krishna had done. "If you send a scorpion out to stick someone, and they don't have it coming, the scorpion will spin around and come back at you. After that Hindu burned me and I survived, their leader in India was shot dead and twenty-five hundred of his followers were consumed in a fire. The Hindu's evil was reflected back."

Returning to Pin, I found my old pal disquietingly concerned. "Don't get too close to Manson and his people," he warned. "You could get hurt." That caught me off guard. Pin and Manson were tight. He usually defended Charlie. It wasn't like him to come down on the guy.

"I've gotten to know him a lot better this time around," Pin explained. "I can see how crazy he is. Behind that screwball face is a man you don't understand. There's something wrong with him. There's an evil there beyond your comprehension. You don't know what you're dealing with. You've never murdered anyone. You don't know what it takes, and what it does to you afterward."

That was certainly true. Since Pin was well acquainted with the homicidal beast that can reside inside a person, his warning had to be taken seriously.

"I told Charlie that if anything happened to you or your family, he'd have to deal with me," Pin added.

That was sure nice of Pin. All the kindness I'd showed him over the years was paying dividends. And Pin's brave threat was not without risk, as Charlie didn't take kindly to such talk.

"Let me worry about that in here. You just take care of yourself out there," Pin said.

I left the prison that evening enveloped in a sense of dread. It wasn't Charlie's mood or even anything he said. I was used to all that. It was Pin's concern that got to me. What did he know that he wasn't saying? Despite our friendship, the snitch code was deeply ingrained in all prisoners, Pin included, so if anything specific was coming down, Pin would try to handle it himself without giving me the details. It was obvious that he'd done precisely that. Hopefully, Manson got the message. I didn't relish the thought of having to clean any more voodoo stews off of my porch — much less deal with something decidedly more sinister.

Recently, a movement of militant white supremacists known as "the Order" approached Manson about being their leader. Searching for a resurrected Hitler, they spoke of a grand coronation that glorified Manson's mystical qualities. The FBI busted some of their members, and their previous guru was burned to death in a shoot-out, leaving them leaderless. They came to Manson searching for a shepherd to recruit "true believers" like Timothy McVeigh, the man who bombed the federal building in Oklahoma City, or Theodore Kaczynski, the infamous Unabomber.

Manson has intensely followed the growth of these burgeoning militias, often sending me articles that he's come across. With a little updating and fine-tuning, his philosophy would fit in perfectly with theirs. If he's ever released from prison as a "harmless old man," I could easily see him uniting these strange groups that fester all over the country and building them into one large, scary army. Just as Adolf Hitler rose from being a misfit and a petty criminal to become the racist dictator of Germany, so these white supremacist groups lust for Manson to become their unifying leader.

We may not have seen the last of him yet.

IN LATE AUGUST 1997, Charles Manson was transferred from Corcoran State Prison to Pelican Bay State Prison—one of the top maximum security facilities in the United States. Set on a bleak strip of land a few miles from the Oregon border, Pelican Bay is basically a series of isolation cages that house the most violent and incorrigible offenders in the California prison system.

Long before this move, I warned Charlie that if he didn't stop threatening officers, dealing drugs, and operating illegal businesses (selling autographed photos of himself at $50 a pop), he was going to end up at Pelican Bay. Naturally, he didn't listen.

I almost feel sorry for him now. Pushing sixty-five, Charlie is starting to show signs that Father Time and the prison system have finally worn him down—something he vowed would never happen. He complains of an ear problem "eating up my brain, man," and writes that his eyes are dimming to the point that he sometimes stumbles and falls. I don't completely buy it. Charlie's whined before, and in the next moment he can hear like a rabbit, see like an eagle, and throw a tantrum with enough volcanic energy for a half-dozen men.

His recent letters and conversations wander into fantasy and utter confusion—but then again, they always did.

How Charlie will handle the isolation and oppression of Pelican Bay at this stage of his life is anyone's guess. I sense that he will die there. However, as Dylan Thomas wrote, he will "not go gentle into the night." Charlie is sure to "rage against the dying of the light."

''You can try to kill me a million times more but you cannot kill soul. Truth was, is, and will always be. You have beaten me, broken my neck, knocked my teeth out. You've drugged me for years, dragging me up and down prison hallways, laying my head on every chopping block you've got in this state, chained me, burned me, but you cannot defeat me. All you can do is destroy yourselves with your own judgment.''

—CHARLES MANSON
AT HIS 1986 PAROLE HEARING

HEN I WAS a small boy, the highlight of the week was a Sunday afternoon walk with my father. We lived in the geographical center of San Francisco near a hill that people called Mount Olympus. The name was not a tribute to the mythological home of the gods. It was a politically incorrect joke on the local milkman. The guy had a bad leg and was known as "Old Limpy." He dragged that leg up the hill so many times everyone began referring to it as Mount Olympus.

My dad and I used to spend many wonderful hours hiking the winding road to the top. There was a magnificent statue set high on a pedestal overlooking the city and the Pacific Ocean. The statue held a torch high over her head in one hand, and a sword ready to strike in the other. It was a riveting piece of art that never failed to captivate me, no matter how many times I saw it.

"Do you know what it means?" my father asked.

"No, Dad, what?"

"It's the statue of light. She carries the torch of truth over her head. The sword is there to protect the torch from those who want to put it out."

Six years later, after the Japanese attacked Pearl Harbor, my father was called into the service. He and other soldiers set up a lookout post on Mount Olympus, scanning the coast for enemy ships and submarines. I was ten then, and used to go up there with him. We spent long hours together looking into the ocean on the night watch. The whole city was blacked out, and the view was glorious. When I couldn't keep my eyes open anymore, I'd curl up at the foot of the statue, braced from the whistling wind, and fall asleep. Those were the best of times.

My father was eventually transferred to the battle front overseas and never returned home. No, he didn't die, but he might as well have as far as a young boy was concerned. He met another woman in a foreign land, divorced my mother, remarried, and moved away. I was devastated.

For years afterward, for decades, I returned to that hill, remembered my father, and fed a pain that wouldn't go away. When I came home from college a grown man, my car mysteriously headed for the old statue. I married and became a father myself, six times over, and still kept coming back. Finally, I arrived one foggy day to find the statue gone. It stunned me, depressing me further, but did nothing to stop my lemminglike treks. Year after year I came, staring up at the empty pedestal, trying to heal a wound that would never stop hurting.

One night, a dream carried me to the haunting spot. I climbed on the pedestal and stood facing the wind and ocean. Suddenly, my limbs froze. I looked down. My arms and legs had turned to stone. The rest of my body hardened as well. Unable to move, I watched as a parade of fathers and little boys came to see the magnificent statue on the hill. Tears were burning into my pillow when I awoke.

The dream was so unnerving that I immediately embarked upon an almost frantic search to find out what had happened to the statue. A trip to the library and some old news clippings directed me to a dank city warehouse that served as a retirement home for broken-down sculptures. Searching though the rubble, I found it. She stood alone in a corner, vandalized almost beyond recognition. Her torch and arm were missing, the sword broken off, her head gone. I wondered at that moment if there was a heaven for statues that no longer served a purpose.

I stared at the battered remnant for over an hour, remembering all it had meant to me. Once, she had been a proud landmark for sailors entering the bay, guiding them safely to shore. For a half century, she stood tall as a symbol of truth. And most important of all, she had been a little boy's bond to a father who abandoned him.

Charles Manson lost his father in a similar fashion when he was four, a fact that he continues to try to hide from the world to this day. For all his bluster and uncaring ways, it's a pain that he's never been able to face. How much of what he became, of what he did, of the rage that never dies, can be blamed on a mother who decided to leave town one day to search for greener pastures, and gave no thought to a sad little boy who was forced to leave his beloved father behind? A sad little boy who was later dumped by that same mother, and became a horribly abused, institutionalized teenager who used to get down on his knees and beg God to send someone who loved him.

From my experience, I'd say virtually all of it.

THE TESTIMONY OF CHARLES MANSON, NOVEMBER 19, 1970

THE COURT: Do you have anything to say?

MANSON: Yes, I do.

There has been a lot of charges and a lot of things said about me and brought against me and brought against the co-defendants in this case, of which a lot could be cleared up and clarified to where everyone could understand exactly what the family was supposed to have been, what the philosophies in regards to the families were, and whether or not there was any conspiracy to commit murder, to commit crimes, and to explain to you who think with your minds.

It is hard for you to conceive of a philosophy of someone that may not think.

I have spent my life in jail, and without parents.

I have looked up to the strongest father figure, and I have always looked to the people in the free world as being the good people, and the people in the inside of the jail as being the bad people.

I never went to school, so I never growed up in the respect to learn to read and write so good, so I have stayed in jail and I have stayed stupid, I have stayed a child while I have watched your world grow up, and then I look at the things that you do and I don't understand.

I don't understand the courts, and I don't understand a lot of things that are brought against me.

Your write things about my mother in the newspaper that hasn't got anything to do with anything in particular.

You invent stories, and everybody thinks what they do, and then they project it from the witness stand on the defendant as if that is what he did.

For example, with Danny DeCarlo's testimony. He said that I hate black men, and he said that we thought alike, that him and I was a lot alike in our thinking.

But actually all I ever did with Danny DeCarlo or any other human being was reflect himself back at himself.

If he said he did not like the black man, I would say, "Okay." I had better sense than tell him I did not dislike the black man. I just listened to him and I would react to his statement.

So consequently he would drink another beer and walk off and pat me on the back and he would say to himself, "Charlie thinks like I do."

But actually he does not know how Charlie thinks because Charlie has never projected himself.

But maybe the girls and women in your world outside . . . Being by yourself for such a long time when you do get out you appreciate things that people don't even see, you walk over them every day.

Like in jail you have a whole new attitude or a whole different way of thinking.

I don't think like you people. You people put importance on your lives.

Well, my life has never been important to anyone, not even in the understanding of the way you fear the things that you fear, and the things you do.

I know that the only person I can judge is me.

I judge what I have done and I judge what I do and I look and live with myself every day.

I am content with myself.

If you put me in the penitentiary, that means nothing because you kicked me out of the last one. I didn't ask to get released. I liked it in there because I like myself.

I like being with myself.

But in your world it's hard because your understanding and your values are different.

These children that come at you with knives, they are your children. You taught them. I didn't teach them. I just tried to help them stand up.

Most of the people at the ranch that you call the Family were just people that you did not want, people that were alongside the road, that their parents had kicked them out or they did not want to go to Juvenile Hall, so I did the best I could and I took them up on my garbage dump and I told them this, that in love there is no wrong.

I don't care. I have one law and I learned it when I was a kid in reform school. It's don't snitch. And I have never snitched. And I told them that anything they do for their brothers and sisters is good, if they do it with a good thought.

It is not my responsibility. It is your responsibility. It is the responsibility you have towards your own children who you are neglecting, and then you want to put the blame on me again and again and again.

Over and over you put me in your penitentiary. I did not build the penitentiary. I would not lock one of you up. I could not see locking another human being up.

You eat meat with your teeth and you kill things that are better than you are, and in the same respect you say how bad and even killers that your children are. You make your children what they are. I am just a reflection of every one of you.

I have never learned anything wrong. In the penitentiary, I have never found a bad man. Every man in the penitentiary has always showed me his good side, and circumstances put him where he was. He would not be there, he is good, human, just like the policeman that arrested him is a good human.

I have nothing against none of you. I can't judge any of you. But I think it is high time that you all started looking at yourselves, and judging the lie that you live in.

I sit and I watch you from nowhere, and I have nothing in my mind, no malice against you and no ribbons for you.

But you stand and you play the game of money. As long as you can sell a newspaper, some sensationalism, and you can laugh at someone and joke at someone and look down at someone, you know.

You just sell those newspapers for public opinion, just like you are all hung on public opinion, and none of you have any idea what you are doing.

You are just doing what you are doing for the money, for a little bit of attention from someone.

I can't dislike you, but I will say this to you. You haven't got long before you are all going to kill yourselves because you are all crazy.

And you can project it back at me, and you can say that it's me that cannot communicate, and you can say that it's me that don't have any understanding, and you can say that when I am dead your world will be better, and you can lock me up in your penitentiary and you can forget about me.

But I'm only what lives inside of you, each and every one of you. These children, they take a lot of narcotics because you tell them not to. Any child you put in a room and you tell them, "Don't go through that door," he never thought of going through that door until you told him not to go through the door. You go to the high schools and you show them pills and you show them what not to take, how else would they know what it was unless you tell them?

And then you tell them what you don't want them to do in the hopes they will go out and do it and then you can play your game with them and then you can give attention to them because you don't give them any of your love.

You only give them your frustration; you only give them your anger; you only give them the bad part of you rather than give them the good part of you.

You should all turn around and face your children and start following them and listening to them.

The music speaks to you every day, but you are too deaf, dumb, and blind to even listen to the music. You are too deaf, dumb, and blind to stop what you are doing. You point and you ridicule.

But it's okay, it's all okay. It doesn't really make any difference because we are all going to the same place anyway. It's all perfect. There is a God. He sits right over here beside me. That is your God. This is your God.

But let me tell you something; there is another Father and he has much more might than you imagine.

If I could get angry at you I would try to kill every one of you. If that's guilt, I accept it.

These children, everything they have done, they done for love of their brother. Had you not arrested Robert Beausoleil for something he did not do . . .

(*Interruption.*)

I have killed no one and I have ordered no one to be killed.

I may have implied on several occasions to several different people that I may have been Jesus Christ, but I haven't decided yet what I am or who I am.

I was given a name and a number and I was put in a cell, and I have lived in a cell with a name and a number.

I don't know who I am.

I am whoever you make me, but what you want is a fiend; you want a sadistic fiend because that is what you are.

You only reflect on me what you are inside of yourselves, because I don't care anything about any of you and I don't care what you do.

I can stand here in front of this court and smile at you, and you can do anything you want to do with me, but you cannot touch me because I am only my love, and it is all for me, and I give it to myself for me, because I look out for me first and I like me, and you can live with yourselves and your opinion of yourselves. I know what I have done.

If I showed someone that I would do anything for my brother, include give my life for my brother in the battlefield, or give where else that I may want to do that, then he picks his banner up and he goes off and does what he does.

That is not my responsibility. I don't tell people what to do.

If we enter into an agreement to build a house, I will help you build the house and I will offer suggestions for that house, but I won't put myself on you because that is what made you weak, because your parents have offered themselves on you.

You are not you, you are just reflections, you are reflections of everything that you think that you know, everything that you have been taught.

Your parents have told you what you are. They made you before you were six years old, and when you stood in school and you crossed your heart and pledged allegiance to the flag, they trapped you in a truth because at that age you didn't know any lie until that lie was reflected on you.

No, I am not responsible for you. Your karma is not mine.

My father is the jailhouse. My father is your system, and each one of you, each one of you are just a reflection of each one of you, and you all live by yourselves, no matter how crowded you may think that you are in a room full of people, you are still by yourself, and you have to live with that self forever and ever and ever and ever.

To some people this would be hell; to some people it would be heaven.

I have mine, and each one of you will have to work out yours, and you cannot work it out by pointing your fingers at people.

I have ate out of your garbage cans to stay out of jail.

I have wore your secondhand clothes.

I have accepted things and given them away the next second.

I have done my best to get along in your world and now you want to kill me, and I look at you and I look how incompetent you all are, and then I say to myself, "You want to kill me, ha, I'm already dead, have been all my life!"

I've lived in your tomb that you built.

I did seven years for a thirty-seven-dollar check. I did twelve years because I didn't have any parents, and how many other sons do you think you have in there? You have many sons in there, many, many sons in there, most of them are black and they are angry. They are mad, and they are mad at me.

I look and I say, "Why are you mad at me?"

He said, "I am mad at you because of what your father did."

And I look at him and I say, "Well," and I look at my fathers, and I say, "If there was ever a devil on the face of this earth I am him."

And he's got my head anytime he wants it, as all of you do too, anytime you want it.

Sometimes I think about giving it to you. Sometimes I'm thinking about just jumping on you and let you shoot me. Sometimes I think it would be easier than sitting here and facing you in the contempt that you have for yourself, the hate that you have for yourself, it's only the anger you reflect at me, the anger that you have got for you.

I do not dislike you, I cannot dislike you. I am you. You are blood. You are my brother. That is why I can't fight you.

If I could I would jerk this microphone out and beat your brains out with it because that is what you deserve, that is what you deserve.

Every morning you eat that meat with your teeth. You're all killers, you kill things better than you. And what can I say to you that you don't already know? And I have known that there is nothing I can say to you. There is nothing I can say to any of you. It is you that has to say it to you, and that is my whole philosophy; you say it to you and I will say it to me.

I live in my world, and I am my own king in my world, whether it be a garbage dump or if it be in the desert or wherever it be. I am my own human being. You may restrain my body and you may tear my guts out, do anything you wish, but I am still me and you can't take that.

You can kill the ego, you can kill the pride, you can kill the want, the desire of a human being.

You can lock him in a cell and you can knock his teeth out and smash his brain, but you cannot kill the soul.

You never could kill the soul. It's always there, the beginning and the end. You cannot stop it, it's bigger than me. I'm just looking into it and it frightens me sometimes.

The truth is now; the truth is right here: the truth is this minute, and this minute we exist.

Yesterday you cannot prove yesterday happened today, it would take you all day and then it would be tomorrow, and you can't prove last week happened. You can't prove anything except to yourself.

My reality is my reality, and I stand within myself on my reality.

Yours is yours and I don't care what it is. Whatever you do is up to you and it's the same thing with anyone in my family. And anybody in my family is a white human being, because my family is of the white family.

There is the black family, a yellow family, the red family, a cow family and a mule family. There is all kinds of different families.

We have to find ourselves first, God second, and kind, k-i-n-d, come next. And that is all I was doing. I was working on cleaning up my house, something Nixon should have been doing. He should have been on the side of the road picking up his children. But he wasn't. He was in the White House sending them off to war.

I don't know the different people that have got on the stand; one friend said I put a knife to his throat. I did. I put a knife to his throat. And he said I was responsible for all of these killings.

I have done the best I know how, and I have given all I can give and I haven't got any guilt about anything because I have never been able to say any wrong.

I never found any wrong.

I looked at wrong, and it is all relative.

Wrong is if you haven't got any money.

Wrong is if your car payment is overdue.

Wrong is if the TV breaks.

Wrong is if President Kennedy gets killed.

Wrong is, wrong is, wrong is you keep on, you pile it in your mind, you become belabored with it, and in your confusion . . .

I make up my own mind. I think for myself. I look at you and I say, "Okay, you make up your own mind, you think for yourself, then you see your mothers and your fathers and your teachers and your preachers and your politicians and your presidents, and you lay in your brain with your opinions, considerations, conclusions." And I look at you and I say, "Okay, if you are real to you it's okay with me but you don't look real to me, you only look like a composite of what someone told you you are. You live for each other's opinion and you have pain on your face and you are not sure what you like, and you wonder if you look okay."

And I look at you and I say, "Well, you look alright to me," you know, and you look at me and you say, "Well, you don't look alright to me."

Well I don't care what I look like to you. I don't care what you think about me and I don't care what you do with me. I have always been yours anyway. I have always been in your cell.

When you were out riding your bicycles I was sitting in your cell looking out the window and looking at pictures in magazines and wishing I could go to high school and go to the proms, wishing I could go to the things you could do, but oh so glad, oh so glad, brothers and sisters, that I am what I am.

Because when it does come down around your ears and none of you know what you are doing, you better believe I will be on top of my thought.

I will know what I am doing. I will know exactly what I am doing. If you ever let me go before you kill me. And then I don't really particularly care anyway, because I still will be there and I will still know what I am doing.

In my mind I live forever.

In my mind I live forever, and in my mind I have always lived forever.

I am only what you made me. I am only a reflection of you.

I have done everything I have always been told. I have mopped the floor when I was supposed to mop the floor. And I have swept when I was supposed to sweep.

I was smart enough to stay out of jail and too dumb to learn anything. I was too little to get a job there, and too big to do something over here.

I have just been sitting in jail thinking nothing. Nothing to think about.

Everybody used to come in and tell me about their past and their lives and what they did. But I could never tell anybody about my past or what my life was or what I did because I have always been sitting in that room with a bed, a locker, and a table. So, then it moves on to awareness: how many cracks can you count in the wall? It moves to where the mice live and what the mice are thinking, and see how clever mice are.

And then, when you get on the outside, you look into people's heads. You take Linda Kasabian and you put her on the witness stand and she testifies against her father. She never has liked her father, and she has always projected her wrong off to the man figure. So, consequently, it is the man's fault again, and the woman turns around and she blames it on the man. The man made her do it. The man put her up to it.

The man works for her, the man slaves for her, the man does everything for her, and she lays around the house and she tells him what he should do, because, generally, she is an extension of his mother. His mother told him what to do and she trained him for twenty years and passed him on to the wife. Then the woman takes him and tells him what to wear, when to get up, when to go to work.

Then when she gets on the stand and she says when she looked in that man's eyes that was dying, she knew it was my fault.

She knew that it was my fault because she couldn't face death. And if she cannot face death, that is not my fault. Why should she blame it on me? I can face death. I have all the time.

In the penitentiary you live with it, with constant fear of death, because it is a violent world in there, and you have to be on your toes constantly.

So, it is not without violence that I live. It is not without pain that I live.

I look at the projection that comes from this witness stand often to the defendants. It isn't what we said, it is what someone thought we said. A word is changed: "in there" to "up there," "off of that" to "on top." The semantics get into a word game in the courtroom to prove something that is gone in the past. It is gone in the past, and when it is gone, it is gone, sisters. It is gone, brother.

You can't bring the past back up and postulate or mock up a picture of something that happened a hundred years ago, or 1970 years ago, as far as that goes. You can only live in the now, for what is real is now.

The words go in circles.

You can say everything is the same, but it is always different. It is the same, but it is always different. You can "but" it to death. You can say, "You are right, but, but, but."

You sat here for nineteen days questioning that girl.

She got immunity on seven counts of murder.

She got. I don't know how much money she is going to make in magazines and things. You set her up to be a hero, and that is your woman. That is the thing that you worship.

You have lost sight of God. You sing your songs to woman. You put woman in front of man. Woman is not God. Woman is but a reflection of her man, supposedly. But a lot of times man is a reflection of his woman. And if a man can't rise above a woman's thought, then that is his problem, it is not my problem. But you give me this problem when you set this woman against me.

You set this woman up here to testify against me. And she tells you a sad story. How she has only taken every narcotic that is possible to take. How she has only stolen, lied, cheated, and done everything that you have got there in that book.

But it is okay. She is telling the truth now. She wouldn't have any ulterior motive like immunity for seven counts of murder.

And then comical as it may seem, you look at me, and you say, "You threatened to kill a person if they snitch."

Well, that is the law where I am from. Where I am from, if you snitch, you leave yourself open to be killed.

I could never snitch because I wouldn't want someone to kill me.

So, I have always abided by that law. It is the only law that I know of, and it is the law that I have always abided by.

But she will come up here and you enshrine her, you put her above you, and you strive to be as good as something below you.

It is circles that just don't make any sense in my reality. But of course again that is my reality and it has nothing to do with you, because you have got your reality and you have to live with what you believe in.

But this woman has got here and she has testified. She said she wasn't sure, but maybe.

Then the magical mystery tour wouldn't be able to be explained to you.

A magical mystery tour is when you pick up somebody else and play a part. You may pick up a cowboy today, and you go around all day and play like a cowboy. You put on a hat and you ride a horse.

This is all we have done. We have played like mom and dad. We have loved each other. We have done everything we could to stay outside the frame of the law, the shakedowns. Nothing has been stolen. I have got better sense than to break the law. I give to the law what it has coming. It is his law. If I break his law, he puts me back in the grave again.

I haven't broken his law yet but it seems as if somebody lays around and somebody needs to fulfill a spot, they snatch it up and say, "This will do. We will put this over here, we can hang this on him. Or we can do this to that."

Then the words go into another meaning and another level of understanding.

Why a woman would stand up and project herself into a man and say, "Actually he never told me anything, but I knew it all came from him."

Her assumption.

Am I to be found guilty on her assumption?

You assume what you would do in my position, but that doesn't mean that is what I did in my position. It doesn't mean that my philosophy is valid. It's only valid to me. Your philosophies, they are whatever you think they are and I don't particularly care what you think they are.

But I know this: that in your own hearts and your own souls, you are as much responsible for the Vietnam War as I am for killing these people.

I knew a guy that used to work in the stockyards and he used to kill cows all day long with a big sledgehammer, and then go home at night and eat dinner with his children and eat the meat that he slaughtered. Then he would go to church and read the Bible, and he would say, "That is not killing." And I look at him and I say, "That doesn't make any sense, what are you talking about?"

Then I look at the beast, and I say, "Who is the beast?"

I am the beast.

I am the beast.

I am the biggest beast walking the face of the earth. I kill everything that moves. As a man, as a human, I take responsibility for that. As a human, it won't be long, and God will ask you to take responsibility for it. It is your creation. You live in your creation. I never created your world, you created it.

You create it when you pay taxes, you create it when you go to work, then you create it when you foster a thing like this trial.

Only for vicarious thrills do you sell a newspaper and do you kowtow to public opinion. Just to sell your newspapers. You don't care about the truth. You take another Alka-Seltzer and another aspirin and hope that you don't have to think of the truth and you hope that you don't have to look at yourself with a hangover as you go to a Helter Skelter party and make fun of something that you don't understand.

(The Judge asks Manson to stick to the point.)

The issues in this case? The issues in this case?

The issues are that Mr. Younger is Attorney General, and I imagine he is a good man and does a good job. I don't know him. I can't judge him. But I know he has got me here. He set me in this seat.

Mr. Bugliosi is doing his job for a paycheck. That is an issue. He is doing whatever he is doing. Whether he thinks it is right or not, I couldn't say. That is up to him.

The only way that I have been able to live on that side of the road was outside the law. I have always lived outside the law. When you live outside the law it is pretty hard, you can't call the man for protection. You have got to pretty much protect your own.

You can't live within the law and protect yourself. You can't knock the guy down when he comes over and starts to rape one of the girls, or starts to bring some speed or dope up there. You can't enforce your will over someone inside the law.

I gave everything I could think of to that old man and that ranch for permission to stay there, and I have given the people that stayed on that ranch my all. When no one wanted to go out in front and fight, I would go out and fight. When no one else wanted to clean the toilets, I would go and clean them.

People would see me and they would see what I do and see the example that I set. They see, when I am cleaning out a cesspool, that I am happy and smiling and making a game of it. Like I was on a chain gang somewhere once upon a time and they come and pass the water. I make a game out of it, or I make a pleasure out of a job. We turn it into a magical mystery tour.

We speed down the highway in a 1958 automobile that won't go but fifty, and an XKE Jaguar goes by, and I state to Clem, "Catch him Clem, and we'll rob him or steal all of his money," you know. And he says, "What shall we do?" I say, "Hit him on the head with a hammer." We magical mystery tour it.

Then Linda Kasabian gets on the stand and says: "They were going to kill a man, they were going to kill a man in an automobile."

To you, it seems serious. But like Larry Kramer and I would get on a horse and we would ride over to Wichita, Kansas, and act like cowboys. We make it a game on the ranch.

Like, Helter Skelter is a nightclub. Helter Skelter means confusion. Literally. It doesn't mean any war with anyone. It doesn't mean that those people are going to kill other people. It only means what it means. Helter Skelter is confusion.

Confusion is coming down fast. If you don't see the confusion coming down fast around you, you can call it what you wish.

It is not my conspiracy. It is not my music. I hear what it relates. It says, "Rise!" It says, "Kill!" Why blame it on me? I didn't write the music. I am not the person who projected it into your social consciousness, that sanity that you projected into your social consciousness, today. You put so much into the newspaper and then you expect people to believe what is going on. I say back to the facts again.

How many witnesses have you got up here and projected only what they believe in. What I believe in is right now. I don't believe in anything past now. I speak to you from now.

Because there is nothing here to worry about, nothing here to think about, nothing here to be confused over. My house is not divided. My house is one with me, myself.

Then I look at the facts that you have brought in front of this court and I look at the twelve facts that are looking at me and judging me. If I were to judge them, what scale would that balance? Would the scale balance if I was to turn and judge you? How would you feel if I were to judge you? Could I judge you? I can only judge you if you try to judge me. That is the fact.

Mr. Bugliosi is a hard-driving prosecutor, with a polished education. Semantics, words. He is a genius. He has got everything that every lawyer would want to have except one thing: a case. He doesn't have a case.

Were I allowed to defend myself, I could have proven this to you. I could have called witnesses and showed you how these things lay, and I could have presented my picture.

You are dealing with facts and positive evidence. If you are dealing with things that are relative to the issues at hand, then you look at the facts. What else do you look at? Oh, the leather thong.

How many people have ever worn moccasins with a leather thong in it? So you have placed me on the desert with leather clothes on and you took a leather thong from my shoe.

How many people could we take leather thongs from? That is an issue.

Then you move on and you say I had one around my neck. I always tie one around my head when my hair is long. It keeps it out of my eyes. And you pull it down on your neck. And I imagine a lot of longhaired people do.

There are so many aspects to this case that could be dug into and a lot of truth could be brought up, a lot of understanding could be reached.

It is a pretty hideous thing to look at seven bodies, one hundred and two stab wounds.

The prosecutor, or the doctor, gets up and he shows how all the different stab wounds are one way, and then how all the different stab wounds are another way; but they are the same stab wounds in another direction.

They put the hideous bodies on display and they say: "If he gets out see what will happen to you." Implying it. I am not saying he did this. This is implied. A lot of diagrams are actually in my opinion senseless to the case.

Then there is Paul Watkins' testimony. Paul Watkins was a young man who ran away from his parents and wouldn't go home. You could ask him to go home and he would say no. He would say, "I don't got no place to live. Can I live here?" And I'd say, "Sure." So, he looks for a father image. I offer no father image. I say, "To be a man, boy, you have got to stand up and be your own father." And he still hungers for a father image. So he goes off to the desert and finds a father image.

When he gets on the stand, I forget what he said, whether it had any relative value, oh, I was supposed to have said to go get a knife and kill the sheriff of Shoshone. Go get a knife and kill the sheriff of Shoshone? I don't know the sheriff of Shoshone. I don't think I have been there but once.

I am not saying that I didn't say it, but if I said it, at that time I may have thought it was a good idea. Whether I said it in jest and whether I said it in joking, I can't recall and reach back into my memory. I could say either way. I could say, "Oh, I was just joking." Or I could say I was curious. But to be honest with you I don't ever recall saying, "Get a knife and change of clothes and go do what Tex said." Or I don't recall saying, "Get a knife and go kill the sheriff."

I don't recall saying to anyone, "Go get a knife and kill anyone or anything." In fact it makes me mad when someone kills snakes or dogs or cats or horses. I don't even like to eat meat because that is how much I am against killing.

So you have got the guy who is against killing on the witness stand, and you are all asking him to kill you. You are asking him to judge you. Because with my words, each of your opinions or diagrams, your thoughts, are dying. What you thought was true is dying. What you thought was real is dying. Because you all know, and I know you know, and you know that I know you know. So, let's make that circle.

You say, "Where do we start from there?" Back to the facts again. You say that the facts are elusive in my mind. Actually, they just don't mean anything. The District Attorney can call them facts. They are facts. You are facts.

But the facts of the case aren't even relative, in my mind. They are relative to the thirteenth century. They are relative to the eighth century. They are relative to how old you are or what kind of watch you wear on your arm. I have never lived in time. A bell rings, I get up. A bell rings and I go out. A bell rings, and I live my life with bells. I get up when a bell rings and I do what a bell says. I have never lived in time. When your mind is not in time, the whole thought is different. You look at time as being man-made. And you say time is only relative to what you think it is. If you want to think me guilty then you can think me guilty and it is okay with me. I don't dislike any of you for it. If you want to think me not guilty it is okay with me.

I know what I know and nothing and no one can take that from me.

You can jump up and scream, "Guilty!" and you can say what a no-good guy I am, and what a devil, fiend, eeky-sneaky slimy devil I am. It is your reflection and you're right, because that is what I am. I am whatever you make me.

You see, it is what happens inside the now that . . . the words just lose meaning. A motion is more real than a word. The Indians spoke with it. They could explain to you with motions what they felt. This is what I intended to do if I could represent myself. Explain to you what is inside of me, how I feel about things.

Because words are your words. You invented the words, and you made a dictionary and you gave me the dictionary and you said, "These are what the words mean." Well, this is what they mean to you, but to someone else, they have got a different dictionary. And things mean different things to different people, and to match the symbols up as you talk back and forward. Then you put a witness up here to say what you said.

I could never say what someone else said. I could only say what I said.

You tell me something and, tomorrow, I try to repeat it, if I didn't write it down, I couldn't tell you what you said. Let alone a year ago, let alone eight months ago, let alone a week ago. I am forgetful. I forget one day to the next. I forget what day it is or what month it is or what year it is. I don't particularly care because all that is real to me is right now.

But then, the case is real to me, and I say, "What do I have to do to make you people let me go back to the desert with my children?"

You have your world. You are going to do whatever you do with it. I have got nothing to do with it. I don't have the schooling in it. I don't believe in your church. I don't believe in anything you do. I am not saying you are wrong, and I hope that you say I am not wrong for believing what I believe in.

Murder? Murder is another question. It is a move. It is a motion. You take another's life. Boom! and they're gone. You say, "Where did they go?" They are dead. You say, "Well, that person could have made the motion." He could have taken my life just as well as I took his.

If a soldier goes off to the battlefield, he goes off with his life in front. He is giving his life. Does that not give him permission to take one? No. Because then we bring our soldiers back and try them in court for doing the same thing we sent them to do. We train them to kill, and they go over and kill, and we prosecute them and put them in jail because they kill. If you can understand it, then I bow to your understanding. But in my understanding I wouldn't get involved with it.

My peace is in the desert or in the jail cell, and had I not seen the sunshine in the desert I would be satisfied with the jail cell much more over your society, much more over your reality, and much more over your confusion, and much more over your world, and your word games that you play.

And each witness got up here and only testified for what was best for them, they did not testify for what was best for me. They testified for what was best for them, their own benefit. So you say, "Okay, and then what else did she say?" She said, "You only see in me what you want to see in me." You only see in her what you put in her, because when you take LSD enough times you reach a stage of nothing. You reach a stage of no thought.

An example of this: if you were to be standing in a room with someone and you were loaded on LSD and the guy says, "Do you like my sports coat?" And you would probably not pay any attention to him. About two or three minutes later the guy loaded on LSD will turn around and say, "My, you have a beautiful sports coat" because he is only reacting. He is only reacting to the individual terminology, the person that he has in the room.

As you would put two people in a cell, so would they reflect and flow on each other like as if water would seek a level.

I have been in a cell with a guy eighty years old and I listened to everything he said. "What did you do then?" And he explains to me his whole life and I sat there and listened, and I experienced vicariously his whole being, his whole life, and I look at him and he is one of my fathers. But he is also another one of your society's rejects.

Where does the garbage go, as we have tin cans and garbage alongside the road, and oil slicks in your water, so you have people, and I am one of your garbage people. I am one of your motorcycle people. I am one of what you want to call hippies. I never thought about being a hippie. I don't know what a hippie is.

A hippie is generally a guy that's pretty nice. He will give you a shirt and a flower, and he will give you a smile, and he walks down the road. But don't try to tell him nothing. He ain't listening to nobody. He got his own thoughts. You try to tell him something, and he will say, "Well, if that's your bag."

He is finding himself. You, those children there were finding themselves. Whatever they did, if they did whatever they did, is up to them. They will have to explain to you that. I'm just explaining to you what I am explaining to you. Everything is simple to me. It is what it is because that is what it is. It doesn't go any farther.

What? That is all there is. Why?

Why?

Why comes from your mother. Your mother teaches you why, why, why. You go around asking your mother why and she keeps telling you, "Because, because" and she laces your little brain with because and: "Because." "Why?" "Because." "Why?" And you don't know any different. If you had two mothers, one to tell you one thing and one to tell you another, then your mind might be left where mine was. If you had a dozen parents that you went around with and couldn't believe anything you were told and then you couldn't disbelieve anything you were told. And it's the same thing with this court. I don't believe what these witnesses get up here and say but I don't disbelieve them either. I won't challenge them. If the guy says, "You're no good," I say, "Okay." If that's what you want me to believe it's okay with me.

I don't care what you believe. I know what I am. You care what I think of you? Do you care what I think of you? Do you care what my opinion is? No, I hardly think so. I don't think that any of you care about anything other than yourselves because when you find yourself, you find that everyone is out for themselves anyway.

It looks that way to me here, the money that has been made, the things that I cannot talk about, and I know I can't talk about, I won't talk about and I will keep quiet about these things. How much all money has passed over this case? How sensational do you think that you have made this case?

I never made it sensational. I was hiding in the desert. You come and got me. Remember? Or could you prove that? What could you prove?

The only thing you can prove is what you can prove to yourselves, and you can sit here and build a lot in that jury's mind, and they are still going to interject their personalities on you. They are going to interject their inadequate feelings; they are going to interject what they think. I look at the jury and they won't look at me. So I wonder why they won't look at me. They are afraid of me. And do you know why they are afraid of me? Because of the newspapers.

You projected fear. You projected fear. You made me a monster and I have to live with that the rest of my life because I cannot fight this case. If I could fight this case and I could present this case, I would take that monster back and I would take that fear back. Then you could find something else to put your fear on, because it's all your fear.

You look for something to project it on and you pick a little old scroungy nobody who eats out of a garbage can, that nobody wants, that was kicked out of the penitentiary, that has been dragged through every hellhole you can think of, and you drag him up and put him into a courtroom.

You expect to break me? Impossible! You broke me years ago. You killed me years ago. I sat in a cell and the guy opened the door and he said, "You want out?"

I looked at him and I said, "Do you want out? You are in jail, all of you, and your whole procedure. The procedure that is on you is worse than the procedure that is on me. I like it in there."

I like it in there—it's peaceful. I just don't like coming to the courtroom. I would like to get this over with as soon as possible. And I'm sure everyone else would like to get it over with too.

Without being able to prepare a case, without being able to confront the witnesses and to bring out the emotions, and to bring out the reasons why witnesses say what they say, and why this hideous thing has developed into the trauma that it's moved into, would take a bigger courtroom, and it would take a bigger public, a bigger press, because you all, as big as you are, know what you are as I know what you are, and, I like you anyway. I don't want to keep rehashing the same things over. There are so many things that you can get into, Your Honor, that I have no thoughts on. It is hard to think when you really don't care too much one way or the other.

(*Interruption.*)

I was released from the penitentiary and I learned one lesson in the penitentiary, you don't tell nobody nothing. You listen. When you are little you keep your mouth shut, and when someone says, "Sit down," you sit down unless you know you can whip him, and if you know you can whip you stand up and whip and you tell him to sit down.

Well, I pretty much sat down. I have learned to sit down because I have been whipped plenty of times for not sitting down and I have learned not to tell people something they don't agree with. If a guy comes up to me and he says, "The Yankees are the best ball team," I am not going to argue with that man. If he wants the Yankees to be the best ball team, it's okay with me, so I look at him and I say, "Yeah, the Yankees are a good ball club." And somebody else says, "The Dodgers are good." I will agree with that; I will agree with anything they tell me. That is all I have done since I have been out of the penitentiary. I agreed with every one of you. I did the best I could to get along with you, and I have not directed one of you to do anything other than what you wanted to do.

I have always said this: You do what your love tells you and I do what my love tells me. Now if my love tells me to stand up there and fight I will stand up there and fight if I have to. But if there is any way that my personality can get around it, I try my best to get around any kind of thing that is going to disturb my peace, because all I want is to be just at peace, whatever that takes. Now in death you might find peace, and soon I may start looking in death to find my peace.

I have reflected your society in yourselves, right back at yourselves, and each one of these young girls was without a home. Each one of these young boys was without a home. I showed them the best I could what I would do as a father, as a human being, so they would be responsible to themselves and not to be weak and not to lean on me. And I have told them many times, I don't want no weak people around me. If you are not strong enough to stand on your own, don't come and ask me what to do. You know what to do. This is one of the philosophies that everyone is mad at me for, because of the children. I always let the children go. "You can't let the children go down there by themselves." I said, "Let the children go down. If he falls, that is how he learns, you become strong by falling." They said, "You are not supposed to let the children do that. You are supposed to guide them."

I said, "Guide them into what? Guide them into what you have got them guided into? Guide them into dope? Guide them into armies?" I said, "No, let the children loose and follow them." That is what I did in the desert. That is what I was doing, following your children, the ones you didn't want, each and every one of them. I never asked them to come with me—they asked me.

(*Recessed.*)

There's been a lot of talk about a bottomless pit. I found a hole in the desert that goes down to a river that runs north underground, and I call it a bottomless pit, because where could a river be going north underground? You could even put a boat on it. So I covered it up and I hid it and I called it "the Devil's Hole" and we all laugh and we joke about it. You could call it a Family joke about the bottomless pit. How many people could you hide down in this hole?

Again you have a magical mystery tour that most of the time there's forty or fifty people at the ranch playing magical mystery tour. Randy Starr thought he was a Hollywood stuntman. He had a car all painted up and like never done any stunts. Another guy was a movie star, but he had never been in any movies, and everybody was just playing a part, you know, like most people get stuck in one part, but like we were just playing different parts every day. One day you put on a cowboy hat and say, "Shoot somebody," or the next you might have a knife fighter, or go off in the woods for a month or two to be an Indian, or just like a bunch of little kids playing. Then you establish a reality within that reality of playacting.

And then you get to conspiracy. The power of suggestion is stronger than any conspiracy that you could ever enter into. The powers of the brain are so vast, it's beyond understanding. It's beyond thinking. It's beyond comprehension. So to offer a conspiracy might be to sit in your car and think bad thoughts about someone and watch them have an accident in front of you. Or would it be a conspiracy for your wife to mention to you twenty times a day, "You know, you're going blind, George, you know how your eyes are, you're just going blind; we pray to God and you're going blind, and you're going blind." And she keeps telling the old man he's going blind until he goes blind.

Is that a conspiracy?

Is it a conspiracy that the music is telling youth to rise against the establishment because the establishment is rapidly destroying things? Is that a conspiracy? Where does conspiracy come in? Does it come in that?

I have showed people how I think by what I do. It is not as much what I say as what I do that counts, and they look at what I do and they try to do it also, and sometimes they are made weak by their parents and cannot stand up. But is that my fault? Is it my fault that your children do what they do?

Now the girls were talking about testifying. If the girls come up here to testify and they said anything good about me, you would have to reverse it and say that it was bad. You would have to say, "Well, he put the girls up to saying that. He put the girls up to not telling the truth." Then you say the truth is as I am saying it, but then when it is gone, tomorrow it is gone, it changes, it's another day and it's a now truth, as it constantly moves thousands of miles an hour through space.

Hippie cult leader; actually, hippie cult leader, that is your words. I am a dumb country boy who never grew up. I went to jail when I was eight years old and I got out when I was thirty-two. I have never adjusted to your free world. I am still that stupid, corn-picking country boy that I always have been.

If you tend to compliment a contradiction about yourself, you can live in that confusion. To me it's all simple, right here, right now; and each of us knew what we did and I know what I did, and I know what I'm going to do and what you do is up to you. I don't recognize the courtroom, I recognize the press and I recognize the people.

THE COURT: Have you completed your statement, Mr. Manson?

MANSON: You could go on forever. You can just talk endless words. It don't mean anything. I don't know that it means anything. I can talk to the witnesses and ask them what they think about things, and I can bring the truth out of other people because I know what the truth is, but I cannot sit here and tell you anything because like basically all I want to do is try to explain to you what you are doing to your children.

You see, you can send me to the penitentiary, it's not a big thing. I've been there all my life anyway. What about your children? These are just a few, there is many, many more coming right at you.

THE COURT: Anything further?

MANSON: No.

We're all our own prisons, we are each all our own wardens and we do our own time. I can't judge anyone else. What other people do is not really my affair unless they approach me with it.

Prison's in your mind. . . . Can't you see I'm free?

Manson's 1986 Parole Hearing Statement

As anyone in the know knows, throughout the state of California, the country, and the world: the lawyers, courts, and government of the U.S. lie and cannot be trusted. (California Department of Corrections included.) To keep this so-called Board of Paroles from telling more lies about me, my family, brothers and sisters in soul in truth and of God, I have come to this hearing to make statements to and for the public record to be marked in history.

I have been kept in handcuffs for over sixteen years and kept for the most part in solitary confinement, as the so-called authorities kept changing the names from solitary to "administrative segregation" to "quiet cells" and other coverups each time the court ordered elimination of solitary time, or the public began to hear about mistreatment. Their fears and guilts were covered up by distortion, lies, and confusion to mislead and misinform the public for more tax dollars and bigger criminal justice business, actually fed by the misfortunes and blood of children.

I've been kept in mental wards, nut wards; I've been beaten, drugged, and have lost track of the times I've been handcuffed to the bars or left to be killed. Inmates have told me that doctors and other C.D.C. staff have tried to have me killed by telling them lies about me killing pregnant women and eating their unborn babies, or have implied threats to their personal safety along with promises of paroles and other favors. I have witnesses to all I say but no court will touch it because they broke their laws to put me back in prison, and each day they break all the laws by keeping me. They violate every human right in the book, yet they keep preaching to the world as if they had no sins and were all good guys.

So, for years doctors and staff have been falling off me with heart attacks, sicknesses, killing themselves or being murdered, as they did me wrong by trying to use this case to set a new prison system and continue to pick up the paychecks. I see all new cops, new staff. For each inmate sent to kill me, the prison system has lost staff. All of the judgments and the blame that is pushed off on me will be reflected back in the fires of the Holy War that you call crime. It suits your fears not to face the actions you are creating and calling up in your prison crime factories, as your deceit is reflected. And then you are paid for the stories of crime sold to the public in TV and movies.

The children of the 1960s that you call the "Manson Family" wanted to stop a war and turn the government and world to peace. They gave their lives when they took lives and they knew it. They gave all to clean up ATWA, air, trees, water, animals, the whole of the life of Earth, in love and concern for brothers and sisters in soul. They gave to get their brothers and sisters out of cages and to touch some intelligence upon the Earth. By living next to the land, we did see the drought and famine coming. For my part, I was complete and willing to take responsibility for any influence I had over THE mind of all, but your courts ran for the money and away from their own fears, guilts, and responsibilities. They didn't want to confront the truth about themselves.

Your government invented the Watergate coverup but never did say what they were really covering up was a Holy War invoked from the soul. When Manson, aka Lord Krishna, Jesus Christ, Mohammed, the Buddha, was condemned by the press and the *People of California vs. Manson*, you condemned yourselves. You condemned yourselves in the so-called Manson Family, putting the son of God on the prison cross again. I broke no law, not God's nor Man's law. God knows this; the Holy Spirit knows; and anyone in the truth knows. What you are buying and selling in God's name you will suffer. With your own judgments convicting yourselves of being Satan, the anti-Christ, you stand your world on fire. I am Abraxas, the son of God, the son of Darkness, and I stand behind ALL the courts of the world. Until I get my rights, no one has rights. I'm God's messenger from and in the truth, brother and son to all men. (666 your computers will print the same read-out to your book brains.) Until I get the same rights my fathers had, I will stand in Nixon's place, convicted as the false prophet, as fire burns and the children starve and the land dies along with the air, as the wildlife becomes poisoned and the trees are being cut so fast that wildlife will not survive NOT WITHOUT WORLD CHANGE.

I did I say "did" invoke a balance for life on Earth. From behind the time locks of court-rooms and from the worlds of darkness, I did let loose devils and demons with the power of scorpions to torment. I did unseal seven seals and seven jars in accord with the judgments placed upon me, upon my circle. All who had no forgiveness will have no heart, and did set loose upon the earth destruction in the balance of their own judgments. These are the people who gave their own children no chance for survival. These are the people locked in death wishes which they project into the minds of the children.

To the faithful I say this, so that understanding can be touched and because I know you have been misled: I did live among you in the will of all, in and out of prison for over twenty years before I was put on trial in 1969. From the 1940s I lived a lifetime in and on your prison cross, kept in your punishments to be your goat, your blame, all your bad, long before your children of the '60s picked me up and my will from the leftover garbage of past wars you waged upon your young. I am a child of the '30s, not the '60s. I told and answered in truth for what I was asked. What they did and do to balance themselves in their own points of view for the life they said they wanted is their own responsibility. You gave them your blame, and all of your problems but no forgiveness. They were you—your reflections—yet you keep your children in cages and want new prison crosses for your own profits, and the same cycles continue as your judgments are pushed off to the unknowing people for more tax money in old and useless jobs. They are also making up more TV movie crime, as if you don't have enough. Know this: from the prison graves the Christhead is no new trip, and the so-called Christians have been and are feeding on the blood of Christ children. You are so misled and caught up in lies that your souls and your justice are locked in the bank. Actors play your leaders in the same war patterns set by the dead.

I could have a parole and have no soul. I'll keep my soul and shirk your parole. You people have no authority from justice. You're crooks running the numbers racket. You got no respect. I don't want into your thoughts as anything but a number and you are dismissed from any service you claim to do in the name of God.

Prison is a frame of thought. I'm out of that. I don't want out of your prison unless I can go with my brothers and sisters. If I have the whole world and not my Family, I would have nothing. I'm not broken. I'm not beaten. My own Holy Revolution against pollution is still in full swing. I am my own government. Even if Reagan is trying to ride on my life. I am my own court and judge, my own world, my own God, in my own rebirth movement started behind the judge's chambers in 1943. God is in me and I'm in God and we both have a spirit of justice for the world.

You can try to kill me a million times more but you cannot kill soul. Truth was, is, and will always be. You have beaten me, broken my neck, knocked my teeth out. You've drugged me for years, dragging me up and down prison hallways, laying my head on every chopping block you've got in this state, chained me, burned me, but you cannot defeat me. All you can do is destroy yourselves with your own judgments.

All that cannot get under me and in God's will will not live over me but for a short time and that will grow to be a thousand hells, for you not only gave me your heads in truth by Dying, but have made me Christ four times in the world thought, Satan four times, Abraxas four times. But over that I already was the 666 for 17 years in government prisons and am still brother in that chamber of thought with knives in darkness. My 666 Beast is running free outside, in one will, with permission to do anything except to destroy water, air, trees, or wildlife, or the people with the marks of the Father on them. My armies move in ways beyond your programmed book brains in a Holy War to redeem life on Earth. For ATWA they move in all things, everywhere, coming from all you don't know, from all you can't or won't try to understand.

There are many people who have already made a lot of sacrifices in order to turn the world around, to redeem their own ATWA. So, the people who lie and have lied will suffer the sufferings of a lot of people who gave. Reborn Christians who are real in their rebirth don't need to find God's words in books. The people who want life on Earth are with me in the will of life and working beyond money. The others can go to their deaths however and wherever they find it. The same God I speak of is all gods in ONE GOD. One world. One court. One government. One order. One mind. Or continue with the madness you have judged for yourselves to live in forever. The time has ended and will catch up to each person's thought as it does.

Before 1969, for over twenty years, I suffered your prison cross. I give that to live, because I didn't know the difference. I forgive and it is in my will to forget. But for the last fifteen years, there is no forgiveness. The IPCR is the green field with a red bull. Until you all accept one God, one government, one order, there will be no order. One religion, or no religion. Religion is God's biggest problem. "Just as a circle embraces all that is within it, so does the Godhead embrace all. No one has the power to divide this circle, to surpass it, or to limit it." To do so will be your destruction.

Note for the record. In the all that was said about me, it was not me saying it, and if you see a false prophet, it is only a reflection of your judgments, for in truth, it is motions, not words, that speak for the Manson family. We each have our own worlds and judgments. I have no judgments outside of what you all have set for yourselves. I'm content wherever I am. Whatever you do or say does not touch my inner circle. I have peace within myself. Peace of mind.

Charles Manson

P.S. The U.S. started the Second World War.

CHARLES MANSON'S 1992 PAROLE HEARING

SUBSEQUENT PAROLE CONSIDERATION HEARING STATE OF CALIFORNIA BOARD OF PRISON TERMS in the Matter of the Life Term Parole Consideration Hearing of:

CHARLES MANSON
CDC NUMBER B-33920
CALIFORNIA STATE PRISON
CORCORAN, CALIFORNIA

TUESDAY
APRIL 21, 1992
1332 HOURS

MEMBERS PRESENT

Ron Koenig, Board Commissioner, Presiding
Joseph Aceto, Board Commissioner
Cleo Brown, Deputy Board Commissioner
ALSO PRESENT

Charles Manson, Inmate
Stephen Kay, Deputy District Attorney County of Los Angeles

PROCEEDINGS

PRESIDING BOARD COMMISSIONER KOENIG: These hearings are being taped, Mr. Manson, so if you would answer up so that it will be recorded, please.

This is a subsequent parole consideration hearing for Charles Manson, B-33920. Received California Department of Corrections on April the 22nd, 1971, pursuant to Penal Code Section 1168 for violation of Section 187; California Penal Code, first-degree murder, counts one through seven and 182.1/187, conspiracy to commit murder, count eight, stayed; Los Angeles County case number A-252156.

On February the 2nd, 1977, this sentence was changed being case number A-252156 from death to life pursuant to Court of Appeal. The prisoner was additionally received on December the 13th, 1971, for violation of P.C. 187, first-degree murder, concurrent with prior term, Los Angeles County case number 8267861, count one.

Counts two and three of case number A-267861 for violation of P.C. 182.1/187/211 and 187, conspiracy to commit murder and robbery and first-degree murder were stayed.

The controlling minimum eligible parole date is December—was December 13, 1978.

Today's date is April the 22nd, 1971 [sic]. The time is now 1332 hours and we are at the Corcoran State Prison.

For purposes—participants in today's hearing are Commissioners Koenig and Aceto and Deputy Commissioner Brown. Representing—the prisoner has declined an attorney, a state-represented attorney or an attorney of his own. Representing the people of the County of Los Angeles is Stephen Kay. We also have several members of the news media attending the hearing today and the CNPR and assistant CNPR, and we have an observer in the room.

For purposes of identification we're going to go around the room, state our first name, last name, and why we are here. I want only participants in the hearing to participate in this.

I am Ron Koenig. I'll start and I'll go to my right. Mr. Manson, when we come to you would you also give your C.D.C. number? Okay.

I am Ron Koenig, K-O-E-N-I-G. and I'm Commissioner for the Board of Prison Terms.

BOARD COMMISSIONER ACETO: Good afternoon. Joe Aceto, A-C-E-T-O. Commissioner, Board of Prison Terms.

DEPUTY BOARD COMMISSIONER BROWN: Cleo Brown, B-R-O-W-N. Deputy Commissioner, Board of Prison Terms.

MR. KAY: Okay. I'm Stephen Kay, Deputy District Attorney of Los Angeles County.

PRESIDING BOARD COMMISSIONER KOENIG: Mr. Manson?

INMATE MANSON: Charles Manson, inmate, B-33920.

PRESIDING BOARD COMMISSIONER KOENIG: Would you spell your last name please?

INMATE MANSON: M-A-N-S-U-N.

PRESIDING BOARD COMMISSIONER KOENIG: Thank you. Today, Mr. Manson, the panel from the Board of Prison Terms that you see before you will once again consider your suitability for parole. Certain things we have to go through, so let me go through this, if you will please.

INMATE MANSON: Uh-huh.

PRESIDING BOARD COMMISSIONER KOENIG: And we have a procedure that we follow. If you follow that it will make it much easier on all of us.

The—you've had nine prior hearings. Let me explain the process so you know what's going on. The hearing is basically broken down into three areas. The first area is the instant offense and I'll incorporate that instant offense.

And then I'll give you—and read the instant offense—and then I'll give you the opportunity to make corrections or additions to the instant offense. Then I'll talk about your prior criminality—

INMATE MANSON: I don't understand instant defense.

PRESIDING BOARD COMMISSIONER KOENIG: Instant. That's the offense that you're in here for, the murders—

INMATE MANSON: Instant?

PRESIDING BOARD COMMISSIONER KOENIG: Yes.

INMATE MANSON: Offense?

PRESIDING BOARD COMMISSIONER KOENIG: Yes. Offenses that you're in here for. We'll then go to your social factors and your prior criminality and then we'll go to the second part of the hearing which is your postconviction factors and your psychiatric evaluation. That will be handled by Deputy Commissioner Brown on my far right.

The third area of the hearing are your parole plans and Commissioner Aceto will handle your parole plans.

From there we go to questions by any one of the Commissioners regarding any part of the hearing, and then questions by the District Attorney. The District Attorney will pose the questions to the panel and when you answer his questions would you please answer the panel.

Do you understand what's going on here so far?

INMATE MANSON: Yes. I have a couple questions.

PRESIDING BOARD COMMISSIONER KOENIG: All right. It's all right. Let me finish and then you can ask. We'll then go to closing statements. The first closing statement will be by the District Attorney and then you'll have the opportunity for the final closing statement. We will then recess. We'll make a decision and call you back. Everybody will clear the room when we recess, make a decision. We'll call you back and we'll read into the record that decision.

There are certain rights you are afforded, Mr. Manson. You were notified of the hearing. I saw where you were notified; however, you refused to sign the notification. Also, you had an opportunity to review your central file and I don't know whether you did or not. Did you review your central file?

INMATE MANSON: I've been checking this thing out that I'm sent here.

PRESIDING BOARD COMMISSIONER KOENIG: Okay. All right, good. You also have a right to appeal the decision within ninety days of receiving that decision.

You have a right to an impartial panel, Mr. Manson. Do you have any problems with the three representatives from the Board of Prison Terms you see before you today?

INMATE MANSON: No, not at all.

PRESIDING BOARD COMMISSIONER KOENIG: Thank you. You'll receive a tentative written decision today. The decision will be effective in approximately sixty days after the Board of Prison Terms' review process has taken place.

You are not required, Mr. Manson, to discuss the matter with the panel if you do not wish to. But you must keep in mind that the Board of Prison Terms' panel accepts as true the Court findings in the case, the fact that you are guilty of these murders. Are you going to talk to the panel today and answer questions?

INMATE MANSON: Yes. Yes, sir.

PRESIDING BOARD COMMISSIONER KOENIG: Would you raise your right hand as best as possible. Do you solemnly swear or affirm that the testimony you give today will be the truth, the whole truth, and nothing but the truth?

INMATE MANSON: Yes, sir.

PRESIDING BOARD COMMISSIONER KOENIG: Thank you. Okay, at this time I'm going to incorporate the instant offense from the decision held on December the 1st, 1982, pages two through six.

INMATE MANSON: I don't have that.

PRESIDING BOARD COMMISSIONER KOENIG: Okay. I'm going to read it to you so you can—if you would listen to—and then I'll give you opportunity to make corrections or additions to the instant offense.

INMATE MANSON: I'm a little nervous.

PRESIDING BOARD COMMISSIONER KOENIG: Okay. Just settle down because it's very informal and we want you to relax as we go through this. Are you still—you're nervous?

INMATE MANSON: Yes. Yes, yes, very. I've been a long time sitting in that cell—

PRESIDING BOARD COMMISSIONER KOENIG: Well, we have a lot of people who—

INMATE MANSON: I'm not used to people that much.

PRESIDING BOARD COMMISSIONER KOENIG: Okay. Let me read the instant offense. If you'll listen please—

DEPUTY BOARD COMMISSIONER BROWN: Mr. Chairman? Mr. Chairman?

PRESIDING BOARD COMMISSIONER KOENIG: Yes.

DEPUTY BOARD COMMISSIONER BROWN: We need to make a correction. The date is the—April 21.

PRESIDING BOARD COMMISSIONER KOENIG: Excuse me, the date today is April the 21st, 1992. Thank you.

Shortly before midnight on August—I'm reading from the second—third page—second page of the Board report dated 12/01/82. Shortly before midnight on August 8, 1969, the prisoner informed his crime partners that now is the time for Helter Skelter. The crime partners were directed to accompany Charles Watson to carry out the orders given by the prisoner. The crime partners at the time were Linda Cabastian—

UNIDENTIFIED SPEAKER: Kasabian.

PRESIDING BOARD COMMISSIONER KOENIG: Kasabian, Susan Atkins, and Patricia Krenwinkel. As the crime partners were in the car getting ready to leave the area, the prisoner informed them, "You girls know what I mean," something to which he instructed them to leave a sign. Crime partner Watson drove directly to 10050 Selio—Selio [phonetic spelling] Drive, where he stopped the car. Linda Kasabian held three knives and one gun during the trip. Watson then cut the overhead telephone wires at the scene and parked the vehicle.

INMATE MANSON: Excuse me. Where we getting this from?

PRESIDING BOARD COMMISSIONER KOENIG: This is from the Board report dated 12/01/82. Do you have a copy of that?

INMATE MANSON: No, I don't. Who—whose signature's on the end of that?

PRESIDING BOARD COMMISSIONER KOENIG: This is a Board report. This is the hearing that was held at that particular time—

INMATE MANSON: Uh-huh.

PRESIDING BOARD COMMISSIONER KOENIG:—and this was the reading of the instant offense at that particular time.

INMATE MANSON: That sounds like a book.

PRESIDING BOARD COMMISSIONER KOENIG: Well, if you'll listen and then you can make corrections.

INMATE MANSON: Yes. Okay.

PRESIDING BOARD COMMISSIONER KOENIG: Okay?

INMATE MANSON: Yes.

PRESIDING BOARD COMMISSIONER KOENIG: All right. Crime partner Atkins and Krenwinkel had been in the backseat with Linda Kasabian, the passenger in the right front seat. Watson then carried some [inaudible] over the hill and to the outer premises of 10050 Selio Drive.

The vehicle containing victim Stephen Parent [phonetic spelling] approached the gate opening into the street. Watson stopped him at gunpoint and Parent stated, "Please don't hurt me, I won't say anything." Watson shot Parent five times and turned off the ignition of his car.

All of the crime partners then proceeded to the house, where Watson cut a window screen. Linda Kasabian acted as a lookout while another female crime partner entered the residence through an open window and admitted the other crime partners.

Within the residence the prisoner's crime partners, without provocation, logic, or reason, murdered Abigail Anne Folger by inflicting a total of 28 multiple stab wounds on her body. Victim Wachezski—excuse me—victim-

MR. KAY: Voitek [phonetic spelling].

PRESIDING BOARD COMMISSIONER KOENIG: Voitek, count two, was killed by multiple stab wounds. A gunshot wound to his left back and multiple forced trauma of blunt nature to the head. Victim Sharon Tate Polanski was killed with multiple stab wounds. Victim Jay Sebring was killed by multiple stab wounds.

On August the 10th, 1969, the prisoner drove his crime partners to a location near the residence of victims Leo and Rosemary LaBanca—LaBianca. The prisoner entered the LaBianca home alone at gunpoint and tied up the victims.

He impressed them with the statement that they would not be harmed and that a robbery was taking place. He then returned to the vehicle containing his crime partners and then directed them to enter that residence and kill the occupants. He informed them not to notify the victims that they would be killed.

Crime partners Charles Watson, Patricia Krenwinkel, Leslie Van Houten then entered the residence and the prisoner drove away from the scene. The crime partners entered the residence and in a callous manner killed Leo LaBianca by inflicting multiple stab wounds to his neck and abdomen. Rosemary LaBianca was killed by multiple stab wounds which were inflicted to the neck and trunk.

The crime partners carved the wood *war*—the word *war* on Leo LaBianca's stomach with the use of a carving fork. At both of the above murder scenes, the prisoner's crime partners used blood of their victims to write the words.

Under case number A-267861, the prisoner was received into the institution on December 13, 1971, for violation of first-degree murder concurrent with prior term. The pistol, knives, and swords were used in the following crimes which the prisoner committed with crime partners Bira Alstea—how do you pronounce that?

MR. KAY: Beausoleil.

PRESIDING BOARD COMMISSIONER KOENIG: Beausoleil, and Atkins and Grogan and Davis. The prisoner directed the crime partners to go to the home of victim Gary Allen Highman—

MR. KAY: Hinman.

PRESIDING BOARD COMMISSIONER KOENIG:—and have him sign over his property. The crime partners followed the prisoner's directions and on July 26, 1969, they contacted the prisoner from the Hinman residence. Prisoner and Davis then went to the Hinman home and the prisoner struck Hinman with a sword severing a part of the right ear and causing a laceration to the left side of his face from his ear to his mouth. The prisoner and Davis then drove away from the crime scene in Hinman's automobile.

On July 27, 1969, after suffering three days of torturous treatment, Hinman was killed by a stab wound through the heart which was inflicted by Beausoleil.

When Hinman was found in the Topanga Canyon home on July 31, 1969, he had been stabbed through the heart in addition to suffering a stab wound in the chest, a gash on the top of his head, a gash behind the right ear, and a laceration on the left side of his face which cut his ear and cheek.

This concludes the reading of the instant offense. Do you have any additions or corrections, Mr. Manson, to the—

INMATE MANSON: I'd like to know who signed that, who put their name on it.

PRESIDING BOARD COMMISSIONER KOENIG: Nobody put their name on it. This was a hearing conducted in 1982. Your hearing was conducted at that particular time and that's the reading of the instant offense as taken from the probation officers report at the time of the trial that you had. Do you have any corrections or additions to that?

INMATE MANSON: No. We could correct the whole thing because it's basically hearsay.

PRESIDING BOARD COMMISSIONER KOENIG: Okay. Do you remember what I said at the beginning of the hearing?

INMATE MANSON: Yes.

PRESIDING BOARD COMMISSIONER KOENIG: I said that we accept as true the court findings in the case. The fact that you were found guilty and you are guilty of those particular murders. If there's any change or anything you wanted to say about—

INMATE MANSON: So all that is reality to you?

PRESIDING BOARD COMMISSIONER KOENIG: Yes. Yes, we accept it as true—

INMATE MANSON: And that—and either—even if it never happened it's still reality to you?

PRESIDING BOARD COMMISSIONER KOENIG: Yes, because you were found guilty by a court of law.

INMATE MANSON: And—okay—and all the things that in that courtroom that went through that courtroom is reality to you?

PRESIDING BOARD COMMISSIONER KOENIG: Yes. Okay. We accept as true—

INMATE MANSON: Now let me—let me just say one thing.

PRESIDING BOARD COMMISSIONER KOENIG: Okay.

INMATE MANSON: Nine black Muslims and three Mexicans signed a writ that said I was Jesus Christ. Is that reality to you as well?

PRESIDING BOARD COMMISSIONER KOENIG: I didn't read that in the Board report.

INMATE MANSON: Oh, well it's in the record. I mean, you know.

PRESIDING BOARD COMMISSIONER KOENIG: Well, we've read—we have your C-file and all the reports were made available to us.

INMATE MANSON: Okay.

PRESIDING BOARD COMMISSIONER KOENIG: And I think we know most about, but that's the reason for the hearing, Mr. Manson—

INMATE MANSON: Okay, okay.

PRESIDING BOARD COMMISSIONER KOENIG:—that you can bring these things out if you wish.

INMATE MANSON: I think if you'll look in your own minds for every point, there's a counterpoint. For every red, there's a black. For every black, there's a red.

In other words, what you're making me into in your reports so that you can write your books and do your Rambo trips and make your movies for public entertainment, is not really what happened and what happened could have been explained but if you will allow me to call a witness?

PRESIDING BOARD COMMISSIONER KOENIG: No. We do not allow witnesses in here—

INMATE MANSON: I mean, it's within the panel. I'd like to question that man in front of the panel.

PRESIDING BOARD COMMISSIONER KOENIG: No. We do not allow that, Mr. Manson. We have a procedure that we follow.

INMATE MANSON: Okay. All right.

PRESIDING BOARD COMMISSIONER KOENIG: Now, if you want to tell about the crime—

INMATE MANSON: Okay.

PRESIDING BOARD COMMISSIONER KOENIG:—then go ahead and tell about the crime. Otherwise [inaudible].

INMATE MANSON: Then I will say it and then if it isn't true, he can interrupt it through you, and then we can talk through you. Is that legal?

PRESIDING BOARD COMMISSIONER KOENIG: You may—you may—[inaudible].

INMATE MANSON: It says here that I can call witnesses on this paper here.

PRESIDING BOARD COMMISSIONER KOENIG: No.

INMATE MANSON: This says I got these rights to do that.

PRESIDING BOARD COMMISSIONER KOENIG: No, you do not. If you would please respond to me there—any additions or corrections to the instant offense that I just read?

INMATE MANSON: Yes. I didn't tie anybody up.

PRESIDING BOARD COMMISSIONER KOENIG: Okay.

INMATE MANSON: I was never on the scene where anyone was killed. I think the law says you can only keep me 17 years or 18 years if I was never on the scene when anyone was killed. I was never on the crime scene of anything.

The closest I came to the crime scene is I cut Hinman's ear off in a fight over some money because the Frenchman—he wouldn't pay the Frenchman and I told him, why don't he be a man about himself and pay his debts? And we had a fight.

So to—in order to hook me up to that they say well, they tortured the dude three days. I was gone from that scene of that crime for three days. I was never on the scene of any crime. I never told anyone directly to do—to go anywhere and do anything.

I always said—and mostly it come from the witness stand—I said like, you know what to do, you have a brain of your own, don't ask me what to do, I've just got out of prison, I don't know what's going on out here. I hadn't been out of jail long enough to really get a perspective of what was happening.

I just was released from McNeil Island and I was in Mexico City prison before that and I was in Terminal Island before that. So I really wasn't up on the sixties as much as you all make me out to be. I had just got out of prison.

Most of those people, I—like Kasabian, I knew her two weeks. I had seen her two or three times around the ranch. I had never even been with the broad, man, that much, you know. People came around me because I played a lot of music and I was fairly free and open because I really didn't know, honestly.

Everyone says that I was the leader of those people, but I was actually the follower of the children because, like I never grew up. I've been in jail most of this time, so I stayed in the minds of the children. And I'm pretty much a street person so violence is no new thing to me. And people getting hurt around me is no new thing.

I've lived in prison all my life. That happens all the time. I've always walked on a line. In Ohio, Kentucky, Indiana, all across this country. Cook County Jail, Chicago, it's always about fighting. That's part of everyday life where I live, you know.

So, a lot of the things that people were doing were just their own little episodes that they get involved in and they looked at me like I was something like a friend or a brother or a father or someone that understood because I learned in prison that you can't really tell anyone anything because everybody's got their own perspective. And all you can do is reflect people back at themselves and let them make up their own mind about things.

So, when Beausoleil come to me with, could I be a brother? I told him certainly, you know. So we were like in a little brotherhood together, like we didn't lie to each other. And whatever he said do, I would do. And whatever I said do, he would do.

But as far as lining up someone for some kind of helter skelter trip, you know, that's the District Attorney's motive. That's the only thing he could find for a motive to throw up on top of all that confusion he had. There was no such thing in my mind as helter skelter. Helter Skelter was a song and it was a nightclub—we opened up a little after-hours night-club to make some money and play some music and do some dancing and singing and play some stuff to make some money for dune buggies to go out in the desert.

And we called the club Helter Skelter. It was a helter skelter club because we would be there and when the cops would come, we'd all melt into other dimensions because it wasn't licensed to be anything in particular. And that was kind of like a speakeasy back in the moonshine days behind the movie set.

And I'm an outlaw. That's—they're right there, you know, and I'm a gangster and I'm bad and I'm all the things that I want to be. I'm pretty free within myself. I cut people and I shoot them and I do whatever I have to do to survive in the world I live in. But that has nothing to do with me breaking the line.

Let me explain something about the penitentiary in my mind. I came to Gilbault in Terre Haute, Indiana, overlooking the federal penitentiary in Indiana. And I was raised by a bunch of monks that taught us how to tell the truth and how to play handball and how to box in a boxing ring.

So, I learned to fight early and I ran off and stole a bicycle and then I went to reform school for that. And I ran off from reform school. And all my life I've been in prison. I've been in jail running off. I never went to school. I've never grown up. I've never accepted the system. I've always accepted the ole man, the ole winos and I accepted the retired veterans that were guards at the prisons and county supervisors and such.

But there's a line that man walks. All men walk a line. And I walk that line in prison. I don't tell on other people. I don't carry tales about other people. If someone's going to kill themselves, I feel obligated by Christian ethics to tell him don't do that, your life is worth more than that. But if he continues to go on a self-destructive path, I step from his way. I get out of his way. I've learnt that in prison.

Someone's got a knife and they're going to do something, I say don't do that. And they say I'm going to do it, I say I'm gone. It's got nothing to do with me. So they call me on the phone and said the guy's got a gun, what do I do? I said, well if he's got a gun he must be afraid of something.

DEPUTY BOARD COMMISSIONER BROWN: Hold on a minute. I think he's kind of straying away from what you had going—

PRESIDING BOARD COMMISSIONER KOENIG: Okay.

INMATE MANSON: I'm right there in Beausoleil's murder.

PRESIDING BOARD COMMISSIONER KOENIG: Yes. I think he's talking—that's all right. [Inaudible.]

INMATE MANSON: I'm right there on the telephone where he called and asked me what to do. This is the point where I got convicted.

PRESIDING BOARD COMMISSIONER KOENIG: Go ahead, Mr. Manson.

INMATE MANSON: It would come from the witness stand that when on the telephone the only thing that ever connected me with Hinman's murder was Beausoleil called me and asked me what to do and I told him, you know what to do. I didn't tell him like [*raising voice*], you know what to do. I told him, man, you're a man, grow up juvenile. Don't ask me what to do. Stand on your own two feet. Be responsible for your own actions. Don't ask me what to do. I just got out of prison. I don't want to go back to jail.

I know what walking that line is. It's a straight razor in the barbershop in McNeil Island. I've worked in a straight razor, I've worked in the barbershop in the McNeil Island. I was with all the ole men that came outta Alcatraz. I don't break the law. The old man tells me, if you don't break the law, you don't have to go to jail. You break the law, you're putting yourself in jail. The law is there and the will of God. You break that law, you're breaking the will of God and you're going to go to jail. When I got out, that was my symbol. Everybody else was doing this and this and different symbols. I would do that. And they'd say, what is that symbol? I'd say, that symbol is, I got one positive thought. I'm in a rebirth movement. I just come outta prison. I got a chance to start over. And I'm starting over and I'm not breaking no laws. So don't come around me with no—nothing. I don't want no money. I'll eat out of garbage cans. I'll stay on the complete bottom. I'm underneath this snake here. I'm not breaking no law.

So a lotta people came to me from the underworld and in the outlaw world and run away from the war, from the Vietnam War. That was—what's his name—them guys that testified for you on them motorcycles. Them Italian kids that came off of that Venice, California. They took the witness stand and they said everything they could get away with to get their cases dropped. There wasn't a witness that took that witness stand—

PRESIDING BOARD COMMISSIONER KOENIG: Okay. I don't want to go into the hearing, Mr. Manson. Just talk about the crime. Any changes from what I read which is—

INMATE MANSON: Well, that's what made that—that's what wrote that down is what all these people said to you guys, you know. They told you all these trips about what I said, and when I said it, and how in the hell—

PRESIDING BOARD COMMISSIONER KOENIG: But any more—

INMATE MANSON:—could you possibly know what I said to somebody 25 years ago in the corner of—when we were only talking to ourselves and I couldn't even remember what that—what I said. I may have said just anything, but I know what I would say now and I don't lie, so I know what I would say then, you know. And I certainly wouldn't tell nobody to go in and do nothing to anybody that I wouldn't want done to me.

PRESIDING BOARD COMMISSIONER KOENIG: Okay.

INMATE MANSON: Listen, listen. I got enough sense to know that if I spit on you, that you—that gives you the God-given right to spit on me back. Anything I do to you, you got the right to do right back to me. And I'm not going get caught up in that. I've been in jail long enough to know if you go over on the other side of that yard and you beat somebody up and you walk that line, pretty sooner or later somebody's going to beat you up.

PRESIDING BOARD COMMISSIONER KOENIG: Okay. Let me go on a little bit, okay, and talk about your prior criminality. You've covered it pretty well. It says here that you started your criminal history when you were very young, is that right? Back in '48 you went to Terre Haute, Indiana Boys School because of a burglary of a grocery store. And then you went AWOL from the school and were placed in Indiana State Reformatory—

INMATE MANSON: Before you get into that, before you rush me off into that.

PRESIDING BOARD COMMISSIONER KOENIG: Okay.

INMATE MANSON: Every time I go to these committees—

PRESIDING BOARD COMMISSIONER KOENIG: Uh-huh.

INMATE MANSON:—I'll wait two or three years for you and I'll sit in the cell and stare at the wall for two or three years just waiting for you people. And then when you get here you can't even give me five minutes.

PRESIDING BOARD COMMISSIONER KOENIG: No—

INMATE MANSON: You're in such a rush, you know, you know.

PRESIDING BOARD COMMISSIONER KOENIG: All right. Then what I—

INMATE MANSON: You have to slow down with my mind and to—to see where your mind is.

PRESIDING BOARD COMMISSIONER KOENIG: All right. All right. You're right.

INMATE MANSON: Let me say this. The courtroom—Charles Older would not have been sitting on that bench had I not went in the courtroom. So, we're kinda like married in this thought together, like we're together whether we want to be here together or not, you know, we're stuck in this madness, you know.

PRESIDING BOARD COMMISSIONER KOENIG: Right.

INMATE MANSON: I don't want this job. I'm not getting paid very much, you know.

PRESIDING BOARD COMMISSIONER KOENIG: No, that's true.

INMATE MANSON: And you're certainly going to get paid if you take your time, so give me time to finish what I was trying to do, will you, please?

PRESIDING BOARD COMMISSIONER KOENIG: Is it on the crime, Mr. Manson?

INMATE MANSON: Yes sir, it is.

PRESIDING BOARD COMMISSIONER KOENIG: Okay. Then—

INMATE MANSON: Yes, sir. It's the very same thing that you read.

PRESIDING BOARD COMMISSIONER KOENIG: Okay.

INMATE MANSON: You know, I kind of anticipated what you were going to say because you've been saying the same thing for 20 years.

PRESIDING BOARD COMMISSIONER KOENIG: All right.

INMATE MANSON: This has grown so much that the people living in my life have moved in with uniforms and penitentiaries. They built whole penitentiaries in the fear that they generated off of this case. So the public can feel safe against this monster, we're going to charge you $200 million to build another set of penitentiaries.

PRESIDING BOARD COMMISSIONER KOENIG: Mr. Manson—

INMATE MANSON: So people living in my life, they don't care whether I broke the law or not. They'll make up a lotta things and sell a lotta books, 58 of them to be exact, and billions of dollars has been made. And it's okay if I have to spend my life in prison—let me finish—just to hold me because I've shown you some strong strength and I haven't surrendered to—to this by—by copping out to you or telling tales on someone else or playing weak. You've medicated me, you've burnt me, you've beat me, you've stabbed me, you've done everything you can do to me and I'm still here. And you're still gonna have to face the truth about this case sooner or later. If not here—

PRESIDING BOARD COMMISSIONER KOENIG: [Inaudible.]

INMATE MANSON:—in the street.

PRESIDING BOARD COMMISSIONER KOENIG: All right, Mr. Manson. I'm going to give you an opportunity to give a closing statement and you can read that or talk about that at that particular time.

We're going to now talk about your prior criminality. I said before, and I think you stated that you were placed in a boys school at an early age, in 1948, for burglary. You tried to escape from there or run away, whatever it was, and you were placed in Indiana State Reformatory.

Again went AWOL in February of '51. You stole an automobile, went to Utah. You were arrested there and you were convicted of the Dyer Act and sentenced to the National Training School for Boys in Washington, D.C.

Your adult convictions there are one, two, three, four, five, six, seven, eight, or nine adult convictions beginning in 1955 and ending in 1969. They've consisted of the Dyer Act— you were sentenced to three years in federal prison for that, attempted escape, five years probation; forgery, mail theft, ten years suspended; Los Angeles probation violation; ten years federal prison, McNeil Island, Washington; South Ukiah, interfering with an officer, three years probation; and in Ventura possession of a driver's license and in Los Angeles, was the instant offense of murders.

Now you said you also spent time in Mexico in a prison.

INMATE MANSON: Yes, I was in Mexico for—

PRESIDING BOARD COMMISSIONER KOENIG: In prison down there?

INMATE MANSON: In Mexico City, prison, yes. Immigration prison.

PRESIDING BOARD COMMISSIONER KOENIG: What was that for?

INMATE MANSON: I had been accused of killing some French people and a couple dudes in Acapulco.

PRESIDING BOARD COMMISSIONER KOENIG: And how long were you in prison down there?

INMATE MANSON: I was there a couple different times.

PRESIDING BOARD COMMISSIONER KOENIG: A couple times?

INMATE MANSON: Uh-huh.

PRESIDING BOARD COMMISSIONER KOENIG: I have here under your personal factors, Mr. Manson, that you were born on—in 1934 in Cincinnati, Ohio. Your mother was Kathy Maddox, who never—and you never saw your natural father.

INMATE MANSON: That's not true.

PRESIDING BOARD COMMISSIONER KOENIG: It's not true?

INMATE MANSON: No. My father's name was William Manson.

PRESIDING BOARD COMMISSIONER KOENIG: William?

INMATE MANSON: Yes.

PRESIDING BOARD COMMISSIONER KOENIG: And did you live with him for a while?

INMATE MANSON: No. You know, it's one of those divorce trips where you see a guy walk by and he's your father and you really don't—you know, I remember his boots—

PRESIDING BOARD COMMISSIONER KOENIG: Yes.

INMATE MANSON:—and I remember him when he went to the war. I remember when he—his uniform, but I don't remember what he really looked like.

PRESIDING BOARD COMMISSIONER KOENIG: Your mother was arrested shortly after the birth and sentenced to prison for assault and robbery?

INMATE MANSON: Yes.

PRESIDING BOARD COMMISSIONER KOENIG: And you lived with your maternal grandparents in West Virginia. You don't have a southern accent, do you?

INMATE MANSON: When I need it.

PRESIDING BOARD COMMISSIONER KOENIG: Yes, when you need it. You later resided in foster homes until you were made a ward of the court in '47. The rest of your juvenile life was spent in various informatories, reformatories and boys schools in Pennsylvania and Indiana. You dropped out of school at the age of nine in the third grade. You married Rosealie Willis in 1954. The marriage ended in divorce in 1956. You have one son, Charles, Jr., which resulted from this marriage, but you have not seen your son since the divorce. Is that correct, Mr. Manson?

INMATE MANSON: I don't know.

PRESIDING BOARD COMMISSIONER KOENIG: Okay. It says here, no military service. You used L.S.D. extensively, mescaline, amphetamines, and barbiturates, but no alcohol. Is that correct?

INMATE MANSON: No.

PRESIDING BOARD COMMISSIONER KOENIG: No? Enlighten me.

INMATE MANSON: I've taken a few tabs of acid, I smoked grass, I smoked a little hash. I don't mess with drugs, per se. I don't do anything self-destructive. I like the cactus buds. They're a spiritual experience, and I—

PRESIDING BOARD COMMISSIONER KOENIG: Peyote?

INMATE MANSON: And mushrooms are okay.

PRESIDING BOARD COMMISSIONER KOENIG: Yes.

INMATE MANSON: I drink scotch whiskey. I like scotch whiskey and I drink beer occasionally. I'm not much of a wine drinker, but now and then some wine with meals is all right.

PRESIDING BOARD COMMISSIONER KOENIG: You get any of that in here?

INMATE MANSON: No, no, no.

PRESIDING BOARD COMMISSIONER KOENIG: All right. We're going to—remember I said there was three areas of the hearing. The second area is your postconviction factors. We may come back to this. I told you one area we have questions.

INMATE MANSON: Do I get to say anything about that?

PRESIDING BOARD COMMISSIONER KOENIG: Oh, yes. We're going to do that in just a little bit. We're going to go to your postconviction factors and your psychiatric factors and your psychiatric evaluation. Now, that's everything that's happened to you since your last hearing, and also the evaluation and Deputy Commissioner Brown will handle that on my far right.

DEPUTY BOARD COMMISSIONER BROWN: Thank you, Mr. Koenig.

PRESIDING BOARD COMMISSIONER KOENIG: You're welcome.

INMATE MANSON: Do I get a minute here—in between there?

DEPUTY BOARD COMMISSIONER BROWN: Why do you want a minute?

INMATE MANSON: To respond to just what that record that you laid out there?

PRESIDING BOARD COMMISSIONER KOENIG: We'll go back to that. You—

INMATE MANSON: There's just no way my mind can handle that.

PRESIDING BOARD COMMISSIONER KOENIG: All right—

INMATE MANSON: In other words, I don't have the papers you have and I can't refer to what you're referring to, you know.

PRESIDING BOARD COMMISSIONER KOENIG: Yes. You may respond to this right now, if you wish. Go ahead.

INMATE MANSON: Okay, okay. What that whole first 11 years being locked up in was trying to get away. You've got a juvenile. You lock him up in juvenile hall, you don't know anything. He's got no parents. He's got nobody telling him the truth. Everybody's lying to him. So the only thing he can do is run away.

So that's all I did. I ran away. And every time I ran away, they just got me and put me in a harder place to get away. So every time I would run away, they would take me and put me in a more difficult place to run away until I got to the federal prison system.

I ran through Indiana and I ran through Illinois and I ran through Ohio. And then when they put me in Washington, D.C., Dr. Hartman put me in Virginia, Natural Bridge Camp with a [inaudible] and that was in 1952—'51. Then I went to Petersburg—Camp Petersburg, Virginia, where they got the military academy.

And then I went to Pennsylvania, then I went to Ohio, and then in 1954 I got out and I [inaudible] knew what I was doing. I'm still nine years old in third grade in my mind. I couldn't very well know what was going on, you know, I never had any help from anyone. No one ever done anything for me.

So what I did was I married the first girl I came to and stole a car and came to California because that's where she wanted to come and I just followed her around like a blind guy because I really don't—California was a—you know, I didn't know what California was. You know, I'm this dumb hillbilly. I thought the pigeons were seagulls and the seagulls were pigeons. I didn't know the difference, you know.

So when I got to California, it was all about fighting in the county jail. I wasn't out there on the street but what, maybe two or three weeks before they had me in the jail back in Terminal Island.

So I went through the lieutenant there and they brought the guys—the lieutenants and the men that were in the uniforms from the dentist office and all the Navy and the doctors from Dr. Hartman, they brought them from back East, they brought them to Terminal Island with a lot of the old-time gangsters that were being released. They're going to Needles, California, and out in the desert, to do different things in the—in the Mafia world, in that old underworld, where they made all that moonshine stuff.

So I learned all the things they learned. So this—I'm picking up all these things from all these older men. So they're laying out to me what's right and what's wrong, and I don't really know what's right and what's wrong, because people that say what's right and wrong, they're not doing what they say. They're doing something different than what they say, you know. So I had to find all this out for myself.

So then when you keep calling me a criminal and keep calling me a bad guy, then I got to be all the things that you think in your mind that I am, which is—that's not really what I am. You got me being a bastard, you got me being a dope fiend. You got me being everything's bad. I'm only five foot tall. I was five seven, then I went to five six, now I'm down to five two. I figure about another 20 years, I'll be about four feet tall, because everybody's just constantly pushing it over on me, like they got permission to get away with doing anything they want to do to me, because I don't have no parents, because I don't have no money, because I don't have no education.

You've got to have some education or some parents or you're not smart. You've got to be stupid if you don't read and write, you know. You've got to be all the things that are bad if you ain't got nobody to protect you, because you find out in that cell, the only person that loves you, Jesus Christ.

And that rebirth movement in 1967 was mine. Now you can tell Carter and all them other people that have been stealing my life every day and living in my reality, you know, that they can read Corinthians 13, chapter verse, you know. And that'll handle that part of it. That's the end of what I got to say then.

PRESIDING BOARD COMMISSIONER KOENIG: All right. You did a good job there. We're going to go to the second area of the hearing now. Mr. Brown will handle your postconvictions.

DEPUTY BOARD COMMISSIONER BROWN: I want to start right in with your C.D.C. 115s. You have about 60 of them. And it doesn't appear that you have been doing very much to change them. I won't go all the way back past 1981. As a matter of fact, I'll start in '83. Your last time you appeared before the Board was 1981, and I'm sure that that panel reviewed all of those 115s with you prior to that time.

There are 60 of them starting from that time. Disrespect toward staff, possession of hacksaw blade. Do you have a copy of those?

INMATE MANSON: No.

DEPUTY BOARD COMMISSIONER BROWN: [Inaudible] violence, dangerous properties?

INMATE MANSON: No. No, I know what all those are though.

DEPUTY BOARD COMMISSIONER BROWN: I want you—I'm going to read a couple this year that you had. March 14, 1992, threatening staff. (*Reading.*) On 03/14/92 at approximately 1510 hours while conducting my duties as floor officer, I was sweeping up a tier [inaudible] when Inmate Manson, B-33920 verbally demanded I go out to the S.H.U. yard and clear the showers now—clean the showers now because in my—in his opinion they're dirty. I informed Inmate Manson that I didn't have time to clean them today. Inmate Manson began to call me a liar and treacherous bitch. Inmate Manson also stated, "I would like to break all the bones in your body starting with your elbow working down to your knees." Then Inmate Manson stated, "Tell that man up there, the patrol group operator, to open this cell door and let me beat you into submission so that you'll be under my power." (*End of reading.*)

Do you recall that?

INMATE MANSON: Yes.

DEPUTY BOARD COMMISSIONER BROWN: Threatening staff—

INMATE MANSON: Do I get to explain it?

DEPUTY BOARD COMMISSIONER BROWN: You want to explain that?

INMATE MANSON: Yes.

DEPUTY BOARD COMMISSIONER BROWN: You got it. Go ahead.

INMATE MANSON: Prison is a treacherous place to live in. You miss one move, and you get stabbed. You've got to be aware of everything that goes on. There's nothing that you can overlook. You've got to be aware of your air and ventilator that you breath, because if you've got emphysema and a Ninja warrior gets in your air, he can stop your air.

So I'm in the shower area. They got some rust that's coming out of the pipes, and this rust is building up and it looks just exactly like instant coffee. If you take a spoonful of that rust and you mix it in with instant coffee and you give somebody a cup of coffee, you can burn their kidneys out, you can kill them.

So there's a deadly substance out in the yard that needs cleaned up, because if I'm aware of this substance, when someone else comes out they see this substance, they may pick some of it up and put it in my coffee. So I try to be aware of everything.

So I asked the woman when she came to work—I said, would you take the hose that you've been watering me down with and squirting me with when no one's looking and go out there and squirt down that yard and clean up that mess out there, to where—and she says, well, no, she wasn't going to do that. I said, well, somebody needs to do that because it's a danger, you know. So she said she didn't want to do it and she called me a liar so I called her a liar back.

Now, whether you want to accept this or not, the deer in the woods—there's a doe and there's a buck. And the buck comes up to the doe and scares the doe and the doe turns around and backs up to the buck. That's a matriarch and a patriarch. I live in a patriarchy. You live in a matriarch. You back up to your women. I don't back up to my women. I don't take no lip from my women. I don't give them none, but I don't take none either.

If they disrespect me, I'll disrespect them back. If they hit me, I'll hit them back.

DEPUTY BOARD COMMISSIONER BROWN: I'm going to interrupt you. I'm going to read these other two, because they're along the same line. You keep your thought, and I'll let you continue to go in that vein for a short while longer, but I'm not going to allow you to ramble all day.

INMATE MANSON: You got it.

DEPUTY BOARD COMMISSIONER BROWN: The second one, February the 1st, 1992, written by an officer by the name of Bass, and you told her, "Bass, you're a fucking punk." She attempted to counsel. You stated, "Open this—Bass, open this fucking door and I'll take that stick away from you and beat your ass with it."

You got another one, February the 10th, 1992, officer by the name of Moony. You became verbally abusive saying, "Get your nose out of my ass, you bitch." When I attempted to proceed with the C.D.C. 115, Manson exposed his penis, and said, "Suck my dick, you white bitch, you're nothing but a witch." Manson then proceeded to spit on me.

You may go ahead with your—conclude your statement that you were making about why this kind of behavior keeps going on, as far as you're concerned.

INMATE MANSON: Prison is a place where they keep men. They chew tobacco, they spit, they cuss, they do bad things. They ride horses, they fall down. It's not a place where women should be working.

Women come in here and we're sitting on the toilet. We have to bare down and take our clothes off and bend over and show our private parts and they stand there and gawk. And it's not a place for a woman. I wouldn't want my mother working in a prison, if I had one. I wouldn't want my sisters, I wouldn't want my old ladies working in a prison.

Prison and the authoritative-type jobs kind of—they like certain kinds of jobs. Some women that don't like men, they like these kind of jobs. They can get over on some men and they feel really good about that, because they didn't like their father and they don't like men anyway. Well, I don't particularly like men either, whatever men is. Or whatever that is to them, it's got nothing to do with what it is to me.

So what it is to me is like—I say a lot of words they say are bad words. To me, they're just words. I don't see good words or bad words. Good and bad is up to the individual to decide whatever he feels like's good words.

So when you're talking to a man, you say, "Hey, you old dirty [unintelligible]." You're saying things that you're rapping, what they call the dozens, you're rapping back and for-wards. Then you got a guy and you're sitting there rapping and you let a stinker, and there's two guys in the room and (sniff-sniff) one of them smells it and looks at the other one, says wasn't me. I mean, there's only two of you there. It could—you know, I mean, how are you going to lie to yourself, you know.

So me and this man is standing there and we're rapping and man-talking back and forwards and this woman come around the corner like I was talking to her. I wasn't talking to her to start with. I was talking to the guy.

DEPUTY BOARD COMMISSIONER BROWN: You have enough sense to understand that when you accumulated this many disciplinaries, that somewhere along the line, somebody's saying that you're doing it wrong. And somewhere in your mind, you need to make some kind of decision that you're going to make a choice to stop.

INMATE MANSON: Uh-huh.

DEPUTY BOARD COMMISSIONER BROWN: Now you can sit up and you can rationalize and you can come up with all of the rhetoric that you want to, but it isn't going to get you out of the hole. You're just going to continue to dig yourself in deeper.

INMATE MANSON: Okay. Can I explain that?

DEPUTY BOARD COMMISSIONER BROWN: Go ahead.

INMATE MANSON: The turnaround, it comes to push, push comes to shove, shove comes looking around to see where you're up above or down below, where you're at and how it turns. Something that says good, says bad, that's good, say what it is, what it is, that's cool.

So when you catch cool you got some fool coming through the door, you don't know what he's doing about what. He just come and fell out of the water like a fish on the floor. And he don't know what he's doing, he got no idea where he's at and he's coming into other people's lives talking about words he don't even know nothing about it.

He comes in to my world, my life, and tells me roo-roo-rah, some old punk-ass motherfucker shit that's going to get me killed if I don't put up some force fields in his mind to get his ding-dong ass off of me. So I tell him, get off of me. If you don't get off of me, I'll teach you how to get off of me. And he leans that, and he turns that around and he tells the inmate, you get up against that wall and shake down.

And then he learns his man from getting the man and when they feel real secure, then they have to get them 115s in before I get to parole, because they want to get them 115s in because they don't want to ever let me go, because if they let me go they lose the best thing they've got because they feel secure as long as they got me locked up in a cell. And they feel like—yeah, they feel like they got the man right there in the box where they can go back and say what's what to who and says where, and you represent and who in what part or whose courtroom, see.

DEPUTY BOARD COMMISSIONER BROWN: All right.

INMATE MANSON: Here's the thing—let me say this to you Chief Thomas [sic]. When we—

DEPUTY BOARD COMMISSIONER BROWN: Hold up, hold up just a minute. My name—

INMATE MANSON: Brown—excuse me, Mr. Brown.

DEPUTY BOARD COMMISSIONER BROWN: My name is written right there and don't you ever call me anything but that name right there. Do you understand?

INMATE MANSON: Yes, sir. Yes, sir. Yes, sir.

DEPUTY BOARD COMMISSIONER BROWN: Now proceed.

INMATE MANSON: Sure. So it comes to this, it's like, I'm not going to try to kid you. I'm not going to try playing nothing with you.

DEPUTY BOARD COMMISSIONER BROWN: And I'm not going to play with you and let me tell you something else—

INMATE MANSON: Now, wait a minute, wait a minute, wait a minute—

DEPUTY BOARD COMMISSIONER BROWN: No, no, no. you wait.

INMATE MANSON: Oh, you want to kick me out of here and [inaudible] go home.

DEPUTY BOARD COMMISSIONER BROWN: No, I'm not going to kick you out of here. No way I'm going to kick you out—

INMATE MANSON: Well, I just don't—you know, like the words you like—

DEPUTY BOARD COMMISSIONER BROWN: Hold up. Will you—

INMATE MANSON: What do you want to prove here?

DEPUTY BOARD COMMISSIONER BROWN: And I'm not going to tell Corrections what to do with you, but we're going to follow some kind of decorum and procedure in this hearing room.

INMATE MANSON: Uh-huh.

DEPUTY BOARD COMMISSIONER BROWN: I'm going to let you go just a little bit longer on this that you're talking about, then we're going to move to your psych reports. Now go ahead.

INMATE MANSON: I reflect the procedure back to stay alive, man, and I've got to get nasty sometimes, because everybody you sending here working over me is not a nice guy, you know. I think if any of you have any experience in jail, you know that jail is not a very nice place to be.

And you have all kinds of different people in all kinds of different levels and I have to deal with all those levels. I have to deal with every kind of psychotic maniac you got in the world trying to burn me up, trying to beat me up, trying to get some attention to get me in any kind of direction he can. And I have to propose a certain image and keep a certain kind of guy stuck up there to keep those bullies off of me. Because if I show any weakness, if I fall down in any perspective, I get ate up because I run with a pack of wolves and I've got to be a wolf.

And when it reflects back to you that I'm a no-good so-and-so and so forth, I'm reflecting a procedure that's reflected onto me. If I don't have any other choice but to get a 115 to stay out of something more dangerous or more terrible, rather than stand—rather than stay out of my cell and fight this big old ugly guy, I'm going to call him a bunch of names so he'll put it on paper. And then when he puts it on paper, I say, whew, boy, I didn't have to go with that physically, then I could do it mentally.

As long as I run my jaw mentally and I get it put on the paper, then physically I can walk around all the violence and I can stay in peace and harmony.

DEPUTY BOARD COMMISSIONER BROWN: Are you saying that you're deliberately keeping yourself placed in a security holding unit?

INMATE MANSON: No, I'm saying that we're all doing this. We all only use each other in different perspectives all the time. If the song's saying, love won't let you go—it ain't got nothing to do with, love won't let you go. It's people who need you that they don't want to let you go.

They need you for different reasons. They need you to feel secure in—because if they got guys they're afraid of, you got two or three dudes over there that are bad and you're afraid of them and you're a correctional officer, but yet you got a guy over here that ain't afraid of you. It's like this woman come to work and she goes over to this guy and tells him, "Turn your radio down," and he tells her, "Shove it right up your ass [inaudible]," run her off.

So she comes over to my cell and because she sees that he's afraid of me, so she takes my radio away and looks back at him and says, "Humph." So then she uses me to stand up over you, because in the darkness on the yard out there, you do what I tell you to do.

When you're on that committee, I'll do what you tell me to do. I'm the man in here. And that's a fact.

[Off the Record]

DEPUTY BOARD COMMISSIONER BROWN: This is Tape 2 in the case of Charles Manson, April the 21st, 1992, California State Prison, Corcoran, California.

We're going to proceed to your psychiatric evaluations. You don't have one. Well, you had one for this year, but you didn't have one completed for the Board of Prison Terms specifically.

Bruce T. Reed, Ph.D., Clinic Psychologist, went over to see you on February the 19th and you refused to be evaluated. Any reason why?

INMATE MANSON: Yes, I had two other doctors trying to evaluate me at the same time. I couldn't—I can't write that many books.

DEPUTY BOARD COMMISSIONER BROWN: What doctors were trying to interview you at that time?

INMATE MANSON: Well, see the front side, you see the doctor coming to me to give me help. The back side, he get his information, he'll go to Turkey. He's over in France writing books about the psychotherapy or [inaudible] therapy—

DEPUTY BOARD COMMISSIONER BROWN: Which doctors came to visit you at the time Dr. Reed tried to get in?

INMATE MANSON: Dr. Christopherson, Dr. White.

DEPUTY BOARD COMMISSIONER BROWN: Where are they from?

INMATE MANSON: Right here. Since then, I think Christopherson's been fired for ethics violation of some sort. Then there's Willis — Dr. Willis.

DEPUTY BOARD COMMISSIONER BROWN: Willis came over to see you this —

INMATE MANSON: Willis has been my psychiatrist. We went through — if you'll check the record, we went through two sessions. He said I was okay for level 3. He said that I was all right for level 3.

What this latest doctor wants is a — what's happening out of Frisco is this law firm is coming up with new psych evaluation with the prisoners union. The prisoners union in San Quentin, they got a bunch of inmates to sign a suit for better psychiatric treatment. What that means is more political power because they're using the psychiatric base to get their doctors in here so they can get doctors up over the uniform, so they can hold the reality up over the courts and the minds of the people that live inside the prisons. Because when they can do that, then they can do Vacaville.

See when I left Vacaville, there was 12 dead doctors there of heart attacks. Dr. Morgan was the last doctor that they found dead in the parking lot with his brains blown out. I went to doctors —

DEPUTY BOARD COMMISSIONER BROWN: Dr. Christopherson saw you on January the 24th of this year.

INMATE MANSON: Yes, sir.

DEPUTY BOARD COMMISSIONER BROWN: And in his report of that date, states that he went over to see you because you were not eating. Staff was concerned.

INMATE MANSON: Yes, he came to see me two or three times about that.

DEPUTY BOARD COMMISSIONER BROWN: But he didn't appear to be concerned because he said you were eating something, either candy bars or canteen or —

INMATE MANSON: Yes, I fast a lot.

DEPUTY BOARD COMMISSIONER BROWN: — or whatever, but he wasn't concerned about your not eating. He talked about your paranoid delusional disorder at that time in his report.

INMATE MANSON: Perspective.

DEPUTY BOARD COMMISSIONER BROWN: He prescribed a plan for you and that was to put you on [inaudible] and said this will have two affects. One, they will support or deny the fact that he is on hunger strike, and they will also give the inmate a chance to get out of his cell on occasions as a form of environmental stimulation.

On the same vein, one, will have more frequent visits to the psychiatrist. This too will monitor signs and symptoms of active psychosis versus malingering; three, if indeed he's on a hunger strike, he should be considered for the M.O.U. What's M.O.U.?

INMATE MANSON: It's some kind of—

DEPUTY BOARD COMMISSIONER BROWN: Memorandum of Understanding? If he does refuse psychotropic—

INMATE MANSON: Medical observation unit.

DEPUTY BOARD COMMISSIONER BROWN: Medical observation unit.

INMATE MANSON: Uh-huh.

DEPUTY BOARD COMMISSIONER BROWN: If indeed he's on a—if he does refuse psychotropic medications, we may ask him [inaudible] our decision, which is adjudged ordered involuntary medication. It should also be noted that we should have a careful monitoring of his intake and output including material from the canteen.

So he's suggesting that you were kind of faking things a little bit.

INMATE MANSON: Whenever you do something beyond someone else's understanding, and they don't want to understand it, they—they'll hate it and look at it as being bad. It doesn't really—it isn't really bad. I fast. I fast to tighten my stomach up. It makes me healthy. It's a spiritual experience. Sometimes I go ten, 15, 30 days. Sometimes I go longer than that. I fast until I can get my mind straightened around.

Whenever—when a bad circumstance comes to me and I have to deal with the mental situation all around me, I'm surrounded by inmates and officers and all kinds of things beyond your comprehension, I have to sit and I have to balance all those things in my mind.

So what I do is I quit eating, and when I quit eating, what happens is that everything trusts, and trust is going one way, but trust it goes the other way too. I'm your economy. If I don't eat, then you don't know whether I'm trusting you, because the only way you know if I trust you is if I eat from your hands.

So I hold all the trust with the food and when I don't eat, then everybody gets scared and they start going through—they're not sure and then I'm paranoid, because anything around me is going to be my fault because I'm the last chicken in line.

One chicken—the dogs bark at the chickens and the chickens get to pecking on each other and then you get the last chicken in line and they just peck him till he's either gone, or they get it straightened around, you know.

And like, being the last chicken in line, I have to take up the slack, so I—what I do is I quit eating. And then all the fat people that can't quit eating, they start going through a lot of changes when I show them I'm about ten times stronger then they ever thought about dreaming about.

DEPUTY BOARD COMMISSIONER BROWN: Let me ask you something, now that you got the fat joke out. What have you done in all the years that you've been on prison that this panel or anybody could look at that would indicate that there's been a change in Charles Manson?

INMATE MANSON: I change all the time, sir. Every day I'm going to change.

DEPUTY BOARD COMMISSIONER BROWN: Well, I can't measure that. You have to tell me.

INMATE MANSON: Can I ask you a couple questions? What did you do before this—so I know what foundation in your mind where I can speak to you from? You got any jurisprudence? You got any correctional officer experience or policeman or what?

DEPUTY BOARD COMMISSIONER BROWN: I don't think you need to know that. All you need to know is—

INMATE MANSON: Can I ask you?

PRESIDING BOARD COMMISSIONER KOENIG: Just answer the question.

DEPUTY BOARD COMMISSIONER BROWN: All you need to know is that I'm sitting on this panel today.

INMATE MANSON: Okay. Well, we'll go to the judge. The judge sits on the bench and he takes in his mind the crime. It comes to him for judgment. If it goes through his understanding and he watches it, judge itself. The judge really doesn't judge it. He judges— he lets the district attorney and it passes through his understanding.

He does this six hours a day, seven days a week, five days a week. He retires 65 years old. He's done that for 8,000 hours. I've done the same thing all my life, 24 hours a day, so I'm about 15 street poor judges in my mind. In other words, I know more about law than anybody in the world. I know more about courts and procedures and criminology and penology and procedure than any card shark dealing devils off the bench in Monte Carlo.

I know more about the economy, more about money, more about the government than any ten presidents you got. You know, in other words, I've sat in solitary confinement and I've watched everything you guys do, and the truth is you're all lying to yourselves, you know. And like—

PRESIDING BOARD COMMISSIONER KOENIG: Mr. Manson, you're not answering Mr. Brown's question.

INMATE MANSON: I'm not?

PRESIDING BOARD COMMISSIONER KOENIG: No. He asked you what have you done in the institution to show the Board of Prison Terms and society that you've changed?

INMATE MANSON: I'm real with you. I don't pretend. I'm not bringing you a bunch of phony garbage. I'm not trying to tell you that I'm a good guy. I'm just myself, whatever that is. I believe in God and I do the best I can every day by everybody I can, you know. When something bad comes up, I react bad to it, you know. I can fight. I can't read and write too good, but boy I can fight. You wouldn't believe how I could fight because I've been fighting all my life to survive, and I live right on that edge of survival, you know. I just survive.

I play a little music when I'm allowed to. I draw real good, but they took my pencils.

Everything I do, if I can do it real good, they'll take it away from me. I used to do—make little dolls of strings, then he come took the string. So I'm not allowed to do anything. I don't have any clothes. I haven't combed my hair in two, three years, you know, I can't comb my hair. I can't do that.

DEPUTY BOARD COMMISSIONER BROWN: Have you been involved in any psychiatric intervention?

INMATE MANSON: Yes, yes. I've seen more doctors than doctors have seen inmates. I was with Dr. Nich there in the back alley over there in Vacaville with [inaudible].

DEPUTY BOARD COMMISSIONER BROWN: Was this in a therapy setting?

INMATE MANSON: Well, I guess you could call it the therapy setting. I was handling all the crazy people and taking care of the kids in the visiting room and [inaudible] in the garden and chapel.

DEPUTY BOARD COMMISSIONER BROWN: Was anybody doing anything with you?

INMATE MANSON: No, everybody was doing what I told them.

DEPUTY BOARD COMMISSIONER BROWN: No, no. Were any of the therapists doing anything to assist you in your life?

INMATE MANSON: No. It was me doing it for them. I had to look out for the veterans just came back from the war and all the wheelchairs and all the doctors. They had a lot of Vietnamese doctors come in, couldn't speak English, so I had to get the medication all straightened around for that, you know, because my life at the bottom, I got to look out for everybody else's life too or I can't get on through what I'm trying to do.

I like to play music, but they took my music away and they took my guitar away. That's the only thing I do. I play a little music. But they're scared of that. Anything I do, they get afraid of and then they'll run and tell the cops that they're afraid of whatever I'm doing and they run, take it away from me and I'm not allowed to do anything. So I just sit in a cell, you know. I don't really need to do anything because I'm doing everything all the way anyway. And my radio—

DEPUTY BOARD COMMISSIONER BROWN: Now you keep talking about not being able to read and write.

INMATE MANSON: Not that well. I read and write [inaudible].

DEPUTY BOARD COMMISSIONER BROWN: You have an I.Q. that's up well over a 100 points.

INMATE MANSON: Yes, I am pretty smart.

DEPUTY BOARD COMMISSIONER BROWN: And you've been in prison all these years. Have you done anything at all to improve your grades?

INMATE MANSON: Grades for what? What am I doing?

DEPUTY BOARD COMMISSIONER BROWN: Well, you keep harping on the fact that you cannot read very well, nor can you write very well.

INMATE MANSON: No, I just—I'm not harping. I'm just explaining that that's—

DEPUTY BOARD COMMISSIONER BROWN: You keep saying it.

INMATE MANSON: —that's where I'm at.

DEPUTY BOARD COMMISSIONER BROWN: Have you done anything to improve your reading and writing skills?

INMATE MANSON: Yes, I read a book. I read a book. It was kind of boring, man. You know, I can think better things than I can read. I mean, reading is kind of like slowing down and people only love each other in books. You can't love each other in reality, because you're all trapped in books, locked up in wars. You're all locked up in the Second World War, man. You're still fighting wars over there, you know.

I was trying to unlock that war. That's what was over there trying to unlock the wars. Bob Arondis [phonetic spelling] came from India and the Dr. Hyler [phonetic spelling] used to come over and tell me what Bob Arondis had to say about, you know, the lovey love center there in Berkeley where they've had to hire minds of the religious perspective there.

DEPUTY BOARD COMMISSIONER BROWN: And so you haven't done any of those kinds of things?

INMATE MANSON: Well, what I'm trying to explain to you without a lot of—I don't want to appear like I'm somebody, but I'm on top of everything. I'm the smartest guy in the world, you know. I can't—I don't think there's anyone in the world—there's no subject I can't tell you everything you want to know about it, you know. I've even fixed a Harley-Davidson motorcycle. I'm short change, I know how to deal off the bottom. I've learned everything that you taught me, Dad.

DEPUTY BOARD COMMISSIONER BROWN: Okay—

INMATE MANSON: Yes, yes, yes, uh-huh, well [inaudible]—

DEPUTY BOARD COMMISSIONER BROWN: Return to the Chair.

PRESIDING BOARD COMMISSIONER KOENIG: Thank you. Okay. Mr. Manson, we're going to the third area of the hearing now, parole plans. Mr. Aceto [background noise/inaudible].

BOARD COMMISSIONER ACETO: Thank you. We have to talk about your parole plans. Do you know the statement that you made to your counselors?

INMATE MANSON: No.

BOARD COMMISSIONER ACETO: You stated that you had no plans for the future. You also stated that you were not interested in paroling and that you would be lost in our society. His main concern at this time is to be released to a general population setting in order to program.

INMATE MANSON: Makes sense to me.

BOARD COMMISSIONER ACETO: That's a good statement, if it's yours. It doesn't sound like you.

INMATE MANSON: Well—

BOARD COMMISSIONER ACETO: Was that your statement?

INMATE MANSON: Yes, basically I said that to that broad, yes, but I might've said something else to somebody else in a different perspective. I generally say to people what they want to hear.

BOARD COMMISSIONER ACETO: Hold it. What broad are you talking about?

INMATE MANSON: Some caseworker woman. Name was Virginia. I think her name was Virginia.

BOARD COMMISSIONER ACETO: Correctional counselor?

INMATE MANSON: Yes, who was it?

BOARD COMMISSIONER ACETO: I'm not going to tell you. It's your counselor, you should know.

INMATE MANSON: Well, yes, I have—there's all kinds of counselors, man—

BOARD COMMISSIONER ACETO: Talk too loud [inaudible].

INMATE MANSON: There's all kinds of counselors, they turn over all the time. They come and go like—I can't keep track of those.

BOARD COMMISSIONER ACETO: Montero [phonetic spelling].

INMATE MANSON: [Inaudible.]

BOARD COMMISSIONER ACETO: Montero.

INMATE MANSON: Montero, I think that's a broad.

BOARD COMMISSIONER ACETO: It's not a broad. It's a woman.

INMATE MANSON: I should say woman, okay.

BOARD COMMISSIONER ACETO: Okay. That's good enough.

INMATE MANSON: Let me explain something.

BOARD COMMISSIONER ACETO: I didn't ask you nothing yet. I just want to get the statement out of the way. Is that your statement?

INMATE MANSON: Partly.

BOARD COMMISSIONER ACETO: Partly.

INMATE MANSON: To that person on that level. I've got other legs. Cockroach got eight legs [inaudible] got six.

BOARD COMMISSIONER ACETO: You said that you would be lost in society today.

INMATE MANSON: My position is taken.

BOARD COMMISSIONER ACETO: You're safe in here without society.

INMATE MANSON: No. It's got nothing to do with safety. I'm not in that [inaudible]. The position that I should be holding is taken by someone else.

BOARD COMMISSIONER ACETO: All right. Let me tell you what you've got here. You may have seen them yourself. You had 45, what your counselor calls, fearful letters. Fearful letters opposing your parole. That right?

INMATE MANSON: I've got a bunch of them, but I think they're all from one person, aren't they?

BOARD COMMISSIONER ACETO: Well, it would appear that they're written by different people at a certain time, except for a few. And it's all based on some rumor you let out of this joint that you were going to be paroled and that you would be accepting a hideout place and money in the bank and that's what you put out as a rumor. Did you do that?

INMATE MANSON: Can't say for real.

BOARD COMMISSIONER ACETO: Can't say for real?

INMATE MANSON: No. There's a lot of rumors that go in and out of different things I've been doing. That's what's hard about this whole thing. They put so much pressure on you that everything I say or do goes—gets twisted around to what people want it to be, what they wanted to have said. It hasn't really got anything to do with what it really is. It's what other people need it to be.

BOARD COMMISSIONER ACETO: This appeared in an article in the paper, I know that. Here it is. Charlie Manson should never return to society. It was written because the news media said that Charlie Manson masterminded through his claim the outrageous murder of Sharon Tate, da-da-da-da-da, according to them [background noise/inaudible] admitted [inaudible] put fear into the system. Now the system may be putting fear into us. That the witness protection program [inaudible] program to release Charlie Manson.

INMATE MANSON: Yes, they offered me a place in Valachi [phonetic spelling].

BOARD COMMISSIONER ACETO: Who was they?

INMATE MANSON: F.B.I.

BOARD COMMISSIONER ACETO: What do you got to do with the F.B.I.? You don't have nothing to do with the F.B.I.

INMATE MANSON: Yes, I do. I was a barber in the federal penitentiary for 20 years.

BOARD COMMISSIONER ACETO: Were you a snitch?

INMATE MANSON: Nope. That's the reason I didn't take the program.

BOARD COMMISSIONER ACETO: Well, anyway—

INMATE MANSON: If I had been a snitch, I'd been gone for Virginia.

BOARD COMMISSIONER ACETO: There was a [inaudible] there in 1990 that almost got out of hand for you.

INMATE MANSON: Well, they come to me two or three times and they wanted me to work and do different—draw profiles for new criminal types. And that Mexican—New Mexico thing jumped off the—they asked for some help. I'm not really a—I'm not a—an informant-type guy.

BOARD COMMISSIONER ACETO: Okay. Now, you're talking what's [inaudible] when you get home, mom and dad? You got a mom and dad? [Inaudible] sir?

INMATE MANSON: I'd like to explain. I really would.

BOARD COMMISSIONER ACETO: You don't have to. I mean, it's—

INMATE MANSON: But I mean, I really want to. I really want to.

BOARD COMMISSIONER ACETO: The question is, do you have folks to rely on?

INMATE MANSON: But you don't understand. Each one of you is somebody. I ain't nobody. I'm nothing. I'm now [inaudible] now [inaudible]. My mother went to prison. She left me. And everybody's lied to me. A few old men in the Second World War were honest with me, you know. The older dudes were, you know—I was used to working the hospital [inaudible] you know.

I've always run with the—I've always run a main line with the guys that were truthful and honest. And like, the reason I haven't been—you haven't been able to kill me is you haven't been able to find me, because every time you send somebody after me they can't find me because I'm not really there in your minds.

Just like you draw a line across the desert and I'm sitting there and you come and draw a line, you say, "You can't get out of there." I say, "I'm aware." You say, "You're locked up." I say, "Locked up in what?" He say, "Well, you're locked up and we're free." And I say, "Oh yeah?" And then you walk back and forth and you play important with my life as if you've got something that I want, you know.

Like you got out and I'm supposed to be in, but yet I'm everywhere and I'm out and in and I'm all around, down to San Diego Zoo, and I'm riding a motorcycle and I'm your children and I'm the trees and I'm your—

BOARD COMMISSIONER ACETO: Okay. Hold it. Hold it up. Hold it up.

INMATE MANSON: I'm crazy and you got to get another doctor. Yes, sir.

BOARD COMMISSIONER ACETO: I get the point.

INMATE MANSON: In other words, like you won't find them on here, man. Not [inaudible]—

BOARD COMMISSIONER ACETO: You do have some letters on your behalf. Okay? Let me find it here. Support letters. Sharon Quimbley—Sharon Quimbley, Cindy White. Do you know a Cindy White?

INMATE MANSON: No. I know Squeaky. She's doing time. She wrote a letter to the president.

BOARD COMMISSIONER ACETO: Margaret Ramone—Ransom? You don't know that person?

INMATE MANSON: No, I don't know them.

BOARD COMMISSIONER ACETO: These are your supporters I'm talking about.

INMATE MANSON: Well, I didn't know I had any supporters. I didn't really need any supporters actually. I thought I was my supporter.

BOARD COMMISSIONER ACETO: George Stimson from Cincinnati, Ohio.

INMATE MANSON: Simpson. Yes. George—St. George. Yes, he's a good man. He's an orthodox religious kind of guy. He's got a very good—very good mind.

BOARD COMMISSIONER ACETO: A relative of yours?

INMATE MANSON: Huh?

BOARD COMMISSIONER ACETO: Is he a relative?

INMATE MANSON: No, no. Spiritually we're allies. I'm allied spiritually with a lot of things.

BOARD COMMISSIONER ACETO: Okay. He wrote a two-page letter for you. Cindy White, again, she has—

INMATE MANSON: I never really applied for this, or asked my friends for any support.

BOARD COMMISSIONER ACETO: Well, I know that, but you do have some people out there that are interested in you.

INMATE MANSON: But you realize where most of those letters come from, don't you?

BOARD COMMISSIONER ACETO: Don't have an idea.

INMATE MANSON: Ulterior motive. I think the doctor sent you one of them, but he sent it to you and he didn't sign his name. He sent it from Sacramento. They hoodwink their own paperwork, and then when it comes back, then he can keep me here and then he can build a medical association with me.

BOARD COMMISSIONER ACETO: You talking about Dr. White?

INMATE MANSON: Yes. He—yes, Dr. White and Christopherson.

BOARD COMMISSIONER ACETO: Did you want to show us something here? The pictures?

INMATE MANSON: Oh, no. I had some pictures here. No, no. These are just—I'm working on a zoo project for the ecology. I've got frogs and I've got hawks and turtles, lizards, and I'm working on the backside of this game, trying to get C.C. camps. We was trying to start C.C. camps when I was in Folsom with Governor Brown. That's when Squeaky and Red and Blue and Gold was out. That's when we were running colors out.

BOARD COMMISSIONER ACETO: Okay. One last thing I have. Somewhere I read that you were getting $500 for an autographed picture on the outside.

INMATE MANSON: Uh-huh.

BOARD COMMISSIONER ACETO: Is that correct?

INMATE MANSON: Yes.

BOARD COMMISSIONER ACETO: How is that done?

INMATE MANSON: Well, you see I live in the underworld. You live in the over world. I do a lot of things under world that you guys don't see. I made about 75 albums in Vacaville and I bootlegged about three times more music than the Beatles put out.

BOARD COMMISSIONER ACETO: Music?

INMATE MANSON: Yes. I had the surfboard of the Beach Boys but I didn't sell it because every time I would go to the music, they'd want to change the music. So rather than change the music, I went into the subculture with it. I got in an old nuclear submarine that I had from the Navy when I was Section 8 in Leavenworth, Kansas, with brother Dynamite and the Mafia coming off of Frankie Costello and the Horseshoe Pits in Pennsylvania in 1952. And it was like, I'm an awful big fellow. I'm really big. I've got a great big body, because my body's underground.

BOARD COMMISSIONER ACETO: Tell me about the albums.

INMATE MANSON: This is music about the ecology, the air [inaudible].

BOARD COMMISSIONER ACETO: The pictures—the autographs were on the albums. Is that what you're saying?

INMATE MANSON: No, no. That's just a backlash of the younger generations, like—

BOARD COMMISSIONER ACETO: You got me mixed up then.

INMATE MANSON: Remember the old movie where the piper—the pied piper, they said you play all the rats into the river and that they would pay you. And then the people never paid the piper so they always kept losing their children. Well, you've lost six generations of children to me, because you won't pay me what you owe me. Because I didn't break no law. I didn't kill nobody. I didn't tell nobody to get killed.

BOARD COMMISSIONER ACETO: Okay.

INMATE MANSON: I didn't get no trial, you know.

BOARD COMMISSIONER ACETO: Okay. Okay, Mr. Manson.

INMATE MANSON: We don't want to hear none of that, see—

BOARD COMMISSIONER ACETO: That's it. I don't have anything—

INMATE MANSON: We don't want to mention anything up in the truth.

PRESIDING BOARD COMMISSIONER KOENIG: We're back to me. I'm the Chairman.

BOARD COMMISSIONER ACETO: I'm all done.

PRESIDING BOARD COMMISSIONER KOENIG: Okay. And this is time for questions by any one of the panel members and the District Attorney. I have a couple questions. Do you feel any responsibility for the murders?

INMATE MANSON: Sure.

PRESIDING BOARD COMMISSIONER KOENIG: Okay. Could you elaborate briefly?

INMATE MANSON: I influenced a lot of people, unbeknownst to my own understanding of it. I didn't understand the fears of the people outside. I didn't understand the insecurities of people outside. I didn't understand people outside.

And a lot of things that I said and did affected a lot of people in a lot of different directions. It wasn't intentional and it definitely wasn't with malice or aforethought.

PRESIDING BOARD COMMISSIONER KOENIG: Okay. You answered it. Do you have remorse, Mr. Manson? Do you feel any remorse for the victims whatsoever?

INMATE MANSON: Now, we've reached an impasse here, man. We're in pawn four, bishop four and seven—let's see. How do I finesse that? You say in your minds that I'm guilty of everything that you've got on paper. So therefore, it would run logic that I would need to have remorse for what you think is reality, and if that be true, then all the oceans' contents, if it were my tears, there would not be enough to express the remorse that I have for the sadness of that world that you people live in.

But I don't have—on the other side of that, I ask you back the same thing, you know. You've been using me ever since I was ten years old. You used to beat me with leather straps, you know. It's like, does anyone have any remorse that I've spent 23 years in a solitary cell and even on Devil's Island, you didn't keep anyone over five years. You broke every record that they've ever set in the planet Earth. You only kept Christ on the cross three days.

PRESIDING BOARD COMMISSIONER KOENIG: Mr. Manson, I think you answered the question. Do you have a—still have a family, per se, that is, the type of family you had at the time of the crimes? Do you still have a family?

INMATE MANSON: Family?

PRESIDING BOARD COMMISSIONER KOENIG: Uh-huh.

INMATE MANSON: That's another one of the District Attorney's—see, when they set that case into the paper were to make it real, they had to get—catch a little words so they could turn all that into—make it into a reality. Hippie cult leader, is a word that they used, leader, family.

PRESIDING BOARD COMMISSIONER KOENIG: Well, I believe I read in the reports where you yourself mentioned your family [inaudible]—

INMATE MANSON: Yes, well, you—

PRESIDING BOARD COMMISSIONER KOENIG: [Inaudible]—

INMATE MANSON:—you keep driving that on me, and then I have to refer to what's already on me.

PRESIDING BOARD COMMISSIONER KOENIG: My simple question is, do you still have a family as existed at that particular time?

INMATE MANSON: Well, I can't—I can't answer that in just a—you know, it would take more time than you want to listen to me—

PRESIDING BOARD COMMISSIONER KOENIG: Well, yes or no? You either have a family [inaudible]—

INMATE MANSON: Well, there's no yes or no [unintelligible].

PRESIDING BOARD COMMISSIONER KOENIG: All right. All right.

INMATE MANSON: Yes, no, or [unintelligible] you know, like you is stuck in yes or no, yes, all right.

PRESIDING BOARD COMMISSIONER KOENIG: All right. Mr. Brown, do you have any other questiens?

DEPUTY BOARD COMMISSIONER BROWN: I have no further questions. Thank you.

PRESIDING BOARD COMMISSIONER KOENIG: Mr. Aceto?

BOARD COMMISSIONER ACETO: No.

PRESIDING BOARD COMMISSIONER KOENIG: All right. Mr. Kay, we're going to go to questions by the District Attorney on something that has not been covered, anything that has not been covered or something that he would like to emphasize. He will pose the questions to the panel and when you answer the panel—the questions, Mr. Manson, would you answer the panel, please.

INMATE MANSON: All right.

PRESIDING BOARD COMMISSIONER KOENIG: Okay. Go ahead, Mr. Kay. Do you have any questions?

INMATE MANSON: And do we get to do this back the other way?

PRESIDING BOARD COMMISSIONER KOENIG: No.

INMATE MANSON: Oh, yes, yes. Now what do all you people think about that? Yes, yes. We have fair play, huh?

PRESIDING BOARD COMMISSIONER KOENIG: This is—[inaudible]—

INMATE MANSON: [Inaudible]—

BOARD COMMISSIONER ACETO: Don't look at the camera. Look at the panel.

INMATE MANSON: Yes, I know, yes, I know [inaudible].

MR. KAY: Thank you. I think the interesting thing for the Board to do here is to question Mr. Manson about the ninth murder he was convicted of. He doesn't mind talking about the Tate-LaBianca murders and Hinman murder because he's never accepted the law of conspiracy and aiding and abetting in California. And he always thought that if he didn't physically do the murder himself, that he wouldn't be guilty. His followers would be guilty, but he didn't really care about that.

But the one murder that he doesn't like to talk about because the evidence came out in court that he personally stabbed Shorty Shea to death. He stabbed him, Bruce Davis stabbed him, Tex Watson stabbed him.

PRESIDING BOARD COMMISSIONER KOENIG: Excuse me, Mr. Kay.

MR. KAY: Yes.

PRESIDING BOARD COMMISSIONER KOENIG: This is time for questions.

MR. KAY: Yes.

PRESIDING BOARD COMMISSIONER KOENIG: Do you have any questions?

MR. KAY: Yes. That's the question I would like you to ask Mr. Manson, what he did to Shorty Shea and how Shorty Shea died.

PRESIDING BOARD COMMISSIONER KOENIG: Okay. You heard the question, Mr. Manson. Would you answer—face the panel and answer, please?

INMATE MANSON: Shorty Shea was not short. He was a great big guy and he's very tough. He had everybody bullied, he had everybody buffaloed and there was a whole bunch of guys around. And he was pushing on Steve and he was pushing on someone else and I moved in and I said, if you go into combat with someone you don't hesitate, and I'm going to show you kids how to do this one time and then don't invoke me to no violence anymore.

And I moved on Shorty and I put him in a—in a situation where he couldn't move. And then I said, "Now can you understand what I'm saying to you?" And he said, "Yeah." I stepped up on the highway and hitchhiked a ride. And about three or four minutes later, somebody stabbed him and he was stabbed to death and he was killed.

Now wait a minute—

PRESIDING BOARD COMMISSIONER KOENIG: Go ahead.

INMATE MANSON: Anybody that knows anything about combat knows that when you go into a combat situation and you're on a line with something, that line can mean your life or your death. If you're on the line of life and death and you're gone and you're up on another line, that other reality's a completely different reality. It hasn't got anything to do with the other side of that line.

I was on that side of the line and it was a violent situation and I did deal with it and I put it into where it was—let me say this—there's only one way I can explain it. Duke in the joint is a guy that can fight with his fists.

PRESIDING BOARD COMMISSIONER KOENIG: Mr. Kay—

INMATE MANSON: Wait a minute, let me explain this.

PRESIDING BOARD COMMISSIONER KOENIG: All right.

INMATE MANSON: This will explain it. The count is somebody who don't fight with his fists. He fights with his mind. He sits up on top of the count. When the count is clear, he runs the radio and the duke does all the physical things, like the first cop does his level, then the sergeant—

PRESIDING BOARD COMMISSIONER KOENIG: Mr. Manson, just a second.

INMATE MANSON: I can't explain it to you, man.

PRESIDING BOARD COMMISSIONER KOENIG: Now, wait a minute.

INMATE MANSON: Don't have a yes or no.

PRESIDING BOARD COMMISSIONER KOENIG: The question was, did you kill Shorty Shea?

INMATE MANSON: No, no, I didn't have—

PRESIDING BOARD COMMISSIONER KOENIG: You didn't personally kill Shorty Shea?

INMATE MANSON: Not personally, no.

PRESIDING BOARD COMMISSIONER KOENIG: Did you order him to be killed?

INMATE MANSON: I know there was a fight, man—

PRESIDING BOARD COMMISSIONER KOENIG: Did you order him to be killed?

INMATE MANSON: No.

PRESIDING BOARD COMMISSIONER KOENIG: All right. Another question, please?

MR. KAY: All right. The last question, because I don't want to take up a lot of the Board's time, but I'd like the Board to ask Mr. Manson whether on the night of the Tate murders at the Tate house, after the murders were committed, did he go to the residence to see what had been done? And if so, what did he do when he was there?

PRESIDING BOARD COMMISSIONER KOENIG: You heard the question, Mr. Manson. Answer—

INMATE MANSON: I had a traffic ticket in San Diego, but ask him why the District Attorney moved the highway patrolman to the East Coast along with the traffic ticket.

PRESIDING BOARD COMMISSIONER KOENIG: Mr. Manson, did you go to the residence afterward?

INMATE MANSON: No, no. Let me—let me explain that to the Board. The reason they want to say that is because they should've let me out of here three years ago because if I'm not on any scene of the crime, he can only keep me 18 years. You've already had me 23, so I can sue you for Hearst Castle, probably.

PRESIDING BOARD COMMISSIONER KOENIG: Okay. Did that answer your question?

MR. KAY: Yes, thank you.

PRESIDING BOARD COMMISSIONER KOENIG: Are there any other questions you have, Mr. Kay?

MR. KAY: No.

PRESIDING BOARD COMMISSIONER KOENIG: Thank you.

INMATE MANSON: Thank you.

PRESIDING BOARD COMMISSIONER KOENIG: Now, this time we're going to have closing statements. First by the District Attorney and then you'll have the opportunity for the final closing statement before we recess. Okay, Mr. Kay.

MR. KAY: Thank you very much. Penal Code Section 3041.5(b)(2), subsection (c) empowers the Board to deny a life prisoner a new parole hearing for five years if you find three things: (1) that the prisoner is unsuitable for parole, (2) that he has been convicted for more than two murders, and (3) it would not be likely that he would be suitable for parole during the period of five-year denial.

Charles Manson, through his actions and [inaudible] to the murders of nine innocent people, plus the attitudes and actions that he has shown while in prison for those murders. By those actions and attitudes, he has demonstrated unquestionably that he is deserving of a unanimous finding of unsuitability by the Board and the maximum five-year denial.

Charles Manson attained his status as America's most famous and feared criminal by his powerful ability to control his followers. And from July 25, 1969, through and including August 28, 1969, led them on a monthlong murderous rampage.

That murderous rampage started at Gary Hinman's residence on July 25. Mr. Hinman was not killed until the 27th, but he was tortured over a three-day period, and then went to the Tate house, where Sharon Tate, Jay Sebring, Abigail Folger, Voytek Frykowski, and Stephen Parent were killed on August 9. Then on August 10, Leno and Rosemary LaBianca, and on August 28, Donald Shea—and I should repeat that the evidence was clear in his trial that Mr. Manson did stab Mr. Shea.

The first three murders involving eight victims were all tied into Mr. Manson's desire to ferment or take advantage of black-white race war. The murder of Shorty Shea was caused by Mr. Manson wanting to get revenge against him.

The enormity and cruelty of these murders almost defies belief. The motive for the Tate and LaBianca murders is enough in and of itself for the Board to deny Mr. Manson parole and Mr. Watson and the three girls parole forever.

Helter Skelter, what was this and how did it start? Well it was started by Manson, who was the guru on L.S.D. trips leading his Family members through the trips. They would listen to the Beatles White Album. And Mr. Manson and the others—and it wasn't just Mr. Manson alone, because they would kind of feed on each other—and they determined, listening to the "White Album," with songs like "Helter Skelter," "Revolution 9," "Black Bird," "Piggies," "Sexy Sadie," "Back in the U.S.S.R.," that the Beatles were the prophets.

It talked about in Revelations 9 and 10 of the Bible—Mr. Manson I heard even is still quoting the Bible. He could quote the Bible very well, but twist it to mean what he wanted it to mean.

INMATE MANSON: [Inaudible].

MR. KAY: Mr. Manson felt that there was going to be this black-white revolution and the Family was going to be the beneficiaries because the blacks were going to kill all of the whites, except for Manson and the Family. And Manson and the Family were going to escape to the bottomless pit talked about in Revelations 9 and 10 of the Bible. And they would live in this bottomless pit for 50 to 100 years in miniaturized form and then they would've grown to the size of 144,000, the 12 tribes of Israel.

And at the end of this 50-to-100-year period, Manson and the Family would come out of the bottomless pit and there would only be blacks left—black president, black senators, black congressmen. But Manson, who is a real racist, thought that blacks were too stupid to maintain power. And as soon as he and the family came out of the bottomless pit, the blacks would rush up to him and turn over all power. Now it was never clear whether he was going to rule the world, but at least he was going to rule the United States.

Now I know this sounds bizarre, but the problem is that Manson and his followers believed in this motive enough to kill innocent people. At the trial we showed that Manson was so serious about this that he went to a sporting goods store in Santa Monica and bought expensive golden rope that he was going to lower himself into the bottomless pit. He rented scuba equipment because he thought the entrance to the bottomless pit was under some underground river in Death Valley and he was looking for the entrance.

He brought topographical maps because he felt that he and the family were going to have to fight their way out of L.A. from the Spahn Ranch to Death Valley to get to the bottomless pit. He got an alliance with the Straight Satans motorcycle gang in Venice that they were going to help protect him and lead him to the bottomless pit. He had one of the Straight Satans members, Danny DeCarlo, who ran a gun room out in Spahn Ranch where he had machine guns and other armaments and DeCarlo would pack bullets.

Now there are four separate occasions of murder here. The first occasion of murder, the Hinman murder, was tied into Manson preparing for war. He needed money because he was buying armaments. He was buying dune buggies. He had his own dune buggy. He had a machine gun mounted on the dune buggy and he had a sheath for his sword that he kept on the side.

Well, he met Gary Hinman, who was a rock musician. He met him at Dennis Wilson's house, the same place he met Tex Watson. Dennis Wilson was the drummer for the Beach Boys. Manson thought that Hinman had come into an inheritance and he wanted his money and his property and he wanted Hinman to join the Family.

So he sent Beausoleil, Atkins, and Brunner to Hinman's house to get the property. Hinman was not interested in doing this. He hadn't come into an inheritance and he didn't want to join the family.

When he wasn't cooperating, Beausoleil called first Bruce Davis—and I know there's been some misconception here about who was Manson's chief lieutenant. Make no mistake about it. Bruce Davis was Manson's chief lieutenant, not Tex Watson. Tex Watson was certainly the major killer here, but when Manson was not at the Family—at the ranch in charge—Bruce Davis was the one in charge. When Manson wanted somebody to study Scientology more—because that's how he used that a lot to control people to get into their minds—he sent Bruce Davis to London to the Scientology headquarters to study Scientology.

Anyway, Manson and Davis then went the second day to Hinman's house and tried to force him to turn over his property and when he wouldn't cooperate, Manson sliced his ear off with Davis holding a gun on him. And then they left and let Beausoleil know, get the property or else, and of course it turned into, or else, with Beausoleil killing him on the third day and Atkins holding a pillow over his nose so he—and his mouth—so he couldn't breathe while he was dying from the stab wounds.

Now Manson always felt that the blacks were going to start the revolution. And when they didn't, he was very impatient. And finally on the evening of August 8, he told his Family members, "The only thing blackie knows what to do is what whitey shows him and I'm"—

that's a quote—"and so we're going to have to show blackie how to do it. Now is the time for Helter Skelter."

And so he told Watson, Atkins, Krenwinkel, and Kasabian to go to the residence. Now the motive for the murders, make no doubt about it, was Helter Skelter, but Manson had an ulterior motive. He was very mad at the prior residents of the Tate house. He had been there before. He knew the layout. He and Watson had both been to a party there. But he was very mad at Terry Melcher who—Doris Day's son and his girlfriend Candice Bergen, because Manson wanted a recording contract from Melcher and Melcher auditioned him and wouldn't give him the contact.

So the reason that this particular residence was picked out was because Manson wanted to send a message to Melcher and Bergen that there but for the grace of God go you. And he knew that they moved out. He knew that somebody else lived there at the time. He didn't know who they were. He didn't know any of these people at the residence. He knew that somebody famous lived there.

And he told his followers that he wanted some gruesome murders. He even talked at one point about gouging eyeballs out and smashing them against the wall. And when they left the ranch, he told the girls—he said, do what Watson tells you to do because he knows the layout of the place and leave a sign, something witchy.

Well, they followed his instructions because the victims at the Tate house suffered 102 stab wounds. Sharon Tate, who was eight and a half months pregnant, was hung while she was still alive. And I should tell you that Watson took a long rope in there because Watson and Manson both knew the living room had high beam ceilings that you could throw a rope over and hang somebody. So that was planned from the very beginning. Susan Atkins wrote in Sharon Tate's blood on the front door, pig, the letters P-I-G. Now this wasn't good enough for Mr. Manson.

PRESIDING BOARD COMMISSIONER KOENIG: Excuse me, Mr. Kay.

MR. KAY: Yes.

PRESIDING BOARD COMMISSIONER KOENIG: We're retrying the case is actually what you're doing. We should be talking about suitability on parole.

MR. KAY: Right. Yes.

PRESIDING BOARD COMMISSIONER KOENIG: We know he killed the people and we accept that—

MR. KAY: Right.

PRESIDING BOARD COMMISSIONER KOENIG:—the findings of the court. So I would like you to speak to suitability, if you would, please.

MR. KAY: I will. I'm just about finished with this area, but this goes to suitability, what he did in the life crimes. That's a part of it, that's a part of your hearing, and I just don't want people to forget what he did, what he's responsible for. I'm not going blow by blow like I would in the Watson hearing and in Van Houten. I mean, I would do that, blow by blow there. I'm not doing it here. But I'm telling about his directions.

On the LaBiancas, he met in the bunkhouse on the ranch and he scolded the people who were there at the Tate murder and told them they had been too messy and that he was going to show them how to do it this night.

And so they went—he led them on a four-hour trip around the county of Los Angeles, at one point even stopping at a Congregational church in South Pasadena and knocking on the door trying to find the minister so that he could kill the minister and hang the minister upside down to the cross in front of the church.

Now in the LaBianca house, he went in by himself, got the drop on Mr. and Mrs. LaBianca with a gun, tied them up, tied their hands, assured them they were going to be okay, that it was only a robbery.

He took one thing from the house when he went outside. He took Mrs. LaBianca's wallet. And the reason that he did this, because he had it later planted in what he felt was a black area, because he wanted a black person to find the wallet and to use the credit cards, Mrs. LaBianca's credit cards, so that the blacks would get blamed for these murders and that would start the revolution.

On the Shea murder, Shea was a ranch hand at Spahn Ranch and knew that Manson and the Family were up to no good, but he knew that Mr. Spahn, who was 80 years old, was too old to do anything about kicking Manson off. And so Mr. Shea conspired with a neighboring rancher to kick Manson off the ranch. That, and the fact that Mr. Shea, who was white, was married to a black woman when Manson just couldn't understand that. For those two reasons, he decided to take care of Mr. Shea.

Now six of the nine victims who were murdered were murdered in the supposed sanctity of their own homes, and seven were complete strangers. Now what has Mr. Manson learned in the 23, almost 23 years, that he has been in prison for these murders? I thought Mr. Brown really hit the nail on the head here.

In my estimation, Mr. Manson has learned nothing. Other than physically aging, and Mr. Manson's going to be 58 this year, Mr. Manson is exactly the same person he was when he was arrested at Barker Ranch in Death Valley on October 12, 1969. He has no respect for authority, he has no respect for society or desire to be part of it, and he has no remorse for directing the murder of any of these nine victims.

His adjustment in prison has been horrible. His record is replete with assaulting prison guards and staff, including punching them, spitting in their face, throwing hot coffee. And I thought Mr. Manson's talk here about spitting on the guard, you would think listening to him that this was some man that he spit on. It was a woman, that he spit in her face.

Mr. Manson doesn't like women. I think that's pretty clear. His record's also replete with threatening staff and guards, either that he's going to kill them or he's going to have somebody else kill them.

His record is—also has in his possession of contraband, he had L.S.D. in his cell in Vacaville and tried to smuggle in a hacksaw blade when he was transferred to San Quentin, and he was caught with escape plans when he was in Vacaville.

Now, Mr. Brown said that he had 60 C.D.C. 115s. I counted 571 but that's pretty close. But one of the important things is that he has nine since his last hearing. And at the last hearing, the Board directed him that one of the things they wanted to see him do was to be disciplinary free. And yet, what has he done? He's picked up nine C.D.C. 115s, the same type of violations that he's had since he's been in prison. He hasn't changed one iota.

What else has he done? He refused to cooperate with the schedule of psychological evaluation and he refused to appear at his 1982 and '89 parole hearing. I think that we have to face the fact that based on Mr. Manson's words and actions that he's really not serious about being paroled.

In 1981, he said that he did want to be paroled, but since he hated people, he wanted to be paroled to Death Valley so that he could live with his friends, the spiders and the snakes or in the alternative, be paroled to space. Here this time he told Correctional Counselor . . .

[Off the Record]

DEPUTY BOARD COMMISSIONER BROWN: This is Tape No. 3 in the hearing for Charles Manson 04/21/92, California State Prison, Corcorcan. Proceed.

MR. KAY: This year in the Board report, he told Correctional Counselor Montero—and I'd like to say about that, that this Board report by Correctional Counselor Montero—this is the forty-fourth parole hearing I've been to for Manson, Watson, Atkins, Van Houten, and Krenwinkel—is the best Board report I've ever read. This is a crackerjack Board report.

Anyway, he told Correctional Counselor Montero that "he has no plans for the future, that he was not interested in paroling and that he would be lost in our society." Well, I can tell Mr. Manson that our society feels the same way about him. We don't want him back. The Board has received over the years over 352,000 cards, letters, petitions signed by individuals, all directed and sent to the Board in Sacramento asking you members of the Board not to parole Mr. Manson or the other four defendants convicted of the Tate-LaBianca murders.

Charles Manson told his followers that Adolf Hitler was his hero and he tried to emulate him. We can see even today he still has a swastika on his forehead. Can we ever risk setting a man like Charles Manson free in society, a man who, in essence, tried to destroy our society? I think not.

I would respectfully ask the Board to find Mr. Manson unsuitable for parole and to give him the maximum five-year denial. Thank you very much.

PRESIDING BOARD COMMISSIONER KOENIG: Thank you, Mr. Kay. Mr. Manson, would you speak to your suitability for parole, please?

INMATE MANSON: Is there any way that we could take a recess where I could use the rest room?

PRESIDING BOARD COMMISSIONER KOENIG: Certainly. We'll recess at this time. The time is now 1507 hours.

[Off the Record]

PRESIDING BOARD COMMISSIONER KOENIG: We've reconvened the panel hearing on Charles Manson after a brief break as requested by the prisoner. All participants are present now who were present prior to the recess. The time is 1515 hours. Go ahead, Mr. Manson, with your closing statement regarding suitability.

INMATE MANSON: You're going to limit me to suitability?

PRESIDING BOARD COMMISSIONER KOENIG: I'll let you ramble a little bit, but I'd like you to stick to suitability.

INMATE MANSON: Is that what you call it, rambling, huh?

PRESIDING BOARD COMMISSIONER KOENIG: Well, no, I didn't mean it that way. I will allow you to talk about what you would like to talk about, as long as you don't stray too far from suitability, please.

INMATE MANSON: As long as I don't say anything, it's okay if I talk?

PRESIDING BOARD COMMISSIONER KOENIG: No. I'll allow you to say—

INMATE MANSON: You see nine dead people. That's just—that's not even the tip of it. That just set one little blaze to this thing that you call Helter Skelter that you created for Rambo movies, so all the Italians can move over from New York and move into the District Attorney's office and this Anglo-Christian girl don't seem to know which whorehouse is— got the red light on it.

The law in my perspective is a [inaudible] like the—there's a court on the inside, like an inmate court. We've always held a court in the inner sanctum of the prison. Peace officers are servants to the will of everyone, the Bible, the church has a chapel and a preacher in it and we abide by the rules and regulations. It goes into the courtroom to do the same. If I abide by the rules and regulations I can walk in harmony with God. If I don't abide by the rules and regulations, sooner or later I have to fall short and go through a lot of changes.

It's best you look into my mind now while you got a chance while I'm still here. I know a lot about law. I know the judge's bench. I know crime and school and doctors and reports and I know bad and good and money and the economy and gambling, prostitution. I see the world from the underworld up.

So I go out in the desert when I get out in '54 and I see birds and I see bees and bugs and trees and then I get locked up. Well, when I get back out again, all these bugs and birds and trees are gone. There are shopping malls where the lake used to be. You're using up all the water. The creeks is over there where the freeway is and you can't swim there anymore, there's no more fish there. And civilization has moved out and it's choking all the life off the earth.

So it's none of my affair. I just got out of jail. I don't know that much about it. A couple of old men I met in Mexico City, we used to deal mushrooms and talk about the planet and the earth and the balance of the earth, and all these kids come around me and I'm playing music. And they ask me, how do I know these things, and where do these things come from? And I said, well, the only thing I know is what I learned in jail, man, you know. My brother's in jail [inaudible] you know, my brother's like, he's God, you know, he lives in jail, you know. And that's all I know is what I've done, you know.

I said, but I'll tell you, if you don't stop cutting them trees down, there's going to be nothing of them left, you know. And a lot of the kids never met anybody that told them the truth. They never had anybody that was truthful to them, you know. They never had anybody that wouldn't lie or snake on them or play old fake games.

So what I did was I was honest with a bunch of kids and they used to come to me and say, we ain't got no place to stay and I said, well, I ain't got no place to stay either. And they say, well, can we stay with you? I said, can you stay with me? They'd say, well, we want to be a family. I said, don't put no tags on my toes, man. Don't give them people nothing to identify them with. If they can come back and put me back in the penitentiary with.

I know what conspiracy is. I got an intelligence, I'm not that stupid. I can understand that bugs communicate. I can understand that trees can hear you. I understand that there are other life forms on this planet besides myself, you know. And conspiracy, I understand the law.

And a lot of things that people have said in the court is [inaudible] the game that they're gaming whether I'm suitable for this planet earth or not probably will outlast what the court's doing for money, because my principle is not locked up in a bank and my soul is not locked up in a government. And my life is not locked up in a penitentiary. You've got my body in a cell, but that's only today, you know. That don't count for no eternity. I'm walking in forever, man.

And this little game that we're playing here on this level, there is more things that are important to you than my parole and there's a whole lot more important to me than my parole. If you want to give me a parole, I might consider taking that and letting you live in my world. If you deny my parole, you go off in your world. Don't come back at mine. If I can get some trees growing over here and C.C. camp and I can work with these guys in a uniform and I can work and do a job in here like I don't get paid for the job that I do in here. But if I'm honest with what I do in here, maybe the preacher will let me out and hoe in your garden again.

And I was helping the kids over there in the visiting room in Vacaville and then people wanted to use me again and play some more politics and tell some more lies, because they wanted to bring Bingham back from France, because he's responsible for killing six people over there when San Quentin came down from death row and Jackson got killed. But we'll cover that up. We won't look at that because he's got the money to get away with things like that.

So we got the juvenile running wild and we're saying, where does the juvenile come from and where does he get his principle from, the old winos that live in the county jail or the retired veterans that were outcasts? And we dig into their hearts and we see how real they are and how comes they got up on the railroad train because they couldn't even get the dog in the house, because she wouldn't let him do anything except what the Queen of England said, and she's fighting against Spain and that's still going into languages and it's so abstract that someone has to carry insanity. Someone's got to be insane. Someone's got to be the bad guy. How can we be good guys?

There's another letter in there that you didn't read about how Manson was burned up and how people threw fire at him, they should've killed him. They didn't tell you that they tried to kill me at least 30 or 40 times. But they hadn't been able to kill me, because you ain't got nobody bad enough to kill me, [inaudible] handcuffed. No two or three of you.

Because I'm right with my God and I'm right with myself. And I didn't break the law. I didn't break God's law and I didn't break man's law.

What you're doing in the political arena with Hollywood to make your Rambo movies with my machine gun, the machine gun was a World War II relic. It would only shoot one bullet at a time. It wouldn't even go pop, pop, pop because it was all worn out, it was so old.

But I liked it because I liked World War I, because that was my father. I didn't worship Hitler any more than I liked MacArthur. MacArthur and Truman was the same father figure to me like the kids look up to Vietnam veterans as their father figure, so I looked up to my grandfather in the First World War and my father in the Second World War.

And wherever there is a man, I am there also. In the truth, I walk with all men. I'm bad. I'm as bad as I got to be when it comes down. I deal. And I can deal from the bottom, just as easy as I can deal from the top and I'd cheat if it comes to where I need to cheat. And I steal if I need to steal if I'm too hungry and I can't feel it any other way, I'll do whatever I can do to survive, just like I've always done. And if I have to pick up steel and roll it down to—do whatever I got to do, that's what I got to do and that's what I'll do.

I seen this, and this is the reality. The air in L.A. basin is dying. Where there used to be bees, the bees can't live. Where there used to be butterflies, the butterflies can't fly. I said to Blue—I said, "Girl I'm going to call you Blue." I said, "You see that sky?" I said, "That sky's dying. If we don't do something about that sky, nobody cares. If you don't care, there's going to be no life left on this planet." I said, "Do you see that water over there?" I said, "They're dumping tons of junk in that water. So you're Blue for the sky and the water and I—

PRESIDING BOARD COMMISSIONER KOENIG: Mr.—

INMATE MANSON: Now wait—I set those people's minds, like he said, I set their minds back on the track with Jesus on a rebirth movement. I set it with a guy called Frank Costello in the Horseshoe Pits. I set it with the Pope in the Vatican. I set it with the Mafia and the gangsters. I set it with every man I'd ever met in my life all the way back to Creepy Carpis when he did the Ma Baker gang with J. Edgar Hoover and the F.B.I. Because wherever there's been a man walking in the underworld from Cook County Jail in Chicago to the super chief that rides to L.A., from Leavenworth, Kansas, to [inaudible] Section 8, the Navy down to the Coast Guard, wherever there's one walking, I've been walking there with it.

PRESIDING BOARD COMMISSIONER KOENIG: Mr. Manson, talk about suitability, please.

INMATE MANSON: I don't know what else I could be if I couldn't be suitable to be your leader, I ain't nothing.

PRESIDING BOARD COMMISSIONER KOENIG: All right.

INMATE MANSON: I'm your president at least three times. That's through Reagan up through [inaudible]. [Inaudible] was only his appointee and he only got there because he was riding on me. That was my horse, that was my divorce court to come back from Nixon, and the only reason J. R. got up out of Texas was because I went across to Africa with two [inaudible] from [inaudible] in 1960.

PRESIDING BOARD COMMISSIONER KOENIG: Mr. Manson—Mr. Manson, excuse me. Would you please talk as to why you should be paroled? If you have nothing to say in that area, then we're going to recess and we're going to deliberate.

INMATE MANSON: Okay. If I'm not—

PRESIDING BOARD COMMISSIONER KOENIG: [Inaudible]—

INMATE MANSON:—if I'm not paroled, and I don't get a chance to get back up on top of this dream, you're going to lose all your money, your farms ain't going to produce, you're going to win Helter Skelter. You're going to win your reality. You're going to get everything that you want right from the pages of that court. That's going to be your reality and you're coming. You're growing up and you're going to be there, just like you want him to be there, that's where he's coming because that's what you're making for yourselves.

PRESIDING BOARD COMMISSIONER KOENIG: All right. We're going to recess for deliberation. We'll call you back after we make a decision. The time is now 1525 hours. The prisoner will leave please.

INMATE MANSON: I don't need those papers.

PRESIDING BOARD COMMISSIONER KOENIG: All right.

[Recess]

[Decision]

PRESIDING BOARD COMMISSIONER KOENIG: We've reconvened the panel's hearing on Charles Manson. All participants are present who were present prior to the recess and the time is 1545 hours.

The panel reviewed all the information received and relies on the following circumstances in concluding that the prisoner is not suitable for parole and would pose an unreasonable risk of danger to society if released at this time.

The [inaudible] offense was carried out in an especially heinous, atrocious, and cruel manner. The offense was carried out in a manner which exhibits a callous disregard for the life and suffering of another. Multiple victims were attacked, injured, and killed in the same and separate incidents. The victims were abused and defiled and mutilated in the offense.

These conclusions are drawn from the Statement of Facts wherein the prisoner [inaudible] participated in the torture, mutilation, and killing of nine victims. Seven of the victims were strangers who were selected by the prisoner at random. The murders were senseless, brutal, directed by the prisoner to satisfy his idealistic vision of a race war.

The prisoner has a record of violent and assaultive behavior, an escalating habit of criminal conduct and violence. He had an unstable social history. He's failed to profit from society's previous attempts to correct his criminality. These included juvenile probation, juvenile camps, C.Y.A. commitment, three prior prison terms, and county jail and parole violation.

As to the unstable social history, the prior criminality included beginning criminal conduct at an early age, sent to juvenile boys school as a juvenile involved in burglary, stealing vehicles, convicted of the Dyer Act and sent to the National Training School in Washington, D.C. Adult convictions included G.T.A., forgery, theft, interfering with a peace officer, attempted escape from prison—attempted escapes from prison, three prior prison terms, probation and parole violation, extensive involvement in drugs and was under federal parole at the time of the instant offenses.

The prisoner has programmed in a limited manner while incarcerated. He's failed to develop a marketable skill that can be put to use upon release. He's failed to upgrade educationally and vocationally as previously recommended by the Board and he's not participated to any extent—has not participated in beneficial self-help and therapy programming.

He failed to demonstrate any evidence of positive change. Misconduct while incarcerated included 60 115s from 1971 to 1992, nine 115s since his last hearing, many for threatening staff, the latest was on 2/11/92 where he received three of a serious nature for spitting on a correctional officer, threatening staff, and resisting staff. The psychiatric report authored— dated January of 1992 authored by Christopherson—is unfavorable. He also refused to attend a 1992 appointment for a psych evaluation.

The panel makes the following finding: that the prisoner needs therapy in order to face, discuss, understand, and cope with stress in a nondestructive manner. Until progress is made, the prisoner continues to be unpredictable and a threat to others. Also therapy, although the panel feels that therapy is needed, we question motivation and amenability.

In view of the prisoner's criminal history, continued negative behavior, and lack of program participation, there is no indication that the prisoner would behave differently—

INMATE MANSON: How can I participate? You've got me locked in a hole, man.

PRESIDING BOARD COMMISSIONER KOENIG: Okay. Listen to me—

INMATE MANSON: You guys get trapped up in all that illusion and it keeps building up and making it worse.

PRESIDING BOARD COMMISSIONER KOENIG: Please listen to what [inaudible].

INMATE MANSON: You've got to live in it.

PRESIDING BOARD COMMISSIONER KOENIG: The prisoner—the hearing panel, according to Section 3041.5(c) of the Penal Code, the hearing panel finds that it is not reasonable to expect that parole would be granted at a hearing during the following five years.

The specific reasons for these findings are as follows: No. 1, the crime itself. The prisoner committed the offense in an especially heinous, atrocious, and cruel manner and that he participated in the killing of nine victims, most victims selected at random to fulfill his idealistic dream of Helter Skelter. As a result a longer period of observation and evaluation is required before the Board should set a parole date.

No. 2, the prisoner has a prior criminal record and spent most of his life prior to the instant offense in and out of correctional facilities.

No. 3, a longer period of time is required to evaluate his suitability. In view of the prisoner's long history of criminality and misconduct, these include 60 serious 115s, nine since his last hearing, and three serious within the last year.

No. 4, a recent psychiatric report dated January of 1992, authored by Christopherson, indicates a need for a longer period of observation and evaluation.

And No. 5, the prisoner has not completed the necessary programming, which is essential to his adjustment, and needs additional time to gain such programming.

Recommendations to you, Mr. Manson, that you become disciplinary free, that you work to reduce your custody level so that the program opportunities will become more available, that you upgrade when—and that's when you can, upgrade vocationally and educationally and you participate in self-help and therapy programming.

This concludes the panel hearing. The time is now 1552 hours. The prisoner may leave. Good luck to you, Mr. Manson.

INMATE MANSON: Good-bye.

PRESIDING BOARD COMMISSIONER KOENIG: Here's a copy [inaudible].

Parole denied five years.

ACKNOWLEDGMENTS

Thanks to my wife, Beth, and our six children for enduring my years of struggle collecting information and writing this book. Thanks to them for forgiving my dark moods and moments of rage. Thanks for support from friends like Robi and Bob Andersen, and Bev and Gary McGuire, who have long put up with my Charlie stories. Thanks to my many other friends and relatives who encouraged me to write, and particularly to my perennial convict friend, Roger Dale "Pin Cushion" Smith, the most stabbed inmate in the California prison system, who taught me more about prison life than anyone else.

Thanks to my many bosses, peers, and subordinates who worked with me throughout my thirty-two-year law-enforcement and prison career, especially Warden Bob Rees, Parole Administrator Ron Chun, Prison Chaplain Nick Ristad, and Doctors Larry Clanon, Joyce Sutton, and Al Rotella.

Thanks to Lisa Kaiser, my first literary agent contact, who referred my manuscript to Dary Matera, who proposed changes in the manuscript leading to its sale, and who then rewrote the book into its finished form. Thanks to Steve Huddleston, Assistant Publisher of the Vacaville Reporter, for research assistance.

Thanks to authors Leonard Bishop and Donna Levin, whose writing workshops and advice helped me get started. Thanks to Nuel Emmons, Manson book author, for photos, friendship, and advice. Thanks to those many Sulpician and Jesuit priests and teachers who taught me the skills and virtues of sanity which sustained me throughout the many years of prison madness. And thanks to my mother, who was always there.

Last and the least thanks to Charles Manson, whose demonic behavior shocked the world's conscience, motivating me to search his life and chronicle his long prison odyssey.

—E. G.

Special thanks to Fran Matera, Ph.D., of the Walter Cronkite School of Journalism and Telecommunications, Arizona State University, for all her assistance and support. And to Will Hart, Lonnie Haney, Ernestina Zamora; Jim Fitzgerald, Dana Albarella, and Charles Spicer at St. Martin's Press; and to my agents Stedman Mays and Lisa Kaiser of Connie Clausen Associates.

In memoriam to my agent Connie Clausen.

—D. M.